Virtualpolitik

Virtualpolitik

An Electronic History of Government Media-Making in a Time of War, Scandal,
Disaster, Miscommunication, and Mistakes

Elizabeth Losh

The MIT Press
Cambridge, Massachusetts
London, England

For information about special quantity discounts, please email special_sales@mitpress.mit.edu

This book was set in Stone Sans and Stone Serif by SNP Best-set Typesetter Ltd., Hong Kong. Printed and bound in the United States of America.

Library of Congress Cataloging-in-Publication Data

Losh, Elizabeth M. (Elizabeth Mathews)
Virtualpolitik : an electronic history of government media-making in a time of war, scandal, disaster, miscommunication, and mistakes / Elizabeth Losh.
    p. cm.
Includes index.
ISBN 978-0-262-12304-4 (hard cover : alk. paper)
1. Information society—Political aspects—United States.   2. Information technology—Political aspects—United States.   3. Internet—Political aspects—United States.   4. Communication—Political aspects–United States.   I. Title.
JK468.A8L67   2009
320.97301'4—dc22

2008031029

10 9 8 7 6 5 4 3 2 1

Dedication

The book is dedicated to my husband Mel Horan, who proofread every page, and to my dad, Samuel Losh, who gave me my first computer, an 8-bit Xerox 820 with enormous eight-inch disk drives.

Contents

Acknowledgments

This book would not have been possible without input from literally dozens of people. I am especially grateful to Ian Bogost, Jennifer Cool, Paul Dourish, Michael Heim, Lisbeth Klastrup, Mark Marino, and Siva Vaidhyanathan, who read sections of this book while it was still in draft form and gave invaluable feedback. Reactions from readers of the *Virtualpolitik* blog who sent e-mails and wrote comments also had a major role in shaping the work. Whether they were correcting the record, engaging in debate, or elaborating a point that I had made, I tried to include their observations wherever possible in this text and show respect for their passion for participation in the public sphere.

One of the most pleasurable chapters to write was undoubtedly the first chapter, which was about the SonicJihad debacle in Congress that revealed almost unbelievable twists and turns in the plot with each hour of research on the case. Fellow detectives Ian Bogost and Gonzalo Frasca helped reveal the incredible misunderstanding that took place in the House of Representatives, and Janet Lindenmuth of the Widener University Law Library provided critical evidence about what had happened in the form of the transcripts of the hearings. The following chapter on digital rhetoric owes much to now retired but forward-thinking faculty members Richard Lanham and Ellen Strenski, who described early experiments with integrating multimedia and software development practices into the teaching of composition at UCLA. The third chapter, which is on Iraq-based videogames designed for combat personnel, was heavily based on interviews with Lewis Johnson, Skip Rizzo, Jacquelyn Morie, and Michael Zyda. Other questions were answered by many others working on publicly funded projects at USC. A telephone interview with Gary Patriquin was tremendously useful in thinking about how PowerPoint functions among members of the armed services stationed in Iraq. I learned a huge amount about hacktivism that I otherwise would have never known from Chris Soghoian of Indiana University and Virgil Griffith of the California Institute of Technology. The chapter on digital libraries was shaped by lengthy interviews with Jean-Noël Jeanneney of Europartenaires; Christophe Dessaux and Sonia Zillhardt of the French Ministry of Culture; Aly Conteth, Neil Fitzgerald, Neil Smith, and Graham Cranfield of the British Library; and Laura Graham of the Library of Congress. Remmel Nunn and August Imholtz of the Readex Corporation also provided valuable background information on the history of manuscript replication. Joseph Henderson and the game developers at the IML in Dartmouth took time out from their busy schedules to let me interview team members and observe the collaborative culture around creating games for emergency first-responders and military physicians. Adam Burrowbridge and Garry Gaber of the Federation of American Scientists also corrected some understandable misperceptions about their game *Immune Attack*. Richard Koffler of Alelo provided updates about the game *Tactical Iraqi*, as did Colleen Monahan for the *POD Game*.

I also am extremely grateful to my colleagues at U.C. Irvine who provided support for the often time-consuming fieldwork away from campus that this book required, especially to my dear friend and institutional partner in the Humanities Core Course, design maven Julia Lupton, and to Campus Writing Coordinator Jonathan Alexander. Although this is too often overlooked in book acknowledgments, I don't want to forget personal thanks to Vivian Folkenflik, who frequently covered my classes when I was away on sleuthing missions. Important institutional support for bringing speakers to campus for dialogues that eventually made their way into the book came from Humanitech and the California Institute for Telecommunications and Information Technology. Special thanks to Barbara Cohen and Steve Franklin for arranging those public events. Funds for essential research trips to learn about digital libraries and government-funded videogames came from the Humanities Center and the Office of the Executive Vice Chancellor and Provost at the University of California, Irvine. Thanks also to Celia Pearce of the Georgia Institute of Technology for inviting me to speak at Living Game Worlds III, where I met many of the people who were essential for finishing this book.

While I am thanking people, I would like to thank some of the people who inspired me to think about fundamental connections between academic scholarship and activism on policy issues in innovative ways. Electronic correspondents Alan Liu, Trebor Scholz, and Geert Lovink were great sources of inspiration as I reached the final stretch of writing. Their encouragement for the kind of interdisciplinary work that is often frustrated by the institutional structures of the academy was particularly crucial. Thanks also to fellow blogger Marc van Gurp of Osocio who provided a much-needed international perspective on many of the issues concerning social marketing and risk communication that are addressed in the book.

I would also like to thank the late Jacques Derrida for serving as such an important mentor to me in graduate school and for encouraging me to write more "dramatic" prose involving my personal background and often uncomfortable questions about political engagement and media culture. Although Derrida is often depicted as having encouraged his protégés to communicate in a cryptic language of radical relativism, the pedagogical reality in my case could not have been more different. It was Derrida who urged me to try to draw in a more public audience through direct and emotionally engaged writing when I was working on my very first conference paper about new media, which was on Supreme Court decisions about testimony via closed-circuit television and what Justice Antonin Scalia called "virtually constitutional" procedures for videorecorded witnesses in child sexual abuse cases. Given the project of this book, it is also interesting to note that this conference paper from very early in my academic career was also about a series of scandals at a public agency, one that described these technological devices as "secret machines" to their young clients without acknowledging how such multimedia technologies could replicate and disseminate information to unanticipated parties.

Portions of this book have appeared or will appear in published form in the following collections, journals, and conference proceedings: *Joystick Soldiers: The Politics of Play in Military Videogames*; *Discourse: Journal for Theoretical Studies in Media and Culture*; *Media/Culture*, *Proceedings of Sandbox 2007: ACM/SIGGRAPH Video Game Symposium*; *Proceedings of the 18th Conference on Hypertext and Hypermedia*; *Proceedings of ISCRAM 2007: 4th International Conference on Information Systems for Crisis Management*; *Proceedings of SIGGRAPH 2006*; *Proceedings of the 2006 International Conference on Game Research*; *Digital Experience: Design, Aesthetics, Practice*; *Literary and Linguistic Computing*; and *Kairos*. Special thanks to the following editors of these publications: Doug Eyman and James Inman, Mark Nunes, Nina Huntemann and Matthew Payne, Scott Weintraub and Jess Boersma, and Chuck Mobley and Mark Chambers.

Finally, this book could not have happened without enthusiasm for this project from Doug Sery, Gita Manaktala, and Alyssa Larose of the MIT Press and the many books that they have published over the years that appear in the endnotes of this one. This book is in dialogue with many of the other publications in their catalog, and I hope that it is part of a conversation that will continue with the work of others.

Introduction: A Fable of Politics, Community, and Virtuality

One day, in 1988, the computers and modems suddenly appeared, as if by magic. They were second-hand Apple IIe terminals, but in my mind it was a miracle to have them at all. At the time, I was fresh out of college and running a chronically underfunded after-school program at a delinquency prevention center under the auspices of the California Youth Authority.

Relatively few of our teenaged clients had committed serious or violent offenses by that age, but many of them were either in trouble with the law or with the schools and were thus considered "high risk" by the state. I had been pestering my boss, who did not even know how to type, about getting a technology lab for months. I explained to every potential donor who would listen how essential these devices would be for students who already were what we then called "socioeconomically underprivileged." Once the computer lab materialized, I quickly hustled up donated software for word processing, spelling, basic math, algebra, geometry, biology, SAT preparation, bookkeeping, and keyboard accuracy.

In February 1989, the city of Santa Monica announced a new program called the Public Electronic Network, or PEN. It claimed to be the first municipally owned bulletin board system in the world. It featured a database of city schedules and documents so that constituents could keep up with the business of governance. It also had chat rooms for discussing public issues like redevelopment projects or services for the homeless. I was excited about getting my high-risk students on PEN and giving them e-mail addresses so they could contact their elected officials and perhaps agitate for better parks, more appealing youth programs, or fairer treatment from the police. I thought that it would be a good way to teach civic-mindedness. Through PEN, thanks partly to my efforts and enthusiasm, dozens of gang members in the greater Los Angeles area had e-mail addresses long before most corporate CEOs. Some of these students grew up to be convicted murderers or murder victims. Many of them attended college and ended up in professional careers. Ironically, one became executive director of a delinquency prevention center himself, complete with computer lab, and eventually served as president of

Figure I.1
Photogragh of student using a PEN e-government terminal, 1989. Courtesy of Karla Gutierrez.

the local school board in the same district where he had once been a struggling student.

At first, the hard-case teenagers did not like PEN at all. Their personal addresses were unwieldy and hard to remember, as were their passwords, which were often lost. The city's electronic materials were extraordinarily dull; even the most impassioned pleas for clean energy or unpolluted beaches bored these young people. Plus, I nagged them incessantly about writing letters to the adults on the city council, which they considered a dreary and potentially embarrassing chore, particularly when I gave them written assignments and form letters that I expected them to fill out.

"Why don't you write about getting that new basketball court?" I would ask them. "How about a cool place for skateboarding?" I would chirp. In response, they would stare at me blankly or with hostility and return to doodling graffiti or napping with their heads on the table.

It looked as if my grand experiment in digital direct democracy was going to be a miserable failure. But then—very abruptly—the students all started actually using the system. Teen mothers, tough gangbangers in baggy clothes, and homeless kids who were living with their parents in cars full of trash were often intently and simultaneously online. They crowded our terminals at the youth center, sometimes for hours, writing in less than perfect prose, but writing nonetheless.

It took me a while to realize it, but it turned out that they were all utterly ignoring my explicit instructions on how to use PEN. They were not writing to public office-holders about matters of civic import. They were writing to girlfriends and boyfriends, cousins and neighbors, schoolmates and church members, and anyone else they could manage to talk into getting a free PEN account, too. Sometimes they were writing notes to themselves, which they would chuckle over days later in rereading. Most damaging to my dignity as a novice teacher was the fact that they most enjoyed writing to people who were sitting with them in the very same room.[1]

Frequently, in a high-tech version of passing notes, I suspect that they used the medium to make fun of me, since I periodically saw my name or one of its jokey variants appearing in their cryptic messages. After all, I was the nearest representative of state authority, with the police power to call probation officers, caseworkers, or school guidance counselors if these students incurred my displeasure. Even though I thought of myself as a well-meaning, idealistic young person close to their own ages, I probably did not look much like an encouraging peer to them. By virtue of my race, class, relative seniority, and institutional affiliation with the California Youth Authority, an agency that also ran the juvenile detention system in the state, I can now see that I probably warranted some mockery. In that sense, their subversive electronic conversations represented a kind of political speech, although it was not a politics I recognized at the time.

According to one member of the Santa Monica city council, this form of seemingly aberrant online behavior was exactly what the rest of the local citizenry decided to do with PEN as well: "The head of the City's computer department, Ken Phillips, intended the PEN system primarily to link residents to City Hall, providing information and answering questions. In reality, PEN has grown to be much more of a citizen-to-citizen phenomenon, with a culture of its own."[2] Apparently the adults were using PEN to rehearse adolescent sex fantasies, parody television programs, conduct religious proselytizing, and affirm gestures of feminist solidarity in several mutually shared free speech zones of anarchic peer-to-peer interaction among neighbors, which often had remarkably little to do with the official commerce of representative government. Occasionally, the entire apparatus of this state-sanctioned virtual community degenerated into outright flame wars of nonstop verbal abuse.

In *The Virtual Community: Homesteading on the Electronic Frontier*, Howard Rheingold focuses on just one aspect of the program, the SHWASHLOCK (which stood for SHowers, WASHers, and LOCKers) proposal from homeless PEN members, as the epitome of "how citizens can agree on a common problem, use their collective resources to propose a solution, and convince the city's official government to help put the solution into practice" by using digital networks for group communication.[3]

From several removes of geography and temporal engagement, the PEN experiment has now been read by cyberculture critics as an important case study in digital democracy.[4] This early attempt at constructing a "digital city," years before the project in Amsterdam described by Geert Lovink and Pierre Lévy, similarly exposes the challenges faced in adapting urban needs shaped by neighborhood demographics and geography to digital platforms and networks.[5] Although some have pointed out how the unstable power dynamic of this electronic community reflected the contingent character of its participatory homeostasis, none have looked closely—in rhetorical terms—at the implied struggle over the very definition of "e-government" among participants.

I would argue that what happened with PEN is just one fable about the law of unintended consequences, a version of a story that gets told over and over again about everyday incidents in digital culture in relationship to formal systems of governance. I think it is a fitting narrative with which to begin, because this is a book about public rhetoric and its subversion, about the way that traditional institutions of knowledge do not always conform to social practices around information, and about how computer technology creates secondary purposes and secondary audiences never imagined by the original senders of an official message or the architects of a given system of state-sanctioned communication.

When I first began to do scholarship about the digital rhetoric of government institutions a decade ago, there was a relatively narrow array of objects of study, largely limited to official government websites with static HTML pages, repositories of online forms, and portals to digital archives. At the time, most researchers were only looking at those artifacts and discourses through the lens of e-government, which focused almost exclusively on human-computer interaction (HCI) questions and a problem-solving mechanistic approach that depended on usability studies. Although—unlike many humanists—I agreed with the HCI specialists that interfaces, operations, and procedures mattered, I was also making what seemed to the technologists to be a strange argument: that these public digital messages represented ideologies and cultural imaginaries and that designers' choices about what was visible and invisible could be about more than just user convenience or access for the disabled. At the same time, I think my fellow rhetoricians were baffled by my interest in what then seemed to them to be relatively impoverished texts at the semiotic level, documents that appeared to lack any distinctive personal voice or coherent narrative, paradigms of impassive bureaucratic neutrality without any allure for scholars of high culture and low culture alike. Nonetheless, I thought there was a story to be found in the many mixed messages being manifested on government websites and the competing positions about appropriate technologies for exhibiting materials from electronic archives.

Now it has become more obvious that the government's role as a digital media-maker is worth examining and that these state-sanctioned texts merit close reading, careful explication, scholarly analysis, and the critical tools of historical and rhetorical perspective. Much of that shift has to do with an explosion of genres. Government agencies now sponsor moderated chat, blogs, clips of digital video, online tutorials, videogames, and virtual reality simulations. There have also been many high-profile political gaffes involving embarrassing e-mails, instant messages, and PowerPoint presentations by elected and appointed officials. At the same time, sophisticated online campaigns for public diplomacy, social marketing, risk communication, and institutional branding are coordinated with major advertising agencies that are target-ing citizens via the World Wide Web. In addition, there are virtual tours of national landmarks and government buildings, and in turn there are agency offices and politi-cal events in virtual worlds like *Second Life*. For future voters, there are hundreds of government websites designed specifically for children. Even digital maps and other representations of "big data" convey messages about political ideology. Frequently this material is parodied, remixed, or recontextualized for new audiences in ways that the original media-maker never intended, in media practices that clearly support subver-sive anti-institutional agendas. The libertarian and communitarian factions on the Internet may anticipate a day that the state will wither away as a result of global dis-tributed networks, but government remains an important digital media-maker and regulator, despite the inherent tension created by adopting those dual roles.

The first chapter in this book is about a case involving an extraordinarily powerful unplanned audience: the Congress of the United States. What appeared to be footage from a terrorist videogame, which was posted on the Internet, generated such alarm during a House Intelligence Committee hearing that it became a sensational news item all across the country. A team of expert consultants testifying at the hearing warned that violently anti-American videogames had been created to persuade impres-sionable young Muslims to become radical jihadists. In the film, made by someone called "SonicJihad," lawmakers saw a computer-generated Middle Easterner blowing up three-dimensional (3-D) animated tanks and destroying the ranks of what appeared to be uniformed U.S. soldiers. It turned out, however, that the actual intended audi-ence was a playful fan community of gamers, and that the film had been edited together by a European hospital administrator with no grudge against the United States, a young man who enjoyed the American-made game *Battlefield 2* and the movie *Team America*, from which he assembled his fan film's digital components. What is disquieting about this hearing is that congressional representatives also expressed concern about far more than regulating videogames. Blogs, webpages, and PowerPoint slides all figure in the legislators' discussion in which they publicly display their anxi-eties about new digital practices both abroad and at home.

Of course, with all these new genres, it's important to define what digital rhetoric is as an object of study. The second chapter, "Hacking Aristotle," provides an interpre-tive framework in which the verbal and visual organization of information and the means of its electronic communication can be analyzed, along with user experiences of interactivity enabled by computers. Yet many who purportedly study the rhetoric of digital discourse ignore its informational dimension, so that a conventional view of the study of hypertext, virtual environments, or networked communication directs attention only to the computer interface rather than to the theories behind its continuing development. In the standard model of digital rhetoric, literary theory is almost always applied to technological applications as an interpretive apparatus without considering how technological theories could conversely illuminate literary texts. Rhetoricians of digital culture debate the merits of multi-user dimensions (MUDs) and object-oriented MUDs (MOOs) or blogs and wikis but rarely address how fundamental paradigms of the public sphere have been reshaped by new ideas from the discourses of codes and algorithms from subcultures of software developers, interface designers, and computer programmers and how pre-scripted possibilities and constraints always play a role in shaping the available rhetorical choices.[6]

This chapter proposes four possible meanings for the term "digital rhetoric": (1) the rhetorical conventions of new digital genres in everyday discourse, (2) public rhetoric via electronic distributed networks or hypertext, (3) the rhetorical analysis of new media in scholarly communities, and (4) the rhetoric of information theory as a distinct field associated with computer science. I argue that the new linguistic ideology inherent in the last definition, which is articulated in mathematical theories of communication, also feeds back to influence the norms and generic conventions of everyday digital discourse.

In the third chapter, I begin an in-depth survey of digital genres by considering how videogames and virtual reality simulations persuade users and communicate ideological messages. In "The Desert of the Unreal," I analyze two military-funded projects at the University of Southern California: *Tactical Iraqi*, a computer game designed to accelerate a soldier's acquisition of spoken Arabic to assist in volatile tactical situations, and *Virtual Iraq*, a virtual reality simulation intended to lessen the effects of post-traumatic stress disorder among combat veterans. Of course, there are significant design differences between the two projects. One is a game, and the other is a simulation; one is pedagogical in its orientation, and the other is therapeutic; one uses third-person perspective, and the other uses first-person. Yet there is also significant overlap between these virtual Iraqs, which were developed by research and development teams in close physical proximity to each other in Marina Del Rey, California. Both use pre-existing, off-the-shelf game technology that has a history in the consumer market, and both initiatives have received extensive national media coverage. Finally, both appear to serve rhetorical as well as pedagogical or therapeutic ends by making individual, private digital experiences, aimed to effect the personal education or rehabilitation of military personnel, accessible to a wider public. These games and simulations also make manifest certain politically uncomfortable aspects of the war in Iraq and otherwise hidden vulnerabilities in the soldier's readiness for combat. Consequently, there has been a lively debate in the game development community—surrounding "serious games,"which serve educational or social purposes—about working on behalf of government-funded projects that support current military efforts.

"The War from the Web" presents the next category of digital genre: the official website. Despite the fact that early advocates of e-government celebrated the liberatory potential of hypertext, and that the architects of digital democracy purported to be inclusive in their development practices, institutional websites deploy many forms of manufactured or pseudointeractivity, such as virtual tours or "turning the pages" exhibitions, which deflect participatory challenges by using the ideological authority of cultural metaphors such as the museum. Furthermore, according to the Pew Internet & American Life Project, increasing numbers of residents rely on government websites for information, so official site designers are able to deliver particularly potent institutional messages. Yet official rhetoric about September 11 on the Internet and its reception history shows how the public face of e-government can be more heterogeneous than its boosters would like to believe. There are many different instantiations of state authority from the vantage point of any individual user's screen. A partial survey of websites from the Federal Bureau of Investigation, the White House, the State Department, the Department of Defense, and the U.S. Central Command in the weeks and months following the attacks of September 11 suggests that official idealism about the promise of a user-friendly, authoritative, and direct digital democracy can not account for mixed messages from different sectors of the U.S. government about race, class, gender, and nationality, particularly when even presidential oratory has been shrunk down to the busy desktop crammed with active, open windows.

"Power Points" extends this analysis of government websites to look at other forms of the rhetoric of display. Certainly, electronic slideshows in the proprietary format PowerPoint have been justifiably lambasted by information designers such as Edward Tufte and Mark Bernstein. It is worth noting, however, that these electronic slideshows frequently also borrow from older print genres such as editorial cartoons, office memos, and educational filmstrips. Although alliances between e-government and the advertising industry in fields like public diplomacy, risk communication, and social marketing are further commodifying traditional civic discourses, the components of electronic slideshows may be circulated, edited, and scrutinized among members of the general public. Furthermore, the genre of the electronic slideshow can be used by political opponents and artists, as two recent documentaries (*An Inconvenient Truth* and *The Yes Men*) demonstrate, and stock icons of data visualization can be repurposed to stimulate public discussion for advocacy or activism.

In the sixth chapter, I argue that for stakeholders inside institutional systems, e-mail would seem particularly well suited to the objective of policy change, since would-be whistle-blowers intent on gaining attention could expose government corruption or avert disaster as quickly as possible. As a medium for instantaneous and intimate global communication, e-mail initially appears to be far superior to traditional epistolary discourse since letters are vulnerable to delays and acts of confiscation by hostile parties. Yet because the genre of e-mail is often perceived as closer to speech than to written communication, its juridical authority is undermined by its status as a virtual artifact, as I explain in the chapter "Whistle-Blowers." Ideally, e-mail would serve as electronic testimony but often it functions as mere evidence, if not hearsay. For example, when *Time* magazine named three women as its 2002 "Persons of the Year" as icons of public rhetoric, it is worth noting that not one of the featured whistle-blowers used e-mail as the primary vehicle for her well-publicized rhetorical acts. In fact, Federal Bureau of Investigation (FBI) Special Agent Coleen Rowley devotes a significant section of her thirteen-page letter to Director Robert Mueller to critical metadiscourse about e-mail. It is also worth fully considering how e-mail exchanges involving Hurricane Katrina became ammunition in a battle of partisan politics and competing disclosures. However, e-mail is not the only Internet channel for whistle-blowing: I will also examine how online videos from services such as YouTube have served a whistle-blowing function for federal and state employees and how a very different social media platform at The Hub for the international group Witness is used to publicize human rights abuses.

While the virtual state becomes increasingly associated with particular signifiers and conventional clichés in visual rhetoric, such as authorized brands or stock genres like the photo essay, netizens are appropriating that same iconography into subversive digital artworks and political satires, which include Web generators, Photoshopped images, photo mosaics, and remixed audio and video files. In "Submit and Render," I describe how these digital ephemera circulate in an unregulated gift economy. In particular, I look at the story of Chris's Northwest Boarding Pass Generator, which was created to publicize a flaw in airport security procedures, but caused its creator to be investigated by federal authorities. These circuits of online political exchange are potentially subject to rules governing intellectual property and state-run procedures for authentification of documents and persons, and thus the status of these satires as constitutionally protected political speech may come into jeopardy. I also point out that perhaps the regulatory impulse is understandable, given that these forms of gift exchange not only make a mockery of official surveillance practices, but can also promote the development of Internet theaters of cruelty, in which disenfranchised political subjects can take revenge on the virtual bodies of the leaders of the body politic.

The features of digital rhetoric can even be observed in institutional databases, which have long been recognized as aesthetic objects as well. The basic thesis for "Reading Room," based on my own research in European and American archives, is that just as the physical building of a national library can serve as a tangible expression of political and cultural philosophy, a given digital library manifests ideological features of the national legacy it preserves and disseminates electronically. For example, millennial discourses have influenced national library building projects in both physical and digital archives. However, a simple analogy between conventional and electronic spaces is inadequate, because national policies on digitizing documents and regulating access engender contradictory impulses in archivists and policy makers. Although critics like Lessig, Stallman, Warner, and Samuelson focus on the centrality of the right to read, the physical space of a document archive is actually constituted by prohibitions on reading. In the case of the Bibliothèque nationale France, the French government makes its digital collection widely and anonymously available, but closely surveils readers in its physical space. In contrast, the Library of Congress celebrates democratic access to its reading rooms and takes an open source approach to the collective labor of cataloging, but corporate business models for Web development undermine the authenticity of these rhetorical appeals to the public interest. Finally, the British Library offers an interface that emulates turning pages of rare tomes but comes late to prioritizing searchable text encoding. Alongside these three eminent national libraries, I consider how privately funded initiatives or those depending on user-generated content create alarm among those who champion public infrastructure. Now that Google Print and the competing efforts of Microsoft are appropriating the cultural work of the state archive and consigning it to the sphere of corporate privatization, it is important to reconsider the potential obligation of government agencies to the public for information access and look at the prehistory of utopianism, proprietary technologies, and eventual obsolescence associated with efforts involving microfilming and microprinting books and government documents. Futhermore, out of the news spotlight, smaller metadata factories are emerging all over the country, even in small New England towns like Chester, Vermont, to digitize important legislative documents and other historical records.

After looking at how things are made public, I examine the competing trend to make things private by compartmentalizing certain forms of discourse as appropriate only for select professionals. In "Waiting Room" the topic is public health websites, educational CD-rom programs, videogames, and virtual reality simulations intended only for licensed practitioners. I consider how expertise is constituted in several computer-mediated projects being developed for medical providers and emergency first-responders with funding from government agencies. Many see this as a logical extension of work already being done with virtual reality in the training of medical doctors and public health workers to decrease the incidence of human error, with the aviation industry as a model of successful implementation. Because many of these projects simulate terrorist acts, I argue that such games and other learning environments can also be read in the context of the genre of public risk communication, which achieved particular importance after World War II during a period of heightened fear of nuclear attack by the Soviet Union. The Interactive Media Laboratory at Dartmouth Medical School has been the flagship for research on these pedagogical applications for virtual reality technology: their teams are producing both the Virtual Terrorism Academy and several software projects in the Virtual Clinic series.

Finally, I close the book with a rare success story about the government as a digital media-maker by looking at the rhetorical techniques of the Jet Propulsion Laboratory (JPL) Mars rover program. To understand the context for the emerging information culture that the JPL experience represents, I return to a prior historical moment from the period after World War II, when the U.S. government invested heavily in an emerging discipline called "information science" and communications engineers were solving the technical problems that would make widespread access to television and eventually other digital video and audio networks possible. The Shannon and Wiener publications of 1948 and 1949 articulated the axioms underlying a new worldview based on probability, contingency, and information.[7] This worldview also had ideological consequences for language, rhetoric, politics, property, and gender, which still shape public culture today and in the near future.

To research this book, I found myself in many wildly improbable situations for a bookish academic, which were far different from the elevated scenes of traditional oratory or poetic composition that I had studied in graduate school. At the huge video-game convention E3, which constructed temporary themed environments to showcase its newest products, I shuffled down the stairs of a gangster's mansion, was herded behind security doors for a top-secret military briefing, strolled down a bombed-out French street complete with "GLACES" signs, and stood gawking in front of a huge half-pipe as skateboarders whizzed by. At the Association for Computing Machinery's Special Interest Group on Graphics and Interactive Techniques (SIGGRAPH) computer graphics conference, I cuddled a projection of a deformed child, fished for virtual fish with a pole, played hopscotch across glowing squares, shouted at an eerily responsive magnetic sculpture, loitered about with people wearing glowing LED messages on vests that said "This is Crap" and "I Want to Fart," and waved a red/green paddle in an audience of hundreds of people to manipulate a massively multiplayer Etch-a-Sketch. I have worn immersive video head-mounted displays while balancing on a skateboard, riding a Humvee, exploring an abandoned house, shaking hands with a Japanese cyborg, and crawling through a sewer tunnel in an unnamed Eastern European city. I have played videogames involving speaking Arabic, decontaminating myself from radiation, leading a UN food aid mission, and balancing the French national budget. I have watched interactive video about removing gall bladders surgically and about having anonymous drug-addled sex with complete strangers. I have visited the websites of apocalyptic cults, racist hate-mongers, conspiracy theorists, seeming fronts for U.S. intelligence agencies, and the White House pastry chef. Through it all, thanks to blogging during the book's progress, I have received tremendously useful feedback from both scholarly readers and members of the general public, along with impressive amounts of hate e-mail, much of which I answered personally with my best bureaucratic politeness.

This book is the result of dozens of interviews over the past ten years and many site visits and demos. I do not consider myself to be an ethnographer, but I do think that a certain amount of fieldwork is necessary to understand debates about digital design questions and the deliberative processes that may be obscured in the final electronic artifact presented to the public. To uncover this media archeology, interviews with team members, observation of their rituals and practices, internal project documents, drafts of papers that may not have been ultimately published, and physical inspection of the site of collaborative sociality around technology can be essential to understanding how the end product on a computer screen may reflect a complex cultural conversation. In other words, I argue that it may be worth examining the electronic library that was *not* constructed, the official website that was allowed to go dead, the online federal training that was abandoned, or the military videogame that was radically changed in response to criticism when analyzing the discourses around the digital infrastructure of what Jane Fountain has dubbed "the virtual state."[8]

This research is intended to bridge several fields that address the study of contemporary electronic communication, ones that predictably often do not talk to each other. Rhetoric, Internet research, game studies, web design, information science, fair use and intellectual property law, and the study of popular culture as it relates to political discourse are all critical disciplines for this project. In writing this book, I have participated in many cross-disciplinary conversations with academic colleagues and government officials, which I hope will be ongoing discussions long after its publication and in spite of inevitable changes in the current political climate.

Although this is a political book, I don't want it to be a shrilly partisan one. If my critique of the virtual state seems to focus excessively on the recent Republican presidential administration, that is to some degree an accident of history, because the presidency of George W. Bush was also a time of tremendous elaboration and improvisation in subversive communicative practices around politics and community in digital culture. Certainly, legislators on both sides of the aisle introduced and voted for new restrictive intellectual property regulations and unprecedented police powers of surveillance. Furthermore, many of the current policies restricting digital rights—ostensibly to protect children, reward innovation by established software manufacturers, or ensure the economic future of the entertainment industry—actually originated in the Clinton administration.

Unfortunately, this regulatory impulse is dominating current political policy so that this *virtualpolitik*, as a new form of traditional *Realpolitik*, occupies itself with the containment and fragmentation of competing digital communities to protect the short-term interests of the managers of the nation-state. It appears to be spurred by anxieties about the subversive potential of information culture to destabilize traditional institutions of knowledge, and it focuses on common activities of the contemporary consumer-producer like file sharing, videogame play, and the use of social network sites.[9] Of course, this policy approach also represents an indefinite postponement of major institution-building for electronic governance. As Peter Lyman has pointed out, during the 1980s and 1990s there were many metaphors of construction—superhighways and libraries and other forms of public works.[10] Now, by focusing on destructive criminality as the chief characteristic of digital culture, we miss what "piracy," "cheating," or "hacking" tells us about constituents' needs to shape their electronic identities to suit their personal politics and to have meaningful interactions with the virtual manifestations of the state.

Without a serious commitment to institution-building, the virtual state is given little to do but surveil its citizens. This is a lost opportunity, as even the PEN experience shows. Today in Santa Monica, the many-to-many features of the old PEN have been absorbed into a traditional government website devoid of interactivity and electronic citizen participation. Although apparently some Santa Monica citizens still hold on to their individual PEN accounts for communication purposes, the city's Information Services Division, which hosts the last vestiges of PEN, publicizes video security initiatives and the collection of web traffic statistics rather than opportunities to open new PEN accounts. To take part in city government requires face-to-face interactions to which there are many obstacles. To be heard, you have to locate the right hearing, come in person, wait in line, keep comments to the restricted number of minutes, and endure listening to possibly hours of city business unrelated to your personal concerns. Citizens can see a one-to-many netcast of city council and planning meetings, but they are no longer invited into chat rooms to converse with officials and each other.

At the local level of the PEN case, it becomes clear that the practice of virtualpolitik and the forms of pseudoparticipation that it substitutes for digital community represents more than a simple reactionary response against new technologies and their related forms of political association. Elected officials could legitimately claim that PEN produced a lot of anarchic discourse that made it impossible to get anything done and that the absence of face-to-face communication contributed to a lack of political responsibility among constituents, and now that governments are digital media-makers themselves they must be in the uncomfortable position of anticipating that their messages may migrate and morph in ways they can not predict.

I am claiming that the ideologies from which political strategies of virtualpolitik claim their legitimacy also have a long history in the Western rhetorical tradition. This is a book about public policy, but it is also a theoretical work that explores why lawmakers and other stakeholders may have basic philosophical objections to these new social media. At the most fundamental level, for example, they may see these media as threatening the basic Platonic distinction between appearance and reality upon which laws and political states are founded. However, I will argue that there are also several countertraditions in that same rhetorical history that address political participation and institutional memory, which could guide us forward in creating a more inclusive and responsive virtual state.

1 Digital Monsters: Show and Tell on Capitol Hill

On the morning of Thursday, May 4, 2006, the United States House Permanent Select Committee on Intelligence held an open hearing entitled "Terrorist Use of the Internet." On the same day, just a few miles away in Alexandria, Virginia, convicted September 11 conspirator Zacarias Moussaoui was to be sentenced to life in prison without the possibility of parole. The Intelligence committee meeting was scheduled in the Longworth Office Building, a Depression-era structure with a neoclassical facade, in Room 1302, a few doors down from where a series of Seth Eastman paintings of Native Americans from the nineteenth century had hung for many years. Because of a dysfunctional Longworth elevator, some of the congressional representatives, including ranking minority member Jane Harman, had been delayed on their way to the meeting. During the testimony about the latest political applications for cutting-edge digital technology, the microphones periodically malfunctioned, and witnesses complained of technical problems several times.

By the end of the day it seemed that what was to be remembered about the hearing was the revelation that terrorists were using videogames to recruit young jihadists. The Associated Press wrote a short, restrained article that only mentioned "computer games and recruitment videos" in passing, although it did give some column space to a distinctive digital hiccough allegedly used by the insurgents in their online materials: " 'This crusade—crusade—crusade—is going to take awhile,' President Bush says in one video, edited to make him repeat the word 'crusade' six other times."[1]

Eager to have their version of the news item picked up, Reuters made videogames the focus of their coverage with a headline that announced, "Islamists using US video games in youth appeal." The article that followed, written by David Morgan, was quickly rerun by several Internet news services, including *Yahoo News*.[2]

As in the Associated Press story, Reuters highlighted the sampling and remixing of the president's voice around the word "crusade."

"I was just a boy when the infidels came to my village in Blackhawk helicopters," a narrator's voice said as the screen flashed between images of street-level gunfights, explosions and helicopter assaults.

Figure 1.1
The video by SonicJihad. Courtesy of SonicJihad.

Then came a recording of President George W. Bush's September 16, 2001, statement: "This crusade, this war on terrorism, is going to take a while." It was edited to repeat the word "crusade," which Muslims often define as an attack on Islam by Christianity.[3]

The Reuters story also described the deviousness of the country's terrorist opponents, who were now apparently modifying popular videogames through their digital wizardry and inserting anti-American, pro-insurgency content.

One of the latest video games modified by militants is the popular "Battlefield 2" from leading video game publisher Electronic Arts Inc of Redwood City, California.

Jeff Brown, a spokesman for Electronic Arts, said enthusiasts often write software modifications, known as "mods," to videogames.

"Millions of people create mods on games around the world," he said. "We have absolutely no control over them. It's like drawing a mustache on a picture."

"Battlefield 2" ordinarily shows U.S. troops engaging forces from China or a united Middle East coalition. But in a modified video trailer posted on Islamic websites and shown to lawmakers, the game depicts a man in Arab headdress carrying an automatic weapon into combat with U.S. invaders.[4]

Although the Electronic Arts executive dismissed the activities of modders as a "mustache on a picture" that could only be considered little more than childish vandalism of their off-the-shelf corporate product, others saw a more serious form of criminality at work. One Internet news service kept the opening warning that "makers of combat video games have unwittingly become part of a global propaganda campaign by Islamic militants to exhort Muslim youths to take up arms against the United States," but changed the title to emphasize enlisting enemy soldiers, from "Islamists using US video games in youth appeal" to "Islamic militants recruit using U.S. video games."[5] Fox News retitled the story to stress the fact that the alert about technological manipulation was coming not only from government "officials" with general knowledge of public policy but also from recognized specialists in the antiterrorism surveillance field: "Experts: Islamic Militants Customizing Violent Video Games."[6]

According to the news reports, the key piece of evidence before Congress was a film of recorded in-game play by "SonicJihad," which—according to the experts—was widely distributed online. During the segment that most captured the attention of the wire service reporters, eerie music plays as an English-speaking narrator condemns the "infidel" and declares that he has "put a jihad" on them, as aerial shots move over flaming oil facilities and mosques covered with geometric designs. Suddenly a rocket is launched, a helicopter explodes, and the action accelerates. Much of the subsequent gameplay takes place from the point of view of a first-person shooter, seen as if through the eyes of an armed insurgent, but the viewer can also see third-person action in which the player appears as a running figure in a red-and-white checked keffiyeh, the head garb already associated by the mainstream news media with jihadists,[7] who dashes toward the screen over the virtual terrain with a rocket launcher balanced on his shoulder. Significantly, another of the player's handheld weapons is a detonator that triggers remote blasts. As jaunty music plays, helicopters, tanks, and armored vehicles burst into smoke and flame.[8] There are no complicated rhetorical formulae to explain the causal rationalizations of a just war imbedded in the gameplay: exclamations in Arabic are limited to simple phrases like "thank you" and "God is great." At the triumphant ending of the video, a green and white flag bearing a crescent is hoisted aloft into the sky.

Within twenty-four hours of the sensationalistic news breaking, however, a group of *Battlefield 2* fans were crowing about the idiocy of reporters.[9] The gameplay footage wasn't from a high-tech modification of the software by Islamic extremists; it had been posted on a *Planet Battlefield* forum in December 2005 by a game fan, who had cut together regular gameplay with a Bush remix and a parody snippet of the soundtrack from the comedy film *Team America*.[10] The voice describing the Black Hawk helicopters was the voice of Trey Parker of *South Park* cartoon fame. Much to Parker's amusement, even the mention of "goats screaming" did not alert spectators to the fact of a comic source.[11] The man behind the "SonicJihad" pseudonym was apparently a twenty-five-year-old hospital administrator named Samir,[12] and what reporters and representatives saw was nothing more exotic than gameplay from an add-on expansion pack of *Battlefield 2*, which—like other versions of the game—allows first-person shooter play from the position of the opponent as a standard feature, which fans of the actual game immediately realized.[13]

In an interview with the creator of the fan film, SonicJihad reveals that much of the rest of the soundtrack came from the 1981 Anthony Quinn film *Lion of the Desert*.[14] He describes himself as a largely secular, assimilated European Muslim of Moroccan extraction, reared in Holland. By his own account, he created what he considers to be primarily a low-tech homage to the experience of gameplay. Unlike the digitally composited smooth motion that correlates "different senses" that "simulate human experience," described in Lev Manovich's *The Language of New Media*,[15] the SonicJihad video is characterized by abrupt cutting and database-style montages made up of iterations of similar sequences—such as shots of different tanks exploding—from different times of day and even in night-vision mode, which are presented in discrete, mutually exclusive, spatially and temporally disjointed contexts. It draws attention to its status as a mediated artifact rather than immerses the viewer in an extremely realistic spatial experience.

While SonicJihad joins his fellow gamers in ridiculing the mainstream media in this early interview, he also expresses astonishment and outrage about a larger politics of reception. He argues that Reuters's media illiteracy potentially enables a whole series of category errors in which harmless gamers are demonized as terrorists.

It wasn't intended for the purpose what it was portrayed to be by the media. So no, I don't regret making a funny video . . . why should I? The only thing I regret is thinking that news from Reuters was objective and always right. The least they could do is some online research before publishing this. If they label me al-Qaeda just for making this silly video, that makes you think, what is this al-Qaeda? And is everything al-Qaeda?[16]

Although SonicJihad dismisses his own work as "silly" or "funny," he expects considerably more from a credible news agency like Reuters: objective reporting, online research, and fact-checking before publishing. Certainly, almost all of the salient details in the Reuters story were incorrect. SonicJihad's film was not made by terrorists or for terrorists; it was not created by "Islamic militants" for "Muslim youths." The videogame it depicted had not been modified by a "tech-savvy militant" with advanced programming skills.

Of course, what is most extraordinary about this story isn't just that Reuters merely got its facts wrong; it is that a self-identified parody video was shown to an august House Intelligence Committee by a team of well-paid experts from the Science Applications International Corporation as key evidence of terrorist recruitment techniques. Moreover, this story of media illiteracy unfolded in the context of a fundamental Constitutional debate about domestic surveillance via communications technology and the further regulation of digital content by lawmakers. Furthermore, the transcripts of the actual hearing show that much more than simple gullibility or ignorance was in play, because legislators demonstrated that they actually were not naïve about the cultural landscape of the Internet or digital media, although the witnesses who found the material may have been. Based on their exchanges in the public record, elected representatives appear to be keenly aware that the digital discourses of an emerging information culture are challenging the authority of long-standing institutions of knowledge.

I have named this principle of reaction *virtualpolitik*, one of the pragmatic, provisional political forces governing the virtual state. I argue that the peculiar behavior of legislators reflects the anxieties and defensive interests of traditional stakeholders engaged in governance, who are grappling with distributed networks and peer-to-peer forms of community organization that further destabilize an already fragmented representational structure. Certainly, fissures emerge during face-to-face political exchanges whenever issues are debated, thus solidifying forms of oppositional loyalty and closing opportunities for genuine deliberation across communities constituted by difference. Beyond party politics, public institutions have long contained many different cultures, and these cultures reflect particular ideologies about concepts like "freedom" or "honesty" that are in turn shaped by factors like national, linguistic, or theological identity; societal attitudes about ownership and authorship; and cultural categories of gender, race, and class. The introduction of technology, from either the margins or the center of political deliberation, will not necessarily usher in a definitive era of a neutral technocratic public sphere, because pre-existing conflicts can actually be intensified when competing parties are no longer separated by time and space and their messages are condensed and expanded during the course of travel through possibly distorting, noisy, or overly constrictive channels for communication.

Deconstructing the House Intelligence Hearing

These hearings are symptomatic of a historical moment in which the transformation of traditional institutions by digital media in networked societies may no longer be hyped by the utopian or dystopian narratives of a decade ago, but emphatic declarations about prohibiting or stimulating specific discursive practices in this new public culture still occupy a prominent place at the podium, news desk, or official web portal. Furthermore, many civic institutions—government agencies, libraries, public universities, and managers of common infrastructure—have created virtual counterparts with many of the same rhetorical conventions or inverse forms of those very same rules. In other words, the official discourses of institutions that provide digital information often function like those of the traditional institutions of knowledge that they emulate.

This argument about the cultural conservatism of political institutions is designed to explain why policy makers' reactions to terrorists' use of networked communication and digital media actually tell us more about our own American ideologies about technology and rhetoric in a contemporary information environment. When the experts came forward at the SonicJihad hearing to "walk us through the media and some of the products,"[17] they presented digital artifacts of an information economy, one mirroring many of the features of our own consumption of objects of electronic discourse, which are in turn easy to copy and distribute. Indeed, the word "products" appears twenty-two times in the hearings to describe jihadist materials, as though competing goods are at issue rather than competing ideologies.

From this one hearing we can see how the reception of many new digital genres plays out in the public sphere of legislative discourse. Webpages, videogames, and web logs are mentioned specifically. The main architecture of the witnesses' presentation to the committee is organized according to the rhetorical conventions of the electronic slideshow, generally known by the trade name PowerPoint. Moreover, the actual arguments made by expert witnesses about the relationship of orality to literacy or of public to private communications in new media are highly relevant to how we might understand other important digital genres, such as electronic mail or text messaging.

In Bruno Latour's tome on *Making Things Public: Atmospheres of Democracy*, "making things public" in the visual culture of civic life means much more than the common idiomatic meaning that the phrase might suggest. Latour is also interested in exploring the broader, more traditional notion of *res publica* and considering how "things public" are literally constructed for and received by political audiences. Using the language of software development, Latour characterizes a range of political and scientific representations, which are "representative" and "realistic" to varying degrees, as manifestations of what he calls "object-oriented democracy." Government websites, government-funded videogames and virtual reality simulations, national digital libraries and databases, e-mail to and from agency officials, and electronic slideshows by public representatives that employ new presentation technologies can similarly serve as "things public." They reveal conflicts and contradictions from which civilian voters and taxpayers are otherwise shielded.

Latour is largely writing about civic spaces in the physical world, but his claims also have been adapted to virtual environments in which his catalog of manifestations of the public sphere emphasizes activities of deliberation and purposive communicative action. Hearings about the Internet and videogames put similar issues about the function of political and civic rhetoric in the digital age on display, and publicly funded projects to create digital artifacts and architectures with hypertext or virtual reality environments can tell us a lot about how we construct shared truths about medicine, science, economics, government, or the arts. These new media may be showcased as part of distracting political spectacles, or they may function to complement the traditional tropes of the *res publica*. For example, digital documents, virtual objects, social puppets, built environments, navigable terrains, and perceptual spaces of computer-generated sites can take the user into the realm of public matters while also exploring the private spaces associated with certain forms of cultural intimacy and rituals of affiliation.

The hearing also invites consideration of privacy, intellectual property, and digital rights, because moral values about freedom and ownership are alluded to by many of the elected representatives present, albeit often through the looking glass of user behaviors imagined as radically Other. For example, terrorists are described as "modders" and "hackers" who subvert those who properly create, own, legitimate, and regulate intellectual property. To explain embarrassing leaks of infinitely replicable digital files, witness Ron Roughead says, "We're not even sure that they don't even hack into the kinds of spaces that hold photographs in order to get pictures that our forces have taken."[18] Another witness, Undersecretary of Defense for Policy and International Affairs Peter Rodman, claims that "any video game that comes out, as soon as the code is released, they will modify it and change the game for their needs."[19] Thus the implication of these witnesses' testimony is that the release of code into the public domain can contribute to political subversion, as much as covert intrusion into computer networks by stealthy hackers can.

However, the witnesses from the Pentagon and from the Science Applications International Corporation (SAIC), a government contractor, often present contradictory images of the terrorists. Sometimes the enemy is depicted as an organization of technological masterminds, capable of manipulating the computer code of unwitting Americans and snatching their rightful intellectual property away; at other times opposing forces are depicted as premodern and even subliterate political innocents. In contrast, the congressional representatives who are listening seem to focus on the similarities to rather than the differences from everyday American digital practices.

According to the transcripts of this open hearing, legislators on both sides of the aisle express anxiety about domestic patterns of Internet reception. In their questions, lawmakers identify web logs (blogs) as a particular area of concern, because they are potentially destabilizing alternatives to authoritative print sources of information from established institutions. Representative Alcee Hastings (D-Florida) relates the polluting power of insurgent bloggers to that of influential American muckrakers from the political right: "And I might add—maybe my question is rhetorical—because, quite frankly, we have a lot of garbage on our regular mainstream news that comes from blog sites, that's—you know, Drudge ain't the truth every day when he writes something, and then it winds up becoming a story that does considerable damage."[20]

Representative Heather Wilson (R-New Mexico) also attempts to project a media-savvy persona by bringing up the "phenomenon of blogging" in conjunction with her questions about the "hottest sites."[21] Wilson clearly understands how Internet traffic can be magnified by cooperative ventures among groups of ideologically like-minded content providers: "These websites, and particularly the most active ones, are they cross-linked? And do they have kind of hot links to your other favorite sites on them?"[22]

Even the legislators' own webpages are electronic artifacts about which they are self-conscious, particularly when the demands of digital labor create disruptions in the smooth functioning of their duties as lawmakers. Representative Anna Eshoo (D-California) bemoans the difficulty of maintaining official congressional websites. As she observes, "So we are—as members, I think we're very sensitive about what's on our website, and if I retained what I had on my website three years ago, I'd be out of business. So we know that they have to be renewed. They go up, they go down, they're rebuilt, they're—you know, the message is targeted to the future."[23] Certainly, congressional representatives recognize that their public presentation to their constituents and other interested parties now depends on these forms of new media display, particularly as more Americans visit government websites after the September 11 attacks.[24] Recent legislation actually requires federal elected representatives to publish information about gifts from contributors on their own public sites, and this trend toward mandating public disclosure via official websites is likely to continue.

In the wake of these hearings, I visited the websites of the House Permanent Intelligence Committee members and found a range of institutional web styles. First, their chosen visual schemes did not reflect any set distinctions based on party affiliation, regional character, or gender. Second, they all used a personal photograph as part of their legislative web identity, but there weren't set rules about where that photograph should go. Despite interest in providing greater institutional uniformity in the government's web presence, the legislative branch is allowed to personalize their members' sites. This heterogeneousness of organization and content provides a challenge to semantic web experts who have attempted to aggregate this legislative data and index it with metadata, particularly when the user-generated content is so anarchic.[25]

Chairman Hoekstra's site uses established institutional color schemes and standardized design elements in a generic website with a children's page added as an appendage.[26] Then ranking minority member Harman's site announces itself as a "Virtual Office" and uses a layout showing cutaway views of the private spaces of her public office, in which each room represents a realm of relevant information for the visitor to explore.[27] The rank-and-file committee members are a varied group who often adopt competing web design strategies. Despite her claim of regular updating in her hearing comments, Representative Eshoo's site uses little dynamic content. Her navigation area is demarcated with stars, and the main field follows the impersonal e-newsletter format of many institutional early adopters rather than an individuated, informal commentary style more characteristic of a blog.[28] Congressman Hasting's site is perhaps the

Figure 1.2
Home pages of the websites of members of the House Intelligence Committee.

most visually arresting from a web design standpoint: he uses gray rather than congressional blue, breaks up rectangular spaces with wavy lines, uses his own handwriting as a design motif, and offers an extroverted video greeting to website visitors.[29] In contrast, Congresswoman Wilson probably has the most impersonally designed page, one which appears to come from a corporate rather than a governmental web style template. Her home page uses a lot of white space and a mustard palette divorced from the usual visual appeals to patriotism characteristic of political sites.[30] Representative Thornberry's site emphasizes his electronic slideshow with a photo gallery,[31] Representative Tiahrt foregrounds a newsroll in a large font right below his main banner,[32] and Representative Silvestre Reyes points readers to his blog, which says nothing about the SonicJihad hearing in the entry for that day.[33] Despite the fact that the design scheme of committee maverick Rush Holt (D-NJ) is remarkably staid and uses the same blue as many other legislators, the line of sight into the opening photo on his home page is oriented so that the user seems to be seated at the table with Holt and his staff. Although such icons have already become institutional clichés, Holt's file folder tabs and prominently displayed open mailbox still suggest an imagined hands-on quality, allowing site visitors to feel as if they could leave mail or browse through the congressman's file cabinets without a policing receptionist or security guard to impede access to the information channel.[34] Unlike Representative Harman's website, which emphasizes the presence of walls through cutaway diagrams, Representative Holt's site generally signals the absence of barriers to his legislative office.

Of course, there is a single federal organization, Webcontent.gov, which provides guidelines about appropriate web design practices, such as avoiding the use of advertising or content that infringes on copyright law. Yet the aesthetic guidance offered on this site avoids being explicitly proscriptive, and even their sample templates are remarkably minimal on details.[35] Furthermore, legislators may cast themselves as webmasters personally engaged in rebuilding and renewing their sites, yet clearly they are aware of the fact that they depend on the resources and expertise of web designers and site managers with organizational and specialized technical skills to produce and maintain the institutional sites that represent the ethos—the character or image of rhetorical credibility—of the legislators' political personae. For example, at one point Representative Wilson asks witness Rodman if he knows "of your 100 hottest sites where the webmasters are educated? What nationality they are? Where they're getting their money from?"[36] In her questions, Wilson implicitly acknowledges that web work reflects influences from pedagogical communities, economic networks of the exchange of capital, and even potentially the specific ideologies of nation-states.

It is perhaps indicative of the contractors' anachronistic worldview that the witness is unable to answer Wilson's question. He explains that his agency focuses on the physical location of the server or Internet service provider rather than the social backgrounds of the individuals who might be manufacturing objectionable digital texts.

The premise behind the contractors' working method—surveiling the technical apparatus, not the social network—may be related to other beliefs expressed by government
witnesses, such as the supposition that jihadist websites are collectively produced and
spontaneously emerge from the indigenous, traditional, tribal culture. Instead of
assuming that Iraqi insurgents have analogous beliefs, practices, and technological
awareness to those in first-world countries, the consultants characterize the population
as childlike.

Platonic Echoes

Rhetoricians notice residual subtexts, particularly the persistent cultural standbys that
date back to Plato. The witnesses' conjectures about competing cultures of orality and
literacy can be analyzed to offer not only a more complete understanding of these
particular hearings but also of the larger rhetorical environment around videogames
and digital culture more generally. According to the experts before Congress, the
Middle Eastern audience for these videogames and websites is inevitably infantilized
because it is limited by membership in a preliterate culture that—like the emerging
Internet society complementing its abortive cultural production—supposedly doesn't
rely on knowledge that is archived in printed codices.

Sometimes the witnesses before Congress seemed to be unintentionally channeling
the ideas of the late literacy theorist Walter Ong about the "secondary orality" associated with talky electronic media such as television, radio, audio recording, or telephone communication. Later followers of Ong extended this concept of secondary
orality to hypertext, hypermedia, e-mail, and blogs since they also share features of
both speech and written discourse. [37] Although Ong's disciples celebrated this vibrant
reconnection to a mythic, communal past in what Kathleen Welch calls "electric
rhetoric,"[38] the defense industry consultants express their profound state of alarm
caused by the potentially dangerous and subversive character of this hybrid form of
communication.

The concept of an oral tradition is first introduced by the witnesses in the context
of modern marketing and product distribution:

The Internet is used for a variety of things—command and control. One of the things that's
missed frequently is how and—how effective the adversary is at using the Internet to distribute
product. They're using that distribution network as a modern form of oral tradition, if you will.
And we'll talk about oral tradition in a little while.[39]

Thus, although the Internet can be deployed for hierarchical command and control
activities, it also functions as a highly efficient peer-to-peer distributed network for
disseminating the commodity of information. The witnesses before Congress want to
emphasize the latter, supposedly underreported feature, which they claim is "missed

frequently." Throughout the hearings, the witnesses imply that unregulated lateral communication among social actors who are not authorized to speak for nation-states or to produce legitimated expert discourses is potentially destabilizing to the existing political order.[40]

Witness Eric Michael later continues with his analysis of the oral tradition and the conventions of communal life in the Middle East to emphasize the primacy of speech in the collective discursive practices of this alien population:

I'd like to point your attention to the media types and the fact that the oral tradition is listed as most important. The other media listed support that. And the significance of the oral tradition is more than just—it's the medium by which, once it comes off the Internet, it is transferred.[41]

Furthermore, this oral tradition can contaminate other media because it also functions as rumor, the traditional bane of the stately discourse of military leaders, which dates back to classical and early modern texts.[42]

The oral tradition now also has an aspect of rumor. A(n) event takes place. There is an explosion in a city. Rumor is that the United States Air Force dropped a bomb and is doing indiscriminate killing. This ends up being discussed on the street. It ends up showing up in a Friday sermon in a mosque or in another religious institution. It then gets recycled into written materials. Media picks up the story and broadcasts it, at which point it's now a fact. In this particular case that we were telling you about, it showed up on a network television, and their propaganda continues to go back to this false initial report on network television and continues to reiterate that it's a fact, even though the United States government has proven that it was not a fact, even though the network has since recanted the broadcast.[43]

In this example, many-to-many discussion on the street is formalized into a one-to many sermon and then further stylized using technology in a one-to-many broadcast on network television in which propaganda that is "false" can no longer be disputed. This oral tradition is like digital media, because elements of discourse can be infinitely copied or recycled, and it is designed to reiterate content. Implicitly, the witnesses are arguing that authority structures depend on the work of published authors, which the oral tradition threatens.

In contrast, Plato argues that it is literacy, not orality, which is the greatest threat to social and political norms by virtue of its alienation of words from authors. The author's potential absence from his own text means that written discourse cannot be always verified as coming from a credible source. In the *Phaedrus*, Plato explains why literacy is so subversive:

The offspring of painting stand there as if they are alive, but if anyone asks them anything, they remain most solemnly silent. The same is true of written words. You'd think they were speaking as if they had understanding, but if you question anything that has been said because you want to learn more, it continues to signify just that very same thing forever. When it has once been written down, every discourse roams about everywhere, reaching indiscriminately those with understanding no less than those who have no business with it, and it doesn't know to whom it should speak and to whom it should not. And when it is faulted and attacked unfairly, it always needs its father's support; alone, it can neither defend itself nor come to its own support.[44]

While contemporary oral culture is considered to be infantilizing, according to the witnesses before the Intelligence Committee, by speaking through the persona of Socrates's Plato presents a different image from the ancient world in which the written text is personified as a parentless child.[45] Socrates's skepticism about a society based on the written codex runs entirely counter to the interpretation of the paid consultants with their collection of jihadist digital materials. The witnesses before the Intelligence Committee elevate Western society on the grounds of its supposed foundations in authoritative and stable printed texts and tablets rather than transient and mutable oral utterances. Yet digital culture is capable of undermining this flattering picture of cultural superiority and toppling the existing hierarchy of knowledge.

I am a rhetorician, which means that I both study and teach rhetoric. Despite the fact that rhetorical knowledge is the ostensible subject of this hearing, I cannot help but notice that my discipline also does not come off particularly well in this testimony, and that rhetoric is often associated with destructive countercultural forces. For example, witness Eric Michael explains the problem that rhetoric poses to national security:

It's also the use of poetry, the use of language, the use of rhetoric, the use of imagery and meta-phor. When we translate their products into English, you lose the true impact. It's the difference between reading the Gettysburg Address in English and a paraphrased translation of it in another language.

And they use this rhetoric to hammer home two big themes. The first is victimization, their grievances, why they fight; and the second one is a call to action, which is what they can do to respond to self-actualize themselves. And what I will argue to you and show you in the products that we're going to show you is that in terms of victimization, it is emotionally set up to evoke a response. They distort the truth, they use selective pieces of the truth, they assemble it in such a way that it is a distortion, or in some cases they create new truth. And they use that emotion then in call to action where they romanticize the struggle and turn it into the most important thing going on in the world today.[46]

Although the witness initially presents "rhetoric" as the use of particular figures of speech, which may be untranslatable and thus are culturally specific, he quickly moves away from relatively neutral commenting on the presence of discrete tropes and topoi to outright castigation of the entire communicative mode. Rhetoric, he tells us, is designed to "distort the truth," because it is a selective assembly or a "distortion." Rhetoric is also at odds with reason, because it appeals to emotion and a romanticized *Weltanschauung* oriented around discursive configurations of "struggle."

The film by SonicJihad is chosen as the final clip by the congressional witnesses because it allegedly combines many different types of emotional appeal, and thus it conveniently ties together all of the motifs and truisms that the witnesses present to the legislators about unreliable oral or rhetorical sources in the Middle East:

And there you see how all these products are linked together. And you can see where the games are set to psychologically condition you to go kill coalition forces. You can see how they use humor. You can see how the entire campaign is carefully crafted to first evoke an emotion and then to evoke a response and to direct that response in the direction that they want.[47]

Jihadist digital products, especially videogames, are effective means of manipulation, the witnesses argue, because they employ multiple channels of persuasion and carefully sequenced and integrated subliminal messages.

To understand what rhetoricians call the larger "cultural conversation"[48] of the hearing, it is important to keep in mind that this argument that games can psychologically condition players to be predisposed to violence is one that was important in other congressional hearings of the period, as well one that played a role in bills and resolutions passed by the full body of the legislative branch after an elaborate process of political deliberation. In the witness's testimony an appeal to anti-game sympathies at home is combined with critiques of closed antidemocratic systems abroad in which the circuits of rhetorical production and their composite metonymic chains are described as those that command users to produce specific, unvarying, robotic responses.

Of course, there is nothing particularly new about many of the objections that Pentagon and SAIC witnesses lodge against rhetoric more generally. Emphasizing the craft of the wily rhetor and the somatic responses of a malleable audience have been standard clichés from the foes of the traditional arts of persuasion for centuries. Several of the accusations made against rhetoric during the hearing are the same ones emphasized by the character of Socrates in Plato's dialogue *Gorgias* against the practices of the Sophists. For example, Plato compares rhetoric to "pastry baking," which serves as a form of "flattery" for "what's most pleasant at the moment." Unlike "justice," which serves the state's interests like "medicine," rhetoric only appeals to evanescent appetites. According to Plato, rhetoric is also a form of "cosmetics," which only attends to superficial improvement, unlike a useful cultural activity like gymnastics, and so is thus "mischievous, deceptive, disgraceful, and ill-bred," which cheats us "by means of shaping and coloring, smoothing out and dressing us, so as to make people assume an alien beauty and neglect their own."[49]

However, this sharp criticism of the artful use of a "crafted" presentation style is ironic,[50] given that the witnesses' compilation of jihadist digital material is in the form of a carefully structured PowerPoint presentation, one that is paced to a well-rehearsed rhythm of "slide, please" or "next slide" in the transcript. In fact, Congressman Tiahrt (R-Kansas) is so impressed with the rhetorical mastery of the consultants that he tries to appropriate it. For example, he reviews the text on the witnesses' electronic slides in scrupulous detail. This allows for the following jihadist slogans to be included in the Congressional Record: "In Abu Ghraib they rape us every day. We have their bastards in our wombs. Most of us are pregnant," and "If they leave Iraq, we will find them and kill them."[51] At one point Tiahrt expresses his wish to replicate particularly persuasive elements of the witnesses' presentation for his own purposes by having copies of their slides. As Tiahrt puts it, "I'd like to get a copy of that slide sometime, because I don't think people realize the breadth and depth of this threat. This is a battle of cultures." Like many post-September 11 policy makers, Tiahrt alludes to Samuel Huntington's thesis about an inevitable "clash of civilizations" between the developed West and the Orientalist East,[52] which in the presenters' logic becomes a literate West and a preliterate digital East. By borrowing segments from the witnesses' rhetoric, Tiahrt plans to magnify this particular aspect of the threat to national security. Thus, in copying the slide, he actually would make their words distinctively his own by emphasizing a particular aspect of the consultants' message.

From the hearing we also learn that the terrorists' websites are threatening precisely because they manifest a polymorphously perverse geometry of expansion. For example, one SAIC witness before the House committee compares the replication and elaboration of digital material online to a "spiderweb":

The numbers and the—and the actual websites change from day to day. They come up and down, and so the researchers are constantly going back and looking at this list of sites that they've got. Over the course of the last year and a half, we've been asked a couple times which websites we found to be most offensive; that list will also change based on the material that's published. Perhaps the most interesting thing to do is watch a piece of material that is posted to one of the websites, and then it literally spiderwebs across the Web as other websites pick it up. And they are all interlinked. . . . Back to the previous comment I made: it's difficult, therefore, to determine if there's central coordination or not.[53]

Like Representative Eshoo's site, the terrorists' sites go up and down, but the consultant is left to speculate about whether or not there is any "central coordination" to serve as an organizing principle and to explain the persistence and consistency of messages despite the apparent lack of a single authorial ethos to offer a stable, humanized point of reference.

Experts and their Discourses

In the hearing, the oft-cited solution to the problem created by the hybridity and iterability of digital rhetoric appears to be "public diplomacy." Both consultants and lawmakers seem to agree that the damaging messages of the insurgents must be countered with U.S.-sanctioned information,[54] and the phrase "public diplomacy" appears in the hearing seven times. However, witness Roughead complains that the protean oral tradition and what Henry Jenkins has called the "transmedia" character of digital culture[55]—which often crosses several platforms of traditional print, projection, or broadcast media—stymies their best rhetorical efforts: "I think the point that we've tried to make in the briefing is that wherever there's Internet availability at all, they can then download these—these programs and put them onto compact discs, DVDs, or post them into posters, and provide them to a greater range of people in the oral tradition that they've grown up in. And so they only need a few Internet sites in order to distribute and disseminate the message."[56]

As this book will show, public diplomacy is not the only example of a carefully produced, state-sanctioned multimedia campaign that manages digital content, as there are a number of alliances between what Jane Fountain has called the "virtual state" and the advertising and marketing industries that create and coordinate messages. Social marketing, risk communication, and institutional branding occupy different niches in this larger alliance between government and the persuasive industries. Many of these forms of discourse have research communities or academic centers devoted to their practices, and digital media are critical to their delivery strategies to the general population. Although SAIC specializes in the reception of information rather than its production, their paid consultants obviously benefited from a similar union of private enterprise and public interest upon which their claim to expertise about rhetoric is predicated.

Amazingly, Representative Tiahrt commends not only the government's public diplomacy effort, but also argues for outright "propaganda" in an information war with jihadists, dictated by the spirit of populism and the mission of the founding fathers.

The average citizen wants us to do something about this. And yet now we hear concerns about propaganda going on here in the United States government. There ought to be propaganda going on. We need to counteract this kind of blatant lies and misleading.

    And we've heard reference to our truth versus their truth. We believe there's a fundamental truth, and it's something that was laid out by our founding fathers and it's this nation's birth right, that we hold certain truths self-evident; that among these truths is that we're all created equal. And we consider them inalienable rights—the rights of life, liberty and the pursuit of happiness. And those things need to be talked about worldwide on the Internet.[57]

By making appeals to natural law that would contradict claims of relativism or competing truths, Tiahrt asserts that a "fundamental" set of epistemological values can be disseminated by the U.S. government to rebellious potential jihadists. He also ascribes the character of secondary orality to this affirmative, pro-U.S. use of the Internet, since these patriotic appeals can be "talked about worldwide."

In some ways the people who did not speak at the hearing about how terrorists were using the Internet were just as significant as those who did. Specifically, a number of non-governmental freelance groups with well-articulated web and mainstream media presences were not represented at the hearing. The SITE Institute, Global Security, and a number of other politically center-right Internet monitoring organizations were not invited to speak, despite extensive media coverage of their investigative activities. In the weeks and months that followed the hearing, there were long profile pieces about these online international detectives in publications such as the *New York Times* and the *New Yorker*.[58]

Perhaps the most obviously politically motivated omission was the absence of representatives from The International Crisis Group, such as spokesperson Robert Malley; only a few months earlier the Crisis Group had released a much-publicized report about jihadist Internet rhetoric that was also highly critical of the U.S. government. This report similarly comments on the transmedia capabilities of jihadists with access to sophisticated digital tools and production facilities, the rapid dissemination of messages, and the use of Internet servers that protect the anonymity of insurgent sympathizers. However, the Crisis Group report "In Their Own Words: Reading the Iraqi Insurgency" reaches a very different conclusion than does the SAIC witnesses' PowerPoint presentation, despite access to very similar evidence on the World Wide Web. First of all, the Crisis Group argues that the spokespersons of anti-occupation forces are a more serious threat because they have an inherent linguistic advantage: namely, there are more English speakers among their staffs than there are Arabic speakers among their U.S. counterparts. Thus, insurgents are able to respond verbally to events in the theater of combat or statements from U.S. or British policy makers much more rapidly than are their Western equivalents.[59] Much of the opposition's rhetorical efficiency has to do with quick turnaround time in Arabic-English or English-Arabic translation, a problem with which U.S. intelligence and public diplomacy experts continue to struggle as a result of the persistent shortage of speakers of Arabic and other Middle Eastern languages on U.S. government payrolls. Second, the Crisis Group also points out that the jihadists were very conscious of their audiences and would immediately change their rhetorical strategy if a particular approach, such as showing graphically violent filmed segments of the beheading of hostages on the Internet, was alienating their core viewership. Third, the Crisis Group report insists that the actions of U.S. forces are often perceived as being at odds with their words, thus minimizing the impact of their public diplomacy efforts. Because the Crisis Group was on record saying that human rights abuses and civil liberties violations committed in the name of the U.S. government had to end in Iraq in order to deprive the enemy of their chief rhetorical asset, it is not surprising that they were excluded from a panel for which the focus was continuing surveillance, not policy change.

The transcript also reveals that the members of the House Intelligence Committee were not, in fact, the original intended audience for the witnesses' PowerPoint presentation. Rather, when it was first created by SAIC, this "expert" presentation was designed for training purposes for the troops on the ground, who would be facing the challenges of deployment in hostile terrain.[60] According to the witnesses, having the slideshow showcased before Congress was something of an afterthought. Yet SAIC and Pentagon witnesses apparently seized the opportunity to repurpose their electronic presentation to appeal to multiple decision makers in different branches of government.

Rep. Silvestre Reyes (D-TX):   Thank you, Mr. Chairman.
And thank you for sharing the presentation with us. I'm curious, has this presentation been seen—or have you shared it with the leadership of DOD, leadership of the intelligence community from the National Director of Intelligence on down?
Mr. Rodman: Yes, we have. I mean, it was developed for the Marine Corps, as we mentioned. But in recent weeks we've shared it with the State Department, Karen Hughes. I called Mike Hayden to let him know about it, and we provided the briefing to some people at the Open Source Center. So it is available. And within DOD, as I mentioned at the beginning, it's available to other units—
Rep. Reyes: Has the Secretary of Defense seen this?
Mr. Rodman: No, I don't believe he has seen it.[61]

Rodman's mention of Karen Hughes, the Undersecretary for Public Diplomacy, acknowledges the connection between intelligence, training, and nationalistic public relations efforts. The Open Source Center that Rodman mentions is a federal organization with a password-protected site; it provides information in the form of "foreign media reporting and analysis" from print and digital media to "policymakers, government institutions and strategic partners."[62] This information may be politically sensitive, but it is not technically secret because it has been published on paper or on the World Wide Web. SAIC has also extensively marketed its expertise in this open source area by dramatically using domestic examples from Internet datasets that reveal warnings about potential employee, school, or community mayhem from messages on blogs and social network sites.[63]

To maintain a share of the government market, SAIC also employs publicity and promotion practices through the Internet and digital media. They use HTML webpages for this purposes, as well as PowerPoint presentations and online videos. The rhetoric of the SAIC website emphasizes their motto "From Science to Solutions." After a short Flash film about how SAIC scientists and engineers solve "complex technical problems," the visitor is taken to the home page, which re-emphasizes their central message about expertise.[64] The maps, uniforms, and specialized tools and equipment depicted in these opening webpages reinforce an ethos of professional specialization that is able to respond to multiple threats posed by the global war on terror. Although the SAIC corporation emphasizes U.S. nationalism in many of its digital appeals, a tab for SAIC EUROPE is always visible to serve as a reminder that this is a multinational company.

A promotional video on the website demonstrates the company's attention to the careful orchestration of multimedia elements and the conventions of corporate rhetorical styles.[65] The film opens with a desolate, windy moonrise that is interrupted by the sound of boots on the ground. During the course of less than two minutes, the company film provides what appears to be a comprehensive overview of its corporate services: "Research and Development," "Commercial Services," "Systems Engineering and Integration," "Homeland Security," "Intelligence," "Logistics," and "Defense Transformation." The entire presentation is orchestrated to stirring music, and a new melody in a new key is introduced during the "Intelligence" section so that the emotional appeals of the video are conveyed through auditory as well as visual means. At one point during the montage of images, the American flag transforms into the SAIC flag so that the symbols of patriotism and corporate brand identity are merged. At the end, the film returns to soldiers in uniform, this time focusing on their faces rather than on their feet, before cutting away to a shot of the earth from space.

However, even as the hearings were taking place, not all of the representatives were accepting the authority of the SAIC analysis. Although he may have been the lone voice of frank and sometimes strident dissent, Congressman Rush Holt openly criticized the way that many domestically produced videogames presented the political enemies of the United States as dehumanized virtual objects to be destroyed, and attempted to undermine the holier-than-thou position of U.S. investigators looking at foreign-made digital media.

Rep. Holt: Okay. I guess, you know, as I look at computer games that are out there, I don't think of them as our finest and proudest output. I'm wondering, are U.S. computer games regarded in some cases as anti-Muslim and supporting a crusading point of view? Is there commentary on U.S. computer games and that sort of thing?

Mr. Rodman: I think I would have to go back and say that we're looking at computer games that are being used for development of materials on the web, and we don't actually spend a lot of time looking at—

Rep. Holt: But if you're looking—if I may jump in here, you're looking at how the United States is portrayed.

Mr. Rodman: Yes.

Rep. Hplt: And one of the ways that I suspect they might present deleterious information is by saying, "Look, here in the United States the kids are playing games that are anti-Muslim or crusading." And I'm just wondering if you see that kind of presentation.[66]

Representative Holt points out that the recycling of digital content in the Islamic world may actually involve the repurposing of the norms of already violent commercial videogames from the West. Holt also may have been aware that some of this violent digital content in commercial games glorifying battlefield violence originally was produced for military training in games and simulations. As Gonzalo Frasca argues, videogames, such as the recruitment game *America's Army*, could even be taken as a form of political propaganda that celebrates a particular form of allegiance to what Holt characterizes as "crusading" political and cultural violence.[67] The counterargument that military recruitment videogames are providing Frank Capra-style persuasive and patriotic information and entertainment for the digital generation still acknowledges that these games only allow for one possible ideological orientation, whether in attack or defense mode, that of a U.S. uniformed soldier.[68]

Close reading of the transcript reveals that other legislators were expressing some skepticism about the authority and infallibility of the SAIC experts. With search engine technology available to regular citizens, access to specialized knowledge about arcane subcultures once far removed by geography no longer seems to be the exclusive purview of trained professionals. Expert amateurs can also gather useful intelligence, particularly from online sources. At one point Representative Eshoo observes, "Well, I mean, you can Google, too, and see what's there."[69] In retrospect, her comment becomes particularly ironic, because SonicJihad later points out that a simple Google search would have correctly identified both the benign source and the jocular character of his *Battlefield 2* fan film, had the government authorities bothered with such a prosaic approach to basic intelligence-gathering. Although the witnesses describe a daunting monitoring task for keeping track of proliferating jihadist sites, legislators seem to have difficulty accepting the impossibility of surgical strikes on the network or useful data-mining operations to identify suspects, given the importance of particular nodes where large and consequently vulnerable servers are located.[70]

Furthermore, the use of statistical hyperbole by the SAIC team may have made the witnesses vulnerable to suspicion from potential naysayers. One witness defends the slippery numbers to an inquisitive Eshoo at one point: "The numbers that we used, our initial list was 200, it grew to 550, and as I said, we're now to 1,500 that we sort of track on a regular basis."[71] Eventually, the number at issue grows to 5,000 in the witnesses' testimony.

Despite her pro-administration Republican political identity, Representative Wilson is especially persistent in asking for specific web traffic information of the kind commonly tracked by network administrators in both the public and private sectors, such as the country of origin of visiting IP addresses or the discrete number of unique page visits recorded. Despite the astronomical number of sites that SAIC contractors claim to be monitoring, Wilson still insists on the utility of concrete metrics and urges them to winnow down the numbers to achieve measurable goals. She appears to grill the witnesses at one point: "I—have you in your research identified where the servers are? If you take—I know you've got 5,000 websites, but if you—you said you've got between 25 and 100 that are the most active and the most virulent. Where are their servers located?"[72]

However, other lawmakers accept the hyperbolic statistics from SAIC at face value and even encourage the numbers to be magnified. For example, Representative

Tiahrt makes the quantities comparatively even larger by minimizing the number of "moderate" oppositional sites and depicting a vast galaxy of anti-American Internet opinion.

Rep. Todd Tiahrt (R-KS): Thank you, Mr. Chairman. Thank you for holding these hearings. I think a lot of people were not aware that this was out there in the universe, in the Internet. And so it's very important that we talk about this. I heard earlier in testimony that you believe there's somewhere between 1,500 and 5,000 of these websites out there that are put out by this radical form of Islam. Is that the range we're talking about in the universe?

Mr. Rodman: I think the total range we're talking about of sites that we would consider to be hostile is over 5,000. And the 1,500—(inaudible)—the number of sites—(inaudible).

Rep. Tiahrt: If somebody was to go explore the universe of these websites, would they come across the website that appears to be in this same vein but is instead a voice of moderation? And, if so, how many would they stumble across in the 5,000-plus websites?

Mr. Rodman: There are—in the web forums that we look at, there are people who do sign on who will provide some points of moderation.

Rep. Tiahrt: What percentage would you guess?

Mr. Rodman: I don't have that answer for you. I'm sorry.

Rep. Tiahrt: I mean, is it matched one for one, for every—(inaudible)—negative?

Mr. Rodman: Definitely not.

Rep. Tiahrt: Is it one for 100, one for 1,000, one for 5,000? It's not very much.

Mr. Rodman: A very small amount.

Rep. Tiahrt: Very small amount.

The number "5,000" is soon elevated to "5,000-plus" by Tiahrt, and the word "universe" is repeated three times to express the enormity of the project with which SAIC grapples. By emphasizing incommensurability of scale, Tiahrt also attempts to deepen the audience's appreciation of the government's limited understanding of what he considers to be an incomprehensible jihadist Internet Sublime that verges on the statistically infinite. Thus, "moderate" parts that might be comprehensible to a layperson may be encountered when we "come across" or "stumble across" them, but they poorly represent the gigantic whole.

Three weeks after this congressional hearing, Reuters ran another story about SonicJihad/Samir's videogame. The story, "Dutch gamer's clash with U.S. government," continued to repeat claims that the game-play footage fosters oppositional rhetoric, and it even seemed to allude to the language of Huntington's "clash of civilizations" in its title. However, Samir himself—who is described by the reporter as a "clean-cut youth" interviewed at a Burger King over fries and a milkshake—obviously doesn't merit the title of terrorist.[73] Samir asserts again that "it was just for fun, nothing political," and that his footage is not a "serious game" intended for education or indoctrination: "It has nothing to do with recruiting people or training people." Nonetheless, the new Reuters story continues to validate the view that Samir's game feeds an agenda of violence and propaganda: "'You can see where the games are set to psychologically condition you to go kill coalition forces,' said Eric Michael of Science Applications International, which is being paid $7 million by the Defense Department to monitor 1,500 militant websites."[74] Although Reuters uses a lower number of "militant" sites than the 5,000 emphasized by Tiahrt and implicitly acknowledges the pressure for measurable intelligence results in return for the SAIC employees' high salaries, the witnesses' testimony is still given a weight of expertise and the concept of videogames as a form of psychological conditioning is reiterated.

By June 26, 2006, the incident finally was being described as a "Pentagon Snafu" in connection with the online video edition of *Nightline* from ABC News.[75] From the opening of the broadcast, established government institutions were put on the spot: "So, how much does the Pentagon know about video games? Well, when it came to a recent appearance before Congress, apparently not enough."[76] In reporter Jake Tapper's coverage, the very language about "experts" that was highlighted in the earlier coverage is repeated in mockery. Although the obscured face of SonicJihad/Samir on the *Nightline* webcast continues to confer upon him an air of criminality, the chief talking head in the segment is "independent expert" Ian Bogost of the Georgia Institute of Technology, who has studied the rhetoric of persuasive games in depth.

If the Pentagon's experts deride the legitimacy of rhetoric as a cultural practice, Bogost occupies himself with its defense. In his book, *Persuasive Games: The Expressive Power of Videogames*, Bogost draws upon the authority of the "2,500 year history of rhetoric" to argue that videogames represent a significant development in that history.

I will attempt to articulate a new form of the art of persuasion that is distinct from both verbal and visual rhetoric. I call this form procedural rhetoric, the art of persuasion through rule-based interactions rather than words or images. This new form of persuasion is deeply tied to the core affordances of the computer: running code. But unlike some forms of computational persuasion . . . I argue that videogames have a unique persuasive power. Not only can they support existing social and cultural positions (the purpose of so-called "serious games"), but also they can disrupt and change these positions themselves, leading potentially to significant and rapid social change.[77]

Given that Bogost and his *Water Cooler Games* web log coeditor Gonzalo Frasca were actively involved in the detective work that exposed the depth of professional incompetence involved in the government's lineup of witnesses, it is appropriate that Bogost is given the final words in the segment, which call upon the ethical obligations of a collective "we." As Bogost says, "We should be deeply bothered by this. We should really be questioning the kind of advice that Congress is getting."[78]

On the *Nightline* segment, Pentagon spokesman Daniel Devlin is still arguing that secondary audiences seek out content that gratifies their violent urges. He points out that Samir's *Battlefield 2* footage was discovered on insurgent websites and thus was evidence of related criminal intent: "They are on hostile websites. That's where we found them, and that's all the research team is looking for."[79] In response to Devlin's assertions that intention can be construed relative to its audience rather than to its author, SonicJihad/Samir points out that a "ten-year-old kid" could do a "Google search" to discover the original audience and motivation behind the video, thus repeating his initial contention that a lack of online research skills was a core problem for Congress, as it was for the Reuters reporter.[80] Of course, Samir continues to protest that his game doesn't deserve any status as a rhetorical object in the *Nightline* segment, and the game-play's persuasive content is also downplayed by reporter Tapper as "not an advertisement for anything."[81] But those interested in a rhetorical reading of this particular form of cultural software might not accept Samir's claim of total ideological and communicative neutrality.

Indeed, some educational specialists praise games like *Battlefield 2* precisely because they allow players to assume the identity of other political and social actors, even when that identity position might be conventionally seen as an opponent or enemy position. For example, literacy theorist James Paul Gee has defended the pedagogical opportunities in even widely reviled first-person-shooter games by pointing out how they manifest situated learning in semiotic domains that encourage risk-taking, discovery, and the transfer of acquired skills. In his reflections about what he learned from playing as the malevolent "Shadow" in *Sonic Adventure 2*, Gee points out the value of more complicated "cultural models," even if they entail a recognition of moral ambiguity: "Of course, video games are just as easy to design to allow you to play a sinner as a saint. Indeed, this fact has generated a good deal of controversy. While the video game world is replete with heroes who destroy evil, it also contains games where you can be a mob boss, a hired assassin, or a car thief."[82]

Because these games present villains as well as heroes, the domestic production of videogames is always potentially regulated, especially in the environment surrounding the SonicJihad hysteria. Just two weeks after Samir's montage of game-play was shown to Intelligence Committee members, the House unanimously voted in favor of H.R. 1145, the SAFE Rating Act, a bill to ban the sale of violent and sexually explicit videogames to minors. Congressional legislation designed to limit consumption of videogames, particularly by the young, has included a number of distinct bills: the Truth in Video Game Rating Act, the Video Games Ratings Enforcement Act, the Family Entertainment Protection Act, and the Video Game Decency Act of 2006.

The Children's Crusade

Certainly, consternation over the youth of potential consumers of anti-American multimedia punctuated the May 4 hearing. The tender age of seven was mentioned several times as if it described a major sector of the potential audience for jihadist

Internet materials. Even nominal critics of administration policy seemed to accept the legitimacy of cultural norms about reaching an acceptable age of media majority when it comes to online participation. For example, Representative Hastings claims that "on the Internet a child can learn how to make a bomb,"[83] and Representative Harman makes an explicit play to the paternalism and maternalism of legislators by commending the witnesses and saying, "Peter, to the extent that you can share with us what you're doing about this, it would be helpful and finally—we're all parents here, and some of us are even new grandparents—the comment made that the target audience is 7 or perhaps younger than 7 is truly chilling, so if you could include that in your response, I'd appreciate it."[84]

The rhetoric surrounding the concept of a "child-safe" Internet has a history of legislative consequences in the past decade.[85] In July 2005, both the Senate and the House passed resolutions urging the Federal Trade Commission to investigate the rating of the videogame *Grand Theft Auto: San Andreas*—a rating making it accessible to minors—as a case of possible fraud.[86] These sentiments about digital threats to children date back to what the Clinton White House called a "Family Friendly Internet,"[87] which was the motivating factor behind the Children's Online Privacy Protection Act of 1998,[88] which is still struggling to overcome Constitutional challenges, though it continues to drive legislative agendas today.[89]

Plato similarly privileges the interests of the young in the regulation of cultural media. He argues in *The Republic* that dangerous forms of public discourse—like immoral tragedies or chaotic epics—can corrupt the polis, the Athenian city-state, by encouraging imitative behavior among immature members of society who may be moved by virtual spectacles, mere imitations of imitations. By arguing in favor of having a virtuous philosopher-king banish corrupting poets, Plato prefigures many of the same arguments appearing in congressional transcripts concerning the fear that terrorists and pedophiles were using the Internet too freely. As Plato puts it, "And in the case of sex, anger, and all the desires, pleasures, and pains that we say accompany all our actions, poetic imitation has the very same effect on us. It nurtures and waters them and establishes them as rulers in us when they ought to wither and be ruled, for that way we'll become better and happier rather than worse and more wretched."[90] Similarly, legislators argue that children exposed to violent or sexual content from virtual environments risk becoming damaged citizens of the state.

Just as regulating the behavior of foreigner enemies reflects fears about irresponsible domestic use, attempts to constrain the behavior of pedophiles actually may sometimes tell us more about legislators' anxieties about the communicative powers of the young themselves. The day before the House Intelligence Hearing about SonicJihad, there was a hearing in the Rayburn Office Building on "The Sexual Exploitation of Children over the Internet: What Parents, Kids and Congress Need to Know About Child Predators." The May 3 hearing was convened by the Subcommittee on Oversight and Investigations from the Committee on Energy and Commerce. It was the third hearing on the subject of how sexual predators use technology to prey upon their victims, and it was assembled in a more capacious room than the SonicJihad hearing. The room was even equipped with a semicircle of fixed leather chairs that contributed to an environment suggesting ceremonious deliberation rather than a mere preliminary briefing.

Although generally the discourse about pedophiles necessarily excludes children themselves, because it is assumed to be preferable to shield the young from objectionable content, some minors outside the regular circuits of adult rhetorical production are deemed capable of bearing witness in the public sphere by virtue of personal firsthand experience with victimization.[91] The star witness for the day was Russian former orphan Masha Allen, whose story may be as much about the failure of the social safety net that allowed her to reside with an adoptive father with a history of abuse as it is about the traffic of images of exploited children on the Internet.[92] In the webcast of the hearing, young Masha makes a compelling witness in favor of focusing on cyberregulation. Her occasional awkwardness as a speaker seems only to enhance her credibility. In the videotaped record, her hair is pulled back by a large barrette, and she peers through off-kilter glasses at the prepared comments she is holding. She is dressed like a typical teenager in an informal scalloped white top, pink button-down sweater, and simple necklace and earrings. Yet she speaks fluently and expertly in this high-pressure rhetorical situation.

"You have to do something about the Internet," Masha insists.[93] This order to legislators for action reflects her confidence in the government's ability to effect dramatic change and solve complex problems. She compares overcoming the technological challenges of surveiling illegitimate online exchanges to the scientific and territorial accomplishments of the space program. As Masha declares, "If we can put a man on the moon, we can make the Internet safe for kids."[94]

Although this request may seem patently unrealistic to anyone who understands how a global distributed network operates, Masha asserts her authority from the standpoint of victimization and comes off as an articulate and credible spokesperson nonetheless.[95] She begins her narrative with her life in Russia, depicting an alcoholic mother who tries to kill her, followed by misery in an institutional orphanage where the other children are themselves abusers and thieves.[96] After arriving in the United States, she describes an isolated life of captivity, starvation, sexual assault, and humiliation with her adoptive abuser, in which her tormentor kept her physically prepubescent: "the size of a five year old when I was ten."[97] She only begins to stammer once, over the question of how "any could let a pedophile adopt a little girl," because the phrasing was mistyped in her printed statement.[98] As Masha points out, much of the adoption procedure, including her abuser's selection of her from photographs of potential candidates for adoption, took place online. In some of the digital images supplied by the orphanage to her abuser via the Internet Masha says she was naked.[99] Like the terrorists who change the names of their operations and move to other websites, the adoption agencies that handled cases like Masha's are represented as roving entrepreneurs in perpetual flux.

It is interesting to note that traditional mass media channels are shown as considerably less threatening than the distributed networks of the Internet in Masha's discourse. For example, Masha says that television exposure was considerably less traumatic: "A lot of people are surprised that I wanted to go public with my story. But I've been on the Internet since I was five years old. Going on a television show wasn't going to hurt me."[100] In other words, her message is that broadcast media do not make children vulnerable in the way that online communication does.

Criminalizing File-Sharing Practices

Surprisingly, this hearing is as much about the rhetoric of illegally downloading copyrighted music as it is about child pornography on the Internet. Before the committee, Congressman Phil Gingrey, M.D. of Georgia argues for the updating of a "twenty-year-old civil statute" with Masha's Law:

Current civil law allows victims of child sexual exploitation to recover damages of no less than $50,000. However, federal copyright law provides statutory damages of no less than $150,000 to be awarded to the copyright holder when a song is illegally downloaded from the Internet. Masha's Law allows the civil remedy for the dissemination of child pornography to be equal to other illegal downloads.[101]

The Kerry-Isakson bill that takes up "Masha's Law" in the Senate also makes explicit the connection between downloading music and viewing child pornography. On Senator John Kerry's website, in a press release on how "Downloaded songs carry a penalty three times greater than exploited children," he exclaims "It's wrong that we have tougher penalties for downloading music than for downloading sick images of infants and children."[102]

Masha herself serves as an advocate for this equation of unauthorized online behaviors in her testimony before the committee:

Usually, when a kid is hurt and the abuser goes to prison, the abuse is over. But because Matthew put my pictures on the Internet the abuse is still going on. Anyone can see them. People are still downloading them—we get notices from the FBI every time someone is arrested for it. I want every single one of them to go to jail and really be punished. But that's a problem too.

I found out last summer that if someone downloads a song off the Internet the penalty is three times worse than if someone downs child pornography. I couldn't believe it! How can this be? That's when I decided that we had to change the laws about downloading child porn. Senator Kerry and Senator Isakson and Congressman Gingery and Congressman Tierney introduced bills in Congress that make the penalty the same as downloading songs. That was a few months ago. There hasn't been a vote on it. I want every single member of Congress to sponsor these bills and I want the Congress to pass them right away. [103]

Despite these expressions of impatience with the progress of elected representatives on passage, her desire for speedy legislative action was ultimately gratified. Masha's Law became law on July 27 that same year, as part of the omnibus Adam Walsh Child Safety and Protective Act, which passed both houses of Congress unanimously.

In her essay "Surfin' the Net: Children, Parental Obsolescence, and Citizenship," Sarah Banet-Weiser has argued that it is children's technological competence and the associated fear of parental obsolescence that spurs constituents' fear of and hostility toward the online cultural practices of the young. She points out that the ideology of the sexually innocent child who is also disengaged from productive participation in corporate capitalism can be historically situated as a relatively recent phenomenon, as Michel Foucault, Philippe Ariès, and other theorists grappling with the history of the institution of childhood in relation to sexuality and death have done.[104] Banet-Weiser claims that blocking and filtering software emphasizes the deployment of covert strategies to maintain these structures of authority. She untangles the cultural logic in which "if adult guidance is no longer needed to navigate the complex ways of the Internet," other forms of moral and intellectual hierarchy might also be threatened.

However, in her testimony, Masha often seems to desire overturning the sanctity of adult authority that Banet-Weiser describes. For example, she claims to want to reverse the position of the viewer and the viewed, so that professional adult voyeurs can become objects of an inquisitive public gaze themselves.

There are a lot of cases of people who downloaded my pictures and I want every single one of them to be punished as much as possible. . . . The people who are doing this should be afraid. We know who they are. A lot of the people downloading these pictures are professionals. They are doctors and teachers and ministers. We're going to put THEIR pictures on the Internet and tell people what they are doing. People stopped downloading songs when they found out they could be sued. We're going to sue these guys too—every single one we find out about. I want to tell them, "You're not doing this in secret anymore. Everyone can find out who you are!"[105]

Despite their relatively unequal positions of social power, given that the abusive adults are "doctors and teachers and ministers," Masha, with her cohort of abused victims, wants to turn the tables on sexual offenders taking part in covert Internet practices by making them afraid and exposing them to view.

Masha is correct that pedophiles are now the ones featured on websites from state and federal authorities. Unfortunately, this circulation of images of pedophiles in the interest of surveillance and retribution has been the cause for vigilante justice, such as a 2006 case in Maine in which two sex offenders were slain by an outraged Canadian dishwasher, who subsequently shot himself when cornered by police.[106] Unlike other government websites, which can be remarkably difficult for visitors to navigate, federal and state registries that map the location of sex offenders are remarkably user-friendly, with easy-to-read Mapquest-style representations of neighborhoods and arteries of transportation.[107] As additional visual aids, mug shots may be posted along with other personal information.

By using the status quo of draconian penalties for the downloading of music as justification for harsher consequences for pedophiles, rather than focusing attention just on those who traffic in a visual economy that depends on the sexual exploitation of children, debate about legalizing some forms of downloading and about new digital practices is stifled with a dramatic equivocation. Rather than allow the public to question the justice of the existing system in which astronomical federal fines are levied for relatively petty individual intellectual property crimes, these consequences are taken as a norm for all types of digital misbehavior. In other words, the logic goes like this: the penalty for this minor crime is really punitive, so we should make it the standard by which we judge major crimes. Of course, that reasoning makes no sense, even on the level of the simple if-then causal statement, assuming that minor crimes deserve minor punishments, and major crimes deserve correspondingly major ones. Furthermore, a law designed to protect the rights of minors to have control over their own persons is connected to another law that disproportionately targets these very minors' digital practices, because teenagers are particularly likely to be skeptical about claims from the film and recording industries that everyday file sharing constitutes piracy.[108] Despite Masha's claim that "People stopped downloading songs when they found out they could be sued," as of 2006, when a number of studies were conducted, there appears to be little evidence to support her assertion that litigation has significantly affected the frequency of peer-to-peer file sharing.[109]

Unfortunately, by equating two dissimilar user behaviors, the common practice of downloading digital music and the extrasocietal transgression of downloading child pornography, Masha's Law sets the stage for new regulatory attempts by the Department of Justice to control file-sharing practices. Like the SonicJihad hearing, Masha's hearing also uses a form of statistical hyperbole in which the number of digital files and cash proceeds from transactions are magnified in each iteration, as the adult witnesses from law enforcement agencies add their own expert testimony to her own.

Although ostensibly aimed only at pedophiles and terrorists, in late May 2006, Attorney General Alberto Gonzales formally requested that Internet service providers and search engine companies keep records of online behavior for up to two years. Not drawn to the public's attention was the fact that once records are kept, they can be subpoenaed for any legal proceeding, including civil cases involving intellectual property disputes.[110] Thus, the prosecution of those who believe that their access or replication of digital materials for creative, critical, or pedagogical purposes is covered under "fair use" could be further facilitated by a government agency. Furthermore, it is worth examining the actual surveiling technologies that are being funded by these programs and praised in the epideictic rhetoric of the Department of Justice. For example, among those being commended by the Attorney General in 2006 was Wyoming agent Flint Waters, who developed software designed to catch sexual predators, software that could also be used to monitor other prohibited peer-to-peer transactions. Dubbed Operation Peerless and later Peer Precision, the system targets file sharing specifically. However, such technical specifics were glossed over in Gonzales' speech honoring "his extraordinary contribution to cybercrime investigations."[111]

Advocates for free culture, the creative commons, or digital rights may be especially troubled by this subtext. For example, Tarleton Gillespie has written about how "cyber-safety" discourses get repurposed by entertainment industry interests who produce supposedly educational materials for K-12 students that urge them to "respect" copyright while ignoring the existence of fair use, particularly in learning contexts.[112] In *The Anarchist in the Library*, Siva Vaidhyanathan has argued that a dangerous conflict between oligarchy and anarchy is putting deliberative discourse in the public sphere at risk. Although Vaidhyanathan believes that file sharing only represents one recent manifestation of peer-to-peer activities that have been perceived by prevailing institutions as subversive for centuries, he argues that powerful interests who would like to control intellectual property are fostering fundamentally undemocratic practices of litigation and legislation through oppressive copyright law. These interests are controlling the discourse of the *bruits publics* by which exchanges of information normally take place in democratic public spheres.

I have had the luxury of similar conversations with composers, musicians, record company executives, and hackers. Few of these rather subtle and complicated terms of debate have worked their way into the rhetoric of policymakers in Washington, D.C., or Brussels, Belgium. Most newspaper accounts of peer-to-peer battles have changed from sports or crime to business stories. It's not yet a cultural story, an ethical story, or a political story.[113]

In other words, Vaidhyanathan documents patterns of discourse from an informal culture oriented around a communal secondary orality, which is sending a very different message about free culture and copyright than the one in the formalized "rhetoric" of policy makers about illegal downloading that gets translated into the print media, perhaps partly as a matter of economic self-preservation for corporate entities.

Public and Private

The other problem with treating child pornography as an object of political discourse on which to base decisions is that it is by definition not visible and not public. Speeches, testimony, and official reports about exploited children show this in their use of certain paradoxical forms of Orwellian language. For example, the FBI program for collecting data is called "Innocent Images."[114] Bruno Latour has talked about "making things public,"but child pornography makes only the pedophile into the antisocial monster who can be shown, while the products which he manufactures and exchanges can only be witnessed by designated experts. Assistant Attorney General Alice Fisher testified to this effect during the Masha's Law hearing:

I have seen some of these images, and, just like the Attorney General said, they make your stomach turn. I don't think many people realize how difficult it is for the law enforcement professionals who have dedicated their careers to this difficult work. It is revolting to view even one of these images. Imagine having to view hundreds and thousands of them—repeatedly, on a daily basis—in order to build the cases against offenders. That is what these dedicated professionals do, and it is challenging and traumatizing on a deeply emotional level. I join the Attorney General in personally thanking all of those in law enforcement and elsewhere who are enduring those challenges and working hard to protect our children.[115]

Similarly, the discourses of terrorists are relegated to the work of expert analysis, such as the interpretations of the SAIC witnesses in the intelligence hearing, but at least some of these jihadist artifacts can be shown to congressional representatives.

Furthermore, the social actors who serve as justification for these hearings never appear to bear witness for themselves. In "The Promises of Monsters," Donna Haraway suggests a possible interpretation that can be applied to the rhetorical function of these atypical Internet users, who are outside society and its norms and yet central to its signifying functions. In her essay, which is designed to question fundamental assumptions about subjectivity, society, and technology, she situates the modern cyborg without accepting traditional critiques of the creature's artificiality[116] and observes that "nature" itself is "a topos, a place, in the sense of a rhetorician's place or topic."[117] Haraway analyzes a range of contemporary rhetorical figures that serve as *objects* of political discourse rather than speaking *subjects*—astronaut, fetus, cells under "attack" by the HIV virus—and considers how certain social actors can be appointed to speak for those designated as not capable of bearing witness in their own names. In one of her footnotes Haraway points to the Latin etymology behind the word "monster": "Remember that monsters have the same root as to demonstrate; monsters signify."

Terrorists and child molesters are similarly monsters who *show*, although perhaps what they show is our anxiety about the cultural slipperiness of digital rhetoric and the fact that electronic communication is a hybrid, composed of public and private practices, characterized by modes of orality and print, oriented toward production and consumption, and coded both for user and machine. In political discourse, these monsters are often used to merely *tell* citizens that there are threatening dangers to public security, which must be dealt with by the institutions of the political state, even as the state apparatus becomes increasingly more virtual.[118]

Of course, when you look for them, monsters are everywhere. In an April 20, 2004 speech about the PATRIOT antiterrorism act, President George W. Bush explains the need for new digital and procedural tools to fight crime. He justifies these new practices by the presence of such "monsters" among us:

We couldn't use roving wire taps for terrorists. In other words, terrorists could switch phones and we couldn't follow them. The Patriot Act changed that, and now we have the essential tool. See, with court approval, we have long used roving wiretaps to lock up monsters—mobsters. Now we have a chance to lock up monsters, terrorist monsters. (Laughter and applause.)[119]

The linguistic play between the words "monster" and "mobster" suggests a substitution of terms, as one surveilling technology, the wiretap, is supplanted by another, Internet monitoring. Similarly, Congressman Gingrey talks about the "monster who adopted" Masha and sexually abused her, and Masha herself says, "For five years, I was held hostage by a monster."[120]

As massive archiving projects, these initiatives are also fostering inverse forms of once dreamed-of digital public library projects that were stymied by a series of policy decisions that delayed building the necessary information infrastructure or guaranteeing universal access. Now while private corporations are pursuing large-scale scanning, digitizing, and indexing of print texts that some may see as deservedly part of the public trust, government agencies are dedicated to the storage of secret documents. In short, the order of responsibility has been inverted: private companies handle the public record, and public agencies manage a private record. For example, the FBI's "Innocent Images" program specifically calls itself a form of "National Archive."[121]

During a short period of twenty-four hours in spring 2006, two congressional hearings showcased many of our policy makers' anxieties about digital rhetoric and the subversive potential of an emerging information culture. Certainly, this anxiety about a digital revolution is understandable, given that the transformation of traditional institutions by digital media and networked societies has been hyped with utopian or dystopian narratives about a radically new public culture and barraged with a range of philosophical objections dating back to Plato. Even long after new communication practices, such as file sharing or videogame play, have become remarkably widespread, if not mundane, the idea of a threat to public safety is promulgated and used as a powerful explanatory narrative to the American citizenry.

2 Hacking Aristotle: What Is Digital Rhetoric?

"You don't need a computer to do computer science."

These words sound paradoxical, but first-year computer science students often hear this truism as they sit in their introductory classes. The dictum is meant to serve as a reminder that they will be studying discrete math, formal languages, data structures, or number theory, as well as computer hardware or software. The saying seems contradictory, but it makes a simple point: computer scientists frequently study *algorithms*, not computers. Without a computer terminal or electricity or a high-speed connection, a curious individual can still learn the fundamentals of creating code, managing information processing, and facilitating networked communication.

So perhaps one could also begin this chapter with this phrase: "You don't always need a computer to do computer rhetoric." Yet many who purportedly study the rhetoric of digital discourse focus almost exclusively on the technological apparatus, so that a conventional view of the subject directs attention to the mechanical responses of the computer to input rather than the theories behind the design and continuing evolution of digital media and networked systems. Specialists in "computers and composition" or "computers and writing" debate about MOOs and MUDs, blogs and wikis, but too rarely consider the epistemological implications of contemporary information science for networked, digital communication, which may operate with some fundamentally different assumptions about systems of signification than do natural language models. In other words, in the standard model of digital rhetoric, literary theory is applied to technological phenomena without considering how technological theories could conversely elucidate new media texts.

What do I mean by "digital rhetoric"? For the purposes of this discussion, I am going to focus on four different definitions of digital rhetoric:

1. The conventions of new digital genres that are used for everyday discourse, as well as for special occasions, in average people's lives.
2. Public rhetoric, often in the form of political messages from government institutions, which is represented or recorded through digital technology and disseminated via electronic distributed networks.

3. The emerging scholarly discipline concerned with the rhetorical interpretation of computer-generated media as objects of study.

4. Mathematical theories of communication from the field of information science, many of which attempt to quantify the amount of uncertainty in a given linguistic exchange or the likely paths through which messages travel.

With each definition, it may seem that I am getting further away from the common experiences of average citizens, but I hope to show that this new ideology about information (definition four) actually feeds back to influence the norms and generic conventions of everyday digital discourse (definition one). In other words, typical lay users have attitudes about information that may be changed by expert discourses, because many on the Internet participate in cultural conversations in which they share ideas about tactics for effective communication through new technological interfaces, ones that indirectly rely on interpretations—and sometimes misinterpretations—of theoretical components gleaned from specialized fields.

Rhetorical Rules for New Digital Genres

At the level of everyday experience, there are many occasions for rhetorical expression through electronic means. I may be an academic researcher, but in my personal interactions as a member of my local community, a typical week might include several situations similar to digital events in the lives of my neighbors. I might contest a parking ticket using an online form, e-mail my minister, notify my health club that there is a mistake on their website, check one son's grades electronically, correct spelling on the other son's PowerPoint presentation homework, make retouching suggestions about family photos, or look for a good local coffee shop recommended by a blog or online newspaper. To participate in these activities I have to be familiar with a lot of different rules that apply to specific kinds of verbal and visual interactions. There are also subgenres to consider—I certainly could not send the same kind of impersonal, businesslike message to my family's minister that I might send to the parking office.

Earlier new media theorists argued that these new genres, particularly digital documents connected by electronic links as hypertext, obviated many of the distinctions between author and reader, sender and receiver. For example, Nancy Kaplan's work on reader-centered hypertext imagines an empowered audience for digital media by extrapolating from the experiences of conventional readers who can still "provide their own scriptures, their own rules, in light of which they are sometimes content to dwell within that other set of rules, imaginary or not, that the texts they are reading supply."[1] As Kaplan acknowledges, her argument owes much to the ideas of the late French theorist and Jesuit philosopher Michel de Certeau, who claimed that ordinary activities, such as walking, cooking, dwelling, talking, and reading, are inherently rhetorical, even though they are ostensibly carried out by nonproducers. For example, in *The Practice of Everyday Life*, de Certeau points out "homologies between practical ruses and rhetorical movements,"[2] and his reading of reading itself indicates that set rules of propriety are constantly being disrupted by the "ways of operating"[3] in the "ensemble of practices"[4] of impertinent readers and other users of cultural systems of meaning.

Kaplan argues that traditional readers "do not literally write anything anywhere and leave no traces that we know of, not even (as far as we can tell) in their own brains."[5] That is to say, a fastidious user of a print artifact, who wants to leave it pristine for the next user or for posterity and does not mark in the book's margins or dog-ear its pages, is an anonymous visitor to the text who does not change the printed codex in any significant way. In this case, the connection between interpretation and rhetoric may be a stealthy one. Unlike a reader acting appropriately and nondestructively with the pages of a traditional book, digital readers now leave many traces in their online viewing habits. Obviously, I alter digital files when I suggest changes to the health club's website, my child's PowerPoint, or the family photos. The cut, copy, and paste features of many computer applications transform the once definitive versions of individual texts into something more editable. Counters and cookies may also keep track of my visits to the online database of grades or the city parking office website. And regardless of whether or not I choose to leave a comment on the blogs I read, just clicking on the author's profile to verify the credibility of the source may include me in a recorded number of page views that will be displayed for the next visitor. Even as a consumer, I am producing rhetorical relics.

At this level, merely interacting with electronic code or files does not seem to explicitly require that I assume a central role as a political speaker in an obviously public sphere, even though all of these virtual places represent physical sites for communal, communicative action: the city hall, the church, the school, the gymnasium, the childhood home that may center a geographically dispersed extended family, and even the neighborhood coffee house or restaurant.[6] At times, out on the periphery, I may not seem to be actively engaged in persuasion or argument, even when I am most absorbed in completing transactions. For example, perhaps I accept my punishment from the state obediently and pay my parking ticket in full with my credit card number. In what sense is this rhetoric?

It could be asserted that some forms of rhetoric do not require an attempt to influence others at all. Among rhetoricians, the narrow Aristotelian definition that focuses on persuasion is disputed, even by some traditionalists.[7] After all, in classical rhetoric, the critical Greek term *kairos* merely describes an opportunity or season for speaking; perhaps an exact time or a key moment for addressing a pertinent issue about war and peace, legislation, or budgetary planning. According to the Liddell and Scott Greek

Lexicon, the word also carries the sense of "due measure, proportion, fitness" in the original language.[8] Although "rhetoric" is often equated with persuasive discourse, the term can also be defined to focus on the timing of a given message and how the language of that message may be shaped by specific contexts and opportunities for social change, which are located in time and space, as well as politics and culture. Rather than privilege the intentions of the speaker, a given utterance might also be responding to an opportunity created by a specific occasion.[9] In describing everyday activities as "rhetorical," de Certeau also draws on the notions of *kairos* discussed by Vernant and Détienne[10] and the importance of "manipulations of language relative to occasions."[11]

The birth of a child or the death of a friend are occasions that can be marked by the creation of a digital HTML-coded artifact that can be experienced via a personal computer or other device connected to the Internet. This ceremonial rhetoric has been traditionally communicated and commemorated through other means, such as engraved announcements or newspaper obituaries. Now static webpages, attachments to e-mail, postings to blogs, and even activity on social network sites may be part of the communal welcoming and mourning rituals of social groups. Discrete, one-time events that take place in the real world may be subsequently recorded and represented in discourses and linguistic exchanges that take place in the virtual one.

These commemorative webpages often incorporate photographs or other visual ephemera associated with the person whose life is being celebrated. Multiple portraits can be used to establish that the person has occupied a wide variety of identity positions. For example, even little James Oakley (figure 2.1) is depicted as a coddled younger brother, restaurant patron, and model for fashionable baby clothes.[12] Like nineteenth-century commonplace books or friendship albums, the dominant sentiment of filiation may be modulated by other authorial and editorial interests. His parents, who appear as "Admin" on James' blog, have included a blogroll that supplies a "Mystery Link" taking visitors to the White House website; above this are links that lead to online news.[13]

As simple-to-launch dynamic sites allow more do-it-yourselfers to create web presences, the path to content on such sites can change and, of course, degenerate, sometimes leading to entirely noncommunicative code. Links can become broken, connections to the source files for photographs can be ruptured, and domain names can expire so that the perceivable rhetorical connections tying the visitor to the newborn are fragmented and that particular history in his or her social community is lost.

Like gravesites that are not properly maintained, this deterioration can also be true of the websites of the deceased. In this *In Memoriam* digital genre, it is important to note that there are many subgenres that reflect disparate ideologies about class, gender, and ethnicity. Victims of crime may be commemorated to locate a perpetrator or to

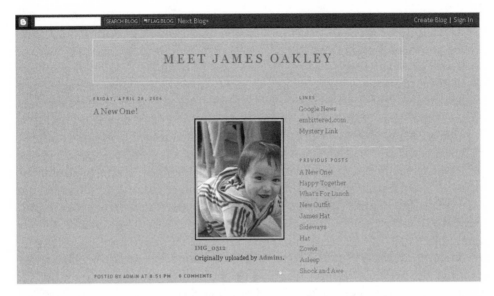

Figure 2.1
Blogspot page for Baby James Oakley. Courtesy of Bill Oakley.

solidify bonds with a given support group. The death of a gang member who has died violently may be recorded in a "memory garden" or other designated location for that particular population on a gang website; these forms of commemoration may seek to end gang violence through positive community-based alternatives, but they may also glorify the drama of live-fast-die-young antiheroes. Although users' accounts are often closed or frozen at death, social network sites can serve as places for mourning and remembrance, so that the digital activities of the deceased are connected and contiguous with those of his or her survivors.[14] On commercial commemorative services such as Legacy.com, online comments may be moderated by live minders to preserve decorum.[15]

When my friend Valerie Margolis died after years with cancer, her parents held a memorial service at a Northern California park in a community center, where champagne was consumed in honor of the deceased, eulogistic speeches were read, and mourners filed by sign boards and tables covered with Valerie's photos, awards, mementos, and writings in which much of the text was handwritten. However, the face-to-face commemoration also had a digital dimension. The service, like many weddings, was videotaped by several people, who could post the clips on the Internet. Some guests brought laptops and showed digital slideshows of Valerie from Burning Man and other contemporary countercultural happenings. Another mourner present at the service, Jenny Cool, had made a website shortly after Valerie's death, featuring photographs of her in life organized into themed galleries, such as "Faces & Friends," "New Hampshire Fun," and "Valerie Plays Olympia" (figure 2.2).[16] After the service, friends contributed photographs for the category of "Burning Man 2004." Like many *In Memoriam* websites, this webpage eschews use of traditional mourning motifs or black, the distinctive color associated with death. Instead, this website occupies itself with gestures to other aesthetics; for example, a digitally altered image of the departed is inserted into Manet's famed painting about sexual and racial power, *Olympia*.

In short, these pages do much more than convey data related to events in history, such as the factual details of the birth or the death of an individual. These websites also serve significant rhetorical purposes that may elevate the creator/sender of the message, endorse particular forms of social association or cultural organization, and even promulgate particular ideologies, sometimes through references or allusions with explicit or implicit political or social import, which words like "Burning Man," "New Hampshire," and "The White House" might suggest, thus bringing some visitors who are strangers, in terms of face-to-face interactions, to the community celebrating the person's life. These newcomers may be brought to these sites entirely by chance, thanks to a scrupulous but literal-minded search engine.

The occasions for rhetoric are not limited to rituals or ceremonies in the contemporary world, because sensitivity to *kairos* could also be important for other time-contingent public events, such as a vote on a proposition, election of an officeholder, or opportunity to present evidence at a trial or lawsuit. In the era of classical Athens, Aristotle's *Rhetoric* categorized three types of rhetorical situation that still exist today: (1) *epideictic* rhetoric for ceremonial occasions of praise and blame, (2) *deliberative* rhetoric intended for legislative assemblies grappling with questions of right and wrong, and 3) *forensic* rhetoric addressing questions of the just and unjust in a court of law. Contemporary citizens may find themselves using similar rhetorical appeals when making webpages for political causes or legal cases.

In the summer of 2006, several people from the same college organization sent e-mails around to the larger alumni group to raise money for a friend's legal defense fund, a person who had been accused of arson and insurance fraud and was standing trial with a former employer. This social group also established a website to enable supporters of the accused to donate money for his defense via a PayPal account.[17] The website they established used photographs of the accused, eulogistic descriptions of his childhood and early career, and several arguments for the improbability of the crime, given his character and lack of economic motive (figure 2.3).

One of the e-mails directing readers to the defense fund site indicates a blurring of rhetorical genres in contemporary digital discourse. The authors of this e-mail write about the epideictic/ceremonial dimension suggested by the upcoming forensic/legal rhetoric of the trial: "We tend to think of holiday gifts, wedding registries, and baby shower presents as symbolic gestures of friendship or support. But the stakes are

One | Faces & Friends
Two | New Hampshire Fun
Three | Valerie Plays Olympia
Four | Burning Man 2004

Valerie Sue
darling, dashing,
daring doll,
taken too soon,
forever young

Figure 2.2
Valerie photos. Courtesy of Jennifer Cool.

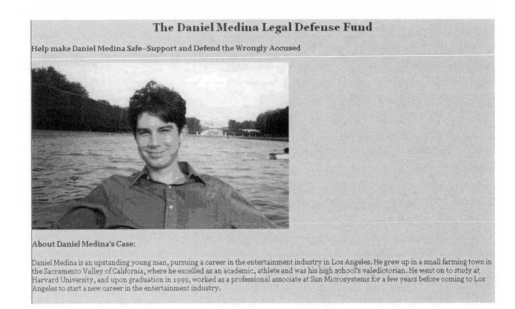

The Daniel Medina Legal Defense Fund

Help make Daniel Medina Safe--Support and Defend the Wrongly Accused

About Daniel Medina's Case:

Daniel Medina is an upstanding young man, pursuing a career in the entertainment industry in Los Angeles. He grew up in a small farming town in the Sacramento Valley of California, where he excelled as an academic, athlete and was his high school's valedictorian. He went on to study at Harvard University, and upon graduation in 1999, worked as a professional associate at Sun Microsystems for a few years before coming to Los Angeles to start a new career in the entertainment industry.

Figure 2.3
Daniel Medina Legal Defense Fund. Courtesy of Farley Katz and Daniel Medina.

suddenly so much higher when a friend is falsely accused of a serious crime. Please help Dan ensure his freedom by making a contribution to this important cause."[18] In addition, the group promulgated their appeals through an electronic mailing list that included dozens of other members of the college organization. Thus, more than one electronic forum can be used to digitally defend a person's character. In this case, ultimately the accused was acquitted.

To have basic competence in digital rhetoric also means to understand the conventions of many new digital genres: these include e-mail, instant messages, static websites, blogs, wikis, webtoons, electronic slideshows or PowerPoint presentations, desktop publications, altered digital photographs, web-engineered video, machinima films, videogames, virtual reality simulations, cave installations, databases, online archives, and many other specific and socially regulated forms of digital text[19] that are composed as files of electronic code.

There is also a plethora of mixed genres, which are ever more rapidly evolving thanks to more sophisticated software, beefier computers, faster network connections, and a richer ecology of media literacy practices, with a general public now able to exploit these technological developments and compose complicated transmedia artifacts or historical pastiches. A blogger may insert a home movie into his or her dynamic text. A Flash webtoon may pay homage to an interactive online game. A 3-D videogame may use a skin taken from a digitally altered image of a public personality, perhaps one derived from an online news service with remnants of the traditional print page. Mapping subgenres can be difficult because they are rarely constituted as neat, mutually exclusive subsets. For example, in classifying videogames many permutations can be made by combining components of dyads like online/offline, first-person/third-person, or single-player/multiplayer.

Even traditional oratory becomes a form of database when recordings of speeches become the raw materials for mash-ups and information visualizations. For example, mash-up videos on sites such as YouTube frequently draw attention to particular forms of repetition, or they recombine syntactical elements to reveal supposed implicit content. When Republican presidential contender Rudoph Giuliani objected to fellow candidate Joe Biden's characterization of his presidential campaign message as "a noun, a verb and 9/11," anti-Giuliani users of digital tools promptly created a number of audio and video compositions consisting of nothing but instances of Giuliani inserting the event into a speech. Former President George W. Bush's State of the Union addresses were frequently remixed, so that one classic version begins with the president of the United States saying, "During these past few weeks, I've been trained by Al Qaeda, and I'm weak and materialistic." Websites also show speeches by American public figures as information trees in which expressions in particular parts of speech are presented as interchangeable.

Some Internet genres reach wide audiences, others are public but site-specific, and still others are intended to be conveyed privately only to single recipients. Some genres conventionally have one author; others have many. Some genres are associated with little or no investment of time, labor, or fiscal resources; others may be extremely expensive to produce. However, the advent of user-friendly tools or amateur-accessible instructions, allowing computer users to create their own content or modify the content of others, can change a given cost-benefit or individual-corporate ratio very rapidly, so that even the manpower requirements and price of production of a once prohibitively expensive videogame could be reduced to the level of personal computing, if the code is made public or back-end programming tasks are given a familiar graphical user interface. Several of these digital genres have stimulated so much media discussion in contemporary civic life that I have devoted entire chapters in this book to them. Of course, many digital genres are still evolving, emerging, and merging, so that likely my tentative list will soon include even more neologisms.

At some level, of course, it is all just code running on machines, but it is important to recognize that some genres become strongly associated with the presence of particular moral values (or their absence) or specific postures about practical worth to society (or cost). What makes the general public think that making a first-person-shooter is intrinsically more morally suspect than word processing a document? What makes the population think that video file sharing is intrinsically worse than exchanging electronic mail? The answers have to do with ideas about language and knowledge that shape the nation's legislative agenda as well. Rhetoric, as Aristotle points out, entails precisely those discursive practices that assign positive and negative characteristics. Studying digital rhetoric involves examining ideologies about concepts like "freedom" or "honesty" that are in turn shaped by factors like national, linguistic, theological, or disciplinary identity; societal attitudes about ownership and authorship; and cultural categories of gender, race, sexuality, and class. As Richard Lanham has argued, "in *practice* the computer often turns out to be a *rhetorical* device as well as a logical one."[20]

So, how do people learn appropriate rhetorical practices in these new digital genres? Critics are only beginning to ask this question and attempt to answer it.[21] The traditional pedagogical model of *error correction* is certainly one approach. For example, a software design class might devote a considerable portion of instruction to techniques for debugging.[22] Teachers and fellow students might endeavor to "break" vulnerable systems or designs. Professional or lay instructors might also provide specific forms of corrective feedback on individual projects, an activity requiring a common metalanguage shared by both teacher and learner. In the corporate setting, the work of error correction may be done by outside consultants who specialize in particular types of interface design or back-end programming, sometimes to capitalize on pre-existing industrial segmentation, and sometimes merely to save face.

Some of these often self-appointed experts choose to create model texts, which are designed to be imitated. Occasionally these models reach the commercial marketplace and become at least temporarily adopted as standards.[23] These "correct" templates may take the form of materials in style guides, such as the venerable Yale *Web Style Guide,*[24] or they may be distributed online by manufacturers of software applications, such as Microsoft or Adobe.

In the field of written composition, this method of imitation has generally been viewed in a more favorable light of in recent years. Despite the fact that throughout much of the twentieth century imitation was regarded as far inferior to invention, many who teach composition and communication now look for continuity with classical and medieval mimetic traditions and express skepticism about uncritically embracing the ideologies of Romanticism and Modernism, which glorify originality.[25]

However, some forms of rhetorical instruction use inverse models of digital style. For example, humorous "antistyle" templates aim to instruct by showing the effects of violating certain authorship taboos to would-be makers of digital content. A computer science professor who teaches technical writing at my university developed a PowerPoint-style slide with numerous "mistakes."[26] Students are asked to identify the problems with the sample slide both in traditional style (errors in grammar, spelling, and usage) and in digital composition (typography, layout, and design).

What's Wrong
With this slide?

List as many things as you can that could be improved on this slide. It was designed to embody as many flaws as possible, of various different kinds. For each flaw, try to list (a) the improvement you suggest and (b) a general principle of design that, if followed, would allow someone to avoid the flaw. Consider:

✡ design,

✡ typography,

☪ layout,

✠ content,

☯ grammar,

✿ usage,

☦ speling,

▥ and anything else that harms the effectiveness of the message.

YOU SHOULD:

◎   Take your time, looking for myriad flaws

◎   Don't talk to your neighbor (not too much, anyhow)

◎   Have a great time ripping it apart!!!!!!!!!!!!

Figure 2.4
What's wrong with this slide? Courtesy of David Kay.

Figure 2.5
The "world's worst website." Courtesy of Michelle E. Blowers.

Another model of don'ts for the digital rhetorician is showcased by the self-described "World's Worst Website," in which jarring colors, chaotic animations, blaring music, flashing text, unnecessary frames, copious advertisements, and outdated information collectively obscure any actual message other than sensory overload.[27] Although this webpage is obviously satiric in its hyperbolic visual and auditory presentation, the site's home page provides discrete chunks of specific advice about web design choices and links to information about web style on other sites.[28]

However, the error-correction model has largely fallen out of favor with composition-ists, particularly since the publication of Mina Shaughnessy's *Errors and Expectations* in 1977, which argued that many intrusive practices of correction were typically based upon subjective judgments and often futile interventions in longstanding behavior patterns.[29] Research showed that even expert teachers disagreed about the precise loca-tion, relative severity, and actual category of individual errors, even though they might all agree that Standard Written English should be the academic idiom of choice. Instead of focusing on error correction, specialists in rhetoric and composition turned their disciplinary attentions to recognizing multiple literacies and validating a wider range of identity positions in activities of authorship. Many also became critical of dominant ideologies about language that reinforced existing and often unjust power structures, which excluded certain social actors from participation in communicative exchanges.

Greater attention to the importance of audience also shaped many of these discussions in the rhetorical disciplinary community. Given this interest in audience, the imagined reader and the norms of reading communities become central. For example, in my own relatively modest experiments with web design in my professional capacity as a writing program director of a large undergraduate course, consideration of my audience shaped design decisions reached with other administrators, artists, programmers, and information technology managers. As higher education master planner Clark Kerr once pointed out, the university really is a "multiversity" composed of niche populations, and often these disparate cohorts have very different interests and goals.[30] Consequently, there may be very different forms of official program website in a university setting, each adapted to a particular group of stakeholders.[31]

During a two-year period, I developed two very different websites for the same undergraduate course, despite working with relatively similar design teams. One page was designed to appeal to prospective students, their parents, alumni, and potential donors by showing how former freshmen looked back on their experiences in the course; another was designed for course instructors, an audience with specialized expert knowledge from many different departments, disciplines, and fields, who needed time-sensitive and easily modified materials for classroom teaching of first-year students.[32]

The page for the general audience of students and parents was graphics-intensive and programmed in Flash with relatively little explanatory text on the home page. Users navigated from the opening screen by clicking on the smiling color photographs of former students. When the photo was activated, the images of the other students faded out into the dark background, while animated text appeared with the individual student's name, major, and advice for potential students on academic research. A link could take the visitor to an HTML copy of the student's prize-winning research paper (figure 2.6).

The page for the audience of instructors was more programming-intensive and required specialized labor to build search features and decide on metadata protocols. It opened with a large amount of explanatory text, which described the features of the database and the rationale for the pedagogical file-sharing project. Graphics were limited to one logo that would identify the project and another to recognize the support of the site's institutional funders. Individual and group photos of the project team members were buried deeper in the layers of the site (figure 2.7).

Although both websites were created for the same undergraduate course and housed on the same server for the electronic educational environment, they followed fundamentally different rules or principles of web design. Of course, rhetoricians since the Greeks have acknowledged this central position of audience in rhetorical production,[33] but digital dissemination now makes it possible to deliver even more targeted appeals than one would deliver when speaking to an interested crowd of heterogeneous

Figure 2.6
Successful students talk about Core.

spectators. Given the importance of addressing potential audiences by "narrowcast-ing"[34] on the World Wide Web and appealing to the sometimes idiosyncratic needs of very specific addressees, an error-correction model would often not be helpful to a web designer who must choose the appropriate combination of image, text, tech-nology, and programming.

Composition specialists have suggested several approaches in lieu of the error-correction model. This proactive attitude about the pedagogy of digital rhetoric was first formulated in the discipline known as either "Computers and Composition" or "Computers and Writing," after the prominent journal launched in 1983 and the conference launched in 1982.[35] Many of the individuals who were active in this upstart movement were early adopters who had knowledge of literary and linguistic comput-ing;[36] often they had relatively little stature in the university because of their interest

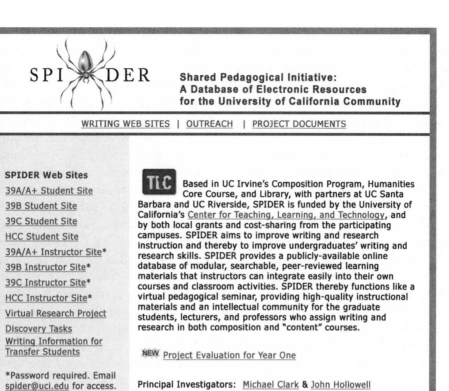

SPI DER Shared Pedagogical Initiative:
A Database of Electronic Resources
for the University of California Community

WRITING WEB SITES | OUTREACH | PROJECT DOCUMENTS

SPIDER Web Sites

39A/A+ Student Site

39B Student Site

39C Student Site

HCC Student Site

39A/A+ Instructor Site*

39B Instructor Site*

39C Instructor Site*

HCC Instructor Site*

Virtual Research Project

Discovery Tasks

Writing Information for
Transfer Students

*Password required. Email
spider@uci.edu for access.

TLC Based in UC Irvine's Composition Program, Humanities
Core Course, and Library, with partners at UC Santa
Barbara and UC Riverside, SPIDER is funded by the University of
California's Center for Teaching, Learning, and Technology, and
by both local grants and cost-sharing from the participating
campuses. SPIDER aims to improve writing and research
instruction and thereby to improve undergraduates' writing and
research skills. SPIDER provides a publicly-available online
database of modular, searchable, peer-reviewed learning
materials that instructors can integrate easily into their own
courses and classroom activities. SPIDER thereby functions like a
virtual pedagogical seminar, providing high-quality instructional
materials and an intellectual community for the graduate
students, lecturers, and professors who assign writing and
research in both composition and "content" courses.

NEW Project Evaluation for Year One

Principal Investigators: Michael Clark & John Hollowell
The SPIDER team: Photographs and Biographies

Figure 2.7
SPIDER: Shared Pedagogical Initiative: A Database of Electronic Resources.

in collaborative projects and their tendency to produce online rather than print publications.[37] It would take almost two decades for these groups' work to be fully integrated into the professional associations affiliated with rhetorical studies. A significant turning point in the recognition of this pedagogical community took place in February 2004, when the Conference on College Composition and Communication (CCCC) issued an official statement declaring the importance of rhetorical instruction specifically for computer-mediated environments. The CCCC position statement included an assertion that the focus of "writing instruction is expanding: the curriculum of composition is widening to include not one but two literacies: a literacy of print and a literacy of the screen. In addition, work in one medium is used to enhance learning in the other."[38]

To provide for the education of students in practical digital rhetoric, Gail Hawisher and Charles Moran advocated an *apprenticeship model* that used the case of e-mail to demonstrate the value of this approach in preparing students for the businesslike rhetoric they would eventually be producing as working professionals.[39] Hawisher and Moran observed that the discursive practices of e-mail were fundamentally unlike those manifested in word processing programs or hypertext editing applications, although students who were careful revisers of such polished offline and online documents were the darlings of composition researchers at this time. In contrast, they characterized e-mail writers as generally overinvested in rapid response or underinvested in careful deliberation, and thus these writers often violated the rhetorical norms of professional or academic communication.[40] In other words, such composers of written texts understood the importance of *kairos* in the sense of "exact or critical time, season, opportunity," but disregarded its other—but equally important—meaning of "due measure, proportion, fitness." Of course, in their analysis of how appropriateness could be sacrificed in the interest of time-sensitivity, Hawisher and Moran would forecast many of the issues involved with blogging, messages for social network sites, and other pseudojournalistic or diaristic chronologically oriented genres. In an apprenticeship model, writers new to electronic communication would learn by watching the composition and revision processes of more experienced writers of e-mail and other electronic genres and gradually advance to crafting compositions of their own in imitation of the carefully nuanced messages of their rhetorical masters.

Unfortunately, this model paid relatively little attention to so-called recreational computing. Furthermore, as Kathleen Yancey and Michael Spooner would later argue, the norms of academic communication can be comparatively atypical, even for the professional world. Spooner and Yancey claimed that classroom e-mail and listservs were a peculiar and limited case, which could not serve as the model for digital literacy practices in the world of work and leisure. They suggested another paradigm, which was derived from their reading of Russian literary critic of the novel and the carnivalesque Mikhail Bakhtin, which I have called the *dialogic model*.[41] (Spooner and Yancey's meta-essay explaining this model actually takes the form of a two-sided dialogue on the page.[42]) Instead of accepting the idea that students should learn through imitation of the media objects produced by more rhetorically expert superiors, Spooner and Yancey posit that students should be engaged in answering their actual correspondents rather than responding to their instructors in artificial, monological, discourse situations. In their minds, e-mail bears little relation to a bounded artifact because it can assume a number of polymorphous forms.

In some cases, it looks like a business letter. Sometimes it's a bulletin, sometimes a broadside, sometimes a joke, a memo, a grafitto, a book. In many one-to-one postings, email shows all the features of the lovers' correspondence you used to read (or did you write it?) every day.[43]

For Spooner and Yancey, e-mail never entirely takes the static form of a single, homogeneous genre, because the rhetorical production of digital rhetoric expresses the heteroglossia of its composition, which takes place in a rhetorical environment of competing voices, overlapping texts, and mixed genres that refuse definitive synthesis. Spooner and Yancey also deny the possibility of "netiquette," upon which Hawisher and Moran's argument rests. They make analogies to telephone conversations or channel surfing instead of traditional written compositions. Unfortunately, this approach would make acceptable composing practices extremely difficult to teach, because it assumes there is no "single rhetorical situation," "coherent set of formal conventions," or common set of "communicative purposes" to shape a given digital message.[44]

In contrast, rhetoricians with a somewhat anthropological bent might see a more explicable set of narratives and rituals governing computer-mediated communication and community behavior. The gift economy of the Internet—which revolves around the paradigm of exchange—seems to present an opportunity for such an analysis, especially since users literally trade digital files, programs, and documents through informal online networks. Ellen Strenski has argued that e-mail functions as a form of communally recognized "epistolary gift exchange" rather than the unstructured, netiquette-less, free-form discussion posited by Spooner and Yancey.[45] In her analysis of this gift economy, Strenski is careful not to idealize these noncommercial linguistic transactions, which are based on social conventions about membership and power constructions of periphery and center. By marshalling the arguments of Marcel Mauss, Claude Lévi-Strauss, Jacques Derrida, and Lewis Hyde, for whom the gift is not always a positive commodity, Strenski argues that like other epistolary genres, e-mail "impels response" and thus may actually coerce the reader into a gift exchange.

According to the pedagogical logic of the gift-exchange model, students learn what is appropriate by participating in actual exchanges, but those exchanges are still governed by the norms of the relevant society or subculture. For example, they learn that a short e-mail usually merits a short e-mail back, and a longer e-mail deserves a longer one, and that it is especially rude not to reciprocate at all, particularly if the sender is a member of the community who is close or important in lived experiences. One group's netiquette may be different from another's, but they both have a sense of the concept. Students learn by gauging how to respond to e-mails from many levels of the social hierarchy. Peers, superiors, and subordinates can give the sender more cues and clues if his or her message elicits a response in turn. Although e-mail may seem like a relatively narrow case, many rhetorical practices associated with code sharing and file sharing more generally could be interpreted through the apprenticeship, dialogic, and gift-exchange models.[46]

As digital media continue to evolve from hypertext to hypermedia and have come to include vivid first-person imagery and even entire computer-generated immersive environments, rhetorically oriented pedagogues have begun to theorize about these newer sites for language practices and about the significance of assuming avatar identities or situating rhetorical experiences spatially. Ironically, classical rhetoric that focuses on public oratory, the appearance and projection of the speaker, and delivery in indoor or outdoor spaces may be remarkably relevant in these contexts. In the massively multiuser online role-playing environment *Second Life*, for example, presidential candidates, United Nations spokespersons, corporate executives, digital rights activists, and cultural commentators have given speeches to virtual crowds who have assembled in virtual fora to hear them.

Janet Murray has discussed how the concept of cyberspace has shaped cultural production and how fictions from popular culture, such as the holodeck on *Star Trek*, may serve as prototypes for new stages for storytelling. For Murray, computer programming functions as a form of performance capable of generating engrossing cyberdramas that deeply resonate with profound human symbolic needs for expression, immersion, agency, and transformation.[47] Like the rhetorician Steven Mailloux,[48] who uses another *Star Trek* episode to make a point about the cultural function of shared stories, Murray argues that such narratives serve as "interpretations of the world"[49] and that interpersonal communication takes place through shared stories.[50] In her pedagogical work with her own students, Murray uses what I would characterize as a *storytelling model*, in which the synthesis and transmission of narratives constitutes almost the entire situation of teaching and learning. Rather than see her students as her obedient apprentices, she characterizes them as incipient masters and praises them as "half hacker, half bard."[51] Unlike traditional oral-formulaic storytelling, the formulaic character of these narratives is constituted as a function of computer code.

Many digital sophists are excited by the possibility of freeing rhetorical instruction from the industrial model of the twentieth-century writing classroom in which education is commodified, intellectual labor is relegated to piecework, and ideologies about efficiency and productivity promote neither. By using a *situated learning model*, James Paul Gee has argued that skills acquired through digital literacy experiences in videogames can be transferred to traditional literacy contexts because the games offer a secure learning environment in which risk-taking, experimentation, and challenging authority are all permissible activities, and yet players can rapidly experience the rewards of participating in expert discourses.[52]

Of course, digital literacy is far from a primary literacy for many citizens, who may be particularly reluctant to engage in videogame play, file sharing, or rapid exchanges of abbreviated information. Yet basic digital rhetorical competence using mobile telephones and personal computers equipped with proprietary software has become critical to our increasingly globalized and technologically mediated society. Those who lack rhetorical skills in digital media can pay a steep price. They may suffer from economic and professional disadvantages. They may lose social capital, since their lack of proficiency may inhibit their choices of friends and romantic partners in their generational cohort. The digitally disadvantaged may suffer from incomplete cultural citizenship without any sense of the touchstone narratives of public life. They may mistrust civic institutions that have adopted an e-government approach to delivering the services of the state. Their problem-solving capacities may be limited by never getting beyond remedial tool literacy in the information literacy hierarchy, and it is likely that they can only envy the recognition associated with publication, authorship, and acknowledged authority that provides gratification to many digital creators.

Manuel Castells has argued that despite rapid amelioration of some inequities in participation in electronic communication, the "digital divide" is being reinscribed along several axes. In particular, he notes that there is a divide between the "interacting" and the "interacted" in which the former "select their multidimensional circuits of communication," and the latter are "provided with a restricted number of prepackaged choices."[53]

For example, as 3-D computer-generated models, animations, simulations, and games become increasingly important in public rhetoric, the issues surrounding productive digital literacy become more complex, particularly now that sophisticated software for photorealistic rendering is important for much more than special effects in movies. Sensibilities in the public sphere are shaped by scientific reconstructions in paleontology, archeology, or microbiology, by reenactments of news stories, by models and animations in courtroom exhibits, by architectural renderings that promote particular visions for urban development, by computer-generated imagery in advertising and corporate promotion, and by a wide range of political imaginaries in which digital experts depict everything from trucks carrying weapons of mass destruction to equipment landing safely on distant planets. Because this complicated software for 3-D design has a relatively steep learning curve, members of the general public rarely understand how this compellingly realistic imagery is created and manipulated.

Even if the population gets beyond rudimentary receptive literacy and finally reaches fully functional productive literacy, their earlier rhetorical mistakes may haunt them. Impulsively posted messages by youthful senders can have remarkably irreversible consequences, as several recent cases demonstrate. For example, danah boyd has described how a MySpace page with gang-affiliated material almost compromised a high school student's college admission,[54] and Tracy Mitrano tells the story of a college senior who was turned down for employment by a prestigious firm on the grounds of his compromising Facebook page.[55]

Public Rhetoric through Electronic Means

The digital literacy of policy makers and other political actors is also not without consequences, particularly when rank-and-file citizens in the electorate discover that disasters and scandals may have involved inappropriate or unprofessional forms of communication by government representatives or their bureaucratic agents. Remnants of digital intercourse may seem to be anonymously authored or fleetingly ephemeral and thus trivial to the interests of the state, and yet these forms of communication can carry distinctive electronic signatures and addresses, or they can be saved and cached indefinitely. Because of the intimacy of the user's experience as either sender or receiver (inside the supposed privacy of home computing or the conventionally agreed-upon social bubble around other forms of ubiquitous contact and interchange via cell phones or hand-held devices) contemporary cyborgs might entertain the false perception that they are not creating documents that can be quickly disseminated and made public or leaving legible traces as readers in texts created by others, both of which can lead to unwelcome media revelations.

The recent political history of electronic media in the public eye has been one of many dramatic rhetorical gaffes. A Florida congressman sends sexually explicit instant messages to underage pages in the House, and a national magazine immediately suggests that it could cost the ruling political party dominance in the midterm elections.[56] A Virginia senator appears to use a racial epithet against a member of his challenger's team documenting a fundraising event with a digital videocamera; footage of the incident is posted on a popular video-sharing site, and ultimately he loses the race and his party's majority in the U.S. Senate.[57] A California governor is recorded uttering ethnic stereotypes about people from Latin America, and the MP3 files demonstrating his cultural insensitivity are posted on an official website, where they can be accessed by his opponent's campaign.[58] A White House policy report on a "National Strategy for Victory" in Iraq, released as a portable document format (PDF) file, is revealed to have an embarrassing and previously undisclosed author, who turns out to be an expert in public relations rather than in the appropriate field of military strategy.[59] A Federal Emergency Management Agency (FEMA) head coordinating the response to Hurricane Katrina in 2005 is exposed as self-absorbed when e-mails about his excessive attention to his fashion choices in preparation for press conferences come to light.[60] As former Secretary of Defense Donald Rumsfeld said, "People are running around with digital cameras and taking these unbelievable photographs and passing them off, against the law, to the media, to our surprise, when they had not even arrived in the Pentagon."[61]

Given the high stakes and high visibility of this new form of public rhetoric, it is no wonder that policy makers have increasingly turned to professional advertising agencies to design authorized government messages intended to provide a professional package for their constituents. To understand these novel alliances between public officials and the persuasive agents of corporate consumer commerce, it is useful to look at four specific twenty-first-century fields in government rhetoric, which I will explain in further detail: (1) institutional branding, (2) public diplomacy, (3) social marketing, and (4) risk communication.

Institutional branding is the practice of closely associating corporate symbolic constructs, often created by marketers, with information about civic institutions, as though public organizations were analogous to manufacturers of a distinctive commodity product distributed in a competitive marketplace.[62] These symbolic constructs can include brand names, logos, trademarks, graphic identities, or distinctive verbal formulas. The aim of branding campaigns is to increase *brand recognition*, which is a measure of public familiarity with a given brand, and *brand equity*, or the set of related positive cognitive associations or fulfilling emotional responses, which may be tied to personal gratification, abstract social values, or both.

The idea of branding a government institution like a corporate product created a scandal among professional diplomats and officials in nongovernmental agencies when Undersecretary of State for Public Diplomacy and former advertising executive Charlotte Beers began to use the language of Madison Avenue to describe soft power campaigns for the hearts and minds of foreign nationals and ethnic minorities opposed to U.S. policy.[63] Journalists were amazed that Beers was comparing Islam to McDonalds during a press conference a few months after the September 11 attacks and that she discussed the branding of America so matter-of-factly. As Beers said, "'poster man'—well, you know, in a way, our poster people are President Bush and Secretary Powell, whom I think are pretty inspiring symbols of the brand, the United States."[64]

Despite the public ridicule of Beers and her eventual exit from office, her basic approach in branding national governments and their official agencies to make them seem distinctive, competitive, and desirable has become the norm. Considering that some branding experts, such as Wally Olins, have traced the practice of corporate identity back to regalia for informal social associations, visual iconography for religious orders, and finally patriotic symbols for nation-states, one could argue that the practice of branding has simply come full circle.[65] Yet this form of public rhetoric does more than merely amplify official messages. The effects of these campaigns often extend beyond would-be laudable goals like providing more vivid information design to the electorate or creating more usable maps and indexes to assist citizens navigating through bureaucracies. Branding, as critics of globalization and corporate capitalism have pointed out, can also be a cultural strategy of economic, social, and political control, in which the rhetoric ultimately serves the purposes of deception by an illusionary narrowing of choices or by furthering obfuscation.[66]

This policy shift toward institutional branding also risks limiting political dissent; at the same time, it fundamentally redefines what is meant by public property held in common. Although the content of government reports and public records has been traditionally free of copyright restrictions, these new branding strategies have placed certain limitations on how intellectual property assigned to the government is managed.[67] For example, the National Security Agency has ostentatiously trademarked several mascots on its children's site. This might sound like a relatively trivial example of a proprietary exercise of power, but trademark protections have already been used in other cases to justify limiting parody, thus stifling constitutionally protected sardonic critiques from political activists and dissenters. Of course, some of the graphic identity of federal institutions, such as the seal of the president, have been protected for a considerable length of time. Nonetheless, during recent years, the number of institutions whose seals are protected under the relevant federal law (Title 18, Section 713 in the U.S. Code), along with the number of protected types of symbolic construct, has certainly expanded.[68]

First Amendment protections for parody, particularly political parody, have traditionally been affirmed by the Supreme Court.[69] Yet the laws concerning federal seals have been used to justify cracking down on parodic content that imitates institutional online publications. For example, on December 12, 2002, the office of the vice president sent a content removal request to the parody website whitehouse.org regarding images and obviously satirical information about Lynne Cheney, the vice president's wife. The letter cited the Title 18 federal law as justification.[70]

Thus, as images themselves are increasingly recognized as capable of serving as arguments,[71] sometimes without any recourse to verbal texts at all, this taboo on using certain images has consequences for public discourse more generally. For example, although skeptic David Fleming has asserted that visual images cannot serve as arguments because a picture in itself "makes no claim that can be contested, doubted, or improved upon by others,"[72] digital technology has changed this assumed lack of interactivity. The software program Photoshop, which makes the alteration of images by would-be critics easier for nonspecialists to undertake, would seem to contradict the basis of Fleming's claim. With Photoshop, the ideological messages of state-sanctioned images can be refined and debated. This digital tinkering interferes with the media consumption model of perfect replication for mass audiences upon which the culture industry depends.[73]

The use of the government's brand identity by others, particularly in cases of digital images used on parody websites, has been closely followed by federal officials, who have made intellectual property claims against several political opponents on the basis of an even broader definition of institutional brand identity that encompasses content other than official seals and traditional insignia. On August 14, 2006, the Department of Homeland Security dispatched a letter to the director of biology for the Federation of American Scientists (FAS) informing the often politically oppositional group that they were in violation of trademark and patent law.[74] The FAS had created a parody website, "Really Ready," which was critical of the rhetorical presentation of the government's official Ready.gov site. Thus, both sites claimed to provide useful advice to citizens about the proper measures to take in preparation for possible terrorism. The federal official from the Department of Homeland Security asserted that the agency had filed service mark applications for several "Ready"-related graphics. Although the notice explicitly acknowledged a more generous free speech prerogative for critics of the administration such as the FAS than the 2002 letter from Cheney's office did, its wording also made more expansive claims, by covering previously unregulated forms of visual public rhetoric and arguing for exclusive rights of ownership of the intellectual property as a government agency endowed with an new form of power different from eminent domain. The letter included the assertion that "we recognize that your organization has every right to advise the public about being prepared in the event of an emergency, we also have to service the American public in the best manner we can, including protecting the Government's intellectual property if that will prevent any future confusion in that regard."[75]

In this official letter, the legal counsel representing Homeland Security is not making a claim to conventional terrain for use in the public interest, such as a national park, deep water port, or any historically significant, environmentally sensitive, or strategically essential territory. Nor is he arguing for requisitioning housing, supplies, or energy or construction resources on the basis of state interest. This is not property for the use of the general public being acquired; this is property that the public is explicitly forbidden to use. There are really two arguments at work here: (1) the government *needs* this virtual property in order to most efficiently convey emergency information to its citizens, and (2) the government has a *legal right* to this property on entirely different grounds, because it has registered the marks with another federal agency and thus hold a superior intellectual property claim.

The principles behind protecting the government's intellectual property can be explained using the framework of rhetorician Richard Lanham's book *The Economics of Attention: Style and Substance in the Age of Information*.[76] Ironically, Lanham claims, real, tangible property has become less valued in an economy oriented around the worth of otherwise scarce attention, rather than of goods or real estate. By the law of supply and demand, virtual property for which you can "count eyeballs" has become the real currency standard, and the culture's commerce has come to depend on accumulation of this form of capital.

Clearly, the "government's property" doesn't mean the same thing as "the commons," which has become a powerful utopian metaphor in the digital age.[77] David Bollier's 2002 essay "Reclaiming the Commons" asserts that the once collectively owned resources of the nation are "rapidly being *enclosed*: privatized, traded in the market, and abused."[78] Bollier claims that recent trademark and copyright legislation—particularly the Digital Millennium Copyright Act, the Copyright Term Extension Act, and the Trademark Anti-Dilution Act—is a manifestation of this trend and complains that legislators have ignored its potentially disastrous effects. He compares such laws to the Enclosure Acts of eighteenth-century England, which fenced off village commons land for active cultivation. Although these laws were justified by state-sanctioned policies of efficiency, they resulted in disproportionate benefits to privileged private interests and the further exclusion of the underclass from public resources. In arguing for an "Information Commons," Bollier takes issue with the thesis of Garrett Hardin's

1968 "The Tragedy of the Commons," which uses the grazing metaphor quite differently.[79] Cold War-era Hardin takes a Hobbesian view that focuses on the consequences of excessive liberty and the impossibility of sharing resources without abuses. His essay is leery of claims to both the inevitable dominance of the state's coercive power and the sustainability of an administrative culture capable of just, equitable, and rational distribution. In contrast, Bollier complains of a lack of liberty in public life, rather than its excess.[80] Branding is a special case of the manifestation of this control.

In principle, *public diplomacy* sounds less hegemonic and more committed to grassroots organizing than do the strategies of institutional branding. If conventional diplomacy might be described as elite diplomacy or the communication between government leaders or top officials, public diplomacy is characterized by the techniques by which a country (or a bloc of countries organized into a military, political, or economic organization) communicates with citizens in other political states or societies. However, because these rhetorical strategies are often specifically formulated to bypass a given country's leadership structure, they may be justifiably perceived as a form of covert force or "soft power." Furthermore, corporate branding experts like Wally Olins have participated in articulating a new public diplomacy strategy for American international policy that attempts to capitalize on the rhetoric of the digital age.[81] Websites, online video, advertisements, news broadcasts and print stories, film and television programs, cartoons, comics, music, and even videogames can be used by public diplomacy specialists in an attempt to sway opinion abroad. Like traditional advertising, sometimes these campaigns involve additional merchandising and product tie-ins.[82]

Those in the academy who are affiliated with public diplomacy efforts often define their task in terms of fostering mutual cultural understanding or promoting peace by avoiding escalation to armed conflict. At the Center on Public Diplomacy at the University of Southern California, public diplomacy is defined as "understanding, informing, and influencing foreign audiences."[83] Persuasion is relegated to a tertiary position, and the emphasis is on "dialogue, rather than a sales pitch."[84] USC argues that "public diplomacy must be seen as a two-way street. It involves not only shaping the message(s) that a country wishes to present abroad, but also analyzing and understanding the ways that the message is interpreted by diverse societies and developing the tools of listening and conversation as well as the tools of persuasion."[85] In contrast, the Edward R. Murrow Center of Public Diplomacy at Tufts University provides a definition of "public diplomacy" in which there is more acknowledgment of the importance of "influence" and the fact that campaigns may be addressing "private" rather than public political actors. John Rendon, chair of the Rendon Group, which has handled public diplomacy efforts in Iraq after the U.S. occupation, puts his role leading his company more baldly: "I am a person who uses communications to meet public policy or corporate objectives . . . I am an Information Warrior and a perception manager."[86]

Rendon's mixed metaphors of corporate management and military might are telling. Some of the actual government contractors who have handled the implementation of public diplomacy campaigns on the ground in recent years have been closely tied to traditional forms of aggressive influence peddling and rely on their prior professional expertise, which is often derived from advertising and marketing, political campaigning, military service or mercenary work, or intelligence gathering turned to sponsoring disinformation efforts. The Lincoln Group was particularly shaken by scandal when it was revealed that it was planting stories in Iraqi newspapers, spending considerable sums of money on bribery, and expending some of its human resources on tasks related to physical intimidation of the populace.[87]

Furthermore, many social scientists are suspicious of the long-term success of programs designed to whet consumer appetites rather that foster intercultural communication. Anthony Pratkanis, a proponent of social influence theory, has been highly critical of the information war in Iraq, which was led by government contractors first from the Lincoln Group and then the Rendon Group. Pratkanis has argued that although it may not have been as disastrous as the actual war fought with bombs and bullets, the campaign for Iraqi hearts and minds was doomed by poor administrative planning. By drawing on the lessons of social influence from World War II, Pratkanis argues that more recent models from advertising, public relations, and soft power will inevitably fail to effect long-term social influence, because these approaches don't indicate any engagement with analyzing the enemy's purpose and the related history of successful and unsuccessful messages in a given rhetorical context.[88] Pratkanis's authority rests on the fact that much of his fieldwork has been grounded in the everyday experiences of citizens engaged in linguistic exchanges and social psychology experiments, with a long track record of published research and demonstrable cause-and-effect relationships. This includes research on domestic populations, such as U.S. con men communicating with the elderly.[89] Despite his background in social psychology, Pratkanis orients his critique of slick public diplomacy by harkening back to what he considers to be the still-true lessons of classical rhetoric, often by quoting Aristotle and citing the beliefs of the Sophists.[90]

Social marketing is the application of commercial marketing concepts and techniques to achieve social change by affecting the behavior or social practices of a target population to get them to lead healthier and more productive lives, obey generally agreed-on social rules, and hopefully cost the state less by saving money otherwise spent on medical care, social services, and incarceration.[91] Social marketing as such officially began in 1972 with the publication of an article in the *Journal of Marketing* by traditional marketing experts Philip Kotler and Gerald Zaltman, who used their corporate experiences to codify strategies for "social change campaigns." Another published authority on social marketing, Alan R. Andreasen, notes that unlike "social advertising," which merely promotes the image of a desired behavior change by emphasizing how social goods function as "products," social marketing adopts a systemic approach that also considers how to best adjust the "price" of the behavior change and make the "place" of behavior change more accessible to the consumer.[92] Social marketers often differentiate themselves from the earlier "social hygiene" or "mental hygiene" movements of the Cold War era,[93] which were closely tied to educational films. [94] For contemporary social marketers, schools are no longer the primary institutions for indoctrination. Thus contemporary social marketing can reach a number of different niche audiences and use the more flexible model of the mobile commodity that may circulate.[95] Even social norms can be treated as exchangeable goods, ironically—in one case—at an academic research center funded by a corporation synonymous with the alcohol industry.[96] Many political progressives have lauded the organized efforts of social marketers, which are directed by one group (the change agent) to persuade others (the target adopters) to accept, modify, or abandon certain ideas, attitudes, practices or behavior. Universities have also granted social marketing status as an academic discipline, although, like public diplomacy, social marketing has also struggled with establishing lasting professional organizations.[97]

Social marketing campaigns are also sometimes closely associated with cause marketing campaigns, which encourage donations of money or labor to support research, treatment, or other social services. Critics of cause marketing complain that issues like breast cancer or other matters of public health and safety may be consigned to private charity or "selfish giving" initiatives that encourage consumers to buy goods from private sector vendors who are sponsors and who give a fraction of the proceeds to the cause.[98]

The irony is that the same advertising industry brought the United States many of the social ills that social marketing strives to ameliorate. After all, smoking and obesity may be seen as medical conditions at least partially caused by stoking the desires for immediate gratification and conspicuous consumption, which the advertising industry feeds. Yet now advertisers are charged with fixing ills that they helped create. Furthermore, because social marketing explicitly uses the same tools and techniques as traditional advertising, this form of public rhetoric can risk reinforcing repressive norms about gender, sexuality, class, race, and age and increasing the amplitude of messages about conformity and homogenization already bombarding the public through mainstream media channels. Although some social marketing campaigns make use of an "adbusters" approach, which uses the tools of the advertising industry to subvert its ideology, many others reinforce existing prejudices. For example, recent campaigns about HIV, smoking, obesity, and skin cancer have all emphasized the importance of maintaining superficial physical attractiveness and even sex appeal as grounds for behavior change, often in lieu of a presenting more serious risks to the public, such as long-term illness or early mortality.[99]

From the standpoint of public rhetoric, it would seem to be preferable to foster open discussion, deliberation, debate, consensus, and compromise rather than deploy implicit, undebated, and even unconscious appeals that may actually intensify existing prejudices through covert means. Moreover, social marketing risks promulgating top-down forms of political organization and sometimes even repressing grassroots opposition to its messages.[100] For example California voters have passed propositions that decriminalize some forms of marijuana possession; at the same time public health campaigns in the state advocate continuing prohibition on medical uses of the drug, despite the fact that the constituents they are targeting already favored greater liberalization at the ballot box. Certainly, social marketers should beware of creating cognitive dissonance, particularly when there is a different emerging consensus at the level of populist initiatives. Finally, the issue here is one of real goods in common as well as virtual ones. Policy makers always must decide how budgets should be apportioned, and the benefits of spending marketing money can be difficult to account for in comparison to concrete goods distributed or services rendered.

At their very worst, because these campaigns depend on the ideology of the competitive capitalist marketplace, social marketing rhetoric may devolve into the same "Brand X versus Brand Y" techniques that present a distorting binary worldview based on either/or logic.[101] Thus even social goods grounded in positive communal values like volunteerism and personal generosity could be presented as being in competition with each other. For example, the 2005 "Blood Saves" campaign, which targeted a young adult demographic, emphasized how much simpler blood donation would be than more idealistic forms of social action, because supposedly really ambitious good deeds inevitably have negative consequences. Television spots show the travails of two do-gooder characters, Julie and Charlie. Charlie wants to stop a labor injustice, but he unintentionally creates environmental pollution; Julie wants to halt environmental pollution, but unfortunately she puts events into motion that cause a labor injustice. The "Why bother to take political initiative?" message is clear, as is the message about limiting personal contributions to society. As *Slate* critic Seth Stevenson asks, "Since when do charities bash the competition?"[102]

Risk communication involves the transmission of vital information to the civilian population before, during, and after emergencies. Its most important design principle is to forestall panic, distrust, or disregard for the rule of law. As governments have responded to anxieties from the public about the likelihood of another catastrophic terrorist attack or a global flu pandemic, risk communication has received more media attention and more public funding, and risk communicators have pursued opportunities to use distributed digital media, particularly now that news is also transmitted rapidly through channels other than television or radio. At the same time, connections to the advertising and marketing industries have been solidified as government officials attempt to respond effectively to public concerns. Ad agencies such as BBDO[103] have handled campaigns for the federal government's risk communication efforts, and the chairman of the mega-agency Interpublic Group sits on the advisory board of the Department of Homeland Security.[104] Although many of these projects are volunteer efforts, taxpayers could be affected if the firms can deduct their pro bono work.

In 1989, the National Research Council defined risk communication as "an integrative process of exchange of information and opinions among individuals, groups, and institutions that often involves multiple messages about the nature of the risk or expressing concerns, opinions, or reactions to risk messages or to the legal and institutional arrangements for risk management."[105] However, risk communication is directly related to social marketing to the extent that many social marketing campaigns are designed to alert the public that they may be at risk of mortality, illness, physical danger, or psychic trauma. For example, the first HIV/AIDS campaigns were designed to explain the difficulty of becoming infected through casual contact, including everyday interactions like shaking hands or using a public toilet.[106]

Risk communication expert Peter Sandman, however, is careful to differentiate between "public relations" and "stakeholder relations." For Sandman, the general public is assumed to be inattentive and credulous, while concerned stakeholders are willing to devote time to more complicated messages; yet this population is also much more likely to be skeptical.[107] In Sandman's essay "Why Are People Over-Reacting to Risk?" he suggests that audiences can respond to risk communication messages in a number of ways.

Roughly two decades ago I suggested dividing the concept of risk into two components. I labeled the technical side of risk (magnitude times probability) "hazard" and the rest of risk (factors like control, trust, dread, voluntariness, and responsiveness) "outrage." People's response to risk, I argued, is mostly a response to outrage. So when hazard is high and outrage is low, people under-react. And when hazard is low and outrage is high, they over-react.[108]

As Sandman points out, risk communication can increase the level of fear as well as diminish it. Although fear-based campaigns in social marketing have been criticized by some, exploiting the psychic energy of fear can be integral to the rhetorical dynamic of risk communication. After all, Aristotle advised rhetoricians in Book II, Chapter 5 of his *Rhetoric* that threats to safety always engage the public with an orator's message, because "fear makes people inclined to deliberation." In these situations when it is advisable that the audience should be frightened, the orator must "make them realize that they are liable to suffering"[109] and that negative consequences have happened to others who were stronger, and are happening—or have happened—to people like themselves, at the hands of unexpected people, in an unexpected form, and at an unexpected time.

Unfortunately, sometimes more thought is given to the graphic presentation of risk communication messages to the general public than those aimed at critical decision makers. In his three-volume encyclopedic series on information design, Edward R. Tufte has argued that many disasters and tragedies could have been avoided with better visual explanations and clearer displays of quantitative and qualitative information to policy makers as well as to the public. In his essay on "Visual and Statistical Thinking: Displays of Evidence for Making Decisions," he cites as an exemplary model the 1854 work of John Snow, who mapped London's contaminated wells to represent cholera transmission in a way comprehensible to urban planners. In contrast, National Aeronautics and Space Administration (NASA) engineers presented unclear data, solely in numerical form, which made it difficult to see potential problems with the *Challenger* space shuttle.[110] When the *Columbia* space shuttle crashed, Tufte blamed bad information design in a garbled PowerPoint slide.[111]

Nonetheless, some risk communication professionals don't advocate complete information transparency of the kind that is valued in open source communities. Although withholding information often leads to mistrust in the government, dispensing it too freely can sometimes stimulate a panic. The federal government has developed a number of "governance dilemmas," involving scenarios such as bioterrorism,[112] which are designed to dramatize the difficulty of the balance. Furthermore, to save individuals, people may risk whole populations—for example, by not observing rules on quarantine; on the other hand, to save populations, citizens may self-centeredly disregard threats to the life and health of other individuals.

During the Cold War period, risk communication focused on threats to public safety and the environmental catastrophe that would result from a Soviet nuclear attack. Some of these risk communication efforts came to be ridiculed in retrospect, such as the 1951 "Duck and Cover" campaign aimed at schoolchildren.[113] Thanks to digital media, present-day risk communication campaigns may be lampooned almost immediately, as in the case of the color-coded Threat Advisory System from the Department of Homeland Security. Although Brian Massumi has described this alert system as an abstracted series of cues intended only to "direct bodily responsiveness rather than reproduce a form or transmit definite content" to reinforce "the irrational, self-propelling mode of fear-based collective individuation,"[114] in many ways it functions as a medium rather than a channel. There are now literally hundreds of humorous alternative versions of the ubiquitous graphic of five colored bars, poking fun at the essential oversimplification of risk communication that the original threat alert represents. A feminist peace group, Code Pink, put their name at the bottom of the scale with their pink label and the words "Peace and Harmony" to remind citizens that the desired state of a lack of conflict is not even represented on the chart.[115] A "Democracy Threat Advisory System" showed a register topped by "Martial Law."[116] A Sesame Street terror alert graphic ranged from an Elmo condition to an Oscar the Grouch.[117] There was even a pro-administration "Liberal Terror Alert" system, which showed photographs of left-wing politicians and pundits.[118] In an attempt to seem to move from risk communication to more neutral information representation, an article from *Wired*, "One Million Ways to Die," is illustrated with a graphic showing that the relative risk of dying in a terrorist attack is comparatively quite low.

There are, in fact, digital parodies that mock all four rhetorical tendencies to which I am pointing in the rhetoric of the contemporary state. There is an online video send-up of the social marketing campaign designed to get young people not to make digital copies.[119] There are other online videos that make fun of the public diplomacy efforts of Al Qaeda jihadists to bypass the U.S. ruling government and appeal to average Americans directly.[120] There are images that mock institutional branding efforts. For example, after I wrote in my *Virtualpolitik* blog about the fact that an extensive part of the United States Agency for International Development (USAID) website is devoted to brand identity rather than techniques for ending world hunger and poverty,[121] my colleague Professor Julia Lupton transformed the message underneath the USAID logo, changed its official seal, and then posted it to her own *Design Your Life* blog with the punning title "Brand Aid."[122] It is worth noting that, in addition to branding, USAID also has expanded its public diplomacy efforts,[123] to which Lupton also alludes with the moniker "Band-Aid Diplomacy."

At the same time, multinational corporations have become important actors in encouraging government agencies to pursue these four rhetorical strategies to influence the public. Some firms have been involved in many different types of collaboration between Madison Avenue and the Beltway. For example, the public relations firm Allyn & Company has produced private sector advertising for conventional print ads and logos for companies such as Wal-Mart and Coca-Cola; political campaigns for parties and candidates in the United States, Indonesia, and the Bahamas; a public diplomacy campaign on behalf of the government of Mexico aimed at changing U.S. public opinion in favor of building a physical barrier between the two countries to one more amenable to liberalized immigration; and a social marketing campaign to discourage unwed mothers from abandoning their newborn babies in dumpsters and other hazardous locations with a "Baby Moses" spot aired on television.

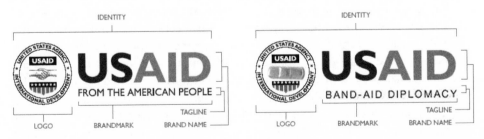

Figure 2.8
"Brand Aid" before and after. Courtesy of Julia Lupton.

Messages can also be designed to encourage stakeholders to express their resistance to these alliances between government agencies and commercial advertisers. There are many parties who resent the cooperation of the state with media consolidation, consumerism, commercialism, or the proprietary ownership of culture. These groups include activists for the creative commons and copyleft movements, bloggers, culture jammers, adbusters, creators of live and virtual political theater, telestreet producers of narrowcast content, smart mobs with cell phones, do-it-yourself (DiY) enthusiasts, open source and homebrew programmers, remix and mash-up artists, and political crowds of all types.[124]

Of course, norms regarding audience participation have ostensibly changed, which is reflected in some of the government's rhetorical appeals to the public through digital media interfaces. Rather than merely listening passively to presidential oratory, visitors to the White House website are encouraged to engage in online "chat" with government officials[125] or take a 360-degree panoramic tour of each of the building's historically important rooms.[126] While some might complain that highly scripted unit operations are in danger of replacing traditional forms of interactivity with government—such as voting, signing petitions, or walking precincts—there are ways that these functions make the visitor cognizant of the constraints of such stylized simulations and open up the possibility for critique.[127]

Ian Bogost has written specifically about "procedural rhetoric" in interactive electronic media, which he distinguishes from traditional verbal or visual rhetoric and even from forms of rhetoric that merely use computer-mediated communication as a presentation technology, to explain how videogames and other interactive media influence users and present particular ideologies.

I call this new form *procedural rhetoric*, the art of persuasion through rule-based representations and interactions rather than spoken word, writing, images, or moving pictures. This type of persuasion is tied to the core affordances of the computer: computers run processes, they execute calculations and rule-based symbolic manipulations.[128]

Bogost focuses largely on the case of "persuasive games," videogames designed to influence players by encouraging them to explore boundaries and other constraints or exploit features created by certain rules of play. He argues that even seemingly recreational videogames can put forward implicit arguments—for example, about the value of public transportation (in *Sim City*) or the structural factors that contribute to obesity in urban culture (in *Grand Theft Auto*). In Bogost's analysis of political games, advertising games, and educational games, he claims that such games may engage players in ways that potentially allow them to read the same algorithms critically and against the grain and thus—through an awareness of a given system's affordances and limitations—imagine alternative explanations or counternarratives.[129]

Although he doesn't name it "rhetoric" initially, Bogost introduces the rhetorical possibilities of games in his earlier book *Unit Operations* by pointing out how users experience rules of play and technical constraints and the ways these limiting structures simultaneously facilitate enjoyment and critique. For example, Bogost describes how machinima artist Jim Munroe creates a film of his gameplay with *Grand Theft Auto*, which violates and yet reinscribes many of the rules of the game. In *My Trip to Liberty City*, the player avoids theft and violent confrontations and instead wanders around the urban environment as a Canadian tourist, a mime, and a priest. Instead of drawing a false moral about the ethical superiority of nonviolent behavior in the virtual cityscape, Bogost shows how Munroe's counternarrative represents a more ambiguous form of rhetorical engagement.

As Bogost notes, governments have developed many videogames for their employees and constituents that cover topics in the public interest from disease control to taxes and budgeting,[130] but the dual function of procedural rhetoric, which naturalizes and denaturalizes specific procedures, extends to other digital genres through which state organizations communicate with their stakeholders. For example, as a member of the teaching faculty of the University of California and thus a worker for a state agency, I was required to complete mandated sexual harassment training, which I could either do in a face-to-face on-campus workshop or from home through an online tutorial. Like most of my colleagues, I chose the remote option.

At the level of verbal and visual rhetoric, I was exposed to argumentative claims related to the definitions, causes, and consequences of sexual harassment and several explanations of the institution's position on the importance of the subject. The program presented dozens of office sexuality scenarios with a number of possible gender configurations. The answers were very clearly telegraphed to the user, however, and wrong responses were often laughably so. Although trial and error didn't seem to be punished, it certainly wasn't encouraged either, because the second-best choice was rarely very tempting. Furthermore, the visual representation of intimate office interactions was very crude because the narratives were illustrated with comics-style graphics.

In clicking on answers in the process of completing the tutorial, I also found myself reading those official verbal and visual claims quite critically. Most of the answers were obvious to me, perhaps because I was already an administrator, but I found their actual obviousness to be extremely ideologically loaded when I looked closely at the individual slides. Why were only women shown wearing inappropriate clothing to work? Why was the female dress code more regulated?[131] Why did the role-playing never present a supervisor (dean, department chair, lab supervisor, or program manager) who was gay or lesbian? Why did homosexuals only appear as actors in the conflict, never as decision makers in the resolution? What did this tell me about the point of view that I was supposed to be adopting and how that point of view was gendered?

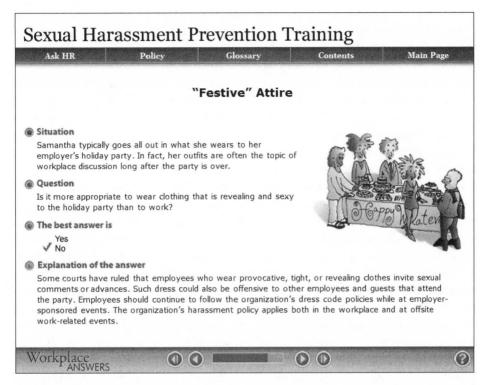

Figure 2.9
Online sexual harassment tutorial for employees of the University of California, 2006, Copyright 2008 by Workplace Answers, Inc. All rights reserved. Used with permission.

I was also aware of a procedural rhetoric at work, which was separate from my analysis of its verbal and visual persuasive appeals. The system was not tabulating "right" and "wrong" answers or checking me periodically with a question to gauge my attention level. The only way it kept score was by showing the total number of minutes passed in my online sessions, the page number I was reading, a progress bar indicating my relative location in the tutorial between the beginning and the end, and a dial with red, yellow, and green segments, so I could be reminded if I was reading too quickly to be properly paced. Of these, the only number that was important for monitoring purposes was the number of minutes total. All that seemed to matter to the computer program was that I complete two hours of online time; I didn't have to demonstrate competence with any particular minimum fraction of the total material. It was even less rigorous than another form of state-sanctioned timed online instruction, traffic school, a procedural rhetoric with which I, like many Californians, was already familiar.

Naturally, everyone who did the tutorial found themselves wanting to game the system, particularly when the essential cheat code was so simple. Those who finished the whole tutorial correctly and conscientiously told others that they were only punished for reaching the end too early, and were then made to go back and repeat sections until their time was up. Rather than thinking about possible ideological critiques of the system, like the ones with which I found myself absorbed, my colleagues invested their attention elsewhere. Some spent their time on other university work while the online clock was ticking: they graded papers during the tutorial or held telephone conversations on professional business. Others realized that they could just open another web window and take care of e-mail or surf the web.

They were clearly getting a message about the choices the university had made in deciding to deploy this particular form of procedural rhetoric. Even though the organization's own managers, potentially including the president of the entire ten-campus University of California system himself, might have completed the same online tutorial under similar and thus seemingly democratic conditions, there might be a disquieting implication that those in power were only concerned with taking an arbitrary statistical measure to prove some technical compliance through a gesture of educating employees about laws preventing hostile workplaces. The "cheaters" resisted partly because they may have figured out that the price of limiting potential liability for future litigation was to be exacted from the labor force in the form of additional hours of work, even though all that would be produced would be a relatively empty signifier, particularly without a real assessment of the distance learning program. Those who took the tutorial might have intuited another purpose of the exercise for university administrators: to avoid serious, substantive, structural changes in the conditions of academic labor relating to gender and sexuality.

Of course, the digital rhetoric of the virtual state aims at much wider audiences than its own employees. As a number of recent studies have shown, traffic to government websites has increased almost exponentially. As the Pew Internet & American Life Project pointed out in its report on "The Commons of the Tragedy," unique visitors to official agency websites jumped dramatically after the attacks of September 11.[132] In anticipation of the needs of these new audiences, many. gov websites undertook dramatic makeovers. For example, "before" and "after" images of the "press conference" section of the FBI website demonstrate how state interests may adjust their visual appeals by using noticeably different layout strategies.[133]

In the earlier version of FBI webstyle, the agency used a design template on their "press release" page[134] that was common among law enforcement and military sites at the time, situating documents against a black background and using sans serif type with 3-D effects, sometimes with a chrome or other metallic finish on the letters. It is important also to note that in 2001 the FBI website was composed of comparatively few pages, many of which suggested the traditional print genre of the wanted poster.

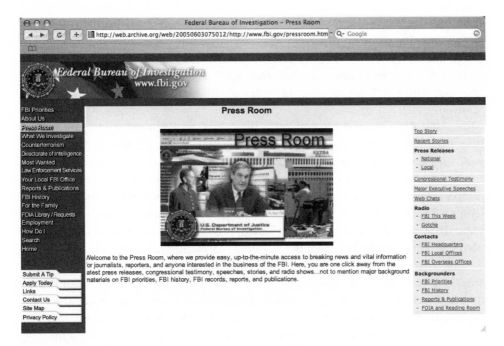

Figure 2.10
2005 Press Room of FBI website after web redesign.

The banner also featured the FBI government seal, which is proprietary to the U.S. government, although it was largely blocked by type, along with a newspaper with a blurred headline held by a pair of disembodied hands.

In contrast, the version from four years later uses a white background, perhaps to conserve the audience's printer ink and to conform with the design philosophy of other federal government sites. (The FBI site is used as an exemplar in several sections of the guidelines at http://www.usability.gov/.) The official seal is shown much more clearly as it is no longer obscured by lettering. This webpage also has come to incorporate the American flag, which many government websites have adopted as a horizontal design motif since the sharp rise in displays of nationalism after the terrorist attacks.[135] What is particularly interesting about this particular graphic is that it serves as a metarepresentation, which presents an image within an image in the layout; thus it reiterates the seal, the flag, and the banner lettering in its basic design. As a state-sanctioned rhetorical presentation it establishes its authority multiple times, with no fewer than three official seals on the page and word repetitions including the phrase "press room" itself.

When one sees the actual word "rhetoric" on the website of a government agency or other public institution, the term is almost never endowed with a positive meaning. The White House website is typical. We are told that "Saddam Hussein's rhetoric is being removed from Iraqi schoolchildren's textbooks,"[136] that "old, tired, stale political rhetoric" needs to be resisted for budget planning,[137] that "rhetoric" needs to be brought in line with "our traditions" during the immigration debate,[138] and that "rhetoric" is opposed to "reality" in our dealings with the Korean peninsula.[139]

Ironically, opponents of government policies restricting cultural production around a burgeoning digital culture often distance themselves from the term "rhetoric" as well. For example, in Lawrence Lessig's *Free Culture*, "rhetoric" indicates that "hard questions" about "balance" are being avoided,[140] that the "rostrum" produces overly "simple" language,[141] and that "great rhetoric" is "wonderfully romantic" and "absurd."[142] Even those, such as Lisa Nakamura, who question the heterosexual white male biases of supposedly politically oppositional "free culture" ideologies use "rhetoric" dismissively. For example, Nakamura talks disparagingly about "libertarian rhetoric,"[143] the rhetoric of the "global village,"[144] and the "rhetoric of the digital divide."[145] In other words, the criticisms of rhetoric from Plato's *Gorgias* seem to be alive and well in the digital age, even if this anti-rhetoric ideology is not sufficient alone to unite those with widely disparate views on other matters of cultural policy.

The search engine on the made-over FBI website also leads back to an early Internet defense of the traditional arts of oratory. A 1996 text file titled "The Four R's for Police Executives," by James D. Sewell, explains the value of rhetoric to the "law enforcement executive." Among other options, Sewell recommends Toastmasters to FBI agents because "skillful oral communication is not so much a product of innate ability as one of desire, training, and practice."[146] At the same time, another 1996 text file associates rhetoric with extremist groups, using language similar to pronouncements about jihadists that would be made a decade later. In "The Lethal Triad: Understanding the Nature of Isolated Extremist Groups," Kevin M. Gilmartin asserts that, as time progresses, "the rocking, chanting, rhetoric-espousing individual becomes unable to question either the group's tenets or its organizational authority structure."[147]

Digital Rhetoric as a Field of Study

In the academy, the value of rhetoric is somewhat more likely to be defended. Today there are faculty appointments advertised for professors of "digital rhetoric"[148] and courses listed in college catalogs on the subject.[149] Yet this particular combination of words is a relatively recent formulation. The genealogy of this specific term can be traced to Richard Lanham and his seminal essay on the subject, "Digital Rhetoric: Theory, Practice, and Property" (1992), which later appeared as "Digital Rhetoric and the Digital Arts" (1993).[150] Lanham's interest in multimedia goes back to at least 1979, when he created a multimedia video with animated digital lettering for his writing textbook *Revising Prose.*[151] A few years later, he attended an early SIGGRAPH conference and realized the power of computer-generated imaging technology. By the mid-1980s, he was reading British science writer Jeremy Campbell's account of information theory, *Grammatical Man: Information, Entropy, Language, and Life*,[152] and in a 1988 keynote address at Duke University, Lanham was imagining how a hypothetical student might be reading a computerized version of *Love's Labour's Lost*. During this period Lanham gave several prominent addresses to prestigious academic organizations, such as the Modern Language Association, where members appeared to be reluctant to embrace his enthusiasm for multidisciplinary explorations.

Like his predecessor Marshall McLuhan, Lanham was a crossdisciplinary popularizer who once even attempted to define "digital literacy" in the pages of *Scientific American*.[153] When Lanham published *The Electronic Word: Democracy, Technology, and the Arts*, it also appeared in an electronic "expanded book" version for Macintosh. That version was produced by the University of Chicago Press and inspired by the now-defunct multimedia software publisher The Voyager Company. Reviews of the digital version of Lanham's text were mixed. Some praised how the "analytical reading and dialogue with the author" was "more efficient" in the electronic form,[154] while others complained that Lanham did not take adequate advantage of the rhetorical opportunities of a digital hypertext.[155] Despite the challenge of working outside the linear academic prose forms that he knew so well, Lanham pursued subsequent collaborations with multimedia software development firms, which included a never-produced volume on *Three Thousand Years of Multimedia* to have been released by Calliope under the direction of Robert Winter and Jay Heifeitz.[156]

Some of the earliest polemics about digital rhetoric were occupied with defensive postures on behalf of the new discipline, many of which involved taking sides in intellectual turf wars within the academy. To understand digital rhetoric in the 1980s and 1990s, it is useful to look at several trends. Traditionalists were attempting to insulate themselves from what they perceived as a triple threat, consisting of an assault on the preeminent authority of print from media studies, the advent of a disruptive new class of practitioner-theorists, and the introduction of unconventional collaborative procedures, which broke even the rules of peripheral university programs like creative writing. Digital rhetoric was also responding to two major influences on the field of rhetorical studies more generally: continental critical theory, particularly the work of deconstructionist philosopher Jacques Derrida, and anti-Socratic revisions to rhetorical history, which questioned the authority of Aristotle as a founding father of the discipline.

At the time Lanham was writing, a series of fin de siècle debates about the mortality of print literature was taking place in literary journals, academic publications, and occasionally the mainstream media. The various death knells clanging over the literary scene included the death of poetry, the death of the novel, and the death of literature more generally. One of the books in this genre that Lanham is reacting to is actually titled *The Death of Literature*. Its author Alvin Kernan blames deconstruction for sapping texts of their symbolic power and thus leaving them vulnerable to a final coup de grâce at the hands of a brutish mass media. Although Lanham also treats poststructuralist critical theory as being of dubious value, he takes Kernan to task for bemoaning declining literacy while also upholding the cultural elitism that denigrates college composition and other sectors of practical rhetoric.

In "Digital Rhetoric and the Digital Arts," Lanham jumps to answer his own central question: "What happens when the text moves from page to screen?" At one level, what Lanham describes in his answer is a classic information bomb in which "the fixed, authoritative, canonical text, simply explodes into the ether."[157] At another level, he imagines a transformation that is creative as well as destructive, because the reader can become a writer now that such texts are "unfixed and interactive."[158]

In formulating a disciplinary realm for digital rhetoric, Lanham appeases the traditionalists by attempting to integrate new media studies into a longer rhetorical history. Yet, at the same time, he is alerting his colleagues that a fundamental paradigm shift is taking place in the present moment. Specifically, Lanham argues that it is the very model of knowledge itself that is dying, and that its close association with the more obviously outmoded codex form is merely serving as a distraction from the fact of knowledge's impending demise. In his work on the "sociality of knowledge," Lanham argues that "electronic information" not only changes what is meant by "author" and "text," but also "desubstantializes" the arts and letters, along with the industrial revolution that produced them.[159]

Lanham is very pointedly *not* responding to another significant factor that shaped the discourses about digital rhetoric at the time, as the ideas of Jacques Derrida and of poststructuralism more generally were becoming part of the canon, studied in graduate programs in rhetoric, and cited frequently in prominent books and theoretical journals in the field. At one point in *The Electronic Word*, Lanham briefly raises the work of Paul de Man and Derrida, only to dismiss their respective efforts on blindness and insight in reading or the inherently unstable character of text as pale imitations of rhetorician Kenneth Burke in the 1930s. [160] He also distances himself from some of his fellow digital rhetoricians, who were using poststructuralism to explain contemporary media culture and information architecture, notably George Landow and Gregory Ulmer.

Despite their different theoretical orientations, both west coast Lanham and his east coast contemporary Landow emphasize the need for brand-new academic institutions in their founding texts for the discipline.[161] As Lanham writes, "If what we hopefully call the 'real world' is moving toward the electronic word, can we continue to plan our curriculum around great books? Can we, in fact, continue to think of the curriculum in our customary linear terms—preparatory courses, intermediate ones, advanced, prerequisites, the whole big catalog enchilada?"[162] Landow also appears to believe that digital rhetoric necessarily involves a complete redesign of the academy and a restructuring of literary education. For example, in the original 1992 edition of *Hypertext*, Landow predicts that hypertext and hypermedia will attract more nontraditional students, foster more situations for collaborative learning, and change the current system of credit hours and timed examinations. Landow also assumes that new digital texts will reshape the literary canon and require that students and their instructors be likewise "reconfigured."

In this classic and frequently upgraded book, which later appeared as *Hypertext 2.0* and *Hypertext 3.0*, Landow examines how electronic documents link to each other and how the reader makes choices among competing texts and alternative logical paths. Landow sees a cultural convergence taking place in which software development and poststructuralist theory are producing analogous if not homologous texts. He frequently cites the work of Derrida, Barthes, and Foucault. Yet Landow asserts that the poststructuralist reader is still oriented through a "rhetoric of arrival and departures." For example, in *Hypertext 3.0*, Landow says that linking "permits simple means of orienting readers by allowing a basic rhetoric of departure" whereby these readers will be directed to "a clearly defined point in the text" that operates through a rhetoric of arrival.[163] Landow's approach to digital rhetoric is prescriptive as well as descriptive. For example, in a section on "How Should We Write Hypertext?" Landow proposes "A Rhetoric and Stylistics of Writing for E-Space."

In contrast, software theorist Lev Manovich considers such digital rhetoric to be an oxymoron, given the paratactic organization of weblinks. He equates rhetoric with stylized hierarchies of tropes that he believes do not transcode to computer interfaces.

Traditionally, texts encoded human knowledge and memory, instructed, inspired, convinced, and seduced their readers to adopt new ideas, new ways of interpreting the world, new ideologies. In short, the printed word was linked to the art of rhetoric. While it is probably possible to invent a new rhetoric of hypermedia that will use hyperlinking not to distract the reader from the argument (as is often the case today), but rather to further convince her of an argument's validity, the sheer existence and popularity of hyperlinking exemplifies the continuing decline of the field of rhetoric in the modern era.[164]

Although Manovich clearly doesn't associate rhetoric with mere distraction or dissimulation, as the term often colloquially appears, he asserts that any rhetoric of new media would need to be invented because real digital arguments do not even exist at present.

However, Manovich's bold assertions in his own "death of rhetoric" narrative are highly questionable, given the facts of electronic texts and the disciplines that study them. Most obviously, hypertext doesn't present the user with all the data at once; if anything, hypertext delays and defers the revelation of information beneath layers of web artifacts, often much more effectively or—in Manovich's terms—seductively than the direct access offered by the easily flippable pages of a book. Furthermore, his characterization of rhetoric as being the handmaiden of the printed word seems particularly counterfactual in light of the number of professional rhetoricians throughout history who have grounded their field in classical oratory and the norms of social interaction in oral culture.

One of the earliest advocates for understanding the role of orality in digital culture was Gregory Ulmer, who is frequently cited by Landow as a precursor to his own work. Although much of Ulmer's analysis is set in the 1980s and thus focuses on the model of television as a media platform upon which to apply Derridean philosophy, rather than hypertext or hypermedia, Ulmer seems extraordinarily prescient elsewhere. Particularly in the current information environment of user-friendly desktop digital tools, his work on sampling and recombinant activities with audiotapes and films remains extremely relevant. He points out that modern-day digital bards can manipulate received content from collective sources and answers the objections of humanists, such as Jerry Mander or Neil Postman, who "condemn electronic orality because they assume that a free society depends on the subject of individualism as it is defined in the Enlightenment tradition."[165] Instead, Ulmer suggests that we must "imagine a different apparatus, beginning with a different technology."[166] He also rereads the canon of classical rhetoric differently, drawing on the lessons of those such as Quintillian who valorized alternative logics, such as those based upon the structure of the joke.

Many of these digital rhetoricians also allude to their involvement with a number of hands-on web-based projects. For example, Landow was particularly important in establishing scholarly "rings" on subjects like the Victorian era or postcolonial literature in Africa and Asia. Landow's involvement with Storyspace, to which he contributed a "descriptive cross-referenced index,"[167] demonstrated the particular significance of this now-proprietary computer application for understanding the confluences of thought about digital rhetoric during its formative period. Storyspace plays a critical role in this short history of digital rhetoric. Both Michael Joyce and Jay David Bolter were active authors in this community based around publicly constructing and revising hypertext narratives and the associated software development project.

Bolter had garnered Lanham's obvious respect, partly because he also appealed to the traditionalists by drawing a longer timeline through which to understand the current late age of print as one in which a conventional notion of "writing space" is revitalized by new technology. Both critics also shared a common enthusiasm for modernism and collage and even insert some of the same images in their books. Lanham went so far as to claim that the computer fulfills "the expressive agenda of twentieth-century art."[168] Both Lanham and Bolter also display a facility for drawing attention to the medieval preprint antecedents of digital texts.

Bolter, however, goes further and claims to understand the processing power of the actual machine, although he often couches his assertions in the positive terms of intelligent design rather than the negative terms of mechanical constraint. For example, he argues that the computer can serve "as a vehicle for human (what computer specialists call 'natural') language."[169] Later he claims that it is "no accident that the computer can serve as an outline processor" because the "machine is designed to create and track such formal structures."[170] Of course, as this book has already implied, more recent digital rhetoricians, who now study the actual algorithms controlling input-output interactions, have a slightly more jaundiced view of the freedom of those who use computers for rhetorical purposes, given the limitations of specific forms of code.

Bolter and Lanham also share an interest in the key term "remediation." Bolter's later work with Richard Grusin complicates his original, relatively straightforward conception of writing space by introducing the theme of remediation, or the way that "digital forms both borrow from and seek to surpass earlier forms."[171] Bolter and Grusin examine how the viewer both looks at and looks through media technologies, and they emphasize that these media technologies function in "networks or hybrids that can be expressed in physical, social, aesthetic, and economic terms" and that the software protocol governing exchanges on the World Wide Web serves a variety of different uses: "marketing and advertising, scholarship, personal expression, and so on."[172] It is interesting to note, however, the absence of the political or messages of the state from their list, despite a number of examples with political content; for example, from the websites of news organs, such as *CNN* or *USA Today*.

Bolter's fellow Storyspace author Michael Joyce focuses on the hybridity of the human subject as well as the new media text, and considers what this lack of homogeneity means for the contemporary cyborg-author. Based on his experiences teaching writing workshops in virtual environments, Joyce looks at how writers for the screen function with "two minds" and how writers connected to computer networks experience what he calls "othermindedness." In his first book on the subject of digital rhetoric, he uses Vannevar Bush's "memex" and Ted Nelson's "Xanadu" as early prototypes for the associative and intermingled qualities of the human mind, which are expressed in dialogic hypertext.[173] Over the course of a decade, his intellectual interests move from the implications of hypertext to the significance of networks. Thus Joyce's more recent work is influenced by studies of emergent behavior and chaos theory,[174] but like Bolter he denies the power of "technological determinism."[175]

The rediscovery of the pre-Socratics was also an important event in the field of rhetoric and composition, particularly for feminist scholars who wanted an alternative historical narrative from which to trace their critical lineage.[176] In this vein, in 1999 Kathleen Welch published *Electric Rhetoric*, which paid homage to Ulmer from its opening epigraph. In her analysis of "electric rhetoric," Welch rejects the Aristotelian/ Platonic/Socratic model as fundamental and proposes Isocrates as the better classical rhetorician through which to understand the current media age. Isocrates, she argues, acknowledges the ways that rhetorical culture may be changed by the advent of a technology of writing, without relying on the rigid, mutually exclusive, binary opposition of writing to speaking, to which Aristotle's teacher Plato held so dear. She characterizes Isocrates as both a Sophist and a precursor of postmodernism for whom the word "logos" represented a "flux of language, thought, and action."[177] Welch posits that our new media culture is fostering what Walter Ong had called "secondary orality,"[178] in which audiovisual electronic media coexist with the literacy of writing but manifest aspects of oral experience as well, just as the era of Isocrates represented a similar juncture in media culture. Furthermore, Welch makes an analogy between how cultural critics complain of the drug-like character of television watching and computer use and Plato's description of writing as druglike *pharmakon*, which is potentially both remedy and poison in the *Phaedrus*.

In the course of this book, I will be coming back to what I see as two possible shortcomings to the bulk of the critical work done in digital rhetoric to date: marked tendencies to overlook the rhetoric of the virtual state and to ignore theories about rhetoric from the discipline of computer science.

First, the objects of study in much new media scholarship are not very relevant to the political interests of the public at large. Art installations in small galleries, hypertext novels with cult followings, and procedural poems by poets considered too minor to be represented in chain bookstores continue to appeal almost exclusively to a rarified, miniscule, and academically oriented niche population of users. Private audiences for demos in university research laboratories or feedback practices in closed online creative writing workshops may also seem inaccessible to average citizens, who are hermetically shut out from such secret knowledge spaces of the elect. And when the objects are relevant, because they represent digital artifacts from popular culture or niche fan communities,[179] they are often divorced from concerns about either the virtual state or the deliberative processes of online communities.[180] As Ulises Ali Mejias points out, there can be significant differences between "masses" and "publics" when it comes to civic participation.[181]

There are some significant exceptions, however, as rhetorical scholarship adapts to the twenty-first century, even though much of this work tends to focus on web campaigning[182] or particular debates about Internet use[183] rather than a broader theory of digital rhetoric. In *Rhetoric Online*, Barbara Warnick uses theories of intertextuality derived from Julia Kristeva and Mikhael Bakhtin to examine web-based public discourses that reuse and remix sources. Warnick also applies a traditional Toulmin model, which has been used in college composition classrooms for many decades, to make statistical generalizations about de-authored discourses in independent news ventures that rely on "flattened hierarchies, wikis, temporary group representation, and collectivism."[184] Unfortunately, her theories about "interactivity" tend to rely more on a knowledge of Kenneth Burke than of the constraints of computer interfaces and the algorithms of computer programs, although her uses of Burke's notion of a "body of identifications" rather than "one particular address" [185] may be useful for complex rhetorical interactions online.

In *Cyberliteracy: Navigating the Internet with Awareness*, Laura Gurak promises to deliver a rhetorical primer for Internet users. As Gurak writes, "Unlike many of the 'how-to' books and 'dummies' guides' on the market, this book is not a technical listing of what to do and not to do."[186] Yet there's also a kind of normative moralism that runs through Gurak's book, along with a tendency to emphasize "cyberliteracy" in singular rather than "cyberliteracies" in plural. Gurak's messages about gender-based harassment, the hazards of "techno-rage," and hoaxes could also be said to play into many of the ideologies that are key to the current reactionary political mood that focuses on cybersafety and Internet security rather than building a commons of public information infrastructures.[187] Furthermore, there are legitimate arguments to be made in favor of conventionally antisocial practices of dissimulation, exhibitionism, and transgression in Internet environments, which are part of the expected social scripts dictating many contemporary conventions for common online behavior.

Second, many interpretive approaches from traditional rhetorical studies have been limited by a peculiar set of disciplinary blinders. The theoretical texts upon which the earlier authors draw tend to be exclusively from literary criticism or critical theory and are thus firmly grounded in traditional humanities departments. Despite appeals to those with interdisciplinary credentials, this work often excludes highly relevant literature from technologists who may have a more intimate understanding of the systemic constraints that govern the representation, processing, or retrieval of information that may be central to communicative exchanges effected through digital media. The discourses of computer scientists themselves—or information scientists, in the terms of the postwar era—tend to be conspicuously absent in scholarly books and articles about digital rhetoric. [188] Yet the field of rhetorical studies considers both the rhetoric of science and the science of rhetoric, and I would argue that the literature of research in computer science has made significant contributions to both. Specifically, I am claiming that a basic understanding of both signal theory and network theory is valuable to any contemporary rhetorician.

Mathematical Theories of Communication

Although Welch argues that digital media practices cannot comfortably fit the traditional Aristotelian model, I would say that it depends on the Aristotelian model in question. Aristotle is also the philosopher who arguably first situated rhetoric in the realm of probability, and as such his approach continues to be relevant to contemporary digital rhetoric and the computer-mediated view of information as a construct of relative uncertainties. In his meditations on possible topoi, Aristotle explains the relationship between probability (*eikos*) and rhetoric in some detail. Aristotle points out that what is improbable does happen and that this specific line of argument can be extended disingenuously by his fellow rhetoricians, such as the Sicilian teacher Corax, into a more spurious construction: what is improbable is probable. Aristotle also shows some suspicion about the dogma surrounding established knowledge and its inclusionary/exclusionary logic of absolute certainty: "Listeners react also to expressions speechwriters use to excess: 'Who does not know?' 'Everybody knows . . .' The listener agrees out of embarrassment in order to share in the feelings of all others."[189]

As Dilip Gaonkar summarizes the epistemological positions of the ancients, "Aristotle replaces Plato's binary opposition between reality and appearance with his own binary opposition between the necessary and the contingent."[190] In other words, to use Gaonkar's opposition, Plato can be seen as the consummate philosopher of knowledge, and Aristotle as the philosopher of information. In his 1959 essay *The Two Cultures*, C. P. Snow described the "intellectual life of the whole of western society" as divided between "two polar groups": those of the sciences and those of the humanities.[191] Now it is possible that institutions of intellectual inquiry will eventually be divided into two even more incompatible communities of scholarly association: the culture of knowledge and the culture of information. In arguing on behalf of "Critical Information Studies," Siva Vaidhyanathan identifies the communities of association that may challenge traditional Platonic institutions of knowledge: "Economists, sociologists, linguists, anthropologists, ethnomusicologists, communication scholars, lawyers, computer scientists, philosophers, and librarians."[192]

Definitions are important here, particularly since in everyday language, "information" is generally treated as nearly interchangeable with "knowledge." Webster's Dictionary, slightly more precisely, defines one word in terms of the other, so that "information" is classified as the "communication or reception of knowledge or intelligence." The Oxford English Dictionary goes further to acknowledge the term's etymological history by including social practices of interpretation in its definition, so that the entry on "information" encompasses the "formation or moulding of the mind or character, training, instruction, teaching; communication of instructive knowledge."[193]

Although I am claiming Aristotle as an early philosopher of information, he did not have the actual word "information" in his lexicon of ancient Greek. In their work on literacy and numeracy, Michael Hobart and Zachary Schiffman have traced the word back to Latin classical culture to consider how antecedents of the term "information" actually functioned in the rhetorics of the ancient public sphere, at a time when the information culture of the Roman world was exploding with new libraries and modes for disseminating written texts, maps, scientific illustrations, art works, and luxury goods:

The term itself traces back to the Latin verb informare, which for the Romans generally meant 'to shape,' 'to form an idea of,' or 'to describe.' The verb, in turn, supplied action to the substantive, forma, which took varied, cognate meanings that depended mostly on context. The historian Livy used forma as a general term for 'character,' 'form,' 'nature,' 'kind,' and 'matter.' Horace applied it to a shoelast, Ovid to a mold or stamp for making coins, while the wily Cicero, among other uses, extended it to logic as 'form' or 'species,' his rendering of the Greek. . . . The practical notion of 'form' as a last, mold, or stamp remained closely tied to its more abstract, logical meaning, which paired content and container.[194]

Hobart and Schiffman claim that the concept of information can be tracked even further back to its historical roots in the origins of writing. Thus information is created at the place where technology and rhetoric intersect.

However, it is the technical definition of the word "information," as it is used by mathematicians and computer scientists in relation to "uncertainty," which is central to my argument. From the perspective of information theory, information is linked to a fundamentally different paradigm for the interpretation of ambiguity in communicative exchanges from that of knowledge. As Bell Labs scientist Claude Shannon explains in his 1948 groundbreaking article, "A Mathematical Theory of Communication," the quantity of information transmitted is determined by the amount of uncertainty at issue in a given situation.[195] For example, I might say that more information is conveyed by the next letter of the sequence C-H-O than by the next letter of the sequence C-H-O-C-O-L-A-T. So, in my example, the components of the first message, C-H-O, could be a restaurant order for "chocolate," but they could just as easily be forming the letters for "chop suey" or "choice steak"; in contrast, the completed contents of the second, longer message C-H-O-C-O-L-A-T appear easier to predict.[196] Shannon's collaborator, Warren Weaver, went so far as to say that information has "nothing to do with meaning," although it does describe a pattern.[197] This is because information refers not to a single message, but probabilistically to an entire set of possible messages. Shannon and Weaver connect information to entropy and thus understand it against a measure of the disorder or randomness in a closed system.

Weaver argues that the redundancy of written English affects how messages are conveyed through text. "Since English is about 50 per cent redundant, it would be possible to save about one-half the time of ordinary telegraphy by a proper encoding process, provided one were going to transmit over a noiseless channel. When there is noise on a channel, however, there is some real advantage in not using a coding process that eliminates all of the redundancy. For the remaining redundancy helps combat the noise."[198]

Ordinary people have some sense of this redundancy in English, from which they infer that the use of acronyms in instant messaging does not significantly lower comprehensibility.[199] One interesting case of how this colloquial understanding of theories of information functions is the "Cmabrigde e-mail" that has been widely circulated in the past decade. The version I received in 2004 reads as follows:

Aoccdrnig to a rscheearch at Cmabrigde Uinervtisy, it deosn't mttaer in waht oredr the ltteers in a wrod are, the olny iprmoetnt tihng is taht the frist and lsat ltteer be at the rghit pclae. The rset can be a total mses and you can sitll raed it wouthit a porbelm. Tihs is bcuseae the huamn mnid deos not raed ervey lteter by istlef, but the wrod as a wlohe.
   Amzanig huh?[200]

Despite the article error of the descrambled "a research," the appeals to authority in the e-mail are obvious. By locating the authors of the supposed study in a prestigious British university and claiming that their findings can be easily demonstrated to the general public in a few lines of text, the notion that most of a given word functions as an empty placeholder is given considerable credence. Unlike the classic example of the telegram that reads "NOTHER DYING" instead of "MOTHER DYING," which Joyce's hero in *Ulysses*, Stephen Daedulus, receives, there is no poetic register on which the ostensible mistakes make secondary meanings. In this popularization of the principle of redundancy, Shannon and Weaver's original message about the robustness of written English as code may be lost, and arguments about Taylorizing the language for greater brevity and efficiency may even be entertained.

The alleged findings have been disputed by a member of the actual Cognition and Brain Sciences Unit at Cambridge University, Matt Davis, who offers his own demonstration of how the e-mail message is a selective sample chosen for its rhetorical effectiveness rather than its actual likelihood as an example of written expression if the intervening letters were randomly generated. Davis even provides a web link to an online generator that will scramble text to conform to the procedural rules. Yet Davis notes that versions of the Cmabrigde e-mail continue to occur in many different languages, including a German variant, which was published as a cartoon in *Der Spiegel*.[201]

Shannon's signal theory model of communication (figure 2.11) can be read as a scheme for explaining rhetorical interactions and the centrality of interference in any information transfer. Like conventional rhetoric, electronic communication is mediated, it travels through channels, it is distorted by noise, and messages must be converted into signals in order to pass from speaker to audience. In order to generalize their work, Shannon's collaborator, Warren Weaver, characterized communication systems as functioning on three different levels.[202] At Level A, the question was "How accurately can the symbols of communication be transmitted?" At Level B, the issues involve "How precisely do the transmitted symbols convey the desired meaning?"

Finally, Level C concerns "How effectively does the received meaning affect conduct in the desired way?" These Level C concerns can be seen as rhetorical concerns if we look at how action is changed by linguistic exchanges in examples from the work of other twentieth-century rhetoricians like Kenneth Burke or the speech act theorists. Although Shannon's actual text is largely occupied with Level A situations, in which the clarity of the signal is the main issue at hand, Weaver argues that information theory has much to contribute to understanding of the entropic character of Level B and Level C discourse.

Strangely, there are some who read information theory and its initial impact on linguistics through interdisciplinary organizations, such as the Macy Conference and the American Society for Cybernetics, as a repudiation of rhetorical models of communication. In explaining the work of Macy participant Roman Jakobson, Lev Manovich has argued that information theory presents a reductive schematic model that is inherently unrhetorical. As Manovich writes, "Ancient and medieval scholars classified hundreds of different rhetorical figures. Roman Jakobson, under the influence of the computer's binary logic, information theory, and cybernetics to which he was exposed at MIT where he was teaching, radically reduced rhetoric to just two figures—metaphor and metonymy."[203] And yet the diagrams that Jakobson himself actually drew, in essays like "Linguistics and Poetics,"[204] seem to suggest an appreciation for the complexity of rhetorical exchanges within communication channels that was complementary to the work of rhetoricians who were his contemporaries.

The importance of signal theory to matters of the public sphere may not always be apparent, although there are situations in which noise in messages to stakeholders contributes to events that eventually cost lives or human resources. For example,

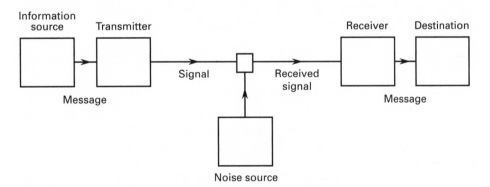

Figure 2.11

Diagram from *The Mathematical Theory of Communication*, copyright 1949, 1998 by the Board of Trustees of the University of Illinois. Used with permission of the author and the University of Illinois Press.

Edward R. Tufte has pointed to the messages from PowerPoint presentations prior to the crash of the space shuttle *Columbia* as indicative of scrambled communicative efforts. A PowerPoint slide shows how a redundant signifier, "significant," masked crucial information buried deep in the hierarchy of bullet points.[205]

In addition to signal theory, a new science of networks also offers opportunities for rhetoricians to share in theories of communication developed across disciplinary lines. For novices, physicist Albert-László Barabási has written a primer on network theory, *Linked: How Everything is Connected to Everything Else and What It Means*. In it, Barabási connects prevailing models of hubs and connectors in graph theory to studies of the spread of disease, the mechanisms of social contact, and the traffic to and from particular websites. Perhaps most interesting to rhetoricians is Barabási's analysis of the persuasive success of the Apostle Paul. The physicist credits Paul's "firsthand knowledge of the social network of the first century's civilized world from Rome to Jerusalem" with the successful dissemination of the Christian faith.[206]

Just as signal theory excites the public's imagination, there are also popular narratives that interpret the research of network theorists for mass audiences. For example, in the 2006 fall television season, a series called *Six Degrees* on the ABC network used the idea that "everyone is connected" to create a drama around the seemingly separate lives of six New York City dwellers.[207] Even before membership in social network sites became mainstream, the series calculated that the general public would have some familiarity with the network concept thanks to awareness generated by a Broadway play and a later film with a similar title about a young imposter who claims to be the son of actor Sidney Poitier, and by fan culture around the ongoing ABC series *Lost*. As in the case of the Cmabrigde e-mail, there are anecdotal references to scientific studies imbedded in much of this popular discourse, although most people who use the term may not know the specific citation that could be made to work by behavioral psychologist Stanley Milgram and others before him.

From Multimedia to Social Media

Rhetoricians may be hesitant to acknowledge contributions to the field of electronic communication from disciplinary sciences in departments far from their own, and they may be particularly leery of the kind of popular pseudoscientific interpretations that I am highlighting, given the humanities' understandable professional biases against empirical claims, broad generalizations about language, and technological determinism. But to exclude these discourses that present models of signals and networks is to overlook research that could enrich research questions in traditional rhetoric as well.

James P. Zappen has characterized the field of digital rhetoric as an assemblage of heterogeneous elements, which nonetheless have a significant contribution to make to rhetorical studies as a whole. As Zappen writes, "Digital rhetoric is thus an amalgam of more-or-less discrete components rather than a complete and integrated theory in its own right. These discrete components nonetheless provide at least a partial outline for such a theory, which has potential to contribute to the larger body of rhetorical theory and criticism and the rhetoric of science and technology in particular."[208]

In contrast, I think that an integrated theory can be defended, although digital rhetoric operates at a number of different registers and includes messages to, from, and within the personal, the governmental, the academic, and the scientific public spheres. However, these registers do not represent discrete, hermetically sealed realms of discourse, because discussions about civic participation, community membership, and appropriate timing inform each other across the multiple levels of disciplinary expertise. As digital rhetoric moves from a model based on one-to-many *multimedia*—typified by audiovisual CD-ROM technology of the 1980s and 1990s—to one based on many-to-many *social media* that include file sharing and social network sites, it is likely that these registers of communal knowledge will be even more interconnected.

On February 8, 2006, the *New York Times* reported that a junior presidential appointee at NASA had resigned his post.[209] The story behind his resignation illustrates how digital rhetoric operates across all four hierarchies of different forms of knowledge work. The political appointee, George C. Deutsch, had irked scientists by telling a web designer to insert the word "theory" each time that the phrase "the Big Bang" appeared on a NASA website. Deutsch had claimed on his résumé that he held a bachelor of science degree from Texas A&M University, which turned out to be a falsehood. A young blogger discovered that Deutsch had attended classes at A&M but never graduated. The blogger, Nick Anthis, was a genuine Texas A&M graduate and Rhodes Scholar who was studying biochemistry at Oxford. His blog, *The Scientific Activist*, earned attention from *Time Magazine* and the journal *Nature* for his coverage of the Deutsch story.

Blogger Anthis is explicit about the fact that *The Scientific Activist* is intended to connect the personal, the political, the academic, and the scientific modes of digital rhetoric. In covering the Deutsch case, he draws on his personal autobiography as a recent college graduate, in which he heard the rumor about Deutsch never graduating, and combines this story with government documents in the public record, which he then relates to his status as an initiated junior member of the academy and the more specialized scientific communities to which he now belongs, communities that might dispute Deutsch on other grounds, such as the experimental evidence for the occurrence of the Big Bang, if the rhetorical context had been more formal and mediated around print rather than the norms of digital community. The circuit of digital production in the Deutsch story began with a website and ended with a blog, but that network of communicative exchanges engaged a number of other social actors, disciplinary communities, and modes of discourse in ways characteristic of rapidly changing social media.

3 The Desert of the Unreal: Democracy and Military-Funded Videogames and Simulations

FlatWorld is housed in a nondescript warehouse on a street that cuts through an area of industrial parks. It is just one site where the built environment of the U.S. military's war zone in Iraq has been recreated to design better government-funded videogames and virtual reality simulations. The cavernous space in Los Angeles is stocked with props and scenery representing remote theaters of conflict: corrugated metal sprayed with Arabic graffiti, peeling Iraqi election posters with citizens holding small flags, synthetic rubble, sandbags, false fronts draped with camouflage netting, and bombed-out dwellings abbreviated to little more than a door or window. Directors' chairs are everywhere. Near the entrance, a visitor can look down the muzzle of a life-sized tank glowing on a screen, which can be made even more intimidating when viewed through 3-D glasses.

Run by the Institute for Creative Technologies at the University of Southern California, Flatworld is known for its Hollywood-style approach to creating digital tools for military training. Rising above the ruins of this ersatz Iraqi neighborhood, toward the very back of the facility, there is an enormous cage-like dome that looks like an off-world colony in a science fiction movie. Known as the "Light Stage," it is covered with light-emitting diodes (LEDs) and has been occasionally repurposed to provide digital effects for big-budget blockbusters, as well as for more realistically lit computer-generated figures for high-tech war games and training simulations. In the adjoining spaces of FlatWorld, odd assemblages of projectors and prosceniums are being used to create Pepper's ghosts, nineteenth-century special effects still used in twenty-first century theme park attractions. Many of the sets are constructed to create "reality sandwiches" that combine digital flats with synthetic environments.[1]

In one FlatWorld demo, as loud Arabic religious chants play, the visitor is instructed to stand, wearing 3-D glasses, in the center of a room made of modular flats with digital displays on which hyperrealistic scenes of urban dysfunction are depicted far into the depth of field.[2] There is real smashed furniture in the center of the room, and tangible broken ceiling panels hang down from overhead. Outside the room, on the virtual street, on the other side of a geometrically decorated fence, helicopters land, cars burst into flames, and unmanned aerial vehicles whiz by like unidentified flying objects. When the door on the right of the set is opened onto another virtual vista, there is an armed insurgent with his face obscured standing menacingly in the threshold; he peppers the walls of the demo room with realistic-looking bullet holes. As the conflict intensifies, the ground actually shakes with concussive force. The visitor is escorted out of this first room into another mixed reality environment, where a child taunts Americans and throws rocks.

In yet another FlatWorld demo a life-sized virtual figure identifies himself as "Sergeant John Blackwell" and reassures us with his expertise; Blackwell claims to be an expert speaker of several languages and to be able to answer questions about his background via a headset using natural language processing software. When Sergeant Blackwell fully introduces himself to visitors from the interested public and the media, he follows a script that provides a remix of patriotic kitsch including some of the following phrases: "I joined up after seeing that movie *Saving Private Ryan* . . . World War II, D-Day—the sacrifices others have made for our freedoms. I figured I had something to give, too. . . . If I change my clothes and my language . . . I'm a noncombatant or an enemy. The question is: what's my mission today?"[3] FlatWorld is imagined as much as an operating system for modern warfare as it is as a physical place grounded in a specific geography of conflict. As one of its architects, computer scientist Jarrell Pair, writes, "The system integrates Hollywood set construction techniques with state of the art computer graphics and immersive display technology."[4] Pair explains that "FlatWorld provides a new type of experience in which gaming and role-playing techniques can be applied to achieve educational and training goals."

In "Welcome to the Desert of the Real," written in the days between "traumatic event" and "symbolic impact," Slavoj Žižek expresses his belief that the September 11 terrorist attacks could finally force Americans to experience some of the violence and privation of the rest of the world, from which the United States has been shielded by an artificial but ideologically comforting socioeconomic, political, and cultural virtual reality environment. His title refers to a famous moment in the movie *The Matrix* in which the once-comfortable hero Neo is finally shown the brutal, mechanical substrate behind the virtual simulation in which almost all of his fellow citizens are still deeply immersed.[5] In the world of the film, only a select population of initiates may see the postapocalyptic environmental wasteland in which human beings have become vegetative slaves who are farmed as an energy source. Žižek points to a number of other "real life isn't real" narratives in popular culture—such as the movie *The Truman Show*, in which the protagonist discovers that he is witnessing an elaborate spectacle rather than authentic and spontaneous experience—as symptomatic of this nagging sense of the unreal in work and leisure in Western consumer society.[6] "So it is not only that Hollywood stages a semblance of real life deprived of the weight and inertia of materiality—in the late capitalist consumerist society, 'real social life' itself somehow acquires the features of a staged fake, with our neighbors behaving in 'real' life as stage actors and extras."[7] He argues that televised reality shows in which interactions are stage-managed and edited for broadcast can also be read as subtle reminders of this unreality effect in operation. Although one could argue that American simulation culture enabled the hijackers, who had trained extensively on flight simulators, to commandeer the planes that flew into the metropolitan landmarks of global commerce and military planning, Žižek posits that the cataclysmic violence could also assert a particular form of experiential authority that would force witnesses to it to see outside the simulation. Despite what he describes as the distracting cinematic spectacle of the demolished skyscrapers, Žižek suggests that if there is "any symbolism" in the center's collapse, he locates it in "VIRTUAL capitalism" or "financial speculations disconnected from the sphere of material production."[8] Thus the impact of the bombings is measured against "the borderline which today separates the digitalized First World from the Third World 'desert of the Real.'"[9]

Ironically, terrorist attacks within the U.S. national borders and two invasions of foreign countries justified by those attacks have probably encouraged the federal government to generate ever more virtual worlds in response. Many of these government-funded virtual reality simulations of Iraq, Afghanistan, and other potential theaters of combat address training for military personnel. By the time I first visited FlatWorld, I was already familiar with two projects at the University of Southern California that were being developed for soldiers with funding from the U.S. military: *Tactical Iraqi*, a computer game designed to accelerate a soldier's acquisition of spoken Arabic to assist in volatile tactical situations, and *Virtual Iraq*, a virtual reality simulation intended to lessen the effects of posttraumatic stress disorder (PTSD) among combat veterans. Both initiatives had received extensive national media coverage and seemed to serve rhetorical as well as pedagogical or therapeutic ends by making individual, private digital experiences aimed to effect the personal education or rehabilitation of military personnel accessible to a wider public. I was also interested in what these government-funded software developers thought about the debate in the serious game development community about working on behalf of government-funded projects that supported current military efforts. I had hypothesized that this conflict dramatized the deliberative potential of this public sphere and thought that games and simulations could manifest what Bruno Latour has called "object-oriented democracy,"[10] in which visual media represent potential sites for popular activism and resistance rather than merely serve as the exclusive stage for state-sanctioned rhetoric.

In recent years, the field of serious games has burgeoned with a number of taxpayer-funded and privately funded initiatives in areas such as military training, the modeling of scenarios for emergency first-responders, disease prevention, physical and mental patient rehabilitation, geopolitical or crosscultural sensitivity training, conflict resolution, and teaching and learning at all levels, from early childhood education to exit certification from medical school. The seemingly oxymoronic term "serious play" has also had resonance in the corporate world, thanks to those like Michael Schrage, who have argued that networked computers with powerful modeling software have fostered a new kind of corporate culture based on simulations, prototypes, and demos, which provides greater flexibility and opportunity for consensus-building when strategizing how best to produce, market, and service commercial products.[11] The niche field of serious games within the game development community has created its own national and international venues for sharing knowledge and showcasing new projects with websites, electronic mailing lists, professional associations, and annual conferences.

Since the U.S.-led invasion of Iraq in 2003, the American government has developed several computer-generated environments that are intended to recreate the embattled nation's terrain—as well as its built environment—in games and simulations designed specifically for military personnel. These alternative worlds are often populated by computer-generated versions of Iraqi citizens, and sometimes these representations employ intelligent tutoring techniques to make the user's interactions with these digital puppets more realistic. Game designers working on military contracts often aspire to what Lev Manovich has described as digitally composited smooth motion that correlates "different senses" that "simulate human experience."[12] Although these games and simulations are often organized by levels, the user's spatial experience is sufficiently sustained to include the exploration of sequences of successive rooms, streets, or even events beyond the horizon of sight.

The *Tactical Iraqi* Case Study

Tactical Iraqi, a language-learning software course and educational videogame, was developed for widespread use by U.S. military personnel. It originated at the Center for Advanced Research in Technology for Education (CARTE) at the Information Sciences Institute of the University of Southern California. Researchers at CARTE had previously authored a range of imaginative but seemingly disconnected distance learning initiatives that featured computer-generated animated agents, software capable of expressive speech analysis and synthesis, and programs organized around the presentation of pedagogical drama. After the invasion of Iraq, it became possible to test large-scale applications of CARTE research to the problem of foreign language learning. A critical shortage of Arabic speakers existed in the U.S. armed forces, and the theater of conflict was coalescing around stressful and confusing situations of urban warfare, military occupation, and postconflict reconstruction in the face of persistent insurgency.

Tactical Iraqi was envisioned as part of a larger Tactical Language Training System (TLTS) under the umbrella of the Defense Advanced Research Projects Agency (DARPA) Training Superiority program, which was intended to develop "just-in-time" training technologies incorporating intelligent tutoring, simulations, and games into preparation for combat readiness. Another "just-in-time" military videogame, *Ambush!*, was launched even more rapidly—after just six months—by BBN Technologies to assist soldiers in locating roadside dangers, such as improvised explosive devices (IEDs), whose presence could be signaled by anything from a seemingly innocuous dead camel to an electric toy.[13] Like *Tactical Iraqi*, *Ambush!* took advantage of an existing platform, the commercial game *Operation Flashpoint*, and used this networked multiplayer system to realistically model interactions between members of a military convoy. Other contracting companies, such as Mäk Technologies, SAIC, and Virtual Heroes have made games and game engine-driven simulations for the military that use technologies and techniques from commercial electronic entertainment. Laboratories, centers, and institutes at universities have also decided to appeal to this potentially lucrative specialized market by incorporating production techniques associated with film, software development, or game studies programs. Ultimately, *Tactical Iraqi* spawned its own privately held company that specialized in tactical language training in order to make forays into the commercial market and to expand its offerings to include languages like Pashto and French.

The 2005 version of *Tactical Iraqi* was built on top of elements from traditional computer-based tutorials and language recognition software, a PsychSim multiagent system, and an *Unreal Tournament 2003* game engine. As designed, the Mission Game (figure 3.1) of *Tactical Iraqi* revolves around an interactive story-based 3-D game where learners practice carrying out a designated mission through a specific avatar, Sergeant John Smith. In an earlier version of the game, the mission was to rebuild a damaged water plant with the assistance of a "Shiite leader of uncertain loyalties"[14]; the 2005 iteration involved rebuilding a girls' school.

The game uses a third-person shooter-style interface that is limited to input from a keyboard, microphone with headset, and mouse. As John Smith, the player navigates through a computer-generated landscape of streets, cafés, and private homes that is rendered with naturalistic lighting, texture mapping, and modeling of 3-D masses. He is also able to interact with flat objects, such as business cards or photographs, and those rendered in three dimensions, such as eyeglasses or cups of tea. In addition to this virtuosity of "perceptual realism," the game was intended to have what Alison McMahan has called "social realism," which she describes as being constituted by "organizing rituals and ceremonies.[15] Many of the rites in the game involve formulaic greetings and the social consumption of nonalcoholic beverages, along with their associated practices of rhetoric.

Negotiating through John Smith's transitions from public to private spaces via his Unreal Puppet poses particular challenges to verbal and nonverbal communication, particularly when trust is limited and the action takes place on a stage with multiple spectators. The learner's limited language proficiency can restrict access to certain

Figure 3.1
Asking for information from two pedagogical agents in the Mission Game of *Tactical Iraqi*, by permission of Alelo and the USC Information Sciences Institute.

critical spaces, and even in the public zone of the *agora*, an environmental bubble where cultural exchanges and mutual appropriation are permissible,[16] John Smith is subject to humiliation that can be reported back to his superior officers and to verbal abuse by native speakers that can include being called a "son of a dog."

To help John Smith in his mission, there are no weapons or martial arts tricks available; the player's only tools are spoken words and gestures, although a female member of the squad can prompt appropriate responses and make suggestions. Paralinguistic learning is an important aspect of the Mission Game, because in rhetorical situations in country, the cultural meaning of particular gestures could prove to be counterintuitive to U.S. military personnel. For example, a "thumbs-up" can have a highly insulting inverse meaning,[17] yet removing one's eyeglasses demonstrates knowledge of a regionally specific gesture of respect.

The rules by which Smith interacts with the native population are directed by what the creators call an "etiquette quotient," which the members of the research team define as follows: "Etiquette refers to the expected 'moves' in context that allow participants to make inferences about group membership, power relationships, formality/informality, degree of friendship, importance of information conveyed, etc. Violation of etiquette can convey lack of regard, lack of acceptance of the proposed relationships, or can convey overriding concerns such as a critical threat."[18] The language used to explain the project emphasizes how game "moves" and "social rules" are interrelated and how these operations can be characterized by expectations that foster inferential reasoning. Ironically, the very research that the *Tactical Iraqi* team cites as inspiration disavow the existence of set rules in highly specific and contextual situations of politeness.[19]

The Skill Builder (figure 3.2) is a set of interactive exercises organized around practice drills in the target language, in which learners say words and phrases and listen to and respond to sample utterances. Vocabulary is chosen to be appropriate for the social context. A virtual tutor evaluates the learner's pronunciation and syntax and gives

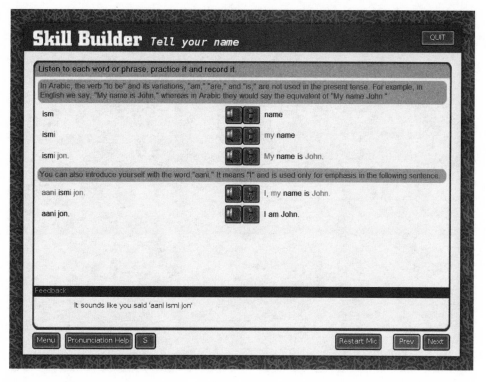

Figure 3.2
A section in the Mission Skill Builder of *Tactical Iraqi*, by permission of Alelo and the USC Information Sciences Institute.

feedback, providing encouragement and forestalling negative affectivity in the learner. Here the player is provided with explicit instruction that focuses on the rules of grammar rather than the rules of play. Principles of social interaction are also explained at a more abstract level in sections on "Cultural Details." The Skill Builder initially proved to be an important factor in achieving measurable improvement in learning outcomes for the military experimental subjects post-test.[20] Nonetheless, the literature on language learning indicates this approach would be incomplete without the experience of play.[21]

A speech-enabled Arcade Game (figure 3.3) gives learners further practice opportunities in Arabic. In the Arcade Game rapid response time is more important than it is in the Mission Skill Builder or the Mission Game. Principle investigator Lewis Johnson also concedes, "You had to put in something you blow up" to provide an enjoyable videogame experience. In the Arcade Game, objects can be picked up by correctly naming directions, and "enemy" elements of different colors periodically appear to

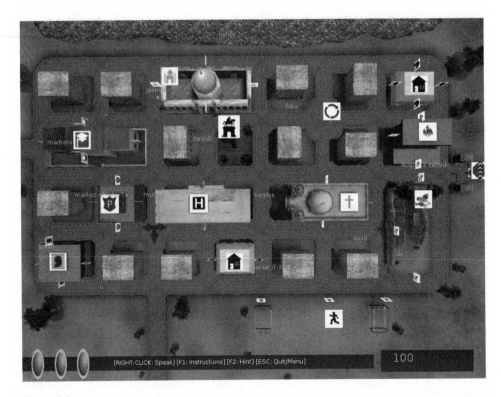

Figure 3.3
The aerial view of the speech-enabled Arcade Game of *Tactical Iraqi*, by permission of Alelo and the USC Information Sciences Institute.

be destroyed. Although ostensibly intended to speed up the acquisition of prepositional and descriptive phrases, the Arcade Game has none of the social interactions that are simulated by the Skill Builder or the Game and directly equates linguistic competence with destructive force. Narrative theorist Janet Murray writes that this kind of digital experience is particularly compelling, because arcade-style action provides a "tight visceral match between the game controller and the screen action. A palpable click on the mouse or joystick results in an explosion. It requires very little imaginative effort to enter such a world because the sense of agency is so direct."[22]

In addition to these photorealistic arenas of play—from third-person, first-person, and God's eye viewpoints respectively—the learner has a number of resources available. The Web Wizard provides a hypertext with English translations, an overview of the structure and elements of a sentence, and notes pertaining to Arabic syntax and grammar for learners interested in exploring the structure and meaning of words and phrases. The MP3 Player Kit allows learners away from computers or visual cues to review the words and phrases to reinforce correct pronunciation and fluency. However, the learner is not truly independent. He or she knows there is constant surveillance by other stakeholders in remote locations. The experimenters and potentially the player's commanding officers can compare the player to other learners with specialized tools. A performance assessment module collects data at each learner's machine, transmits the information to a central TLTS database, and produces individualized performance scorecards with multidimensional benchmarks based on aggregated data.

The *Virtual Iraq* Case Study

Virtual Iraq (figure 3.4) also adapts off-the-shelf game technology for military users. However, unlike *Tactical Iraqi*, *Virtual Iraq* employs what Michael Heim has called "strong" VR [virtual reality],[23] because the user wears an immersive head-mounted display in which visual data correlates to head movement. In addition to optical information, the participant is exposed to the sounds, sensations, and even smells associated with progressively more harrowing combat-related experiences from duty on patrol in Iraq for an extremely vivid and interactive experience. Although forcing patients to relive traumatic experiences might seem counterintuitive to generally held assumptions about psychic healing, such programs have been shown to be highly effective, particularly in conjunction with traditional talk therapy.[24] According to its proponents, this kind of exposure therapy facilitates not only memory construction but also the essential narrative activities that foster psychological integration after traumatic events. In addition, VR seems to provide an objective and consistent format for documenting the sensory stimuli that the patient is exposed to, which is not possible when the therapist must extrapolate from limited verbal information supplied by the patient describing his or her internal state. Finally, less social stigma may be

Figure 3.4
Scene from *Virtual Iraq*, by permission of Albert Rizzo of the Institute for Creative Technologies at USC.

attached to therapeutic activities linked to videogame play or "training" activities associated with conventional masculine gender roles.

Exposure to traumatic cues can be carefully calibrated in the VR therapeutic environment, but the immersive nature of the experience typically leads to a strong sense of what Jonathan Steuer has described as "telepresence," in which "vividness" and "interactivity" are maximized.[25] In *Virtual Iraq*, computer graphics are projected in a head-mounted display, and the user can decide where to look in the virtual environment. This visual information is augmented with motion tracking, localizable sounds, vibration platforms, and, in some scenarios, scent delivery technology. Patients can travel through this virtual world on foot or via motor vehicle. The therapist can manipulate a "Wizard of Oz" interface to increase the verisimilitude of the patient's experience by adjusting the weather conditions or time of day to best approximate the trauma scenario. Like gameplay in *Battlefield 2*, the user can experience combat through several temporal frames to filter the visual stimuli. The patient can be taken from dawn to dusk, be situated in a clear day or one that is overcast, and be led by artificial light or navigate with night vision goggles. Atmospheric effects like fog or sandstorms are also possible. Unlike *Battlefield 2*, of course, none of these programs allow the soldier to experience the environment from any perspective other than that of a uniformed U.S. soldier.

The auditory environment is designed to immerse the patient in the associated stimuli of the traumatic experience. Abrupt explosive events occur within a full orchestration of ambient sounds that includes dogs barking, bullets whizzing, car engines sputtering, sirens, children crying, flies buzzing, spectators saying "cowboy go home," and the muezzin's call to prayer from a minaret. Using the stereo headset implanted in what appears to be a standard army-issue helmet, noises, such as the sound of a lumbering Humvee, are perceived differently from different positions in the virtual space.

Because researchers assume that smell is an important link to the limbic system and thus to memory and emotions, plans for verisimilitude extend to olfactory cues delivered via a "Scent Palette," a USB device with a cartridge that can deliver up to eight distinct odors. At the time of the demo at FlatWorld, these cues included "burning rubber, cordite, garbage, body odor, smoke, diesel fuel, Iraqi food spices, and gunpowder."[26] According to principal investigator Albert "Skip" Rizzo, future versions of the game should include the smell of cooking lamb, which is a "big one" for the psychic landscape of many returning veterans.

Despite the development of new input devices that allow users to interact bodily in virtual worlds, the kinesthetic experience of *Virtual Iraq* is constrained by what appears to be a traditional game panel interface in which walking is simulated by pushing buttons. The motor vehicle simulation, which I had tried prior to my first visit to Flatword, involves a platform that replicates the motion of the vehicle, bumps in the road, jolts due to obstacles, and the force of a concussive blast from an improvised explosive device. To create the spatial experience, the designers of *Virtual Iraq* assembled art assets from *America's Army* and *Tactical Iraqi* but used the control architecture of the FlatWorld simulation, Numerical Design Limited's Gamebryo engine, and considerable content exported from the game *Full Spectrum Warrior* to increase both vividness and interactivity for participants. This use of *Full Spectrum Warrior* demonstrates how game development can come full circle, since the commercial X-Box game being repurposed by researchers originated from a military training game.

Virtual reality therapy has been already used for PTSD in many political contexts that replicate a variety of geographic locales.[27] Those in New York suffering from PTSD from the September 11 terrorist attacks might have been treated by reliving the experience with the *Virtual World Trade Center* created by the Program for Anxiety and Traumatic Stress Studies at Cornell University. *Virtual Bus Bombing*, which was developed by the University of Haifa, allows Israeli citizens to grapple with witnessing suicide bombing attacks. These VR therapeutic technologies were first developed for veterans in *Virtual Vietnam*.

Both *Tactical Iraqi* and *Virtual Iraq* recreate segments of the landscape, built environment, and population of Iraq in 3-D worlds, but they also invite other notable comparisons. Both projects were developed by teams in close physical proximity under the auspices of the same university, and both computer programs turned out to require a high degree of trust from user-participants. Both software packages use off-the-shelf game technology with a history in the consumer market. Moreover, both military-funded applications have attracted considerable news coverage in the mainstream media.

Of course, there are significant design differences between the two projects. One is a game and the other is a simulation; one is pedagogical in its orientation and the other is therapeutic; one uses largely third-person perspective, and the other uses first-person. Furthermore, *Tactical Iraqi* switches more rapidly between discursive contexts and visual perspectives, while *Virtual Iraq* is designed to be continuous and immersive.

However, both of these publicly funded "virtual Iraqs," which are made in America, are also intended to increase efficiencies in activities of memory, particularly those embodied through practices of recognition, recollection, and remembering. Both programs implicitly address mnemonic techniques related to inhabiting these VR worlds: *Tactical Iraqi* is designed to prompt soldiers to remember specific Arabic words and phrases; *Virtual Iraq* is intended to trigger memories and appropriate coping mechanisms in combat veterans suffering from PTSD.

The Palace of Memory

The method of loci in *ars memoriae* is a technique for remembering often associated with the classical rhetorical tradition. According to advice in ancient, medieval, and early modern rhetorical manuals, the loci were physical locations, usually in a familiar and highly articulated public area, such as a church, palace, forum, or garden. The method for this art of memory was famously credited to Simonides of Ceos by Cicero in *De Oratore*, who tells the story of how Simonides used his precise geographical memory of the relative orientation of specific objects in a particular scene to locate the bodies of his former dinner companions in the chaotic rubble of a collapsed building:

In the mean time the apartment in which Scopas was feasting fell down, and he himself [the patron of Scopas], and his company, were overwhelmed and buried in the ruins; and when their friends were desirous to inter their remains, but could not possibly distinguish one from another, so much crushed were the bodies, Simonides is said, from his recollection of the place in which each had sat, to have given satisfactory directions for their interment. Admonished by this occurrence, he is reported to have discovered that it is chiefly order that gives distinctness to memory; and that by those, therefore, who would improve this part of the understanding, certain places must be fixed upon, and that of the things which they desire to keep in memory, symbols must be conceived in the mind, and ranged, as it were, in those places; thus the order of the places would preserve the order of things, and the symbols of the things would denote the things themselves; so that we should use the places as waxen tablets, and the symbols as letters.[28]

To use this artificial memory or method of loci, one walks through an edifice or area several times, viewing discrete landmarks within it, in the same order every time. After several repetitions, the assumption is that one should be able to visualize each of the places in a logical sequence reliably and remember the associated content. Thus to memorize a speech the text is broken into pieces, each of which is symbolized by vividly imagined symbols or signs. In the mind's eye, the orator places each of these images into the loci. Objects of discourse can then be recalled in a precise order by imagining walking through the building again, visiting each of the loci sequentially and viewing each of the images that was placed in the loci, thereby recalling each piece of the speech in the proper order.

It may be a fallacy to assume that the expanded capacity for storage and increased compressibility of digital media, along with the promise of ubiquitous computing and more powerful search engines, will eventually make the organic exercise of memory in human cognition obsolete. While facts and experiences may seem to be conjured up as quickly as pages from Google or del.ici.ous, the increasingly spatial character of electronic environments, the secondary orality of new forms of nearly instantaneous communication, and the fundamental need for epistemological coherence in a complex, amorphous, and rapidly changing information environment will likely make variants of the method of the loci continue to be relevant to contemporary cyborgs. Unfortunately, these military-funded games and simulations do not always capitalize on the particular efficiencies in learning and other forms of psychic integration, which the method of loci offers. Although experimental data continues to suggest that subjects who employ this ancient method still have significantly better recall than those in control groups,[29] opportunities for using it in the Arcade Game component of *Tactical Iraqi* are missed.

As Frances Yates has argued, in the case of Renaissance magical or occult memory systems in the early age of print, new technologies, such as the printing press, do not necessarily displace this key component from the canon of the rhetorical tradition.[30] Similarly, Mary Carruthers claims that the commerce of written texts in vernacular languages actually increased interest in *memoria* during the Middle Ages.[31] She also asserts that the labor involved in systems of memory tends to be underestimated because of our contemporary viewpoint in which invention is valued over retention, and memory is seen as passive behavior rather than an activity of craft and conscious construction.

In 1997, Janine Wong and Peter Storkerson updated the theory of the method of loci to apply to hypermedia and interactive multimedia by claiming that recent forms of spatial organization provided "semantic context" in which communications can be made more intelligible.[32] Wong and Storkerson argued that this revival of these traditional rhetorical techniques was first suggested by Vannevar Bush in his argument for a new epistemology of "association" in information science. The ancients can be seen as precursors to contemporary information design theorists because the loci were chunked or grouped in sets of items, no more than what the mind's eye could encompass in one glance in the medieval equivalent of "working memory." Similarly, Ian Bogost argues that the experience of the flâneur wandering through urban landscapes is useful for understanding the "configurative structure of procedural texts" like videogames.[33] Bogost believes that the reader/player/user is given a "set of options" for negotiating contemporary human experience in which the "chance encounter" can be "embodied as a unit of cultural currency" epitomized even in the work of Baudelaire, Benjamin, and Bukowski. The image of the Palace of Memory also receives a prominent place in Nicholas Negroponte's *Being Digital*, as an example of the importance of "navigating in three-dimensional space to store and retrieve information."[34] Recently computer scientist Eric Fassbender has developed a "Virtual Memory Palace" simulation designed for corporate speakers and other potential public orators who wish to avoid the scripted boredom of a typical canned PowerPoint presentation.[35]

The *Virtual Iraq* simulation itself was developed from another modern-day form of the method of loci used by the USC software development team with both stroke victims and children with attention deficit hyperactivity disorder. In this form of "distance medicine," patients can negotiate around the spaces of virtual living rooms, offices, and classrooms to locate specific objects that were situated in the virtual space. However, the researchers point out that memory is rarely depicted as a single entity in their discipline, because "memory is often broken down into traditional cognitive psychology categories such as iconic, working, procedural, declarative, prospective, and episodic memory domains."[36] Yet they also cite research showing how memory and spatial ability can be seen as closely integrated neurological assets.

In the virtual environment of traumatic combat for *Virtual Iraq*, the mnemonic assets acquired in moving through the 3-D world are associated with emotional rather than intellectual value systems. In the final analysis, this virtual reality simulation is designed to solve a much more difficult problem than merely remembering traumatic circumstances, since the user must ultimately also distance him or herself from these violent events by relegating them to the past using the discursive device of the personal narrative. As Cicero tells of the orator Themistocles's interactions with a disciple who inquires what the art of memory could do for him, the rhetorician retorts that the student would oblige his teacher much more "if he could instruct him how to forget, rather than to remember, what he chose."[37]

The spatialization of memory is also important for other projects associated with the USC group. For example, Jacquelyn Ford Morie's *The Memory Stairs* (figure 3.5) stages the artifacts of a stranger's nostalgia in two elaborate wallpapered rooms, which are stocked with old magazines, knickknacks, and children's toys. Morie's eight different planned immersive environments repurpose some elements of an earlier

Figure 3.5
Scene from *Memory Stairs*. Courtesy of Jacquelyn Morie.

Virtopia project. Via a head-mounted display, the user is inserted into an imagined life chronology structured by discrete memories. According to Morie, these spaces seemingly inhabited by ghosts are "designed to represent an aesthetic journey through a lifetime of memories."[38] When I explored the virtual spaces of Morie's *Memory Stairs* environment, I could even look out the window. However, I was extremely conscious of the two-room constraint, and often found myself on top of tables in my eagerness to move freely around the virtual space.

Morie describes her objectives in the project as "defining an expressive grammar for emotionally evocative virtual environments." It is worth noting that she has also worked on a number of projects for the U.S. military, including *DarkCon*, in which the user-trainee encounters a variety of objects similarly tied to evocations of pathos and a generational past, which include a "baby doll" that "squeaks when stepped on" and "family photo albums" that lie "discarded in the mud."[39] Although the *DarkCon* story unfolds in an Eastern European city, where the user must negotiate movement through a cramped sewer tunnel and be prepared for both "civilian refugees" and "militant rebels," lessons learned by Morie's teams potentially also apply to the research of those building Iraq games and simulations.

In a *Los Angeles Times* editorial, policy analyst Max Boot praises this spatialization of military training and the translation of pedagogically structured orientation experiences into virtual space. Specifically, he uses the example of *Tactical Iraqi* to argue that such situated learning enables participants to develop forms of cultural literacy that soldiers would otherwise be lacking. Boot enthuses about visiting "the Expeditionary Warfare School, where captains study Arabic by playing a sophisticated computer game complete with animated characters."[40] Boot claims that this computerized language instruction exemplifies the critical training simulating "the human terrain" of the Iraqi theater of conflict.

However, the human terrain that Boot emphasizes, which can now be inhabited through virtual reality interfaces, would ideally allow for certain forms of improvisation impossible in many fixed media representations, allowing individuals to respond to the physical and social landscape with certain forms of situated experimentation and even contemplate resistance to norms of movement. In his work on space and boundaries, Michel de Certeau has outlined the elements that define the inhabited space of the built environment and argues that individuals' tactical practices, or practices opposing regulation and ideological control by the interests in power, respond to the city's physical and social landscape with certain forms of situated resistance. For de Certeau, the way that individuals use and move through the space defines the city. As in the method of loci, de Certeau compares verbal linguistics to the "rhetoric of walking" in which the physical movement of different individuals defines and embeds meaning into a space. He claims that spatial order "organizes an ensemble of possibilities (e.g., by a place in which one can move) and interdictions (e.g., by a wall that prevents one from going further)"[41] so that "the walker actualizes some of these possibilities. In that way, he makes them exist as well as emerge." De Certeau asserts that everyday actions make lived spaces readable and thus believable and memorable. These actions by a marginalized majority are designated as "tactics," and they are often the only available tools of a population that doesn't have access to the strategies of those in power who can operate outside of a specifically situated environment.

More rapid and unconstrained types of movement are also possible in virtual environments. Other kinds of military simulations that recreate the space of combat may move through territory with more apparent mastery of space, such as by flying. For example, Patrick Crogan has argued that flight simulators have a particular primacy in digital experiences of play and to the relationship of war to peacetime cultural practices of entertainment.[42] The experience of walking or driving slowly, however, is uniquely well designed for recognition and reintegration of specific memory cues.

Identity in Play

It could be argued that the third-person player format of *Tactical Iraqi* invariably draws attention to issues of identity, since the player can see John Smith's external characteristics while also being expected to identify with his inner affect. This ability to view what Bob Rehak calls "the spectator's own body" in videogames can be equated with the psychoanalytic experience of the mirror stage and related imaginary constructions of self.[43] Because identity is always the product of the bifurcation of internal and external categories of self, a measure of how we see ourselves as similar to and different from others in particular communities of membership, the third-person perspective spotlights identity politics in a way that the unmediated perspective of first-person play cannot.

We know that John Smith is a white male who is often comparatively physically imposing. We can see that Smith is neither young nor old, and—from the context of the mission—we know that he is not located on either extreme in the chain of command. There are also many things that we do not know about John Smith: his marital status, his political affiliation, his sexual preferences, his previous military tours of duty, and the region of the United States from which he comes. The learner is allowed to construct those features as he or she practices social interactions at Jasim's house, where the learner has finally entered an Iraqi home.

As A. Suresh Canagarajah has argued, the "self" is composed of a number of interpretive and rhetorical taxonomies. Identity (such as "racial" or "national" or "ethnic" identity) is only one component of many. Canagarajah argues that the "self" is actually an amalgam of "identity," "role," "subjectivity," and "voice."[44] In other words, Sergeant John Smith occupies an obvious identity position as a white American male, but he also has a social role to fulfill in rebuilding the school with the villagers' cooperation. Additionally, he has a particular consciousness of his own subjectivity and some understanding about how his agency is enabled and constrained (in the case of the game, by his linguistic competence, albeit temporarily). John Smith also has a "voice" that can express resistance and accommodation in a second language; he can be "heard" by autonomous agents capable of response in the context of their own ideologies. Researchers evaluating the success of *Tactical Iraqi* also indicated that the test subjects who served as players could also be defined by a similarly complex matrix of identity, role, subjectivity, and voice; the successes and failures of different test groups were cataloged with attention to all these aspects of self.

Manuel Castells has theorized that increasingly networked "informational societies" are characterized by "the preeminence of identity as their organizing principle," which he defines as "the process by which a social actor recognizes itself and constructs meaning primarily on the basis of a given cultural attribute or set of attributes to the exclusion of a broader reference to other social structures."[45] For Castells, linguistic identity presents a special case: "I would make the hypothesis that language, and particularly a fully developed language, is a fundamental attribute of self-recognition, and of the establishment of an invisible national boundary less arbitrary than territoriality, and less exclusive than ethnicity."[46] Language, Castells argues, provides "the linkage between the private and the public sphere, and between the past and the present, regardless of the actual acknowledgement of a cultural community by institutions of the state."[47]

As John Smith acquires knowledge of Arabic and participates in social networks, he also takes on a new identity as an Arabic speaker, but this identity is always understood to be extrinsic, only a supplement to his core identity as an English-speaking military officer. At most, this identity serves as a temporary dramatic persona; at the very least it serves as a tool that merely provides a means to an end. Although John Smith participates in the activities of the village, he does not take on a new citizenship, even after he is welcomed into the house of the village leader and has participated in rituals of social bonding.

In the United States, the following joke is sometimes told: "If a person who speaks two languages is 'bilingual,' and a person who speaks three languages is 'trilingual,' what do you call a person who speaks one language?" The answer, of course, is "American." Despite the fact that the U.S. citizenry is increasingly transnational and bilingual, this joke reveals an ideological truth: to some extent, to speak another language is to cease to be an authentic American, as the long history of English-only initiatives demonstrates.[48] The U.S. Congress may have declared a recent year, 2005, to be the official "Year of Languages," but governmental funding for bilingual and second-language education remains insufficient, and many college programs in second-language learning for critical world languages, ones with hundreds of millions of speakers, remain desperately underenrolled despite nominal governmental support. In Castells' terms, this monolingual identity can be seen as so primary that it assumes a special moral authority in U.S. policy and populism, although it could also be argued that this linguistic national identity erodes its moral authority by subverting the language identities of its own bilingual and transnational members.

Techniques for embodied language learning are actually nothing particularly new; they predate digital virtual environments by decades. For example, in the 1970s Bulgarian psycholinguist Georgi Lozanov championed "Suggestopedia," a technique that emphasized the learner's embodied physical state, bodily comfort, and sensory perception to encourage receptivity and to lower learning anxiety and resistance.[49] Suggestopedia also used gameplay and encouraged learners to assume an identity within the target language, just as foreign language software simulations do. For example, if one wanted to learn Russian with Suggestopedia, one could assume the identity of a native speaker whose upbringing would have encouraged him or her to be proficient in the language since childhood. In some ways, *Tactical Iraqi* represents a more timid form of embodied learning: curricular materials only attend to auditory and visual stimulation, and learners are restricted to occupying an identity located on the periphery of membership in the target language, not at its center.

As James Paul Gee has argued, situated learning environments can be created with the tools of a traditional classroom, given that the right set of productive learning practices are in play to minimize anxiety about educational risk-taking and to maximize the intuitive character of the interface for the knowledge that is to be confidently owned.[50] Yet even if *Tactical Iraqi* is judged to be superior to traditional instruction, which is as yet unproven by independent researchers, it is worth asking if the videogame solves the central problems posed by the actual theater of conflict: (1) a critical shortage of Arabic speakers and (2) confusing rules of engagement in the situations of search and patrol. For example, the decision makers' authority could be called into question if the particular rules of the game are not taken as givens. What if there were recruiting and retention problems to blame for these staff deficiencies of Arabic speakers, or if mistakes made in diplomatic negotiations with local populations were a more significant causal factor in the difficulties of urban warfare?

Trust and Face

Tactical Iraqi differs significantly from commercially produced language-learning software featuring interactions with digital characters in circumstances of virtual travel, although these language-learning programs incorporate similar speech recognition technology so that the learner may converse with the program's computer-generated characters and practice skill development in modules focusing on particular forms of grammar, syntax, and usage. Although the "Skill Builder" of *Tactical Iraqi's* 2005 version appears to be similar to these interfaces—in which the appropriate videotaped reactions of a human actor can be situated in textual information, such as a glossary or a written transcription of appropriate dialogue[51] —there are significant differences in the structure of the pedagogical drama.

The on-screen interlocutors who populate programs like those developed by the Living Language series only sit docilely behind ticket counters or hotel registration desks. Native speakers never do more than register mild dismay or embarrassed confusion when the learner struggles with pronunciation or syntax because interactivity is limited to polite exchanges. In contrast, autonomous pedagogical agents in *Tactical Iraqi* may shout at the learner's avatar, make angry accusations, or threaten the learner's avatar with physical harm, so that the learner may be forced to flee the actual site of the communicative exchange and retreat to the Skill Builder or attempt to re-take that particular stage of the Mission Game all over again from the beginning to the interchange.

The initial measure of a player's "health" in *Tactical Iraqi* was the "emotional arousal level"[52] of the other autonomous agents John Smith encounters on his mission; the "arousal level" meters of the early demo version were later replaced by "trust" meters in more recent game prototypes. Researchers explained the development process:

As we conducted formative evaluations of the TLTS, we frequently saw a need to improve feedback, and developed new feedback methods in response. For example, when learners carry out actions in the Mission Game that develop rapport with the local people (e.g., greet them and carry out proper introductions), they want to know if they are making progress. Some cues that people rely on in real life, such as the facial expressions of the people they are talking to, are not readily available in the game engine underlying TLTS (namely, Unreal Tournament 2003). We therefore developed an augmented view of the non-player characters' mental state, called a trust meter. . . . The size of the grey bar under each character image grows and shrinks dynamically depending upon the current degree of trust that character has for the player. Note that this lessens the need for intelligent coaching on the subject of establishing trust, since learners can recognize when their actions are failing to establish trust.[53]

Project team members describe how they must compensate for particular shortcomings in the player's digital experience—in this case, insufficient granularity in the interlocutors' facial expressions. They adapt the system design so that vividness and interactivity can continue to be closely correlated in play. Although John Smith is not otherwise equipped with hypersensitive superhuman abilities, he is magically able to visualize particular nonverbal cues about trust that are signaled on meters in the course of gameplay. Therefore, he is particularly empowered to achieve success in the game by inspiring the greatest trust from the greatest number. It is worth observing that there are a number of other serious and commercial games that use a trust meter as part of gameplay. They include *The Thing* (2002), *Tom Clancy's Splinter Cell: Double Agent* (2006), *Global Conflicts: Palestine* (2007), and *ELECT BiLAT* (2008). Trust in videogame play can operate in either zero-sum or non-zero-sum situations, in which players are encouraged to pursue a variety of strategies, from preemptive violence based on Hobbesian skepticism to cooperative efforts that include mutual decision-making and consultation with cultural and linguistic others.

It is interesting to note, however, that the game designers' initial conceptions held "face" to be most critical component in judging discrete linguistic interactions as polite in the world of *Tactical Iraqi*. Unlike "trust," which relies on the perceived presence of social guarantees and assumes that the rational actors are oriented around intention, "face" can be seen as a more appropriate standard for a game about autonomous agents from different cultures because face is a public measure of culturally specific self-esteem and social prestige,[54] while trust gauges one's comfort depending on others in a shared system of highly rationalized values. The researchers apparently intended first to follow the typology of Brown and Levinson, in which face is defined in terms of so-called face-wants, which may be positive (the desire to feel appreciated) or negative (the desire to remain unmolested).[55] Thus politeness is a social strategy dependent on mutual cooperation between the speaker and the hearer. Depending on whether the speaker's politeness strategy aims at preserving the positive or negative face needs of the addressee, Brown and Levinson identify positive or negative politeness respectively.

These politeness researchers advise that the safer strategy is generally negative politeness, such as avoiding constraining another person's freedom of movement, rather than positive politeness, such as paying a compliment or giving a gift, which could easily backfire. They claim as a general principle that "it is safer to assume that H prefers his peace and self-determination than he prefers your expressions of regard."[56] Yet on military "knock and talk" missions into private homes led by armed soldiers, those in the civilian population will necessarily have their freedom constrained in ways that they are likely to resent. Certainly there are similar linguistic situations that could perhaps serve as models, such as police work, in which individuals sometimes must be questioned, searched, and detained. Strangely, however, *Tactical Iraqi* emphasizes positive politeness, with the exception of one lesson on conducting house searches and one on procedures if weapons are found.

Although Brown and Levinson draw on a number of fields—among them anthropology, sociology, and linguistics—they also acknowledge an intellectual debt to the field of rhetoric.[57] In synthesizing their matrix of power (P), social distance (D), and relative imposition (R), they label these "variations in interactional style which we call ethos."[58] Repeatedly, they assert that many of their research questions have not been addressed in any significant manner since Aristotle, who first formulated a manner in which pragmatic reasoning could be operationalized.

The use of the Brown and Levinson construct in a virtual environment with artificial intelligence (AI) puppets is an interesting choice by the *Tactical Iraqi* team, given both the sociolinguists' interest in the constitutive character of the "virtual offense"[59] in situations of day-to-day politeness and how Brown and Levinson believed that research in artificial intelligence by their contemporaries had been hampered by overinvestment in individual cognition and an underinvestment in the study of social interaction.[60] In the fictional conceit of *Tactical Iraqi's* virtual world, the Arabic-speaking characters John Smith encounters seek to engage him in social practices of praise, and they also generally preserve a respectful distance from him. However, when mutual politeness strategies fail, they reflect badly on parties from both sides: Smith and his party flee with almost Monty Python-ish cowardice, and the Arabic characters become transformed into angry, cursing buffoons, so that the narrative of *Tactical Iraqi* is filled with what Brown and Levinson call "face-threatening acts" (FTAs) that might be seen to impinge upon or take away honor, or status.

Critical Play

For rhetoricians who study new media, a program like *Tactical Iraqi* immediately raises a number of red flags. First, the game engine comes from the ultraviolent *Unreal Tournament* series in which opponents are dehumanized alien life forms and annihilating weaponry is central to gameplay. The engine operationalizes weaponry and bodily liquids in an entirely different procedural rhetoric from that envisioned by the *Tactical Iraqi* team. The development team at CARTE told reporters that it took the game designers working on the *Tactical Iraqi* mod almost eight months to remove all the coding that directed graphic displays of violence or gore, a process that was slowed by lack of access to the source code. Even after it appeared that the entire Unreal arsenal of weapons had been confiscated, principal investigator Johnson admitted that "one of the testers discovered that if he stomped on other characters, they would explode in blood and guts."[61] Despite having acquired the source code, some elements of the Unreal substrate of combative spectacle might remain undisturbed, and thus the theatrical perspective of the game could distance the subject from his or her linguistic interactions and reinforce a logic of spatial domination rather than one of participation in literacy as a form of mutual social exchange.

Second, the computer-generated animated pedagogical agents of *Tactical Iraqi* are incapable of speech acts that are not scripted by the U.S. military; for all their sophisticated AI they cannot ask the learner hard questions about the unpopular geopolitical agenda being pushed by U.S. policy makers in the Middle East, a species of verbal challenge that native Arabic speakers might easily ask in live face-to-face situations. Although project documents tout the fact that each pedagogical agent comes equipped with "its own goals, private beliefs, mental models of other characters, and evolving relationships with and attitudes towards other characters (including the learner),"[62] no pedagogical agent is provided with the persuasive tools that might prepare learners for serious challenges to U.S. political ideology or better engage learners in substantive critical thinking about cultural difference. Pedagogical agents who manifest resistance can do little more than shout "CIA!" at Smith. Even Hasan, a character who asserts that it is "impossible to accept America's occupation of Iraq" is given nothing to say beyond this relatively undeveloped objection.

Third, as many recent critics have observed, *Tactical Iraqi* can be read as representative of the current U.S. "military-entertainment complex" in which entertaining military-style simulations are seemingly implicated in real acts of violence and coercion in the developed and the developing world.[63] Although the game is explicitly nonviolent, *Tactical Iraqi* provides the soldier with an interpretation of remote political actors and settings that reshapes their indigenous meaning. By simulating complex sociolinguistic interactions in such a cartoonish form, the program risks further replicating the "hyperreal" within the current dynamics of Iraqi occupation, just as Baudrillard's "precession of simulacra" would predict.[64]

Fourth, verbal and physical aggression are still closely linked by a logic of substitution in *Tactical Iraqi* that can be seen as a legitimation of armed force. Materials on the *Tactical Iraqi* website make this connection more explicitly. As one DARPA researcher observes, "The idea is to put behind every steering wheel and behind every trigger finger in a foreign country a little bit of that culture and language."[65] This assertion may be particularly troubling if policy makers believe that only a "little bit" of "culture and language" is necessary behind the powerful tools for control and domination that are represented by the synecdoche of the "trigger finger" or "steering wheel."

Yet *Tactical Iraqi* is not a conventional military combat game. It does not express values of selflessness or heroism or even loyalty to the nation-state. Other military simulations lionize patriotic displays or measure the player's success in conventional terms of battlefield honor. These games may also emphasize how strategic choices by key personnel and commanding officers affect other agents in the game, and that in situations of extreme risk it is necessary to make utilitarian calculations, but such maneuvering also generally serves the larger national interest at the expense of enemy combatants. In many ways, however, the other members of Smith's squad are less important for his success in the mission than are the Iraqi civilians he encounters, independent agents upon whom he depends for local cooperation and material supplies. Despite these interchanges, cultural empathy is limited: in the game of *Tactical Iraqi*, the player can never assume the position of the presumptive enemy. Unlike off-the-shelf products, such as *Battlefield 2*, learners can never play the game as Hasan or Jasim or any of the other indigenous characters in the game. As the player acquires new linguistic skills, he or she is not necessarily given any insight into the subjectivity of those who might be seen as otherwise radically other.

Testing the Prototypes: Gamer Culture and Primary Reception

Despite widespread cheerleading for the tremendous potential of videogame learning,[66] preference for this particular medium of instruction is far from universal at present. Research has shown that even when videogames are enormously popular with a particular instructional demographic, such as undergraduate students,[67] it does not follow that the players themselves perceive any connection to learning or expressly desire educational content in play.

Therefore, the initial trust problem encountered by *Tactical Iraqi* researchers involved players who avoided the game space entirely when using the program, often by hiding out in the Mission Skill Builder. Project documents indicated that "the learners were generally reluctant to start playing the game, because they were afraid that they would not be able to communicate successfully with the non-player characters."[68] In fact, rather than anticipating that play would be a pleasurable experience, "Learners usually started playing the game only when experimenters insisted that they do so."[69] To overcome this problem, researchers focused on replicating introductory social rituals in the virtual environment and applying forms of conventional etiquette to the world of the simulation. As the research team from *Tactical Iraqi* writes, "We found that if the experimenter introduced them directly to the game and encouraged them to try saying hello to one of the characters there, they got engaged, and were more confident to try it."[70]

Other players were eager to engage with the Unreal puppets, but were not as enthusiastic about language acquisition skills. When asked to participate in gameplay by researchers and commanding officers, this group of players chose to merely "game the system" by joining collaborative activities that postponed rather than promulgated learning. A project paper about the evaluation of *Tactical Iraqi* records that the game "when played in beginner mode gave learners the impression that they simply needed to memorize certain phrases to get through the game. After the first day the subjects showed up with printed cheat-sheets that they had created, so they could even avoid memorization."[71] Like gamers who aspire to simply exploit a system's shortcuts by relying on cheat codes to arrive at the conclusion of the game more rapidly,[72] these Fort Bragg soldiers had decided to take advantage of systemic loopholes and subvert the very learning process that others might undertake in good faith.

In October 2004, another test was scheduled at Fort Bragg that was deemed to be much more successful than the first. Test subjects were drawn from an all-male group from the U.S. Army Special Forces. To the experimenters, these men seemed to represent a superior class of learner and were characterized by researchers as having "intelligence greater than the average soldier." Those who evaluated the game claimed that this particular group worked with *Tactical Iraqi* as a single, coherent unit more effectively. These soldiers were praised for making "better use" of the Mission Game and for not relying on "cheat sheets."[73]

It could be argued that these soldiers were more like the John Smith envisioned by the game designers, since in his backstory Smith is a sophisticated specialist in "economics and public finance" in the military who has launched a career as a "financial and loan consultant" when off-duty back in the United States. Perhaps these Special Forces subjects were able to endow the burly, bumbling Smith of gameplay with some of the incipient, intangible, exceptional qualities that Smith's designers had endowed him with in his backstory.

Like all the human figures in *Tactical Iraqi*, Smith has an elaborate character profile in the library of project paperwork produced by the software development team. However, this narrative substrate is invisible to the player. According to these internal documents, game designers have envisioned Smith as a soldier who joined the military as a reservist and for economic reasons, to support his family and to defray his educational expenses. In this backstory, Smith's early attempt at a career in music and his choice not to delay parenthood after marrying appears to have derailed his predictable class aspirations, given that designers have imagined Smith to be from a privileged background in which his father is an attorney and his mother serves in the Massachusetts State Legislature.

Yet as players we know remarkably little about John Smith's personal history before he enters the game space. The backstory with which the designers have equipped him is never narrated to the player; thus the game's avatar functions as a cipher in play. And yet the Mission Skill Builder teaches the learner that to earn trust in realistic linguistic interactions and to preface business discussions appropriately, it is necessary to disclose public aspects of personal life to interlocutors. Units on "Describing Yourself" and "Building Rapport" make the obligation for personal revelation and open discourse from a clearly defined identity position manifest. The learner is helped with descriptions of these positions of self by units on "Learning about Your Host" and "Kinship and Occupations."

In the critical fourth scene, "At Jasim's House," the learner must independently endow Smith with a range of specific kinship relations. The player must decide if Smith is married or unmarried and can give him different gender configurations of offspring or can assign him brothers and sisters. These family members can also be endowed with a range of occupations (which are associated with certain class designations): doctor, soldier, teacher, lawyer, engineer, and merchant. The learner can even offer to show Jasim a photograph of his family in the United States, although this image is not clearly visible on-screen. If the learner omits the social niceties of establishing Smith's personal background when faced with Jasim's polite but mildly probing questions, Jasim will refuse to use his authority as a senior official to help the mission go forward, because the learner has too abruptly initiated business discourse before a sufficiently intimate rapport could be established.

Researchers admit that the player could be placed in the uncomfortable position of being expected to provide personal details about John Smith that are not included in the available narrative ingredients of the game, so that when this situation is carried to its logical conclusion, it would seem that the only way to convince others of the authenticity of a given self would be to forge information about one's fictionalized alter ego. So, if John Smith asks the village headman how old his son is, he should realistically expect a similar question about the ages and genders of his own children in return, and thus Smith would be expected to give a definitive answer requiring elaboration by the player on the blank slate of the avatar's character.

It is useful to look at even more submerged cryptohistories in *Tactical Iraqi's* design process and to consider what was changed about the game during its multiyear development. Although initially there were plans to create a parallel version of the game with a female protagonist, Major Kate Jones,[74] game developers are no longer actively pursuing a version with a female mission leader. Researchers cited cost and design issues, the demographic features of the typical service person, the social dynamics of what could be called "military drag" in which those who put on a uniform assume its gender position, and a perceived female acceptance that the armed forces are dominated by masculinist ideology. However, from the perspective of applied linguistics, this permanent postponement seems an area of serious concern, especially given published research identifying significant gender differences in Arabic language use.[75] Even the voice-recognition technology to which the microphone connects has difficulty recognizing correct utterances from female players, so that male speakers are the acknowledged norm and female speakers are an aberration. Nonetheless, promotional materials about *Tactical Iraqi* prominently feature endorsements by female service people for the program, including female instructors from West Point and Fort Carson, Colorado. Yet what Arab linguist Amy Perkins seems to be asserting is actually the suitability of the game for those of the *opposite* sex. As she says, "These guys aren't going to sit in class learning Arabic."[76]

Certainly, a substantial body of criticism now exists about the manifold benefits of playing and learning across gender lines through videogame play. As James Paul Gee and many others have argued, transgender play is both common and educational, so female service people playing as Smith may be empowered and enlightened by the experience.[77] The *Tactical Iraqi* program features a female voice in the 2005 Skill Builder that encourages awareness of gender difference in the tutorial mode. And in the Mission Game, Sergeant Smith is accompanied by a three-dimensional Sergeant Samia Faris, whose presence is acknowledged from the opening scene at the Hai Al-Nahar café and whose cultural knowledge as a native speaker cues the learner about how to properly engage in Smith's identity building in Jasim's house.

In the sidekick's backstory, we learn that Faris is a cultural hybrid, a woman born in Baghdad to a Chaldean Christian family but raised in Canada and California after her family's flight from the Iraqi regime in 1988. Like Smith, she is also a reservist who was motivated to join the army to pay for her education. The narrative of Faris's agency is only an off-screen backstory, however. Frequently, virtual women in *Tactical Iraqi* are either invisible or their presence is limited to performing the traditional roles of female characters dating back to epic narrative conventions, in which women can only serve as guide, as goal, and as obstacle. In other words, female agents can redirect the trajectory of the hero or misdirect him from his goal, but they cannot participate as central agents in the pedagogical drama their own right. For example, Faris is limited to making suggestions about what Smith should say and do, and the potential presence of female members in Jasim's household only represents possible social gaffes to be avoided.

A complicated backstory has also been written for local leader Jasim's college-educated wife, Munaa, who is the principal of the girls' school and an obvious stakeholder in Smith's mission. The game designers have given Munaa many soap opera elements in the narrative: she is both wife and cousin to Jasim, and—in a move toward metanarrative made by many videogames—she is fan of elaborate plot-driven Mexican telenovelas that have been dubbed into Arabic. But Munaa has no actual lines in the 2005 script of scene four of *Tactical Iraqi*, and virtual women remain largely ancillary to the action in the present version of the game.

Furthermore, although some subversive practices may seem undesirable to skill-and-drill educators who uniformly value attentive obedience, many theorists in game studies argue that rebellion against authority is essential for learning. From this pedagogical perspective, the category of transgressive play is fundamentally different from the category of cheating. In his essay on Lara Croft, James Gee claims that transgression is actually central to effective learning and that defiance of authority figures is critical for the acquisition of specialized knowledge in gameplay.[78] In other words, to play the game as Lara Croft successfully, the player must sometimes ignore the Professor's instructions or only listen selectively or even risk open disobedience. Squire and Jenkins believe that even games like *Grand Theft Auto* can help students understand political resistance in history games and simulations about the American Revolution.[79]

In contrast, games developed by the U.S. military actively discourage transgressive play for obvious reasons, because the chain of command depends on submitting to orders from those in authority without questioning their directives. For example, a player in *America's Army* who experiments by shooting his commanding officer in the first few seconds of the game forecloses any future opportunities for learning, because he immediately finds himself in the brig. Although *Tactical Iraqi* focuses on suggestions and responses rather than orders from other military personnel to foster a sense of autonomy in gameplay, John Smith only experiences negative consequences from not following explicit instructions, and the Pavlovian mechanisms of the game are consistent with a language learning methodology that emphasizes obedient responses to stimuli as a reinforcement to learning.

Yet the approach of the Tactical Language series of games is assumed to serve as a model for learning languages more generally. In its most recent testing phases, the pool of human subjects for *Tactical Iraqi* was even expanded to include adolescent civilians. In a February 2006 interview principal investigator Johnson said, "I think it's fair to say the younger you are the more natural it is. We've tried the program also with teenagers, and it's really remarkable to watch. You know that before long they've already made contact with the local leader and are ready to sit down and plan the reconstruction. They really take to it."[80] Because many in serious games are committed to exploring paradigms that go beyond the stereotypical audience of the adolescent male, it is somewhat surprising to see the *Tactical Iraqi* team actively courting this audience, although it may make sense in terms of its business plan of moving toward a commercial model.

Secondary Reception in the Mass Media: Showing and Telling

In recent years, the news media has presented considerable coverage about these simulated environments. Items on *Tactical Iraqi* appeared in *Newsweek*, *USA Today*, the *Los Angeles Times*, the *New York Times*, *National Geographic*, and *Forbes*, and on the BBC, National Public Radio, Public Radio International, and ABC News.[81] *Virtual Iraq* was featured in broadcast news stories from the BBC, NPR, CNN, ABC, CBS, Reuters, and even Al Jazeerah, and in print in *The New Yorker*, *Newsweek*, *The Washington Post*, *The Nation*, and *Le Figaro*.[82] This coverage is almost uniformly positive and never presents contrary viewpoints from advocates for traditional language learning or talk therapy. However, since news stories about new technologies tend to emphasize characteristics that promote ideologies of progress, this slant is not distinctive to these computerized programs with their hostile physical environments from the Iraqi physical and cultural landscape.

What is perhaps more significant about this coverage of military digital experience is the way that this publicity creates the possibility for a particular form of public display, which purports to show that difficult, if not intractable, problems are being addressed during the war effort. The problems that seem to be ameliorated in both weak and strong VR environments include foreign language incompetence, combat-related PSTD, the threat of roadside attacks by improvised explosive devices, unsuccessful negotiations with Iraqi locals, exacerbation of existing religious or tribal rivalries, confusion of insurgents and civilians, physical immobility from dismemberment or spinal cord damage, and—for battlefield medics—inadequate preparedness for real-life triage situations. Critics could argue that displaying virtual problem solving is not necessarily the most effective way to solve actual problems, and that these games and simulations may function as a distracting show or spectacle to serve the political ends of power elites.[83] Furthermore, if Ian Bogost has argued in *Persuasive Games* that interacting with rule sets while playing videogames opens up opportunities for critique,[84] it would seem that television audiences have a very different experience. As passive spectators, viewers only see and hear selected snippets of the game and have little sense of how the underlying algorithms affect user behavior in sustained play situations.

Moreover, television broadcasts tend to be even more laudatory than print in publicizing these game adaptations, for many of the same reasons that prepackaged video news releases may be aired: the researchers' video of gameplay or sample animations of the digital experience offer no-cost footage illustrating an interesting news story that appeals to a range of youth-oriented constituencies. In one ABC News broadcast, announcer Bill Blakemore reads directly from the testimonials on the *Tactical Iraqi* website, which include the improbable claim that a typical soldier would learn more Arabic "in one day" with *Tactical Iraqi* than a "whole tour in Iraq."[85]

During my first FlatWorld visit, I was allowed to watch a television reporter from a local CBS affiliate in San Francisco film the *Virtual Iraq* foot patrol interface, which consisted of two laptops and a head-mounted display, and interview Rizzo and his collaborator computer scientist Jarrell Pair.[86] Toward the end of the interview the reporter asked Pair to pose as a soldier wearing the gear while Rizzo explained the therapeutic procedure, and Pair jokingly lamented that it was a role that he had had to play previously with other reporters. When Rizzo expertly threaded his microphone wire through his shirt, the reporter commented, "You've done this before," to which Rizzo responded that he had been a "subject in videos over the years." Despite his obvious experience interacting with the media, Rizzo seemed sometimes to forget that he should speak in short soundbites designed for the attention-limited average television watcher and that his vocabulary should reflect a layman's knowledge. For example, at one point in the interview, Rizzo used the term "habituate," and the reporter reminded him that "'habituate' is a word that you know, and I don't." At another juncture Rizzo also showed himself to be willing to go off-message. When the reporter asked if the procedure was like "scaring a person with a heart condition," Rizzo realistically responded that "it could be." However, he followed up with a lay-friendly analogy to going up the "terror stairway one step at a time" and emphasized that this was for already impaired patients who needed to be able to hear a "car backfire in a café" without "feeling like they were back in Fallujah."

To the reporter's credit, he seemed less concerned with the dramatic props in the FlatWorld environment, and focused his attention on the more mundane laptop screen, although he conceded "normally I'd kill for a backdrop like that." Yet the television reporter seemed particularly eager to capture the dramatic explosions and helicopter entries and exits scripted into the game in his demo footage. "Do the explosion again," the reporter asked, and after Rizzo made the helicopter land for the first time, he said "I can make that happen again," much to the reporter's pleasure.[87]

Eliminating human figures also seemed to be a key discursive act in the system demos, which I first noticed when I did the convoy demo with the motion platform, when roadside antagonists were made to magically disappear. At one point during the FlatWorld demo a car exploded and a terrified civilian ran around the scene on the screen display holding his head. Then Rizzo said, "On a keystroke, we can eliminate the civilian if we want," and promptly did so. Unlike *Tactical Iraqi*, the utterances of non-English speaking others are not given much attention in the virtual space. Even the members of the research team did not know what the virtual insurgents depicted were saying in Arabic.

Perhaps the lived space of deliberative experience could be read as being at risk, because the mass media almost infinitely replicate traumatic scenes of spectatorship in cinematic reconstructions to depersonalize and dissociate violence and recast it as more palatable melodrama.[88] If such games and simulations serve as advertisements for the Iraq war to be consumed by American media users, they might also further particular nationalistic agendas by relegating action in combat to cinematic fictions in which collateral damage is either unrepresented or safely virtualized. In contrast, Bob Rehak has argued that it is precisely the alternation or even simultaneous experience of "participatory and spectatorial" digital experiences that gives game environments their value for human subjectivity and potential for ethical significances.[89] So those who study on-screen experiences may interpret these software programs and their associated publicity differently, given these competing assumptions about the value of spatial and narrative experiences in virtual environments.

Backlash in the Professional Game Development Community

In professional and scholarly communities devoted to videogames and virtual reality simulations, the publicity for these projects has stimulated considerable debate about the appropriateness of lending intellectual capital to these military-funded endeavors. Critics of software development related to the war in Iraq have argued that producers, designers, and programmers were collaborating with an invading army by contributing their code to members of the military hierarchy. Defenders of the projects argued from a position of pragmatism: they pointed out that (1) such programs aided working-class soldiers on the frontlines, not policy makers in the power elite; (2) many programs were specifically designed to reduce civilian casualties; and (3) the Internet and a plethora of other technological advances now enjoyed in cyberculture were once the products of militarily planned and funded projects. Nevertheless, this distrust of what Timothy Lenoir and Simon Penny have called "The Military-Entertainment Complex" runs deep, both in the academy and in hacker culture.[90]

Manuel Castells, like many historians of the digital age, has shown the defense industry to be a key player in the theory and practice of software development throughout its entire evolution.[91] To counteract this militaristic influence, considerable energy has been devoted to developing alternatively themed games about nonintervention or peaceful mediation, such as *A Force More Powerful*, *PeaceMaker*, and graphically less ambitious games like *September 12th* or *Madrid*.[92] However, these games received relatively little attention in the mainstream media, except in the context of discussing violence in commercial gaming.[93]

Not all of the cultural conflict between parties working in these new digital media may be necessarily directly related to specific geopolitical catalysts like the invasion and occupation of Iraq or to the deepening of a civilian/noncivilian divide in knowledge work. As Stuart Moulthrop observes, the "declaration (or acclamation) of war may distract attention from preexisting conflicts inherent in information culture."[94] In other words, stakeholders arguing about the morality of participation in projects like *Tactical Iraqi* or *Virtual Iraq* may actually have more fundamental disagreements about making meaning within a shared disciplinary field. These verbal opponents might even disagree about how technology works upon society in general. For example, some may be instrumentalists who see specific technologies as tools that can be directed by the conscious will of individuals and cause particular changes by intervening in the material world; others may be functionalists who think that cultural institutions use technology mainly to promote social stability and group norms.

It could be argued that the relatively short history of game studies has been characterized by a series of three—sometimes recursive—contentious debates. In the first great debate about videogames, which began in the 1980s,[95] the issues in question about art and representation go back at least to the famous argument between the ancients Plato and Aristotle. On the side that assumes Platonic *mimesis* as the operative principle, games imitate "real" life and in turn encourage players to act in the "real" world in ways that imitate gameplay. The opposing side assumes that Aristotle's theory of *catharsis* is more applicable; these critics adopt a viewpoint that assumes that games provide a socially acceptable outlet for experiencing even destructive behavior and thus help players understand the consequences of antisocial actions. The second great debate, which goes back to Gonzalo Frasca's 1999 ludology manifesto, pitted "narratologists" against "ludologists" in an academic turf war. Supposedly, either critics believe that games tell stories that are organized by archetypal structural elements in a plot line in which players identify with particular characters, or they believe that games potentially subvert cultural narratives because their "rules" can also allow for reciprocity and subversive play.[96] A third great debate seems to be now under way, spurred by the existence of "serious" games that are using game technologies more broadly for training, education, therapy, rehabilitation, social marketing, consciousness-raising, and public diplomacy. Instrumentalists argue that games function as tools giving the player enhanced abilities as an individual to effect change in virtual or real worlds, while others—whom I call game studies functionalists—argue that games function to maintain a society's homeostasis and protect existing institutions and ideological paradigms.

When the BBC ran an online feature praising *Tactical Iraqi* on February 19, 2006, it unintentionally triggered a furious debate in the game development blogosphere. At first the reaction was either positive or subdued. Nick Montfort of *Grand Text Auto* describes the piece as a "great" article and praises project team member Hannes Vilhjálmsson.[97]

The reaction was very different on *Water Cooler Games*, a forum for discussing persuasive gaming in politics, advertising, education, and public health. In his opening salvo in answer to the BBC piece, web log editor and game developer Gonzalo Frasca declares that all ethical designer-programmers should cut all ties to military projects like *Tactical Iraqi*. In his act of public shaming, he castigates those involved with defense projects as collaborators and closes with a virulent malediction against them that excludes them from his interpretive or productive communities. "You are not and will never be my colleagues. The Army money that funds your projects is tainted with blood and what you are doing is just simply wrong. Unlike the poor guys taking the bullets in the frontline, you guys had an education. You should know better. Shame on you!"[98]

Even before debate erupted at *Water Cooler Games*, Mark Marino had publicized his discomfort and his own divided allegiances on *WRT: Writer Response Theory*: "Part of my trouble is that I'm torn. Having seen the system and having learned a few words through it, I must say that I like it as a teaching system. I like that it isn't a shooter. Also, I like the words 'cultural sensitivity.' The trouble is 'cultural sensitivity' becomes a new kind of operational system in the command and control schema of larger military objectives."[99]

Several *Water Cooler Games* readers quickly argued against Frasca from an instrumentalist position. Their postings promote an interpretation in which *Tactical Iraqi* serves as a tool intended to forestall violence and armed conflict rather than a tool to prepare for it. One commentator stresses the necessity of "the ability to communicate with Iraqis." Another prefers to "supply" Arabic as "one of the more innocuous and ultimately healing things" thinkable. A third writes that soldiers "have a far better chance of realizing the human impact of what's been done there, and finding ways to help instead of hurt, if they can communicate with the people there."[100] In this view of language, translation serves as an absolute good and harmful speech acts are unimaginable.

Frasca takes issue with their claims that translation is always an absolute good and even tries to use their very instrumentalism against them. He responds to these assertions of benign intent and execution with his own skepticism and insists that there is "no such thing as an ideologically neutral piece of software." In keeping with Lev Manovich's work on "transcoding," Frasca seems to believe that technology shapes cultural systems of signification as well as the more apparent inverse formulation. Rather than accept the instrumentalist view of his opponents, Frasca retorts with a unit operations reading of their discourse and the discourses of the *Tactical Iraqi* researchers in the media: "Breaking the process into small pieces is a very old military technique for convincing accomplices that they are not doing nothing [sic] wrong. Each little piece of the process seems harmless but the whole process can be monstrous."[101] Then, in what seems to be self-conscious hyperbole, he explicitly compares the game's proponents to Nazis who were just following orders.

Andrew Stern, a coeditor of *Grand Text Auto* with Montfort, subsequently interjects himself into the *Water Cooler* debate and offers his perspective as a researcher currently receiving defense funding himself. Unlike the instrumentalists, he appeals to Frasca's pragmatism and to his understanding of the complexity of systems.

As you know, military funding (e.g, DARPA) is relatively pervasive in computer science in general, helping fund many researchers, including some you know. (The project I'm consulting on is Army-funded.) Such research, like the interactive narrative research I'm working on for ICT, can be applied to many other domains. (Wasn't the Internet itself originally a military-funded project, to create a robust computer network in the event of nuclear war, that the world now reaps the benefits of? The morality of this stuff is complicated.).[102]

Rather than examine the effects of programs like *Tactical Iraqi*, Stern focuses his rhetorical strategy on the causes of other software development projects. Like Moulthrop, Stern also acknowledges that debate about participation in the war effort among game developers and critics might relate to other pre-existing epistemological conflicts: "Perhaps my participation in such projects is a form of implicit approval of the war, but it's also potentially helping improve the situation, and the results can theoretically be applied to help other battles, such as, oh, the Ludology vs. Narratology conflict."[103]

In answering Stern, Frasca grants Stern's complexity argument some credence and acknowledges their common membership in a community of friendship and scholarship—although he teases Stern about his narratological alliances. Yet he remains adamant that moral decision-making is still at issue. As Frasca writes, "I would never doubt about your intentions but I still think that you made a wrong choice. As a friend, my only comment to you is that I think that most of these people cannot be trusted and I recommend you to stay away from them. The safest choice, in my view, is to step aside."[104]

At this point, fellow blog editor Ian Bogost tries to serve as a mediator in the dispute by pointing out the interconnectedness of distributed digital media interests and the way that those networks might implicate Frasca himself. Furthermore, Bogost argues, "Among the more pacifist folks I know, one of the 'strategies' for dealing with the ethical issues DARPA and other military funding raise is to think of such research as subversive: they'll take the military funding and use the resulting research for initiatives that undermine the military. I wish I had some examples to point to for the discussion, can anyone suggest some?"[105]

Bogost's rhetorical question remains unanswered on the *Water Cooler Games* comment page, but at this juncture *Tactical Iraqi*'s Vilhjálmsson himself chimes in. He explains his general rationale in terms of behavioral rewards, both for his labor as a game designer and for the work of the soldiers who play the game.

Being a peace activist myself, I had to overcome a great deal of stigma before accepting technical lead on the project. But two things in particular made this easier: (1) When I met in person a group of soldiers that had just returned from duty in Iraq I was struck by their awareness of the mess they were in and their desperation to get out of there alive—and to them, being able to make friends not enemies was absolutely crucial for their own survival. It was this cry for help at a very personal level, not at the level of government, that touched me. The game rewards non-violence over violence—in fact, you fail the game immediately if things start to take a violent turn. I got a certain kick out of removing all weapons from this Unreal Tournament mod. I was pleasantly surprised to see that the soldiers were not too annoyed by this, instead they really got into the groove of finding out how to say things like 'pleasure to meet you.' I hadn't seen anything like it since I first saw a group of die-hard FPS [first-person-shooter] veterans huddled around The Sims playing doll house. In my mind, coming up with an engaging alternative to violent gaming is a challenge worth tackling.[106]

Vilhjálmsson's approach would seem to subvert conventional norms of violent videogame design. By using the "doll house" analogy to The Sims, he even seems to suggest that gender norms are being upended in the experience of participating in gameplay in Tactical Iraqi.

Of course, many videogames still operate from the radical perspective of total Hobbesian skepticism and exploit kill-or-be-killed misanthropic assumptions. These games construct a virtual drama in which it is always better to engage in preemptive aggression if social actors lack reliable guarantees of mutual respect and cooperation. In the dominant culture of the United States, it could be argued, this logic is replicated in everything from reality television, based on the contestants' cutthroat strategies as "survivors," to presidential speeches about "preventative war." Nonetheless, the rise in cooperative games—massively multiplayer online role-playing games in particular—has dramatized the benefits of the social contract and interdependence in online gaming and perhaps in digital experiences more generally. Combat may be equally bloodthirsty in many games, but players discover the obvious advantages of maintaining social bonds, fostering situations of trust, and bringing others in their cohort back to life in situations of duress.

Games like Tactical Iraqi have the potential to connect the personal to the political and to integrate the actions of individuals engaged in particular speech acts with the rhetoric of the nation-states they represent. Such games could conceivably represent the forefront of an emergent social realism that Galloway argues is essential if videogames are to be recognized as a mature aesthetic form and as an ethical expression of artistic communication and mass instruction.[107] The world of Tactical Iraqi is not a zero-sum game. The success of John Smith depends on his satisfying the social needs of others. In fact, his "health" in the game is measured by the attitudes of the other autonomous agents on the screen. Trust is both the precondition of play and the currency of the game in mimetic and diegetic play. Ironically, different scenarios of trust played out not only for the virtual John Smith, but also for the real-life military players, who were asked by their superiors to engage in a particular form of digital experience and to risk failure in situations of rhetorical and interpretive vulnerability with which they were profoundly unfamiliar.

Although constructing spaces—be they physical or virtual—that direct the movement of human users invariably manifests hegemonic strategies that constrain individual subjects, the possibility of exploration through the "rhetoric of walking" also opens up possibilities for new scripts. For example, principal investigator Rizzo has described how patients experiencing *Virtual Vietnam* would mentally insert particular human figures or other objects, such as a water buffalo, into the rice paddy VR simulation, and principal investigator Johnson has explained that the early resistance of learners to entry and further penetration of the virtual environment was overcome by creating opportunities for unconstrained, informal interactions with the virtual characters and new training worlds designed to ease the user's transition to the virtual space. The creation of 3-D spaces in virtual environments not only allows for certain forms of tactical improvisation by users within the simulated space, but because of the intense media attention that these projects have received, it also includes the general public in this rhetoric of walking and introduces a broader audience to the complicated matrix of trust relationships that suggests the presence of sentient others in these virtual Iraqs.

Language Games in *Tactical Iraqi*

At one point in the game, if the player is successful in his or her interactions with a man at a sidewalk table, the man will hand the player his card. Yet, assuming this virtual card is written in Arabic, at no point in *Tactical Iraqi* does the player acquire the skill to read it. The act of reading, which is so central to many classic computer games, such as *Myst*,[108] is totally irrelevant in *Tactical Iraqi*, even though this Arabic language-learning program is ostensibly a literacy game.[109] Although the program website describes the approach of *Tactical Iraqi* as one that merely "deemphasizes written language," it may be more accurate to say that in the 2005 version of the game the program actively avoids any pedagogy aimed at secondary literacy goals. This is the case despite the fact that the imperceptibly smooth integration of reading and response in videogames has been characterized by literacy specialists like Gee as indicative of their dramatic value as a teaching tool.

It could be argued that the focus of the program on face-to-face interactions and paralinguistic cues promotes primary literacy more effectively because the learner must participate in both receptive and productive modes (with the unintended consequence of sometimes inducing reluctance in some learners). Yet in a game that is about exploring a semiotic landscape and interpreting situated cues, it seems like a lost opportunity to ignore such a significant language realm as written discourse. Compared to giving characters complex culturally specific gestures, which require fine motor coordination in the 3-D game engine, a relatively trivial redesign could draw the player's attention to the way that the setting is already labeled for secondary literacy skills in a meaning-rich environment of building signs and printed ephemera.

To some extent, the soldiers who play *Tactical Iraqi* are being encouraged to "game" the language to reach the next level and ultimately the final goal of tactical success. But to achieve significant foreign language acquisition, it is also important to participate in language games that may not have objectives or designated winners or losers. Wittgenstein claims that linguistic rule-learning originates in the simple language games of childhood, such as call-and-response memorization, the rhythmic naming of objects, and playground rhymes.[110] The total number of language games Wittgenstein considers to be "countless," because such games include an endless combination of verbal activities in a list encompassing asking, praying, speculating, reporting, thanking, joking, and translating, among many others. By building on Wittgenstein's work, Lyotard identifies several language games that are played by social actors: these include the denotative game (where the focus is on what is true or false), the prescriptive game (where the focus is on good and bad, just and unjust), and the technical game (where the focus is on what is efficient and inefficient).[111]

The game's digital entity, representing a combination of the learning soldier and the prepackaged avatar John Smith, participates in a variety of language games. After his training in the childlike Skill Builder, John Smith must be able to affirm that he is from a particular nationality in the occupying forces and to deny that he is a member of the CIA. He must make choices about people, materials, and environments that demonstrate a capacity for the discriminations of just social conduct that are located in discourse. And finally, he must get the building built as efficiently as possible and direct the process of rebuilding, much as the "builder" does with his "assistant" in Wittgenstein's opening example of a simple language game around construction activity.

Philosopher Jacques Derrida presents two seemingly contradictory statements about language acquisition in one of his last theoretical works: "1. We only ever speak one language" and "2. We never speak only one language."[112] For Derrida, the human subjects of language are both always and never bilingual. Regardless of the associated mother language of our apparent ethnicity or national origin, our phenomenological experience of discursive practices is simultaneously uniform and multiform. In other words, John Smith and the players who assume his identity in the game likely function in a complex linguistic universe with multiple codes and conventions that seems relatively seamless to them in their experiences of it. It is not unreasonable to assume that specialized training and personal experience in the armed forces has made these soldiers familiar with many languages. Specific dialects might include otherwise arcane military jargon and technical acronyms, highly ritualized forms of salutation for those higher in the chain of command, and even scatological and misogynistic oral folklore from the base. Gee has gone so far as to argue that gameplay, like advanced professional training, equips a learner with the specialized vocabulary of an expert language. By this logic, John Smith and the players who inhabit him experience the continuity of their linguistic experiences. Expert or foreign language simply expands the number of correspondences of words to things; it does not change the character of the experience of perceptual or social realism.

When Arabic speakers were asked to review the game for accuracy and authenticity, some expressed surprise at the naiveté of the game's design. These critics argued that the local Arabic-speaking authorities to whom John Smith is directed would know some English and would, at the very least, be familiar with hybridized language strategies and engage in code-switching to maximize opportunities for communicative success. Although Iraq achieved independence from Great Britain in 1932, global forms of English still permeate many aspects of official and unofficial culture. Furthermore, "G.I." dialects, such as "G.I. Japanese," are important for facilitating linguistic play in military deployment situations. All around the world, much of the communication that takes place between local people and military personnel reflects provisional language strategies like pidgin or simplified English, or creolized native languages. Yet the game is designed to reinforce formal and grammatically correct sentence constructions. What John Smith encounters in the game space is "pure" Arabic without English slang, loanwords, or code-switching substitutions.

The *Tactical Iraqi* researchers explained that even the simplest hybridized linguistic interactions would strain the capabilities of the speech recognizer, whose technical requirements had already consumed a considerable portion of the program's budget and time on task by personnel during the project's history. At first, the Arabic speech recognition software even rejected many correct utterances. When the system was demonstrated to me in fall 2006, however, the game was excessively tolerant of linguistic mistakes, and thus I was told it would require more tinkering. The algorithm for scoring pronunciation had to be adjusted several times in the development process, even though the system was specially designed with AI technology that aided the machine in recognizing the features of a learner's individual voice. In other words, before the learner could learn, the machine had to learn to recognize the idiosyncrasies in the speaker's personal speech patterns.

At the very end of the game, on the last level, Sergeant John Smith, the successful language learner, is to be celebrated as a village hero for his competence in rebuilding the girl's school in the face of material and cultural obstacles that could have prevented achieving the mission's goal. If, as Gee and Johnson argue, games are in fact inherently pedagogical, language skills acquired in this game should be transferable to other contexts, like the context of real missions in real villages in Iraq. Educational media theorists like Gee argue that videogame skills require such complex interactions that they transfer relatively easily. Once a complicated protocol is learned for inflexible virtual agents, discursive practices can be applied in riskier situations in a more fungible real world. However, other researchers see this very complexity of game rules as a natural obstacle to the transference of skills for educational purposes,[113] particularly when distinct genres of gameplay evolve so rapidly and novelty is so highly prized by the gaming community.

The data on *Tactical Iraqi* appear too limited to judge definitively. Early published results reflected information from tiny sample sizes, and it is obviously difficult to generalize from just a handful of learners about a project with so many curricular components and so many variables of learning. These variables include obedience to authority, group dynamics, the learner's status in the eyes of researchers, the learner's conceptions of self, and, especially, trust in the learning situation.

The political issues around these virtual Iraqs continue to be contentious. For example, during a presentation about *Tactical Iraqi* to an international audience in Copenhagen, Denmark, I was accused by European game theorists of failing to be critical enough of the game's pro-American political ideology, despite having given a peer-reviewed paper that included an analysis of the game's shortcomings with which the *Tactical Iraqi* team was quite unhappy. As a rhetorician who studies new media, I expressed an irksome "hope that this military simulation, which is intended to forestall violence and armed conflict rather than prepare for it, will not be the last game in its genre" that I thought could be divorced from my U.S. citizenship.

The closing lines of that paper suggested another way that the game could be read, one in which the public rhetoric of a military-funded videogame invites deliberative discourse as well. "Although I have expressed concerns about its technological and ideological hard wiring, I think that this program also stimulates critical discussion about how trust and self are constituted by digital experiences and how language is integrated into virtual environments of all kinds, even when conventions about rules and randomness in virtual spaces do not match up neatly with the principles governing linguistic play."[114]

Res Publica: Videogames and the Material Culture of Civic Life

In his explorations of the visual culture of civic life, Bruno Latour means more by "making things public" than the common idiomatic meaning of the phrase might suggest. He is also interested in exploring the broader, more traditional notion of *res publica* and considering how "things public" are literally constructed for and received by political audiences. Using the language of software development, Latour characterizes a range of political and scientific representations, which are "representative" and "realistic" to varying degrees, as manifestations of what he calls "object-oriented democracy." For Latour, "democracy" can be seen in terms of its Greek etymology as a form of civic participation that is as much about division as it is about a unitary ethos.[115]

It may seem strange to think about government-funded videogames as being like civic murals, commemorative columns, or triumphal arches, but games like *Tactical*

Iraqi and simulations like *Virtual Iraq* can similarly serve as "things public." They also reveal conflicts and contradictions from which civilian voters and taxpayers are generally shielded. 3-D environments created for videogames can encourage practices of study and debate about these concrete, albeit virtual, objects. Like other simulation environments created for the U.S. military, they may ultimately also become shared spaces that include visitors from the public. Latour is writing about obviously public spaces:

Scientific laboratories, technical institutions, marketplaces, churches and temples, financial trading rooms, Internet forums, ecological disputes—without forgetting the very shape of the museum inside which we gather all those *membra disjecta*—are just some of the forums and agoras in which we speak, vote, decide, are decided upon, prove, are being convinced. Each has its own architecture, its own technology of speech, its complex set of procedures, its definition of freedom and domination, its ways of bringing together those who are concerned—and even more important, those who are not concerned—and what concerns them, its expedient way to obtain closure and come to a decision.[116]

This deliberative function has even found a place in at least one military-funded Iraq game. The University of Southern California, which produces *Tactical Iraqi* and *Virtual Iraq*, is also developing the Enhanced Learning Environment with Creative Technology, or *ELECT BiLAT*, to help soldiers improve their skills at bilateral negotiations with the Iraqi population. The premise of the game can be explained as follows:

Imagine you are a soldier assigned to rebuilding efforts in an Iraqi town or you're an officer tasked with keeping the peace in an unstable city. Earning the trust and respect of the citizens you are trying to help is of the utmost importance. Should you bring a gift to your meeting? Should you shake hands? Does the person with the highest title actually hold any power, and how do you find out? Cultural sensitivity and situational understanding are among the necessary tools in your arsenal.[117]

The question, of course, is, are videogames the best tools for teaching the principles of participation in dialogue or modeling deliberative give-and-take processes? Although recent research by Ren Reynolds and others looks at collaborative play and collective rule-making in massively multiplayer online environments, it's difficult to break creating democratic institutions into a series of unit operations.

To their credit, both *Tactical Iraqi* and *Virtual Iraq* open a door to traditional private spaces to the larger public and allow outsiders to see inside the classroom or clinic. As Michel Foucault has argued, regulation by professional disciplines polices vision and only permits certain authorized specialists to see into otherwise privileged spaces and realms of the body and psyche.[118] Videogames and simulations make these sites of linguistic conflict and psychic trauma visible to those outside the educational or medical establishments. Indeed, principal investigator Rizzo has argued that his work on *Virtual Iraq* can be read as a form of political resistance, as it makes the hidden costs of warfare visible to the public. He even attributes the interest of the foreign press in his project to this subversive aspect of the program.

As public renderings, these virtual Iraqi vistas and labyrinths are not copies or exact replicas of public and private spaces in the real world. Although the architecture and topography of the virtual world exploits the surface realism of the *Unreal Tournament 2003* game engine, *Tactical Iraqi* does not attempt to recreate actual locations in Iraq in its 3-D environment. Despite the fact that game designers worked from photographs of remote locations in the Middle East, the experience of virtual tourism is constrained. In other words, *Tactical Iraqi* does not attempt to recreate specific buildings or landmarks, unlike the simulated doubling of public spaces from foreign countries in games like *Tony Hawk's Underground 2*.

To maximize relevance for mission transference, it was apparently necessary for the *Tactical Iraqi* designers to create a sufficiently generic Iraqi playscape to prepare soldiers who could be deployed anywhere in the country. Elements of an earlier game set in Lebanon, *Mission to Arabic*, were also part of the design history of *Tactical Iraqi*, so that the game may unintentionally further a digital experience of postmodern cultural pastiche. Moreover, researchers plan to apply the *Tactical Iraqi* game to other contexts in the Middle East and even intend to offer instructional modules in other languages, such as Pashto, which would be designed for service in Afghanistan, where the natural ecology and man-made space are very different from Iraq. Software developers in *Virtual Iraq* similarly avoided mimetic realism and sought to create generic rather than specific landscapes to heal their client's wounded psyches. In other words, despite being in control of a multisensory barrage of hyperreal stimuli, the ideal therapist still wants there to be some neutral canvas on which the patient can recreate details from his or her memories of the seminal crippling traumatic event.

The virtual objects, social puppets, built environment, physical terrain, and perceptual spaces of this computer-generated Iraq can take the user into the realm of public matters while also exploring the private spaces associated with the user's own memories: intimate spaces of private living and traumatic spaces of violent combat. By making these intimate, humanizing spaces of private life visible in Iraq, particularly in the fourth scene in Jasim's house, the members of the general public who are likely to admire the impressive government-developed technology might at the same time see a kind of virtual home worth preserving rather than treat this local political leader's residence as something to be exploded in traditional shooter play. In other words, creating political spectacles can have positive as well as negative implications. If government-funded videogames and virtual reality simulations serve as forms of public display, as critics we need to grapple with how best to interrogate that visibility and understand the potential for rhetorical exchanges, although we may well have to wait for political spectacles that are more sophisticated than the current military offerings.

4 The War from the Web: An Atlas of Conflict, Government, and Citizenship

A few months after the terrorist attacks on New York City and Washington, D.C., the large-scale art piece "Listening Post" was installed at the Brooklyn Academy of Music. Created by statistician Mark Hansen and multimedia artist Ben Rubin, the first "Listening Post" consisted of over two hundred screens channeling words from almost-live feeds pulled from thousands of Internet chat rooms, registering activity (predominantly in English) in the flotsam and jetsam of cyberspace. The glowing patchwork of words and phrases displayed as undulating text, and periodically visitors heard a symphony (or cacophony) of synthesized voices reading the screens aloud. Viewers described the Hansen/Rubin installation, when it appeared at the Whitney, as like "seeing the Internet from space."[1] After it opened at the Skirball Cultural Center in Los Angeles, Hansen characterized this blinking, chanting machine as a representation of "spaces for public discourse" from a "virtual crowd," specifically—using the theories of the composer Xenakis—a "political crowd." Hansen and Rubin also said that they used algorithmic compositions to organize the chat into "scenes" to "allow the data to speak intelligibly" and to "zoom in" and "zoom out" on specific news events and syntactical constructs of grammatical agency, like "movements" organized around the phrases "I am" or "I like."[2]

Because of the unique timing of its post-9/11 premiere, "Listening Post" also showed the polyvocal character of Internet discourses about political and religious extremism, nationalism and globalization, and human agency in the face of terror. There were literally thousands of points of view about the attacks of September 11 and the subsequent "War on Terror" on display—these shifted constantly among the electronic ephemera about a multitude of other quotidian subjects culled from online communities. These staccato sound bites could only begin to mourn, announce, explain, blame, lecture, hector, and apologize before being replaced by other fragments from the Internet.

Official rhetoric on the Internet about September 11 and its reception history similarly shows how the public face of e-government can be more protean than its boosters would like to believe, simply because there are many different incarnations of state authority visible from the vantage point of any individual user's computer screen. A partial survey of websites from the Federal Bureau of Investigation, the White House, the State Department, the Department of Defense, and the U.S. Central Command in the weeks and months following September 11 suggests that official idealism about the promise of a user-friendly, authoritative, and direct digital democracy cannot account for the many mixed messages—particularly those concerning ideologies of race, class, gender, and national identity—that those same federal government websites in aggregate convey.

This is not to say that the democratic possibilities of the Internet are not appealing, particularly if a crowded, open marketplace of ideas serves as an attractive metaphor for the site of public rhetoric. In 1995, Lawrence Grossman waxed enthusiastic about these potentals in *The Electronic Republic,* in which he foresaw a future in which new communications technologies and distributed networks would enable direct democracy to supplant an eroded representative democracy that was already in decline from the effects of voter referendums, sophisticated public opinion polling, and other manifestations of populism on the rise.[3] Many e-government enthusiasts heartily agreed with Grossman and predicted that civic life would soon return to a golden era not seen since the ancient Greek city-states.

Others have not been so certain that democratic institutions necessarily benefit from new technology. Long before the publication of *The Electronic Republic,* Abramson, Arterton, and Orren's *The Electronic Commonwealth* expressed concerns that the removal of barriers of time and space by modern media could subvert both the quantity and quality of public deliberation.[4] In the post-September 11 era, Bruce Bimber analyzed data suggesting that political participation has not been significantly affected by Internet access.[5] Specifically, he asserted that little voter mobilization could be directly attributed to the Internet. Bimber worried that, like television, the Internet encouraged passive consumption of political culture. As an opposing case of a noticeably transformative information revolution in American politics, he pointed to how nineteenth-century penny newspapers solidified party allegiances, encouraged the exercise of opinion in the context of urban communities, and led to higher percentages of voter turnout among eligible citizens.

Even those who believe in the transformative potential of technology raise alarms about its unintended consequences on political life. Siva Vaidhyanathan alerted his readers that democracy is being "hacked" by agents for diametrically opposed oligarchic and anarchic interests, so that promising new technology could conceivably weaken political society further as government in the public interest devolves into mutually exclusive hierarchical or peer-to-peer organizations.[6] From the perspective of identifying the oligarchic threat, Richard Davis had previously warned that forms of centralized power from the era of corporate broadcasting merely colonize new technologies.[7] From the viewpoint of vigilance for emergent anarchy, Anthony G.

Wilhelm cautioned that distributed networks could accelerate the fragmentation of civic life and the loss of a common public sphere.[8]

Perhaps the most systematic attack on e-government boosterism has come from Darin Barney, who has argued in *Prometheus Wired* that although "network technology is widely believed to be the medium through which a democratic revolution is being, or will be, enacted," "this belief cannot be sustained on economic, ontological, or political grounds."[9] Barney cites the fact that the word "cybernetics" and the word "government" have a common etymological root, the Greek *kubernētēs* or "steersman," and then flatly states that the similarities between the two terms end there. Barney argues that "liberalism" has been confused with "democracy" by e-government advocates and that the potentially negative effects of technology on political societies have been prematurely discounted.[10]

With the advent of blogs, social network sites, and smart mobs that use mobile communication technology, the political sites of popular engagement have become very different from the centralized models initially imagined by government planners. Geert Lovink has argued that this digital culture shaped by a post-September 11 political climate manifests a distinctively "nihilist impulse" in its social media production.[11] With a much more optimistic vision of Web 2.0 than Lovink presents, Henry Jenkins has claimed that even seemingly parasitic fan cultures can serve as a model for how the collective intelligence of a burgeoning transmedia society can express potent preferences and set norms that redirect the procedures of governance.[12] Furthermore, as distributed media becomes more distributed with mobile devices, Howard Rheingold claims that ubiquitous computing subverts the possibility of a single, surveiling panopticon, and that forms of emergence he calls "cooperation amplifiers" will inevitably frustrate antidemocratic "computerized reputation systems."[13]

Unlike these relatively complex political ecosystems at issue for e-government advocates and critics, federal websites seem like comparatively two-dimensional, flattened-out expressions of what Jane Fountain has called the "virtual state," the systemization of post-Weberian bureaucracy in cyberspace, organized predominantly around the maintenance of "files."[14] Adoption of particular information technologies by government agencies, Fountain argues, has so far been limited to plug-and-play functions. Thus, she claims, "whenever possible, decisionmakers have used information technology in ways, however innovative, that leave deeper structures and processes—such as authority relations, political relations, and oversight processes—undisturbed."[15] Fountain's prehistory of the development of government websites focuses on events related to the National Performance Review (NPR), an agency founded in 1993 under the Clinton administration, and the NPR's associated rhetorical tropes of "reinventing government" during the Web 1.0 era. She describes how government websites were initially designed for corporate entities seeking access to information about regulatory strictures in the form of a searchable database, and only later were these prototype sites reengineered to serve a broader demographic of citizens who wanted online forms, electronic payment options, and digital access to records and services.

The user's experience of government websites is largely defined by the screen's visual interface. Unlike more immersive virtual reality experiences, government websites are delineated by the presentation of an HTML webpage (or successive layers of multiple computer windows framing discrete webpages) on a desktop screen.[16] As Lev Manovich notes, despite the promise of elaborate futuristic scenarios with 3-D graphics, wearable computers, and immersive multisensory environments, "the screen is rapidly becoming the main means of accessing any kind of information."[17] For Manovich, we are becoming a "society of the screen," which is often unconscious of its ideological ramifications. Manovich argues that the screen is not "a neutral medium of presenting information," because it is "aggressive" in that it "functions to filter, to *screen out*, to take over, rendering nonexistent whatever is outside its frame."[18] He traces two different genealogies for the computer screen in *The Language of New Media*: the silver screen of cinema and the radar screen and its associated metaphors of surveillance.

Since September 11, government websites have become an increasingly important and explicitly rhetorical window on public agencies for many Americans. A Pew study on Internet use conducted in the month immediately following the September 11 attacks, "The Commons of the Tragedy," concluded that not only were more Americans getting their news online as they switched to "on alert" status, but government websites were also getting dramatically higher numbers of unique visits, as anxious citizens sought official information from remote agencies of authority.[19] The numbers are compelling: the report claims that thirteen times as many people visited the FBI website and four times as many visitors clicked their way to the official site of the White House.[20] The report denies that September 11 was a "breakthrough moment" for the Internet, however, because television and the telephone were still the primary vehicles for news across all demographic sectors, even among heavy Internet users. Yet these heavy traffic patterns of surfing to authoritative sites in Washington, D.C., continued, and many new sites and webpages were created by government entities as the showdown with Afghanistan began. Furthermore, between August and October, the White House website had undergone a major transition in the appearance of its home page, which had gone from a list of news links organized by date, in which material for children was prominently featured, in a design that was very similar to the Clinton-era website, to a more comprehensive media portal that was noticeably branded with distinctive images of the flag and the White House portico.[21]

From my own study of government websites since the September 11 attacks, I take issue with Mark Boardman's thesis in *The Language of Websites* that the "real publishing revolution" is only taking place in personal sites because institutional pages are still harnessed to print culture and the monolithic forces of authorized hegemony.[22] In contrast, I argue that institutional websites are more than mere extensions of a single public relations apparatus: they can present controversial speeches, damaging reports, public apologies, declassified documents, and even certain compliance statistics mandated by law. One can find everything from the poetry of Bertolt Brecht to Al Jazeera transcripts on websites from the federal government. Official federal websites show the heterogeneity of institutional rhetoric at the highest levels.

The Desktop President

In the winter of 2002, like several of my colleagues in the University of California, I taught a seminar about the terrorist attacks on the Pentagon and the World Trade Center, which had taken place only a few months earlier. There were actually four different seminars about the rhetoric of the September 11 and the subsequent War on Terror on my campus that quarter, but mine was the only one to focus explicitly on web-based delivery systems, networked communication, and hypertext. My aim was to teach students to analyze the rhetoric of public figures and agencies and to locate primary sources on the World Wide Web. I assumed that these specific skills would best help them understand the events of the particular historical moment, and I also intended to provide a basic interpretive framework that could be applicable to other news stories and give them a background in classical rhetoric and information literacy that could be useful elsewhere in undergraduate coursework. All the materials for the course were available online from a hypertext syllabus. The university provided a technologically enhanced classroom in which we could look at webpages from the Internet projected on a screen and discuss them as a group. Students used a class electronic discussion list to send URLs of relevant websites to each other, and then the sites were analyzed by students online and in class. Undergraduates were graded on the electronic discourse that they produced in response to class discussion and several produced websites of their own. This class experiment, in turn, was featured in *Kairos*, a web-based journal about rhetoric and composition, in a hypertext I wrote about "Teaching, Terrorism, and Technology."[23]

I was initially amazed by the extreme precision of my students' memories when I taught a unit on presidential speeches from the period. Four months later, these undergraduates seemed to remember each vocal inflection, nuance of tone, stammer, hesitation over a word, and emotive pause in the speeches of George W. Bush. Unlike my students, I could not remember the exact delivery or use of specific oratorical flourishes from past newscasts of the president's speeches. However, it seemed as if the chief executive's performance still resonated with my class months later. As we studied what had seemed to me to be lifeless scripts from the official White House website, they commented on both throat-catching and throat-clearing moments as though the discrete experiences of hearing them on television or the radio were still vivid. The mystery was solved when my web-savvy class pointed out that I could easily click "Listen to the President's Remarks" or "View the President's Remarks" on the White House website by activating the silhouette of a speaker or television screen. Thus my students had no need for long-term recall of specific features of oratory that were instantaneously available for playback. In Plato's terms, the device for reminder was easily accessible, and so they had no need for aural, cultural memory. The multimedia organization of the White House webpage also meant that my students could judge the text of the speeches alongside the visual and auditory performance by the president at his desk or podium.

The relationship between classical rhetoric and contemporary political oratory is complex, particularly when it is filtered through the webcast format, in which the speaker competes on the desktop with other electronic ephemera. Even in this intimate single-user setting, the ethos associated specifically with presidential oratory represents a negotiation between multiple personae and audiences. As the chief executive of the United States, the president must claim the "I" position as a speaker of individual action and yet he must also represent America as a collective of citizens

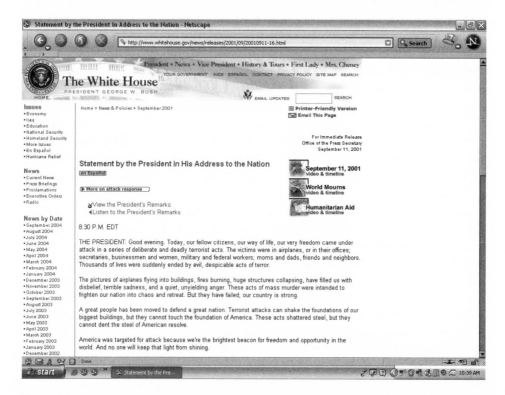

Figure 4.1
White House website with September 11 speech.

and testify from the perspective of the common "we," as the first speech demonstrated:

Today, our nation saw evil, the very worst of human nature. And we responded with the best of America—with the daring of our rescue workers, with the caring for strangers and neighbors who came to give blood and help in any way they could. Immediately following the first attack, I implemented our government's emergency response plans. Our military is powerful, and it's prepared. Our emergency teams are working in New York City and Washington, D.C., to help with local rescue efforts.[24]

Like other broadcasts from the Oval Office, the viewer can see the top of the Resolute desk in front of the president, made from the timbers of the HMS *Resolute*, and the president's flag behind him. Unlike footage from a conventional television broadcast, the camera for the first September 11 webcast is slightly off-center, and the frame frequently shifts. Compared to slick network coverage, this White House presentation has an incongruously off-market character, despite its obvious official sanction.

As either live event or virtual replay, presidential rhetoric must draw on the natural speech idiom, but it must do so in a form that demands elevated oratory, what speechwriters call "laying marble." Although former President Bush had cultivated a homespun Texas image, in a speech delivered September 20 before Congress he employs a topos straight out of ancient rhetoric of the classical period in which an orator raises the shield of the fallen hero and remembers him to the crowd by name. "And I will carry this: It is the police shield of a man named George Howard, who died at the World Trade Center trying to save others. It was given to me by his mom, Arlene, as a proud memorial to her son. This is my reminder of lives that ended, and a task that does not end."[25]

The speechwriting team—and the former president himself—[26] revised the texts of speeches from the week of September 11 many times with an eye to the larger linguistic history of presidential rhetoric.[27] The first presidential speech delivered after September 11 opens with several sentences marked by asyndeton, the omission of conjunctions for dramatic effect. The speech jars the reader with a barrage of uncoordinated ideas and images: "Good evening. Today, our fellow citizens, our way of life, our very freedom came under attack in a series of deliberate and deadly terrorist acts. The victims were in airplanes, or in their offices; secretaries, businessmen and women, military and federal workers; moms and dads, friends and neighbors. Thousands of lives were suddenly ended by evil, despicable acts of terror."[28] Later speeches use polysyndeton, or the conscious use of conjunctions, to elongate sentence rhythms and create stately rhetoric appropriate to national mourning: "Grief and tragedy and hatred are only for a time. Goodness, remembrance, and love have no end. And the Lord of life holds all who die, and all who mourn."[29]

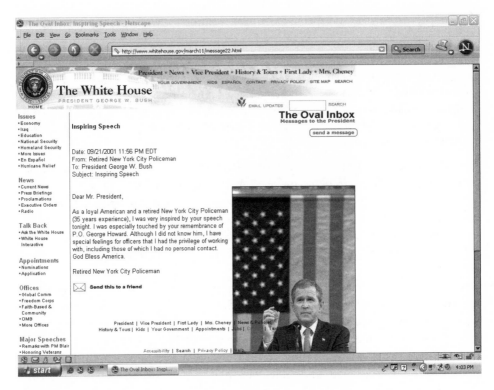

Figure 4.2
White House website with oratorical display.

Although they are preserved years later and playable on a computer anywhere, the speeches have a strong temporal and spatial orientation. Speeches of September 11 and 17 begin with "Today." By the second sentence, the speeches in the National Cathedral and before Congress also have oriented themselves in time: "today" and "tonight" respectively. This sense of rhetorical occasion, what the Greeks called *kairos*, has a particular role in presidential oratory that is aimed at times of disaster.[30] According to the *New York Times*, elements of highly situated oratory from World War II statesmen like Franklin Delano Roosevelt and Winston Churchill played a role in the composition of the September speeches.[31] The place is also important: the Oval Office, the South Lawn, the National Cathedral, the chambers of Congress. Each location orients the president's rhetoric for his webcast presentation either with or without audience reaction.

Students with access to both the "script" and the "performance" available on the website viewed the process of composition and rehearsal as integral to the delivery of presidential oratory. With both text and video available, they noticed that the president may have mischosen a preposition in his first speech with his "daring/caring" parallelism at the moment of performance, since the "caring *of* strangers and neighbors" made more grammatical sense to them than the "caring for strangers and neighbors." They also noticed a hitch in the opening of his speech at the National Cathedral, as he paused against his speech rhythms, seemingly to find his place in the text.

To use the terminology of Aristotle's *Rhetoric*, which the students learned in the course of the seminar, the projected character or ethos of a successful website president both supports and subverts the integrity of the speaking self as the center of discourse. In his speech of September 20, the president announces his oratory as simultaneously exceptional and superfluous: "In the normal course of events, presidents come to this chamber to report on the state of the Union. Tonight, no such report is needed. It has already been delivered by the American people."[32] Viewed from the desktop, the perspective of the American people, who are assumed to be creating public oratory, see a president who is as intimately close as a YouTube confidante or as distant as a public figure seen on a video clip from an online news source.

Presidential rhetoric about September 11 on the whitehouse.gov website also displays certain assumptions about the sympathies of the audience at home for different classes of economic actors. In his speech on the night of the attack, the president said, "The victims were in airplanes, or in their offices; secretaries, businessmen and women, military and federal workers; moms and dads, friends and neighbors."[33] Although George W. Bush lists "secretaries" before "businessmen and women" and places them in a parallel structure, the social taxonomy that provides his rhetorical context makes clear that these are mutually exclusive groups that demarcate social class. On September 16 the president announced that "tomorrow the good people of America go back to their shops, their fields, American factories, and go back to work." Thus, although the actual victims of the attacks on the World Trade Center were associated with transnational postindustrial capitalism, President Bush draws on images of an earlier economic era by calling Americans back to "shops," "fields," and "factories."[34] The firefighters and police officers who died in the disaster were generally portrayed as classless by virtue of the uniforms they wore.[35]

In the years after September 11, these official video documents of presidential speeches on the Whitehouse.gov site have also fostered debate about whether or not they are the fixed historical artifacts that most viewers would assume them to be. After the 2003 invasion of Iraq, President George W. Bush was filmed giving a speech onboard a military vessel in which a banner reading "Mission Accomplished" was visible overhead. In 2006, as the war in Iraq was losing public confidence, video bloggers argued about whether or not video clips hosted on the official presidential site had been cropped to remove the embarrassing banner.[36] Some compared the seemingly altered footage to Soviet-style revisions of visual history, while others

complained that the office of the executive had been unfairly tarnished by the allega-
tions and that use of a CNN news feed was to blame for the suspicious-looking
awkward framing.

The Hijacking Letter on the FBI Website

It is ironic that some of my own interest in the high-tech rhetoric of September 11
began with a crudely copied handwritten letter on four pages of lined notebook
paper. Like other Americans described in the Pew Report, I was "on alert" and a regular
visitor to sites for online news and websites from government agencies. Two weeks
after the 2001 airplane attacks on the World Trade Center and the Pentagon, the official website for the Federal Bureau of Investigation announced that an incriminating
letter had been discovered in three places: the luggage of alleged pilot and chief plotter
Mohammed Atta, a car rented by some of the suspects found parked at Dulles airport,
and the wreckage of the hijacked plane that crashed in a Pennsylvania field after its
passengers resisted their onboard captors in midair.

The author of the letter was anonymous, although some handwriting analysts subsequently claimed that its lack of punctuation suggested that it had been dictated to
another person and that its Arabic characters were likely produced by a female scribe,
perhaps one with limited education.[37] According to a translation published in the
New York Times, the "hijacking letter" is also full of positive affirmations. Its intended
reader is instructed to be "patient," "optimistic," "happy," "calm," "assured," and
"confident." The letter advises its readers to embrace passivity, obedience, love and
charity toward their "brothers" in the mission, to avoid revenge as a motive for action,
and to deny aggressive self-interest. The writer often uses the language of nonviolence
in the context of particular instructions for violence: "If you slaughter, do not cause
the discomfort of those you are killing, because this is one of the practices of the
prophet, peace be upon him."[38]

Official U.S. rhetoric often obliquely criticizes cultures within the Islamic world by
focusing on issues of literacy.[39] There is some latent pseudo-Platonism in many of these
implied critiques, since cultural forms of textual practices related to rote memorization
of the Qur'an are subtly disparaged in comparison to literacy practices in the United
States.[40] Plato's dialogue *Phaedrus*, which focuses on the limitations of writing as a
technological innovation, describes written text as a mere mnemonic tool that relies
on external marks to create a lifeless facsimile of living speech. Plato asserts that such
writing serves as a device not for memory but for "reminder" and thus encourages
forgetting rather than remembrance.[41] In my reading of the hijacking letter, I found
Plato's characterization of written text as a recipe for reminder came almost immediately to mind, because the letter is largely a list of instructions and reminders in order
to implement an inventory of preparatory tasks. In the translation of the letter that

Figure 4.3
FBI website with announcement of the "Hijacking Letter."

appeared in the *New York Times*, the hijackers were explicitly instructed to "remember" nineteen separate times and to "remind" themselves four additional times.

The letter also conspicuously lacks many features of style associated with the grandiloquence of public oratory. It does not participate in discourses about just warfare or jihad aimed at a global audience.[42] Instead, it provides inspirational scriptures for an individual facing death, as well as a numerically superior enemy, with phrases like "a large band have won over a small band" and "Satan scares his followers" and "Do not think that those who died for the sake of God are dead."[43] It invites the reader to consider theological questions but only in the context of private subjectivity. The letter asks, "Did you think you could go to heaven before God knows whom amongst you have fought for Him and are patient? . . . Did you think that He created you for no reason?"[44]

The logic of the hijackers' letter initially puzzled many Americans. The media widely labeled it a "suicide letter," although the emphasis of the text was clearly focused on martyrdom rather than suicide. Within days of the attacks, however, public intellectuals were producing essays—many of which were disseminated online—that questioned American unwillingness to engage in similar discourses about sacrifice. As Slavoj Žižek wrote: "Witness the surprise of the average American: 'How is it possible that these people display and practice such a disregard for their own lives?' Is the obverse of this surprise not the rather sad fact that we, in the First World countries, find it more and more difficult even to imagine a public or universal cause for which one would be ready to sacrifice one's life?"[45] Writing in the *Washington Post*, Salman Rushdie went so far as to suggest an entire inventory of possible causes worth dying for:

The fundamentalist seeks to bring down a great deal more than buildings. Such people are against, to offer just a brief list, freedom of speech, a multi-party political system, universal adult suffrage, accountable government, Jews, homosexuals, women's rights, pluralism, secularism, short skirts, dancing, beardlessness, evolution theory, sex . . . What will we risk our lives to defend? Can we unanimously concur that all the items in the above list—yes, even the short skirts and dancing—are worth dying for?[46]

What Stanley Fish has described as a "strange trio" of public pundits—Bill Maher, Dinesh D'Souza, and Susan Sontag—all faced widespread condemnation for arguing that the hijackers were hardly "cowardly," as they had been presented in the mainstream media.[47] Rushdie, asserting the ethos of a fellow "New Yorker" rather than former *fatwa* target in his opinion piece, similarly suggests that it is "we" Americans who are the cowardly ones.

In contrast to Rushdie's call for "unanimous" consensus from an open democratic forum that will answer his rhetorical questions with its public voice, the hijacking letter continues to be a private document, even after publication of the official 9/11 Commission Report seemed to explain the terrorists' other recruitment techniques and hijacking procedures.[48] Information about the letter's authorship and the closed cultural context of the terrorist cell in which it was produced remains sketchy. Long after its initial discovery, questions have been raised about precisely when all the September 11 terrorists were even aware that they would not personally survive the mission.[49] Thus this particular set of instructions in the hijacking letter may have had an even more select audience in a cell within the cell.

Nonetheless, this letter can be read in the context of many other public documents that were available on the Internet during the same period: speeches, transcripts of press conferences, official leaflets, video presentations, photo essays, and brochures. Although many of these documents were not born digital, as objects of discourse they became accessible to large numbers of U.S. citizens and foreign nationals via official sites on the World Wide Web. Many of these documents were not intended for the eyes of U.S. audiences. For example, the leaflets dropped on Afghanistan were nevertheless available on the Centcom website. In some cases, print copies of documents were actually barred from distribution in the United States, since State Department products intended for foreign audiences are explicitly contraband under the Smith-Mundt Act of 1948.[50] In this ironic inversion of the current copyright wars,[51] authorized print was actually forbidden and virtual replication was facilitated by federal laws that were enforced within the borders of the United States.

"Defeating Terror, Defending Freedom" and a Transcript of Charlotte Beers from the State Department Website Aimed at Audiences Abroad

Near the end of the course, my students watched "Defeating Terror, Defending Freedom," a short film in Flash and Quicktime formats that was posted on the International Information Programs website for the U.S. Department of State. In the visual narrative, which moved quickly over key events, tension seemed to build, climax, and be resolved. The sequence moved from attacks abroad to attacks at home to international reaction to the history of the conspiracy and the case against Bin Laden to diplomatic coalition building to the beginning of the bombing campaign, and finally to a photograph of clasped hands of many colors. Students observed that the film used appeals to pathos with great success. The film's dramatic music crescendoed at key moments. Slides and text emphasized the colors red, black, and white. Scenes cut rapidly back and forth between images of the physical destruction of civilian and military edifices and corresponding scenes of victimization: emergency personnel treating injured people or funerals for fallen comrades. Short excerpts from speeches by George W. Bush and Tony Blair punctuated the action. What is extraordinary about the depiction of the enemy in "Defeating Terror, Defending Freedom" is his absence. The crimes depicted are all committed by a largely unseen and faceless opponent—an absolute Other—who serves as a cipher in the film's narrative.

The film had been introduced to the public by Undersecretary of State for Public Diplomacy and Public Affairs Charlotte Beers at a press conference two months after the attacks. It represents part of a concerted campaign toward what has become known as the "new public diplomacy," in which techniques specifically derived from contemporary advertising and marketing industrial models are to be used in what is assumed to be the public interest.[52] Along with social marketing, risk communication, and institutional branding, public diplomacy represents a new form of twenty-first century public rhetoric, which is often conveyed via new digital media. The transcript of the press conference, which was available online at the State Department website (figure 4.4), announces the launch of a new publicity campaign. Beers explains one form of this new public diplomacy pitch, which will be disseminated through the Internet: "We also have a sort of a musical version of what has happened here, not that it's a subject worth music. It's just that you need to use pictures and music and tone."[53] Beers presents what is literally a "melodrama" in the sense of a theatrical presentation

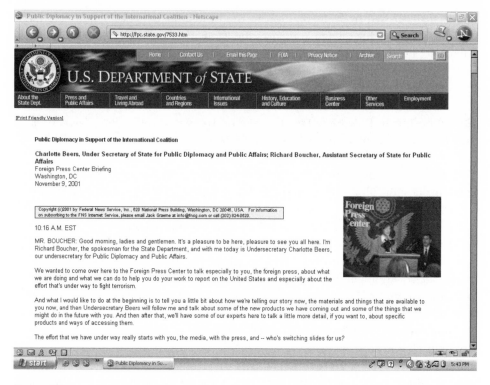

Figure 4.4
Press conference with Charlotte Beers on the State Department website.

with music that exploits temporal disjunctions of asynchrony (in which it is too late to foil the previous plans of the terrorists) to effect maximum emotional impact on an empathetic audience.[54]

The students in my seminar responded very cynically to the melodramatic aspects of "Defeating Terror, Defending Freedom." They immediately noticed that Al Qaeda targets were always shown with rubble and bloodied victims, but U.S. military operations in Afghanistan were symbolized by a sanitized single flare in the night sky. They also observed a possibly strategic emphasis on portraying victims of color in the presentation of attacks abroad. For example, the attack on the USS *Cole* is represented in the film by a close-up of the tear-stained face of an African-American boy who is shown over the triangle of a folded American flag.

The visual rhetoric of "Defeating Terror, Defending Freedom" provides yet another representation of an asymmetrical binary (with an obviously superior "Freedom" pitted against "Terror") invoking Samuel Huntington's paradigm of a post-Cold War "Clash of Civilizations." Despite its title, Huntington's 1993 article in *Foreign Affairs* makes clear that the "civilization" of the Islamic world is at best inferior and at worst a threat to institutions of the developed world. Indirect references to Huntington's "clash" frequently appear in contemporaneous presidential speeches and statements as well. For example, in his speech of September 20, the president announces the terms of the contest: "This is the world's fight. This is civilization's fight. This is the fight of all who believe in progress and pluralism, tolerance and freedom."[55] In the same speech, the larger audience that the president addresses via television is instructed to choose between sides that have been presented as polar opposites: "Every nation, in every region, now has a decision to make. Either you are with us, or you are with the terrorists."[56] The appeal of structuring an argument logically along lines of mutual exclusivity by orientation to "civilized" or "barbarian" ideology creates instant audience identification and a simple trajectory of analogical and causal reasoning. The terms "civilized" or "civilization" were also part of the general lexicon of the executive branch: according to the White House website, the word "civilization" appears 183 times in presidential and vice presidential speeches from the period.[57] For example, on September 15 the president said "I think every civilized nation in the world recognizes that this was an assault not just against the United States, but against civilization."[58]

In those same remarks, the president contends that a "group of barbarians" has declared war on the United States. The following day the president made his now famous gaffe in which he declared: "We haven't seen this kind of barbarism in a long period of time. . . . This *crusade* [author's emphasis], this war on terrorism is going to take a while."[59] Of course, in the era of rapid communication, Osama bin Laden immediately seized on this rhetorical pratfall as an apparent admission of an East/West divide and repeated the words "crusade" or "crusader" as representative of official U.S. ideology in videotaped statements broadcast on Al Jazeera for months afterwards.[60] As a frequent user of video technologies that were first distributed through exchanges of material objects across a network of sympathizers, bin Laden carefully managed a rhetorical persona that both explicated and parodied this East/West dichotomy.[61] In contrast, Edward Said saw, latent in the government's "clash of civilizations" ideology, a more complicated form of Orientalism that revives linguistic artifacts of mutual cultural suspicion from a now-defunct Cold War.[62]

Not all government entities present statements on the World Wide Web that assume that there exists a fundamental divide in the global audience between competing and mutually exclusive ideologies. Although Charlotte Beers of the State Department oversaw the production of "Defeating Terror, Defending Freedom" and was responsible for its bifurcated worldview, she also addressed the world audience as a unified whole in her public statements. In the news conference in which she provides the overview of her new U.S. public relations effort, she assumes certain universals in rhetorical appeal. Much of her discourse seems to be based on truisms of market research and audience analysis by the advertising industry and the associated premises about the predictability of the global consumer's desires. As former advertising executive Beers argues, the "brands" presented include American statesmen: "And 'poster man'—well, you know, in a way, our poster people are President Bush and Secretary Powell, whom I think are pretty inspiring symbols of the brand, the United States."[63]

The radical commodification that Beers presents obliterates cultural differences between "West" and "East." Her tropes about the statistical growth of Islam draw on her corporate background in market-oriented rhetoric so that she seems to conflate sacred and secular discourse in the transcript available on the State Department website:

Their conversion rate is astonishing—a 30 percent conversion in each year is about the fastest growing religion in this country, and a good number for any sales team. I thought this was wonderful—McDonald's has figured out how important this is, and they've already put together foods that are appropriate for the Muslim community.... Here's a sales curve any corporation would envy. These are the percent of mosques founded in the US over the last few years.[64]

Rather than present *Jihad vs. McWorld* in agonistic tension,[65] Beers interprets the rise of Islam in America as a corporate success story.

Yet Beers' appeal to self-interested logic can also be modified by the appeal to pathos in "putting forward" other equally commodified "values" of the United States.

One of the things that strikes me is that as essential as our offices are, our policy statements, our people who speak every day in behalf of the United States policies, these tend to be communications that are extremely reasoned and rational, and yet we know that much of the other side of this argument is intensely emotional and comes from a very different place than rationality and reason. I think one of the things that means is that we have to put forward something we might have all taken for granted, which is the US values. They're just as important as our policies.[66]

Rather than present a "clash of civilizations," Beers assumes that the global audience is choosing between two packages of associated "values" and "policies," based on a judgment of their intellectual and emotional merits. Although the "other side of the argument" is presented as inherently less rational, it is legitimated to the extent that it has located rhetorical appeals to emotion worth appropriating.

When literary and legal scholar Stanley Fish decided to answer accusations that postmodernist thinkers were unresponsive to the cataclysmic events of September 11 and perhaps even responsible for them, he affirmed his own principles of enlightened relativism. Like Beers, he emphasized shared virtues and values (like "justice," "rationality," and "courage") while also noting—as Beers was perhaps unable to—that "the invocation of universals doesn't settle disputes, but extends them."[67] Fish contended that an equitable definition of these abstract terms by an impartial arbiter is an epistemological impossibility. In other words, "justice," as defined by what Beers calls "the other side," is a fundamentally different entity from the definition of "justice" put forward by her own State Department, since according to Fish there are no truly culturally or linguistically disinterested parties.

"Defeating Terror, Defending Freedom" is no longer available on the State Department website, and Beers herself disappeared from the diplomatic scene after she failed to buy sufficient airtime in Islamic countries for her "Shared Values" documentaries about American life, which were designed to run on television worldwide during Ramadan.[68] Compared to state-run television, the Internet offered more porous national borders for State Department messages, and local embassies and news services often maintained mirror sites that replicated content. Yet Beers herself may have been overly optimistic at her first news conference when she maintained, despite objections from reporters about obstacles posed in developing countries by the digital divide, that her projects would be widely publicized by Internet marketing through "banner ads on other websites" and links on other webpages.[69] "Defeating Terror, Defending Freedom" also became anachronistic as the war with Iraq supplanted the war with Afghanistan.

I asked my students who they believed the intended audience for "Defeating Terror, Defending Freedom" would be. Students responded that they believed that the film was intended for a viewer from abroad, because many of the images involved mourning in other countries and meetings of U.S. administration officials with foreign leaders. But students were skeptical that this film might persuade potential jihadists or their allies. The reason for their assertions had nothing to do with the unshakability of conviction that has been associated with the theology or political ideology of the enemies of the United States. Rather, they doubted that potential terrorists would have Flash-compatible computers or high-speed Internet connections. Like the reporters who questioned Beers, they argued that the assumed audience for this film could not possibly live in a third-world environment, which they associated with primitive technologies. However, the actual plotters of September 11 were in many ways like my affluent University of California undergraduates. Like them, many of the hijackers were the college-educated offspring of families from the affluent professional classes. Like my students, many of them almost certainly had access to high-speed Internet connections.[70] Consequently, Beers' State Department developed materials aimed at this literate and technologically adept Islamic audience.

Leaflets to Afghanistan at the Centcom Site

The number of times that rhetoric has been explicitly referred to in the news media as a feature of political discourse has increased exponentially since September 11. Texts like *Collateral Language* and *War of Words* draw attention to the rhetorical dimension of these recent political events. The specific rhetoric of our aerial address to the people of Afghanistan functions around some of the same tropes of traditional first-world and third-world class oppositions that my students took for granted. Leaflets dropped by the U.S. military in Afghanistan as part of their psychological operations campaign emphasize the crudest possible presentation of capitalist values in their exhortation to "get wealth and power beyond your dreams," while also positing a precapitalist interpretive horizon for any potential recipient in Afghanistan. These flyers assume that the recipients would not understand the value of "millions of dollars," which could benefit the backward populace of a "village" or "tribe" with "livestock," "doctors," and "school books." Other flyers on the Centcom site emphasize the class gulf between the assumed recipient, who could potentially die in the battlefields wearing rags, and the Westernized, affluent Osama bin Laden in a white business suit. Bin Laden, the Centcom flyers argue, perpetuates the class structures of the capitalism that he claims to abhor.

The image of the "foreigner" or "stranger" is also central to the leaflets dropped in Afghanistan. However the U.S. message about how foreigners should be treated is often contradictory, perhaps in order to exploit both native hospitality and xenophobia. Early leaflets announce that "the partnership of nations is here to help" and show a friendly foreigner with a light-skinned hand grasping the darker hand assumed to be like that of the presumed audience.

FRONT

GET WEALTH AND
POWER BEYOND
YOUR DREAMS -
HELP THE ANTI-
TALIBAN FORCE
RID AFGHANISTAN
OF MURDERERS
AND TERRORISTS

TF11-RP09

BACK

YOU CAN RECEIVE MILLIONS OF DOLLARS
FOR HELPING THE ANTI-TAILBAN FORCE
CATCH AL-QAIDA AND TALIBAN MURDERERS
THIS IS ENOUGH MONEY TO TAKE CARE OF
YOUR FAMILY, YOUR VILLAGE, YOUR TRIBE
FOR THE REST OF YOUR LIFE -
PAY FOR LIVESTOCK AND DOCTORS
AND SCHOOL BOOKS AND HOUSING FOR
ALL YOUR PEOPLE

Figure 4.5
"Wealth and Power" leaflet from Centcom website.

Such early images stressed the role of the friendly foreigner, like this flyer in which a soldier from the "West"—in a uniform without the insignia of any particular country—is shown shaking hands with a traditionally clad Afghan man. The light blue of the soldier's camouflage uniform suggests the colors of a United Nations peace-keeping force and reflects the design of the surrounding landscape. The rhetoric of the flyer uses two terms that are central to the idiom of the American address to Afghanistan: "Nation" and "People." In this case the appeal is to the people of Afghanistan from a collective of nations.

Later leaflets encourage the Afghan people to drive Taliban-supported foreigners from their lands and assert nation-building practices without external intervention. In this leaflet, gender and nation are explicitly connected, although in modes unlike those promulgated by Western liberalism on other U.S. government websites. "Your women and children" have a "future" and yet belong to the presumed audience like chattel.

FRONT

BACK

The Partnership of Nations is here to assist the People of Afghanistan

Figure 4.6
"Partnership of Nations" leaflet from Centcom website.

FRONT

BACK

Figure 4.7
"Drive out the Foreign Terrorists" leaflet from Centcom website.

Because most of the victims in the World Trade Center attack were male, female victimization was de-emphasized in the U.S. media. In contrast, leaflets dropped on Afghanistan repeatedly emphasize the vulnerability of women and children. In one flyer women and children shield Al Qaeda from the forces of just retribution; in another they are shown unshielded from the wrath of pro-Taliban misogyny.

These leaflets specifically emphasized the need to expel external cultural influences. In another example, Osama bin Laden, who is shown wearing headgear that identifies him as a Saudi, is portrayed as a dog owner or a chess master. Still other leaflets served to clarify the distinction between "good" foreigners and "bad" foreigners. Although the message is printed in the national colors of the flag of Afghanistan, the bags of food in the front central image are printed in red, white, and blue with "USA" clearly visible as a national brand.

Race also plays a powerful role in the rhetoric of post-September 11 leaflets on the Centcom site. In the leaflets dropped by U.S. Armed Forces in Afghanistan, the visual motif of the lighter hand grasping the darker hand is repeated over and over again. One leaflet shows a "typical" American family of Anglo-Saxon descent. Three of the

FRONT

BACK

Figure 4.8
Leaflet depicting U.S. aid from Centcom website.

four family members wear white, and the male members of the family wear clothes reminiscent of tennis whites. Students in my seminar howled with laughter when they saw this picture. This kind of family is hardly "typical" in Southern California, and Asian students are a particularly large demographic segment of the U.C. Irvine campus, where over 50 percent of freshmen come from homes in which a language other than English is spoken.

Nation-building practices are also represented metaphorically in the Centcom leaflets. In one image, builders from three different ethnic groups cooperate to erect a communal building. In another leaflet, the national colors are presented separately as different colored threads to be woven into a single, coherent rug. In another example from the Centcom site, printed in the Afghan national colors, the "world" is shown with a lighter hand clasping the darker hand of the country of Afghanistan. The exact

FRONT

BACK

Figure 4.9
"FRIENDSHIP" leaflet from Centcom website.

hemisphere of the "world" is unclear, so that north/south or east/west orientations remain ambiguous. In this leaflet both hands, presumably each from an Afghan citizen, are shown as dark. Afghan ethnic differences are not translated into racial differences in the flyers.

The Intenet makes the dissemination of print ephemera accessible beyond the physical landscape for which these messages are intended. This contextual slippage exposes certain tensions in message management by government agencies and how certain populations are assumed to be pre-technological and responsive to other kinds of logics of gender, race, class, and nationality from those promulgated by the State Department's public diplomacy efforts.

"Muslim Life in America" on the State Department Website

"Muslim Life in America," another project from Beers' post-September 11 publicity efforts, presents a very different portrait of Americans in their daily lives. Unlike the Anglo-Saxon prototypes depicted on the Centcom flyers, "Muslim Life in America"

Figure 4.10
"Muslim Life in America" website from the State Department.

shows considerable racial and ethnic diversity in the U.S. population. The State Department's depiction of the lives of followers of Islam in the United States focuses on explicitly "mainstream" discourses and communities, with an emphasis on conventional units of association in families, communities, schools, and businesses.

The American public landscape of "Muslim Life in America" also shows off multiculturalism in the man-made environment. For example, mosques are presented as part of the U.S. national architecture.[71]

"Muslim Life in America" continues to be posted on the State Department website, although it is available in surprisingly few languages for a publication intended for a multilingual world.[72] The multiracial character of the American people was also presented in the State Department's now-defunct webpages on "Faces of Islam." The racial diversity of both Islam and America was graphically displayed in "Faces of Islam," but many of the images actually came from corporate image banks and were ethnic representations designed for advertising or promotional purposes. The headshots largely showed Muslim U.S. residents in the context of educational activities. In other places

Figure 4.11
Page of mosques from "Muslim Life in America."

on the site, Islamic scholars supported the U.S. position on September 11 terrorism, so this emphasis on activities of scholarship from primary school to university was given a mainstream political dimension. Significantly, women's faces were uncovered in all but one of the photographs, so that information about gender norms in the United States was also disseminated.

Al Jazeera Transcripts on the Defense Department Website

There is a surprisingly intimate relationship between U.S. government websites and the Al Jazeera satellite channel, which has been accused of jihadist sympathies by those same federal agencies. Transcripts of interviews of prominent government officials by the contentious Qatar-based Al Jazeera television network are often posted on federal government websites. For example, two interviews with Condoleeza Rice have appeared on the White House website, and eighteen separate transcripts of full-length exclusive Al Jazeera interviews—with U.S. diplomats like Colin Powell, Richard

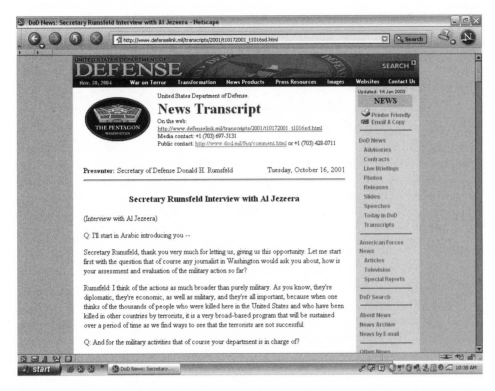

Figure 4.12
Transcript of interview with Donald Rumsfeld on the Department of Defense website.

Armitage, and Christopher Ross—have appeared on the State Department website. Even the transcript of a confrontational interview with Donald Rumsfeld, the combative U.S. Secretary of Defense, was archived on the Department of Defense website alongside optimistic press releases and slideshows with sanctioned content, despite the fact that commentary from the Al Jazeera interviewer critical of U.S. foreign policy occupies a considerable portion of this virtual real estate.

I would argue that this particular Rumsfeld interview dramatizes pressures on the dichotomy between the domestic and the geopolitical created by a particular rhetorical situation. In the interview, which would logically be intended for an Arabic-speaking public in the Middle East, Rumsfeld mentions his wife two times in discursive situations that verge on the bizarre. To the interviewer, in response to a question about "doves" and "hawks" in the U.S. administration, Rumsfeld says, "I work with Colin Powell every day. We have views that are very similar on most things. We differ from time to time, but then I differ from time to time with my wife on various issues, so that doesn't mean much."[73] Rumsfeld compares Secretary of State Colin Powell to his wife, so that Powell is put in a feminized position by this comparison (as a "dove" to Rumsfeld's "hawk"), while Rumsfeld's masculinity is also subverted by the egalitarian presentation of his spouse as an oppositional figure with whom he differs "from time to time."

In the second case, Rumsfeld contrasts the press's opinion of him as a "bad guy" in the political context of Afghanistan and the Middle East with the supposedly less-biased opinion of his family.

I don't know, there's something about the press that they like to get up in the morning and create conflict between people. It's apparently a lot easier for people in the media to write about personalities than it is about concepts and strategies and direction. If you personalize a thing into good guys and bad guys, it's an easier story, I suppose, for a journalist, but it's not terribly useful. I've been kind of amused by it all from time to time, and my wife and children know I'm basically a nice person.[74]

In this snippet of the interview, Rumsfeld defends himself as a "nice person" and suggests that his wife and children would testify to the goodness of his character. In both cases, Rumsfeld introduces his wife as a figure of either potential rhetorical opposition or corroborative testimony, yet in this interview she is a silent partner who is never quoted in her own words or able to enter the public sphere with explicit opinions worth citing.[75] This insertion of elements of the domestic into geopolitical discourses humanizes Rumsfeld, but these comments also seem to suggest an off-the-record quality that appears incongruous on an official government website. At the very end of the transcript, when asked for concluding remarks, Rumsfeld says he is "sweet and loveable." After both men laugh, the interviewer jokes about Rumsfeld's recurring theme: "We will interview Mrs. Rumsfeld to get her version." On the DoD website this strange vignette about matrimonial life is linked with the same authority as a formal policy announcement about troop strength or strategic offensives in major cities.

Rewards for Justice

The emphasis on the role of the small donor in large web-based fund-raising campaigns to aid rescue workers and other victims of the September 11 attacks fosters the impression of a culture in which the individual's social and economic contributions are not structured primarily by class differentiation.[76] This emphasis is even taken to children with the "Dollars to Afghanistan" program from the White House website, which appeals to young Americans' collective identity. Similarly, the State Department-sponsored "Rewards for Justice" site at first used many of the tropes of the disaster relief donation site by valuing the contributions of the individual to the project of national surveillance. Although it was later reorganized as a collection of virtual wanted posters, which clearly reference a form of traditional print ephemera, the

"Rewards for Justice" website initially had a more ambitious aim of providing instruction to promulgate a new culture that could capitalize on distributed media models of vigilance and surveillance among everyday citizens. Groups of potential patriotic informants were oriented along the right navigation in ways that emphasized American social and spatial mobility, such as "commuter" or "frequent traveler."[77]

The obscene inverse of U.S. government websites that spotlight terrorist hunting can be seen in websites designed by the terrorists themselves. Housed on offshore servers and proxied by anonymizing servers, jihadist websites are hard to trace but easily accessible, and their existence is further publicized by news outlets from the United States and abroad. Since the beheading of journalist Daniel Pearl, these websites have sometimes served as graphic desktop-sized theaters of cruelty in which gruesome executions are featured in gory detail not seen perhaps since the images of decapitation in the mass media of the French Revolution. Despite their generally crude web design, video files of beheadings sometimes show considerable editing and postproduction work. For example, one video showing Daniel Pearl's last moments provides a frame with an elaborate montage of Israeli tanks, so that the execution in the center of the user's screen is placed in a specific context of visual rhetoric and political history.[78]

Terrorism specialists have long argued that television has uniquely contributed to stateless combatants' tactical shift from rural guerrilla campaigns to spectacles of urban terrorism that afford them greater publicity, and have even claimed that terrorism and the network news media exist in a mutually beneficial symbiotic relationship.[79] As terrorist rhetoric becomes increasingly adapted to the distributed model of communication predicated by the Internet, however, it is worth considering how terrorism itself will change in response. Terrorist tactics, targets, and visual and verbal rhetoric will inevitably shift. Already jihadists are relying increasingly on the intimate space of the safe house as a backdrop for performing acts of extreme violence, just as the adult entertainment industry first discovered that many web users had a visual compulsion to consume "amateur" content shot in everyday domestic spaces.

In light of the departure of Charlotte Beers, it would seem that the United States' own use of networked digital media to promote a counterterrorist ideology abroad has been largely unsuccessful. At home, the self-aggrandizing Internet displays of U.S. patriotism that the Pew Report describes do little to affect world opinion, particularly since these patriotic displays rely on context-specific national symbols and icons with little global appeal.

It could be argued that my selection of digital ephemera about September 11 from government websites is far from representative and that inappropriately racist, sexist, or commercial messages are generally excluded from the U.S. government agencies' mainstream web façades. Indeed, based on the distance of many of these documents from home pages or essential navigation, it would seem that government web designers already archive this kind of potentially embarrassing political content so it can be accessed as part of the public record without being showcased as authoritative federal rhetoric. Yet with commercial search engines providing the main access to webpages on government sites, it is difficult to control how U.S. policy makers' discourse is seen by computer users at home and abroad, even though some government websites now contain code that makes them invisible to Google. By and large, from any given keyword search, it is hard to predict which face of e-government will appear when visual artifacts of publicity and oratorical performances by officials are so easy to access, review, and replay.

5 Power Points: The Virtual State and Its Discontents

In the "Medic Training" unit of the military-funded army recruitment videogame *America's Army*, the player must watch three different PowerPoint lectures, after which he or she must pass multiple-choice tests, which are based on the actual examinations given in order to earn a basic certification credential in the real army. Players in the 3-D environment of this "first-person-mission" game, so called because army officials didn't want it labeled as a "first-person-shooter," must sit attentively behind long faux wood-grain tables in office chairs while still wearing their battlefield digital camouflage, and listen as speakers at a podium deliver detailed talks on "Airway Management," how to "Control Bleeding," and methods to "Treat Shock," which are accompanied by 2-D electronic slideshows transported into the game environment from the rhetorical conventions of corporate America.[1]

It certainly is not the only example of PowerPoint in the realm of play associated with virtual worlds and the 3-D avatars that inhabit them. As part of their community membership in the online virtual world *Second Life*, some residents share their advice in Internet forums about how to give effective PowerPoint presentations in this computer-generated environment, even though their prospective audience may include drag queens, mobsters, nudists, food items, and extraterrestrial life-forms.[2]

As an electronic genre, Microsoft's prepackaged presentation software PowerPoint has generated considerable ridicule as an object of satire in mainstream culture. A video remix of speech from the movie *Star Wars*, in which rebel spaceship pilots in the Resistance who are fighting the fascistic intergalactic Empire are briefed on plans for the dramatic attack on the ominous Death Star battle station, parodies the original by remaking it with humorous bullet points, inserted arrows, and diagrams. The signature mystical slogan and benediction of religious and cultural community in the *Star Wars* films, "May the Force be with you,"—which has had such power in the participatory culture of fan communities involved in the media franchise—becomes a series of nested bullet points in which "The Force," "with you," and "hopefully" are stacked in decreasing font size.[3] Like the recruits in *America's Army*, the members of the audience of fighters in the parody film sit in rows in uniform and communicate varying levels of attention to the presentation through an assortment of postures of listening.

It would be difficult to write a book about digital rhetoric and political life without mentioning PowerPoint, given its major role in policy briefings and public statements, and yet it is one of the most commonly castigated genres associated with electronic communication. Perhaps part of the general derision about PowerPoint has to do with the fact that this software assumes the presence of the speaker rather than his or her absence, and thus it is fundamentally unlike other electronic genres in that it is founded on an assumed form of rhetorical redundancy, particularly if the speaker reads aloud the words already printed on the preprepared slides.

In his essay on "The Cognitive Style of PowerPoint," information designer Edward Tufte complains that the medium encourages totalitarian cultural practices because it distorts important public messages and recasts them as garbled Orwellian NewSpeak. Tufte makes this point visually with the poster that also serves as the cover of his essay, which shows an obedient Stalinist audience lined up in formation on a parade ground before a monumental sculpture in an illustration punctuated with thought balloons such as "FOR RE-EDUCATION CAMPAIGNS NOTHING IS BETTER THAN THE AUTO-CONTENT WIZARD!" and "THERE'S NO BULLET LIST LIKE STALIN'S BULLET LIST."[4] Tufte's booklet also features an actual mock-up of a jar of "PowerPoint Phluff," which, like Richard Lanham's opposition of "fluff" and "stuff," points to an economics of limited attention for new media objects.[5] In addition to claiming that PowerPoint's style sheets disable critical thinking, Tufte also argues that PowerPoint is fundamentally bad information design that partially explains the crash of the space shuttle *Columbia* and other mistakes by government officials who depend upon this stilted genre to communicate information that is critical to policy decisions.[6] In his precursor essay "PowerPoint is Evil," Tufte complains that the software scrambles numeracy as well as literacy by obscuring the "statistical integrity and reasoning" that a traditional table can provide.[7] By 2006, Tufte was arguing that PowerPoint was also worthy of suspicion because of the ways that it expresses the corporate ideology of the Microsoft corporation.

The metaphor for PowerPoint is *the software corporation itself*. To describe a software house is to describe the PP cognitive style: a big bureaucracy engaged in *computer programming* (deep hierarchical structures, relentlessly sequential, nested, one-short-line-at-a-time) and in *marketing* (advocacy not analysis, more style than substance, misdirection, slogan thinking, fast pace, branding, exaggerated claims, marketplace ethics) [emphasis in the original].[8]

Citing "Conway's Law," Tufte argues that corporations produce designs that inevitably copy the structures of the organization's communication systems.

Among the electronic slideshows that Tufte includes in his "Cognitive Style" booklet is former U.S. Secretary of State Colin Powell's "Iraq: Failing to Disarm" speech, which was delivered to the Security Council of the United Nations on February 5, 2003. Powell's presentation, which makes the argument that Iraq is hiding weapons of mass destruction contrary to the conditions of UN resolutions, also implicitly makes the case that any subsequent invasion of the country would be justified. Of course, no such weapons were ever found during Operation Iraqi Freedom, so in retrospect Powell's presentation seems to be a very elaborate political fiction with little value as meaningful risk communication. Now archived at the website of the U.S. Department of State, the slideshow begins with transcripts of suspicious telephone calls made by Iraqi military personnel. Then it shows a series of otherwise ambiguous aerial photographs to which yellow labels have been affixed to identify irregularities. The slides that follow show computer-generated images of trucks alleged to contain components for biological weapons. For this part of Powell's presentation, digital artists created realistic renderings—complete with shading and shine effects—with cutaway 3-D views to show the incriminating contents alleged to be inside the vehicles. Then the PowerPoint slides return to aerial photographs and telephone transcripts before a section on "Delivery Systems," which emphasizes maps showing zones of potential contamination and violations of the no-fly zone that had been imposed on the country. Near the end of his talk, slides display several genealogical charts showing the relationships between suspected terrorists that all connect back to filiations with Jordanian Abu Musab al-Zarqawi, an acknowledged Al Qaeda operative. Concluding sections on "Nuclear Systems" and "Human Rights Violations" were represented by little more than headings since Powell did not have photographs or diagrams to bolster his case in these sections. Unlike other PowerPoint presentations produced by the Bush administration during that era, there were no numerical representations of large datasets in formats such as bar charts or pie graphs. In the same speech, Powell also famously used content seemingly plagiarized from a Middle East policy journal without attribution,[9] but the borrowed policy analysis is not visually represented in his final selection of slides.

Software executive Mark Bernstein has pointed to how the "simple talking points and simple beliefs" that are particularly well suited to PowerPoint contributed to the disastrous occupation of Iraq under the Coalition Provisional Authority. In "Unlinked and Entangled: How Codex Technology and Contemporary Critical Theory Contributed to the Breakdown of the Anglo-American Occupation of Iraq," Bernstein also insists that this dependence on electronic slideshow technology shows a particular moment in the history of computational media. As Bernstein claims, "At the heart of the failures lay a distrust of the codex book engendered by the late age of print: a fear that comprehensive analysis is either impossible or leads to policy paralysis, and a belief that the contingency of truth means that a policy can be achieved by proclaiming its success."[10] Bernstein argues that the electronic ephemera related to the occupation show the authorities' failures at "recording everyday

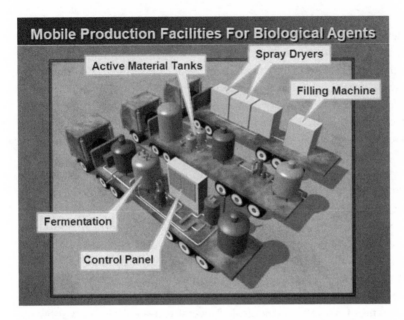

Figure 5.1
Slide from Colin Powell's PowerPoint Presentation before the United Nations.

information" after the invasion of Iraq. In his ideal digital document platform, he asserts that the model of the book should be supplemented with records from the calendar and the ledger to avoid the pitfalls of replicating a scenario in the Joint Task Force that was cynically described by one officer as "fifty-five yahoos with share-ware."[11] Bernstein also points out that post-invasion looting targeted the country's information infrastructure by sacking the Iraqi Ministry of Information along with government computers, archives, records offices, and museums, because the native population could see these informational resources as valuable while their American occupiers could not.

In "Bullet Points over Baghdad," *New York Times* columnist Paul Krugman has complained that White House policy documents were too closely resembling the Microsoft corporate public speaking product.[12] Indeed, the text of the presidential report explaining the "National Strategy for Victory in Iraq" featured bullet points, check marks, and arrowheads, and used boldface, italics, and underlining, often redundantly.[13] The "Victory in Iraq" document would turn out to have an even more complicated electronic rhetorical history. Another *New York Times* reporter discovered, by paying a little attention to the code on the PDF file, that the unacknowledged author of the document was actually an academic expert in public relations rather than military strategy.[14]

- *__The Security Track__* involves carrying out a campaign to defeat the terrorists and neutralize the insurgency, developing Iraqi security forces, and helping the Iraqi government:
  - ✓ *__Clear__* areas of enemy control by remaining on the offensive, killing and capturing enemy fighters and denying them safe-haven;
  - ✓ *__Hold__* areas freed from enemy influence by ensuring that they remain under the control of the Iraqi government with an adequate Iraqi security force presence; and
  - ✓ *__Build__* Iraqi Security Forces and the capacity of local institutions to deliver services, advance the rule of law, and nurture civil society.

- *__The Economic Track__* involves setting the foundation for a sound and self-sustaining economy by helping the Iraqi government:
  - ✓ *__Restore__* Iraq's infrastructure to meet increasing demand and the needs of a growing economy;
  - ✓ *__Reform__* Iraq's economy, which in the past has been shaped by war, dictatorship, and sanctions, so that it can be self-sustaining in the future; and
  - ✓ *__Build__* the capacity of Iraqi institutions to maintain infrastructure, rejoin the international economic community, and improve the general welfare of all Iraqis.

➢ This Strategy is Integrated and its Elements are Mutually Reinforcing
  - Progress in each of the political, security, and economic tracks reinforces progress in the other tracks.
    - ✓ For instance, as the *__political process__* has moved forward, terrorists have become more isolated, leading to more intelligence on security threats from Iraqi citizens, which has led to *__better security__* in previously violent areas, a more stable infrastructure, the prospect of *__economic progress__*, and expanding *__political participation__*.

➢ Victory Will Take Time
  - **Our strategy is working:** Much has been accomplished in Iraq, including the removal of Saddam's tyranny, negotiation of an interim constitution, restoration of full sovereignty, holding of free national elections, formation of an elected government, drafting of a permanent constitution, ratification of that constitution, introduction of a sound currency, gradual restoration of neglected infrastructure, the ongoing training and equipping of Iraqi security forces, and the increasing capability of those forces to take on the terrorists and secure their nation.
  - **Yet many challenges remain:** Iraq is overcoming decades of a vicious tyranny, where governmental authority stemmed solely from fear, terror, and brutality.
    - ✓ It is not realistic to expect a fully functioning democracy, able to defeat its enemies and peacefully reconcile generational grievances, to be in place less than three years after Saddam was finally removed from power.
  - Our comprehensive strategy will help Iraqis overcome remaining challenges, but defeating the multi-headed enemy in Iraq – and ensuring that it cannot threaten Iraq's democratic gains once we leave – requires persistent effort across many fronts.

➢ Our Victory Strategy Is (and Must Be) Conditions Based
  - With resolve, victory will be achieved, although not by a date certain.
    - ✓ No war has ever been won on a timetable and neither will this one.
  - But lack of a timetable does not mean our posture in Iraq (both military and civilian) will remain static over time. As conditions change, our posture will change.
    - ✓ We expect, but cannot guarantee, that our force posture will change over the next year, as the political process advances and Iraqi security forces grow and gain experience.
    - ✓ While our military presence may become less visible, it will remain lethal and decisive, able to confront the enemy wherever it may organize.
    - ✓ Our mission in Iraq is to win the war. Our troops will return home when that mission is complete.

Figure 5.2

Text from the *National Strategy for Victory in Iraq*.

Making the case for invasion was not the only use of PowerPoint in shaping policies and "just war" ideologies associated with the Iraq occupation. In 2004, a series of military briefings justifying stepped-up efforts to eliminate military resistance in the Iraqi city of Fallujah would ultimately reflect several stages of authorship in the electronic document trail. First, photographs designed to publicize violations of rules of engagement and human rights abuses were repackaged in a military PowerPoint presentation coproduced by the U.S. 1st Marine Expeditionary Force (IMEF) and a group within the Multi-National Corps Iraq (MNC-I Effects). "Telling the Fallujah Story to the World" was much forwarded among veterans groups and others sympathetic to the war effort.[15] Shortly afterward, the Fallujah electronic slideshow was disseminated by the conservative blog *Little Green Footballs*, which customized the presentation using PHP code to make the case bluntly that Fallujah fighters had abused their position in civilian communities by using mosques for military cover.[16] A few days later, top military leaders posted a very similar seventy-six page PowerPoint presentation with less text, and thus less editorializing on the images, that ended with the same four pages showing Iraqi civilians receiving boxes and sacks of foreign humanitarian aid. During the actual Department of Defense briefing, this presentation was whittled down to a mere eleven slides.[17] Military planners also improved the appearance of the presentation by using solid fonts in place of distracting outline typefaces.

Despite its relatively large file size and incompatibility issues as proprietary software, PowerPoint presentations frequently circulate in ways that cause them to reach new audiences and be deployed for new purposes. Of course, if disseminated as PDF files, PowerPoint slides are relatively difficult to alter as rhetorical artifacts, but these electronic slideshows are also transmitted among interested parties in their original .ppt format, which invites editing and alteration. Furthermore, although this software has been associated with entrenched hierarchical interests that emulate corporate structures of power, it can also be understood through the dynamics of peer-to-peer electronic exchanges, such as the ones associated with the circulation of the Fallujah PowerPoint through blogs and e-mail.

For example, some journalists have praised the way that PowerPoint software has been used by rank-and-file personnel deployed for duty in Iraq to propagate messages informed by social contact with the indigenous population that argue for fundamental policy changes in defiance of military planners. In December 2006, ABC journalist Martha Raddatz praised a young captain, Travis Patriquin, for authoring "How to Win in Anbar Province."[18] Raddatz claimed that by using "stick figures and simple language," Patriquin's presentation articulated the same goal in Iraq as did the president, but did so more successfully by emphasizing pragmatic approaches situated in experience living with the local populace. Sadly, Patriquin died in the line of duty as a result of an improvised explosive device near his vehicle, but his PowerPoint presentation outlived him and was widely disseminated in the region and among military circles

Figure 5.3
Final slide from "Operation Al Fajr Roll Up."

in the United States. According to his father, Captain Patriquin initially designed PowerPoint presentations to explain to his young daughter why he was stationed in Iraq and then began showing them to adult audiences. The slides show "Joe" of the American army and "Mohammed" of the Iraqi army as stick figures wearing trapezoid-shaped body armor and pentagon-shaped hats that denote their respective military identities. During the course of Patriquin's PowerPoint, Joe and Mohammed are vexed by "insurgent" stick figures, who appear holding the heads of other stick figures, a visual reference to the jihadist videos of the beheading of captives in the country, which were also circulating on the Internet. Fortunately for the U.S. military, a sheik who controls a construction company as well as the activities of a local militia is enlisted to aid coalition forces. The sheik and his allies are indicated with triangles to denote traditional Iraqi headgear. By the end of the presentation, all the cooperative stick figures have acquired stars, much like sheriffs in Western films, and a happy ending to the conflict is declared. A year later, as U.S. General David Petraeus was presenting laudatory PowerPoint presentations about the success of new military strategies in the country, which included some of the strategies of cooperation and cooption that Patriquin had been advocating, Raddatz returned to praising the Anbar

What's that in Joe's hand? Oh, a transitional authority law! It was written by the CPA (25 year olds from Texas, and Paul Bremer) and it says NO SHEIKS! ONLY ELECTED GOVERNMENT!!! "Thats OK", says the Sheik. "Can I have some contract work?"

Figure 5.4
"How to Win in Anbar" PowerPoint, by permission of Gary Patriquin.

PowerPoint and insisting that Captain Patriquin "deserves a great deal of credit" for the success of Petraeus's so-called military surge.[19]

Unlike Patriquin's simplified stick figure allegory of conflict and resolution, Petraeus's September 2007 PowerPoint contains a number of slides with complex data representations, such as bar charts or line graphs. In fact, some might argue that if Patriquin's presentation was intended for maximum clarity, Petraeus's electronic slideshow often contained a certain amount of obfuscation in its graphic elements. For example, "Overall Weekly Iraq Attack Trends" shows information from dozens of weeks, with the numbers of targeted government installations, IEDs located, small arms attacks, and mortar and rocket fire aggregated by relative size and differentiated by color.[20] Maps also provided illustrations of border tensions with Iran and Syria and color-coded registers of "ethno-sectarian deaths." However, a journalist from *The Washington Post* expressed specific concerns about how civilian casualties were being computed, given the fact that different government agencies seemed to be working with different sets of numbers; she also voiced suspicion of the general lack of public disclosure about how the databases that produced these statistics were constituted.[21] Careful reading of the explanatory captions on the charts in Petraeus's presentation also inspired ridicule from bloggers. At the bottom of one slide, the statistics are acknowledged to include numbers from "IED hoaxes," along with "IED explosions" and "IEDs found." In other words, the graph could seem to display the fact that soldiers were being tricked by fewer hoaxes, which would have no effect on actual levels of potentially lethal violence and would hardly laud American troops by pointing to their initial gullibility in the conflict. Critics noted that this inclusion made the apparent drop in events related to improvised explosive devices more dramatic and more legible on a PowerPoint slide. Others noted that the last slide, about proposed military draw-downs in troop sizes, looked like an authoritative plan for the future until one noticed that there were only question marks rather than actual dates on the later graph bars. While other bloggers were focusing on inconsistencies in individual slides from Petraeus's presentation, one Washington analytics strategist emphasized the failure of an overall rhetorical strategy that the software legitimates and "the control of the narrative that PowerPoint affords the presenter." As he writes, "The deck becomes an imperative; any foray into discussion must return within minutes to the predetermined story line if we're to get through the deck.[22]

Certainly, PowerPoint and other similar software programs have become tools not only for communicating but also for formalizing political agendas. For example, the

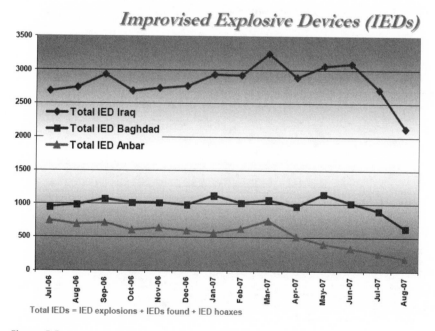

Figure 5.5
Slide from "Charts to accompany the testimony of GEN David H. Petraeus." Courtesy of the Multi-National Force—Iraq.

White House frequently uses the format of this proprietary software program for official business in briefings involving a wide range of federal agencies. On the White House website there are PowerPoint presentations about reporting systems for air quality management, software being used by the Department of Justice, cybersecurity initiatives, critical analyses of universal service programs in the telecommunications industry for low-income people, and training for civil servants in the use of online forms. The rhetoric of these PowerPoint slides often recycles diction from the corporate world about "customer feedback," "business areas," and "best practices." In one slide on the budget allotted to information technology, an arrow runs up a geologic landform with cutaway layers that show a three-stage plan for "Foundation," "Adoption," and "Transformation" via e-government in succeeding years.[23] This visual narrative of a clear increase over time—or decrease if the situation deems that reduction would be more desirable—serves as an important organizing principle in many PowerPoint presentations from the U.S. federal government. As in the case of the Petraeus PowerPoint slides, which indicate a reduction in violence in Iraq, linear progression or regression provides an important organizing principle in the digital rhetoric of the virtual state.

The ludicrousness of using PowerPoint for political oratory is dramatized by Peter Norvig's "The Gettysburg Powerpoint Presentation" in which he depicts Lincoln

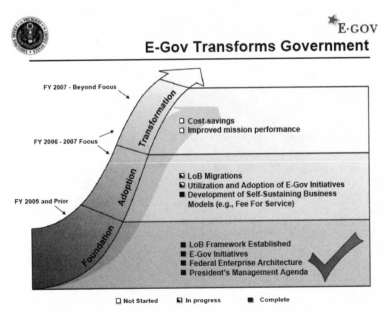

Figure 5.6
PowerPoint slide from the White House for the 2007 IT Budget Report.

delivering a clumsy, stilted corporate talk instead of the rousing rhetoric of the memorial speech, much revised by the president[24] in order to convey the gravitas of a nation
at war and its anticipation of postwar political reconciliation. Norvig's accompanying
essay, "PowerPoint: Shot with Its Own Bullets," compares this diction "with almost
no pronouns or punctuation" to the world of Kurt Vonnegut's "Harrison Bergeron,"
where a dumbed-down dystopia full of incoherent messages is perpetuated through a
constant barrage of babble aimed at its citizens, who are rendered equal by virtue of
enforcement of the lowest common denominator.[25] He points out that Stanford's
Clifford Nass acknowledges that PowerPoint "lifts the floor" for the common man
faced with an occasion for public speaking but also "lowers the ceiling" by removing
the discursive processes associated with producing nuanced rhetorical expressions.[26]
In Norvig's *reductio ad absurdum* electronic slideshow, the Great Emancipator uses the
program's AutoContent Wizard to produce a plodding succession of points conveyed
in a garish color scheme with hard-to-read fonts.[27]

Another academic, John Raffensperger from the University of Canterbury in
New Zealand, thought that Norvig was being somewhat unfair to PowerPoint, which
can also serve as a more user-friendly multimedia platform that integrates video
and audio content with traditional oratory.[28] Raffensperger points out that Norvig

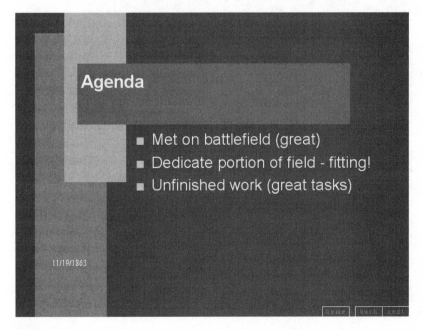

Figure 5.7
Peter Norvig's PowerPoint satire of *The Gettysburg Address*. Courtesy of Peter Norvig.

himself uses the staccato bullet style of PowerPoint in his own presentations on behalf of NASA.[29] In other words, although PowerPoint is frequently used to make a case for action in a business sales pitch, court of law, or public policy meeting, it also has an important deliberative function in the sciences, where slides are collaboratively created and open to processes that imitate many of the aspects of peer review associated with print journals. To respond to Norvig, Raffensperger remakes Lincoln's PowerPoint into an elegy to the slain soldiers that uses public domain images from the Library of Congress and reenactments of the speech by a live actor.

However, Raffensperger does not address Norvig's central objection: the AutoContent Wizard and the ways it would distort the content of Lincoln's speech. A naïve user of the software would be hobbled by choosing a preordained set of rhetorical defaults. This set of model slides from Microsoft includes prepackaged presentations for "Recommending a Strategy," "Training," "Certificate," and "Brainstorming Session." The AutoContent Wizard even has a set of templates for "Communicating Bad News," which does for public rhetoric what the sympathy card does for private epistolary communication.

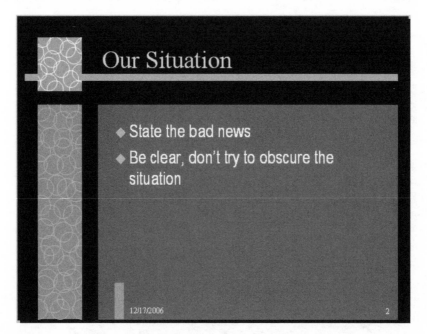

Figure 5.8
Slide from the "Communicating Bad News" template from the PowerPoint AutoContent Wizard. Microsoft product screenshot reprinted with permission from Microsoft Corporation.

The artist David Byrne, once lead singer of the band *Talking Heads*, is now also known for using PowerPoint as a medium to convey irony along with aesthetic expression. Rather than accept the commonly held notion that Microsoft's product is a "neutral tool," Byrne is interested in its "biases and tendencies." Although he cites the AutoContent Wizard as "the most obvious bias" and "the easiest to see," he is interested in more "subtle sets of biases at work" that have to do with aspirations to professionalism and promises of universal happiness. In his book *Envisioning Emotional Epistemological Information*, Byrne presents a series of visual fantasies in which corporate arrows melt into surreal arrangements, subtexts of psychic insecurity are given garish color and volume, and a parade through the taxonomy of clip-art physiognomies is presented like a human zoo.[30] There are also political stakes made visible in Byrne's work. For example, at one point Washington landmarks appear in one of his PowerPoint presentations. For Byrne it is the status of organizations as hegemonic entities that shape discourse. As he says, the "shape of the cake pan" may matter as much as the ingredients.

The general critique of PowerPoint in academia and the arts over its off-the-shelf constraints on rhetoric, cognition, and epistemology is also reflected in the mainstream print media. Writing for *The New Yorker*, Ian Parker claims that PowerPoint is able to reconfigure the brain's most basic taxonomies for organizing meaning.

But PowerPoint also has a private, interior influence. It edits ideas. It is, almost surreptitiously, a business manual as well as a business suit, with an opinion—an oddly pedantic, prescriptive opinion—about the way we should think. It helps you make a case, but it also makes its own case: about how to organize information, how much information to organize, how to look at the world.[31]

If the literacy specialist James Paul Gee argues that "discourse functions as a kind of identity kit,"[32] it would seem like this particular cut of "business suit" used for the conventions of communicative exchange is covertly controlling. Parker sees PowerPoint as epistemologically loaded, a way to control the unruly data that are freely accessible in an information culture and constrain it with a set of oppressive norms. Although philosopher Michael Heim's extended meditation on the phenomenology of word processing, *Electric Language*, argues that there are many possibilities for engagement with digital texts, such as "clustering" or "blockbusting,"[33] PowerPoint software often reminds its users of its constraints rather than its freedoms.

However, precisely because of these constraints, there are some Power Point enthusiasts among those interested in fast-paced visually oriented presentation styles. For example Tokyo-based architects Astrid Klein and Mark Dytham have encouraged an international cadre of hip designers to host "pecha kucha" nights around the world. Klein and Dytham use the Japanese word for "conversation" to describe their events in which rapid-fire PowerPoint presentations satisfy a particular rhetorical need by filling the "demand for a forum in which creative work can be easily and informally shown, without having to rent a gallery or chat up a magazine editor."[34] In exchange, Klein and Dytham insist that presenters observe a strict set of rules by limiting themselves to a total of twenty slides, which are only shown for twenty seconds each. This approach to presentation software with a live speaker has had a rich transmedia legacy as well. Concept maps and YouTube videos record the location and content of pecha kucha events. Klein and Dytham have even issued an art book, *Pecha Kucha Night: A Celebration*. Unlike government PowerPoint representations that may be restructured to become official reports, in transferring content from the screen to the printed page Klein and Dytham emphasize large-format images rather than bullet points.

Nonetheless, the very connection between globalization and PowerPoint that the transnational gatherings of pecha kucha groups celebrate should also invite certain kinds of critical appraisal by those who are interested in sustaining local cultures and economies. The parodic possibilities of PowerPoint for skewering multinational corporate groupthink are key elements of the stunts of the antiglobalization activists The Yes Men, who create hoax websites and produce documentary films about their exploits posing as soulless capitalists with ridiculous strategies or policy decisions, which are often blandly accepted at face value at conferences or media events. In addition to pretending to be representatives of the World Trade Organization, The Yes Men have masqueraded under the guise of major brands, such as McDonald's or Enron, and use PowerPoint and 3-D animations to satirize the institutions they are ridiculing, such as the fast-food industry or politically well-connected energy conglomerates. Posing as "Hank Hardy Unruh" of the WTO, a member of the group delivered a PowerPoint presentation in Tampere, Finland on August 16, 2001, which seemed to argue that a reintroduction of slavery would be advantageous to the worldwide business community, since market freedom is more important than human freedom.[35] It included cartoony representations of events from the U.S. Civil War and thus mimicked a common feature of the allegorical character of PowerPoint style by using actual clip art tagged with keywords like "adversaries," "conflicts," "competitions," and "controversies" to depict the epic battle between the North and the South that Lincoln chronicled so poetically in the Gettysburg Address.

In contrast, the competing slideware product from Apple, Keynote, has become associated with progressive political agendas and policy reform, although this connection appears to have little to do with the actual features of the software. As a tool for representing statistics and argumentative elements, Keynote has been loudly criticized by Tufte and other information designers for being burdened with many of the same problems that characterize PowerPoint.[36] However, Keynote has become associated with a technique sometimes called "slides—as chorus" in which the presenter does not read from the text on the slides, but rather uses them to punctuate a talk

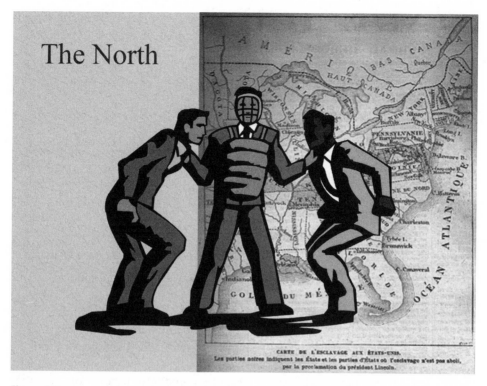

Figure 5.9
Slide from The Yes Men presentation on the "Globalization of Textile Trade," by permission of
The Yes Men.

with short pieces of text or striking images. This technique has become particularly associated with digital rights advocate and Stanford law professor Lawrence Lessig and his signature talks on "free culture " that question the applicability of current copyright regimes to the practices of digital culture and commonsense notions of the law.

Another well-known Keynote user is at the center of the documentary film about global warming *An Inconvenient Truth*, which is largely devoted to an electronic slide-show talk delivered by former Vice President Al Gore. However, instead of always relying on on-screen graphics to show the geometric progression of planetary temperature irregularities, Gore most memorably chooses to use the physical space of the lecture hall to show the statistical elevation. In the film this involved using a theatrical scissor lift to show the relative precariousness of his actual physical person up high in the oratorical space. Compared to the clunky bullet points and repetitive sentence fragments of the Bush administration's PowerPoint rhetoric, Gore offers a remarkably fluent presentation incorporating digital presentation technologies that capitalize on "pull" as well as "push" media. The audience for the film *An Inconvenient Truth* also gets to see Gore modeling idealized online behavior in the mode of detective work, as he incorporates new research and revelations about political influence, such as the editing of documents about climate science by former energy lobbyist Philip Cooney. During the course of the documentary Gore reads the online *New York Times*, surfs Google Earth, and even moves the building blocks of his digital slideshow around. Like activist subversives The Yes Men, Gore mixes 3-D animation in with his graphs and charts, although he deploys the device both for humor (a cooking frog) and for pathos (a drowning polar bear). As the credits roll with animated graphics, the audience is pointed toward the project's website for more information.

Certainly, it can be tempting to use the conventions of slideware technologies to try to tell complicated stories as simply as possible. Proponents of controversial positions on issues have been known to deploy the rhetoric of PowerPoint to further specific political master narratives. For example, the much disseminated "History in a Nutshell," which is translated into thirteen languages, advances arguments about geography, chronology, and relative refugee population sizes to claim that Palestine has no rights to self-determination as a culturally and politically distinct autonomous nation-state.[37] Although it was actually created in Flash for online presentation without the accompaniment of a live speaker, it uses many recognizable slideware conventions, such as navigation by triangle icons forward and backward. "History in a Nutshell" was created by Udi Ohana of the Israeli design firm Studio Homage, a company that specializes in "custom website design and sales presentations, using advanced Photoshop and Flash animation techniques" oriented around "telling a story."[38] The group also produced "Nutshell Too," which goes back to 1250 BCE to establish the grounds for Israel's territorial claims.[39] Other presentations on "Anti-Semitism" and "Hamas" are also available on the studio's website, along with an electronic slideshow on suicide bombing called "Imagine" that features jarring sound effects. The audience for the "Nutshell" presentations was often reached through e-mail, blogs, and pro-Israel websites, modes of digital communication that solidify allegiances and often polarize political constituencies in the irreconcilable ways that Geert Lovink has described in *Zero Comments*.

PowerPoint is without question an important genre in political rhetoric, but it is used so frequently in so many discursive contexts that it is difficult to make broad generalizations about how it functions at the level of theory. Because the speaker is generally present rather than absent, a live orator is able either to be closely identified with his or her text or to manifest some critical distance from the words and images projected nearby. In big-budget films, the convention used to be that the stealthy hacker breaking into the top-secret database was the only model for how computational media functioned in political discourse. Now we are seeing PowerPoint presentations serving the purpose of exposition in blockbuster films, and the possibilities of public rhetoric rather than just private data are being exploited in cinematic narratives. PowerPoint is obviously a very public genre, one intended to be viewed by others, unlike the private contents on an individual user's monitor. But it is not just a simple one-to-many form of communication because there are many cases in which presentations migrate among computer users and accrue multiple authors in the process

6 Whistle-Blowers: Traditional Epistolary Discourse and Electronic Communication

On the face of it, e-mail would seem particularly well suited to the aims of a would-be whistle-blower intent on exposing corruption or averting disaster as quickly as possible. As a medium for instantaneous and intimate global communication, e-mail initially appears to be far superior to traditional epistolary discourse because letters are vulnerable to delays and acts of confiscation by hostile parties. Even when a scandal unfolds relatively rapidly, the requirement of physically transporting the artifacts that carry messages over a distance, inherent in this long-standing form of communication, could potentially worsen the crisis at hand.

For example, in early October 1692, twenty people had already died by the time Boston merchant Thomas Brattle wrote his influential letter condemning the Salem witch trials. From the beginning of his letter, Brattle makes his reluctance to come forward very clear.

I should be very loath to bring myself into any snare by my freedom with you, and therefore hope that you will put the best construction on what I write, and secure me from such as would interprett my lines otherwise than they are designed. Obedience to lawfull authority I evermore accounted a great duty; and willingly I would not practise any thing that might thwart and contradict such a principle.[1]

This early American whistle-blower's missive was addressed not to the presumed logical recipient, Governor William Phips, but to a considerably less august unknown clerical correspondent, and Brattle's incendiary letter circulated in manuscript form for three weeks before the governor finally dissolved the Court of Oyer and Terminer that had indicted the witches and addressed the "strange ferment of dissatisfaction" that had subsumed the colony during his frequent absences.[2] Indeed, such historical narratives generally would seem to illustrate the impossibility of affecting public policy decisions rapidly with manually written communications, particularly when the writer was a subject of governmental authority rather than its agent.

In the counterfactual narrative in which Brattle magically has e-mail, are the potential victims of abuses of power aided much more rapidly? I would argue that the answer is probably "not really." Widening the temporal chokepoint that slows the rate at which information can be transferred technologically is rarely the most important precondition for successful organizational change. As Miceli and Near point out in their 1995 treatise on effective whistle-blowing, far more important is the whistle-blower's custody of evidence of wrongdoing and his or her legal basis for complaint.[3] Of course, in addition to having the advantage of speed, digital communication also obviates certain differences in cultural power, as any tenured professor or endowed chair who receives demands for immediate action from disgruntled students can attest. Potentially, any individual with an e-mail address, from a university president to a corporate CEO, can be accessed by any petitioner through electronic means, which leads to what Dubrovsky calls the "equalization phenomenon" of e-mail.[4]

Yet when *TIME* magazine named three women as its 2002 "Persons of the Year," citing them as icons of public rhetoric who "reminded us what American courage and American values are all about," it is worth noting that none of the magazine's featured whistle-blowers used e-mail as the primary vehicle for their well-publicized performatives. The three women are depicted on the cover of the magazine looking at the camera with their arms crossed defiantly, but they are also dressed in business attire that indicates their continuing associations with large organizations. Although these whistle-blowers contacted higher-ups about their knowledge of corporate or governmental wrongdoing through conventional epistolary means, I would argue that their whistle-blowing discourse still shows the influence of e-mail and displays certain features of its generic instability between writing and speech. For example, like disinhibited writers in cyberspace, these women appear to "flame" their employers by using aggressive rhetorical techniques that appear borrowed from the conventions of electronic communication.

Although they could be called real-life contemporary incarnations of eighteenth-century Richardsonian heroines, risking possible contamination by participating in exchanges of potentially public correspondence while also surmounting gender and class barriers through their revelatory letter-writing, I would complicate that narrative and question an overly simplified viewpoint that female letter-writers necessarily employ epistolary discourse primarily for "political emancipation" or to "further a political action."[5] This is not to say that the women on the cover of *TIME* did not have a political impact. All three of them testified before Congress. But they also had proximate rhetorical purposes related to the trajectories of their own careers that are difficult to link easily to a larger feminist emancipatory narrative.

For example, Sherron Watkins, a vice president at Enron, earned her whistle-blowing reputation by sending a memo to chief executive Kenneth Lay about the looming accounting scandal that would soon devalue Enron's stock and ultimately lead to the indictment of key company personnel. Watkins opens her letter with two confrontational rhetorical questions: "Has Enron become a risky place to work? For those of us who didn't get rich over the last few years, can we afford to stay?"[6] In the space of a seven-page letter, Watkins raises twenty-four separate questions. Much like the approach of Salem witchcraft critic Thomas Brattle, who deploys seventeen questions in his own message to the authorities, Watkins' letter uses an interrogative tone when speaking in her own persona, while also positing a hypothetical outside audience who might be asking questions as well. At the end of her memo she writes:

Don't you think that several interested companies, be they stock analysts, journalists, hedge fund managers, etc., are busy trying to discover the reason Skilling left? Don't you think their smartest people are poring over that footnote disclosure right now? I can just hear the discussions—"it looks like they booked a $500 million gain from this related party company and I think, from all the undecipherable half-page on Enron's contingent contributions to this related party entity, I think the related party entity is capitalized with Enron stock." . . . "No, no, no, you must have it all wrong, it can't be that, that's just too bad, too fraudulent, surely AA & Co. wouldn't let them get away with that?" "Go back to the drawing board, it's got to be something else. But find it!" . . . "Hey, just in case you might be right, try and find some insiders or 'redeployed' former employees to validate your theory."[7]

Watkins' excerpts from this imaginary dialogue between future investigators of Enron concludes her memo with a dramatic flair that may sound dissonant to readers accustomed to the dominant corporate idiom, which privileges language marked by passive voice and third-person address. As *Forbes* magazine points out, this passage also demonstrates that Ms. Watkins may not deserve the title of "whistle-blower" at all, since by definition, *Forbes* writes, "a whistle-blower is someone who alerts the public. She never did."[8] If anything, the conclusion of Watkins's memo actually warns Lay about the threat of future whistle-blowers and the potential need to silence them with preemptive action.

In her biographical account of the scandal, *Power Failure: The Inside Story of the Collapse of Enron*, Watkins claims that she had tried using e-mail as a channel to reach the Enron power brokers in the past, but had not found it a successful strategy for making her concerns known to higher-ups. In the book, she describes how a "year or so back, she'd sent an anonymous e-mail to Skilling and Lay about the sale of some South American assets."[9] Of course, this description of her earlier intervention regarding Enron's "Project California" invites certain questions. In what sense can an important e-mail ever be anonymous? If she sent it from a free account using a public computer, what would cause a CEO or CFO to read her message at all?

By choosing not to use e-mail in her later famous memo, Watkins also risked having her message intercepted or compromised. In fact, to ensure its survival, Watkins sent another copy of her famous whistle-blowing letter in an interoffice memo, which identified her as the author, to a colleague, where it was subject to all the usual risks of disclosure of a missive committed to paper as a physical artifact. Watkins describes the perilous trajectory of this other document. "His secretary either missed or ignored the large CONFIDENTIAL stamp on the front of the envelope. She left it on McMahon's desk in plain sight. McMahon never saw the envelope. He read the memo and then passed it on to a few of his friends, who were probably passing it on to others right now."[10] Although the message reaches her coworker, Watkins describes how it is delayed and then how it is disseminated, much like e-mail travels when it is stripped of its context and forwarded to multiple parties.

Watkins frequently depicts e-mail as a genre that reinforces corporate discourses of denial rather than supports trusted communication, and often e-mail plays a significant role in Watkins' account as a signifier of disingenuousness. For example, she describes having to listen to CEO Kenneth Lay assure employees "that the company is in the strongest shape it's ever been in;" however, she was well aware that he "was reiterating an e-mail" he had sent to Enron staffers earlier.[11] She also shows that e-mail can allow writers in the business world to make rebuttals without the personal responsibility entailed in a face-to-face interaction, or even one involving the materiality of letterhead and a physical signature in ink.

I was shown Causey's e-mail response on August 20, 2001, five days after I had identified myself as the anonymous letter writer and two days before I met with Ken Lay. I was asked if Causey's response satisfied my concerns. My response was visceral—I thought Causey's rather technical-sounding response was akin to a man accused of beating his children who, when confronted, insists nothing is wrong because he's got their future college tuition fully funded. *Huh?*[12]

Although Watkins is no longer anonymous, this e-mail answer does not address her directly. Instead she is "shown" the message and its "technical-sounding" responses to her concerns by an unidentified person who also asks if she is "satisfied." Instead of being pacified, Watkins responds viscerally and compares herself to a witness reporting child abuse instead of corporate malfeasance.

Among the three Time Persons of the Year, FBI Special Agent Coleen Rowley most clearly adopts the whistle-blower persona in her epistolary discourse. At the end of her thirteen-page letter to FBI Director Robert Mueller, Rowley concludes, "Although I would hope it is not necessary, I would therefore wish to take advantage of the federal 'Whistleblower Protection' provisions by so characterizing my remarks." As the Minneapolis Chief Division Counsel who handled the pre-September 11 investigation of the alleged twentieth hijacker Zacarias Moussaoui, Rowley is uniquely situated to challenge Mueller's authority, which she does. Unlike Watkins' unsigned and undated missive, Rowley assumes the ethos of one familiar with professional decorum by using all the markers of business correspondence from salutation to signature.

However Rowley reveals that she is also—to some extent—a naïve correspondent in the rhetorical situation of approaching a figure of paternal authority. As she asserts, "I have never written to an FBI Director in my life before on any topic." She further indicates that her disenfranchised class and gender identity should be important to those who interpret her letter-writing motives. As Rowley explains herself, "I have also been lucky to have had four children during my time in the FBI and am the sole breadwinner of a family of six."[13] As a female writer she uses the grammatical construction of "having had" children to indicate her literal labor of giving birth, and the mathematics of supporting a "family of six" on a civil servant's income would suggest that Rowley has overcome significant socioeconomic disadvantages as well.

Rhetorical criticism about epistolary discourse frequently focuses on the writer's ethos, the projected credibility and character of the author in a given situation. From the historical context of Toby Ditz's interpretation of merchants' letters in colonial Pennsylvania[14] to the close reading of a soldier's letter from the Vietnam War by John Poulakos,[15] analysis of ethos in real-world letter-writing has obvious advantages for critics who want to examine how identity formation and discursive practice are related. Analyzing the discourse of whistle-blowers similarly involves looking at how writers construct a speaking self that will be judged by the reader to be singular, authentic, and trustworthy.

Despite her protestations to subservience, Rowley is significantly more direct in her ad hominem attack on her addressee than Watkins is with Lay. By the second paragraph, Rowley confronts her organizational chief bluntly: "To get to the point, I have deep concerns that a delicate and subtle shading/skewing of facts by you and others at the highest levels of FBI management has occurred and is occurring." Rowley's concentrated mix of abnegation and confrontation in her writing style is perhaps best represented by a sentence like "With all due respect, this statement is as bad as the first!" Rowley poses fewer questions than Watkins, and she sometimes punctuates them with both a question mark and a mark of exclamation ("?!"). These ejaculatory sentences defy Mueller's authority and ridicule his plan to create an "FBI Supersquad." Some of Rowley's most trenchant criticism is reserved for her "Notes" section, which includes a definition of "careerism" from Webster's dictionary and an account of her initial personal reactions to the disaster of September 11. [16]

By definition, of course, whistle-blowers' letters are generally more one-sided than conventional letters. The rhetorical dynamic of traditional epistolary exchange assumes response, what Janet Gurkin Altman calls the essential "reciprocality"[17] in which to "write a letter is not only to define oneself in relationship to a particular you; it is also an attempt to draw that you into becoming the I of a new statement."[18] However, sending a whistle-blowing letter demands an administrative act, not a speech act, in response.

In the FBI whistle-blower case, Rowley lets her presumed reader Mueller see that she has composed her argument carefully and that she deliberates even as she writes: "The term 'cover up' would be too strong a characterization which is why I am attempting to carefully (and perhaps over laboriously) choose my words here." Of course, by even mentioning the term "cover up," she affixes the damaging label to Mueller's behavior,

even though she qualifies the word as "too strong a characterization." Mueller's altera-
tions of language for rhetorical purposes in his discourse, specifically in what Rowley
identifies as his "Congressional testimony and public comments," are depicted in her
letter as "facts . . . omitted, downplayed, glossed over and/or mis-characterized" for
"improper political reasons."

In contrast, Rowley describes her own rhetoric as "from the heart" and "completely
apolitical," although she also describes herself as one who is mindful of the rhetorical
situation in which she composes texts. What I find particularly interesting about
Rowley's metadiscourse in her letter to Mueller is the contradictory attitude toward
the genre of e-mail expressed within it. I am positing a reading of Rowley's text in
which e-mail, unlike the larger frame of her conventional epistolary discourse, is presented as primarily arhetorical—either because electronic mail lacks the necessary
deliberative character of traditional correspondence or because it completely consum-
mates any given exchange by speaking for itself.

The first time Rowley discusses e-mail in her letter to Mueller (in numbered item
4), she is describing her own activities as a writer in the context of her position in the
Minneapolis office at the FBI.

In one of my peripheral roles on the Moussaoui matter, I answered an e-mail message on August
22, 2001, from an attorney at the National Security Law Unit (NSLU). Of course, with (ever
important!) 20–20 hindsight, I now wish I had taken more time and care to compose my
response. When asked by NSLU for my "assessment of (our) chances of getting a criminal warrant
to search Moussaoui's computer," I answered, "Although I think there's a decent chance of being
able to get a judge to sign a criminal search warrant, our USAO seems to have an even higher
standard much of the time, so rather than risk it, I advised that they should try the other
route." . . . What I meant by this pithy e-mail response, was that although I thought probable
cause existed . . . I thought our United States Attorney's Office . . . might turn us down.[19]

As she looks back at this e-mail written in the month prior to the September 11 attacks,
Rowley expresses her wish that she had "taken more time and care to compose my
response." She also offers reader Mueller what she considers to be a more complete
interpretation of what she "meant by this pithy e-mail response." Implicitly she is
blaming the communicative context of e-mail communication, while also deflecting
attention from her own rhetoric and expertise (alluded to by references to her "answer,"
her "assessment," and her "advice") by directing her reader's scrutiny to the rhetoric
of the U.S. Attorney's office, which potentially "turns down" the local FBI office.

Although her e-mail is "pithy," Rowley is implying that it is still a poor record of
her communicative intentions for two reasons: insufficient "time" and insufficient
"care." The first factor, the temporal acceleration that is characteristic of the near-
instantaneous transmissions of information in digital culture, has certainly been
important in the theoretical work of Virilio, Castells, and Baudrillard. On the level of

everyday practices, as Hawisher and Moran point out, "rapid turnaround" is "characteristic of the medium."[20] Of course, time is not the only factor that garbles electronic communication. Sproull and Kiesler note that "although computer-based communications may permanently archive all electronic messages, people perceive the experience of sending and receiving messages as an ephemeral one. . . . When people perceive communication to be ephemeral, the stakes of communication seem smaller."[21] Rowley obviously saved the relevant e-mails or had access to the archive, because she can quote from both sides of her electronic exchange with the NSLU, but it is only with "20–20 hindsight" that she can appreciate the magnitude of the communication error that took place.

Agent Rowley's regret about her careless writing of this e-mail demonstrates Hawisher and Moran's main point as pedagogues: it is critical to teach the skills of electronic rhetoric, particularly when writers are either overinvested in rapid response or underinvested in careful deliberation. Although e-mail is increasingly the main channel of official communication in many fields, few professionals encounter specific instruction about composing in the new genre during the course of their chosen careers.

Although Rowley presents herself as ill-prepared for the communicative tasks that she must undertake and shows the genre of e-mail to be subject to misinterpretation, just a few paragraphs later, she reverses herself and validates the role of e-mail in documenting institutional memory. In her second discussion of the genre (in numbered item 6), she presents electronic mail as a reliable representation of the historical record, one that is superior to representations of "live" face-to-face contact.

Eventually on August 28, 2001, after a series of e-mails between Minneapolis and FBIHQ, which suggest that the FBIHQ SSA deliberately further undercut the FISA effort by not adding the further intelligence information which he had promised to add that supported Moussaoui's foreign power connection and making several changes in the wording of the information that had been provided by the Minneapolis Agent, the Minneapolis agents were notified that the NSLU Unit Chief did not think there was sufficient evidence of Moussaoui's connection to a foreign power. Minneapolis personnel are, to this date, unaware of the specifics of the verbal presentations by the FBIHQ SSA to NSLU . . . Obviously verbal presentations are far more susceptible to mischaracterization and error . . . The e-mail communications between Minneapolis and FBIHQ, however, speak for themselves and there are far better witnesses than me who can provide their first hand knowledge of these events characterized in one Minneapolis agent's e-mail as FBIHQ is "setting this up for failure."[22]

While face-to-face verbal presentations with a high degree of vividness and interactivity are, according to Rowley, "far more susceptible to mis-characterization and error," e-mail communications with considerably less "telepresence"[23] can "speak for themselves" as "far better witnesses." Although Rosalind Picard and other specialists in affective computing have argued that e-mail is an "affect-limited form of communication" with the added disadvantage that the "mood of the recipient" affects the "perception of tone," Rowley presents it as an objective record that conveys a large amount of information to investigators.[24]

Rowley's depiction of the interpretive transparency of e-mail has two decidedly different aspects: in one case, e-mail poorly represents Rowley's admirable intention to assist her peers and the public; in the other situation, e-mail precisely and unambiguously presents the nefarious designs of central FBI managers to capitalize on hierarchical relationships of power by "changing wording" and creating a rhetorical context for "setting this up for failure." I would argue that Rowley's distinctions about the truth value of e-mail are significant, although she is obviously making a self-interested argument that instructs the implied reader to read her e-mail differently from the e-mail of others.

Furthermore, I would suggest that Rowley's bifurcated attitude about the genre of electronic mail is analogous to similarly conflicting assumptions about how "rich" or "lean" a medium e-mail is, which are linked to the fact that e-mail is perceived as a hybrid genre that functions differently in different contexts. In other words, in certain cases it is perceived as speech that functions in the highly contingent temporal present of a dialogue between parties, and in other cases, it seems to be treated as a time-stamped print record of chronological facts that can be understood in absolute terms. About this hybridity, Ellen Strenski writes:

That the electronic medium is hybrid is obvious. The hybrid qualities of the resulting electronic text, however, are not so apparent and are worth examining more closely. Clearly, e-mail format is novel: part-memo, part post-it, part-letter, part-answering machine transcript. But e-messages are hybrid in an even more radical way. Particularly deserving of attention are two special features: the distinctive logic governing the organization of these messages, and the special collaborative quality of the interactive exchange that renders these texts meaningful . . . In e-mail as in dreams, the organizing principle is association rather than demonstration, metonymy rather than metaphor."[25]

Although e-mail may be a genre of "association rather than demonstration" in Strenski's view, Rowley affirms that it shows perhaps more powerfully than it tells.

Specifically, Rowley appears to make a legalistic distinction between testimony and evidence that could conceivably be important for other policy scandals in which e-mail must be interpreted in the context of a larger public sphere. If judged as testimony, the disembodied words of an absent speaking subject are inadmissible as hearsay. If judged as evidence, the logic goes, e-mail has certain technical features that make it appear as conclusive as a tapped phone call.

In particular, I am suggesting that Rowley's default assumptions about e-mail could be significant for beginning to understand the larger role of electronic epistolary exchange in a range of recent public policy scandals. For example, leaked e-mail from the UN headquarters in Cheltenham and from U.S. detention facilities in Abu Ghraib or Guantánamo has similarly been presumed to "speak for itself," even when it is presented without its surrounding rhetorical context. Although the whistle-blowers of 2002 didn't use e-mail as a tool for presenting arguments for change to the authorities, e-mail was already serving a central role in many whistle-blowing efforts as evidence of alleged wrongdoing.

During the 2005 Hurricane Katrina disaster in New Orleans, one prominent government official's e-mail worsened the image of the White House significantly because of its general frivolity of tone and the fact that it seemed to indicate that the head of the Federal Emergency Management Agency (FEMA), Michael Brown, was frequently more concerned with style than substance in his role as a public figure. Brown's cynical one-to-one communications contrasted sharply from his seemingly heartfelt one-to-many media appearances in which he expressed empathy for the plight of the endangered and dispossessed. In contrast to his magnanimous diction in public, private messages exchanged with aides and colleagues often emphasized Brown's personal appearance and individual comfort. Probably his most famous e-mail was one sent to the chief of FEMA's public relations as a follow-up to this either narcissistic or self-deprecating message about his outfit, which he would wear in news coverage: "got it at Nordstroms . . . Are you proud of me?" An hour later, Brown wrote in a frequently reprinted e-mail that he was wearing "lovely FEMA attire" that showed him to be "a fashion god." In his joking with the recipient, Brown added, "you'll really vomit." In fact, Brown's electronic mail was so damning that the Center for Public Integrity published 928 pages of e-mail messages to and from the FEMA chief.[26] One message with the subject line "Sounds like you have a good signal there" from Brown to his chief of staff reads like a self-absorbed microblogging status line: "Yes, sitting in the chair, putting mousse in my hair." In an interview with the center, Brown complained that the e-mails released "do not paint an accurate picture of his efforts during the disaster," because "additional e-mails—chiefly those sent to the White House and senior Department of Homeland Security (DHS) officials—were withheld, making the record an unfair reflection."[27]

In fact, the hundreds of pages in Brown's entire e-mail record reveal a slightly more complicated story about his history as a prominent electronic correspondent. For example, Brown frequently engages in e-mail metadiscourse in the released documents, particularly when he becomes defensive about his e-mail responsiveness. At one point he explains, "sorry I cannot respond to the literally hundreds of emails arriving in my inbox from the general public." At another time he expresses pride in managing his inbox with decorum and concern: "I don't know you; and I'm certain you don't know me. I have read all of your emails as they've arrived." As a general pattern, Brown also seems to have difficulty with exchanges in which he can't respond in kind and simply mirror the sender's sentiments. For example, his answers to e-mails mentioning religious sentiments do not show those feelings to be necessarily reciprocated by Brown.

Brown's "fashion god" gaffe was perceived to be so serious that the how-to netiquette book *Send: The Essential Guide to E-mail for Office and Home* begins with a series of three regrettable e-mails written by the FEMA director.[28] Much of this popular trade book is concerned with how to properly observe recognized, although relatively new, conventions of e-mail politeness and how to send difficult types of e-mail to handle apologies or reject requests graciously. However, the authors of this how-to book for civilians also devote considerable attention to government e-mail and messages from policy makers, which range from the e-mail apology sent by Pope John Paul II over injustices committed by clergy in Oceania to the altering of forwarded e-mail by scandal-plagued lobbyist Jack Abramoff.

However, when federal employees are most careful to observe decorum in e-mail communication, it can obliterate the value of the genre as a method of rapid and confrontational disaster mitigation. For example, investigators of the crash of the space shuttle *Columbia* have looked closely at e-mail exchanges between engineers, since poor communication was identified as a contributing factor in the disastrous accident. In the subsequent investigation, one of the most famous e-mails appears to be one that was never sent, from Rodney Rocha, one of the chief engineers at NASA. His discouragement with the genre is understandable, given how ineffective it had proved to be for him in his whistle-blowing efforts. On the fourth day of the *Columbia* flight, Rocha had sent an e-mail asking if the crew would be visually inspecting the left wing for damage caused by foam striking the vehicle during takeoff. He never received an answer to this e-mail. By the sixth day, Rocha was using the e-mail channel primarily to express his exasperation with the lack of serious responses to his continuing requests for damage assessment. In the same e-mail, he asks, "Can we petition (beg) for outside agency assistance?"[29] Although the message was addressed to three people and copied to three others, the Columbia Accident Investigation Board faulted Rocha with "routing the request through the Engineering department," which "led in part to it being viewed by Shuttle Program managers as a non-critical engineering desire rather than a critical operational need." Shortly after being informed via e-mail that no outside imaging help would be requested, Rocha sat down and began to compose the following message:

In my humble technical opinion, this is the wrong (and bordering on irresponsible) answer from the SSP and orbiter not to request additional imaging help from any outside source. I must emphasize (again) that severe enough damage (3 or 4 multiple tiles knocked out down to the densification layer) combined with the heating and resulting damage to the underlying structure at the most critical location (viz. MLG Door/wheels/tires/hydraulics or the X1191 spar cap) could present potentially grave hazards. The engineering team will admit it might not achieve definitive high confidence answer even with additional images, but without action to request help clarify the damage visually, we will guarantee it will not.

Can we talk to Frank Benz before Friday's MMT? Remember the NASA safety posters around the site stating "if it's not safe, say so"? Yes, its that serious.

Rodney Rocha

Structural Engineering Division (ES-SED)

— ES Div, Chief Engineer (Space Shuttle DGE)

— Chair, Space Shuttle Loads & Dynamics Panel

Mail Code ES2 Phone 281–483–8889

[Handwritten note]

"Draft Memo

Not sent through email

Discussed with Carlisle Campbell and ES management"[30]

Rocha uses many of the rhetorical flourishes of a traditional whistle-blower. He debases himself by referring to his "humble technical opinion." He expresses the questions that he raises as the questions of others. He references traditional print ephemera by mentioning the NASA safety poster. And yet ultimately no e-mail was sent by Rocha that day, although the report claims that he did print out his message and show it to others in the face-to-face office situation. In explaining the rationale for not sending his warning, Rocha told investigators that "he did not want to jump the chain of command" and he felt that he should "defer to management's judgment."[31]

Looking back on their electronic discourse about potential safety issues, the NASA employees often describe their e-mail by using terms equally applicable to oral conversations, words such as "discuss" or "talk." Although these engineers communicate in an environment of extreme governmental surveillance, as the record of precise screen shots of the computers of NASA workers in the actual process of composing e-mails indicates, peer-to-peer models of communication serve as the dominant paradigm (although frequent cc'ing indicates that others on the hierarchical ladder are also often included in the conversation). In the official report on the catastrophe, e-mail is a key part of the narrative. The e-mail record also reveals the office culture of NASA and the dissemination of visual ephemera, such as cartoons. Abbreviations and acronyms that serve as examples of what the report calls "NASA language" are frequently translated, along with more common Internet chat expressions such as "FYI." Members of the doomed but frequently oblivious crew were also e-mailed as part of the larger circuit of exchanges. On at least one occasion astronauts onboard were sent videos of the foam debris incident that would be identified as the main cause for the spacecraft's failure. They would be unaware that engineers were exchanging e-mails with all-caps messages that talked about "pucker strings pulled tight" among NASA bigshots and the fact that they would not "let a loved one land like that."[32]

E-mail now is frequently cited as evidence in criminal trials, and recent high-profile convictions indicate that regrettable e-mail can be taken as compelling evidence by juries. Since the Iran-Contra scandals of 1986, government officials have destroyed thousands of official e-mails in various attempts to avoid prosecution or legislative oversight. Because of the perceived evidentiary character of e-mail, it is frequently used as evidence by whistle-blowing organizations that are using websites to expose human rights abuses or government corruption. For example, the American Civil Liberties Union posted fifty-four e-mails from the Federal Bureau of Investigation that dealt with harsh interrogation techniques used on terrorism suspects and justifications for these procedures from the executive branch of government.[33]

Of course, some whistle-blowers dispense with one-to-one communication entirely and favor websites designed for the public rather than private e-mails to policy makers. A few websites that are established by federal whistle-blowers themselves include documents and media stories about government scandals. For example, Turkish-American translator Sibel Edmonds is associated with the Just a Citizen website, which disputes the use of the "state secrets" provision to quash objections raised by whistle-blowers about security breaches, inefficiencies, and bureaucratic slowdowns that took place after the 9/11 attacks.[34] On her website, Edmonds is shown demurely seated on a couch in a black dress. In addition to journalistic pieces about her case, links to a French film about Edmonds entitled *Kill the Messenger*, and comments from legislators and the kin of victims in defense of her reputation, Edmonds includes her personal correspondence addressed to congressional chairs and officials in the Department of Justice and Department of Defense that is delivered by the postal service.

Other websites obsure the ethos of the whistle-blower to protect the anonymity of sources that provide whistle-blowing documents and emphasize collective intelligence over individual credibility. However, the multiple authorship structure that such sites often deploy poses risks in representing a number of personal agendas and rhetorical motivations simultaneously. Furthermore, online disclosure of some kinds of whistle-blowing documents—such as the contents of secret police files from the Stasi in the former East Germany—is not considered to be feasible because of significant privacy concerns about disclosure; victims or unrelated parties could have highly confidential personal information revealed on the Internet.

For example, the website Wikileaks was temporarily closed down by a judge's order after it published records that seemed to indicate that a bank in the Cayman Islands was involved in possible tax evasion and money laundering. A representative from the bank complained to the news media of possible "harm from the widespread dissemination of private and confidential banking information, including account numbers, personal identification numbers, account transactions and history, and account balances," which could cause "identity theft and electronic theft of account balances" after a "disgruntled employee" posted the documents.[35] However, the Electronic Frontier Foundation was ultimately successful in a legal challenge to the judge's shutdown of the entire site via the internet service provider that was hosting the Wikileaks.org domain, which an editorial in the *New York Times* compared to "shutting down a newspaper because of objections to one article."[36] Other documents on the multilingual and multinational Wikileaks site include official information about U.S. federal guidelines for the treatment of detainees in terrorism cases, materials about corruption in Kenya and Bermuda, and the numbering systems used for NATO equipment.[37] The site interface used the familiar tabs of "article," "discussion," and "history" from Wikipedia, along with a tab for "view source."

Soon after Wikileaks was launched in December 2006, it inspired a watchdog group that often wrote critically about the site and the hundreds of thousands of documents that it published online. WikiLeak.org characterized itself as a "discussion blog about the ethical and technical issues" of the Wikileaks project. This site apparently maintained a certain amount of critical distance from its object of study, because it described itself as "not yet affiliated with the secretive and media manipulative" wiki for "mass document leaking."[38] However, during the legal troubles that Wikileaks faced and its highly publicized forced blackout in the United States, the once-critical WikiLeak.org blog listed the domain names of mirror sites for the whistle-blowing original to help visitors find documents, relevant articles, and position papers that the Wikileaks.org site had made available.

Online video has also become a prominent medium for whistle-blowers, although it manifests some of the same conflicts between its evidentiary and testimonial qualities that I have described to be at issue in the digital rhetoric of e-mail. In other words, often online video is not used by its creators as a means of intentional communication with the public to diffuse or discourage abuses, scandals, or disasters in the making. For example, human rights advocate Sam Gregory asks if "intention" should "matter any more." As he points out, "the most salient 'human rights' videos that have generated action recently have been shot by perpetrators."[39] As evidence, Gregory lists "torture videos by Egyptian police or the Malaysian Squatgate footage—or for that matter Abu Ghraib or the Saddam execution videos." Much like the e-mails released in reports about the Hurricane Katrina or *Columbia* debacles, these videos were not initially intended to be seen by others. They were private communications to be disseminated only among brutalizers, much as the largely one-to-one electronic mail messages were only supposed to be destined for those within the inner circles of incompetence, impotence, image maintenance, or conspiracy in the U.S. federal government.

Of course, not all whistle-blowing online video is produced by parties on the wrong side of the ethical divide, particularly since the "vlog" format often emphasizes the pose of a person speaking directly into the camera. In the YouTube video "Guantanamo Unclassified," a lawyer for detainee Adel Hamad shows interviews with defenders of his client who dispute the U.S. government's case that Hamad is an Al Qaeda supporter. The video emphasizes its testimonial authority by opening with footage of attorney William Teesdale that is actually shot on the shores of Guantánamo Bay, where his client is detained.[40] Another YouTube video shows a Lockheed Martin engineer who had worked on a contract for the U.S. Coast Guard detailing his safety and security concerns about the project in an extended first-person statement.[41] AT&T whistle-blower Mark Klein speaks out on "retroactive immunity and domestic surveillance" on Senator Christopher Dodd's YouTube channel.[42]

However, as Sam Gregory argues, in many parts of the world allowing one's personal identity to be revealed could have fatal consequences, given the history of human rights abuses by authoritarian regimes. Gregory operates The Hub, a video-sharing site maintained by Witness.org, an international group for human rights and civil society initiatives. Gregory, a documentary filmmaker who produced work shot in conflict zones in Burma, not only provides his subjects with cameras and a venue for publicizing human rights and civil liberties violations and antidemocratic practices around the world, but also emphasizes connections to advocacy and concrete action that can be taken by those who have seen what the witnesses have shared online. As Gregory points out, using computer and social networks to foster initiatives for civil society can have consequences for the protection of his subjects' privacy and anonymity as well.[43] Gregory asserts that those who shoot video in conflict zones must be made aware of negative as well as positive possible consequences. Practices involved in informed consent are detailed in a chapter on "Safety and Security" in a book on *Video for Change* that Gregory's group produced.[44] Even if online filmmakers do not show their faces, information about IP addresses and computer-mediated communication can be used to track down whistle-blowers.

In the United States, undercover reporting has also been an important strategy in online video linked to whistle-blowing cases, particularly for organizations involved in animal rights issues. In February 2008, digital video shot by The Humane Society of the United States (HSUH) of the treatment of sick, so-called downer cows spurred the largest beef recall in American history after clips propagated across the web. The recall targeted the Westland corporation, the number two supplier of beef to the school lunch program. As an example of witness journalism, the extremely graphic footage taken by the HSUS investigator, which shows live cows being dragged by chains or abused by forklifts, seems to have been enabled by smaller digital video recording devices that obviously escaped notice by his coworkers.[45] Although perceived as less influential to U. S. policy makers, People for the Ethical Treatment of Animals (PETA) has also tried to use online video and new mobile technologies to raise the profile of animal rights issues by showing chicken processing facilities in which a bored underclass of workers abuse the animals on the production line.[46]

E-mail archives, document wikis, and online video channels are not the only ways that electronic whistle-blowing is facilitated by the Internet. New data visualization and geotagging technologies can emphasize the geographic distribution of possible activities that merit whistle-blowing attention by emphasizing the neighborhoods in which otherwise invisible activities of political influence or unjustified redistribution of public wealth may be taking place. In connection with the 2007 Farm Bill, the Environmental Working Group created the Farm Subsidy Database, which revealed that many who were collecting federal subsidies lived far from agricultural areas.[47] The large progressive political blog *The Huffington Post* published a map of donors during the 2008 presidential election that showed where donors lived in specific regions of the country and how much they gave to individual candidates.[48] The Sunlight Foundation has created a map showing otherwise unreviewed and anonymous earmarks that may be attached to appropriations bills going through Congress.[49] In the Federal Funding Accountability and Transparency Act of 2006, this principle was generalized to authorize a government website to be launched in 2008 that would show where earmarks originate.[50] Such sites maintain a dispassionate neutrality in their spatial representation of numerical data and insist on their nonpartisan character.

Electronic communication's rapidity, broad access to channels of power, and global reach would seem to challenge existing institutional structures of political power in a number of ways. But in order to change public opinion in the long term, it is also important to take note of why some efforts at digital rhetoric are more successful than others and why some are perceived as having more credibility or sustained viability. In the tradition of English common law in which American jurisprudence is grounded, there is a right of confrontation built into the process of accusation. To bear witness is grounded in two acts of vision: the witness must see some wrong and visually apprehend it personally, and then he or she must testify to that wrong and be willing to be seen by the accused.[51] When videotaped or closed-circuit testimony was first allowed in certain U.S. courtrooms, it faced a number of legal challenges that went all the way up to the Supreme Court, where Justice Scalia complained that such procedures may be only "virtually constitutional."[52] Computer-mediated communication poses a number of similar challenges. It represents simultaneously action and text, speech and written code, the immediate and mediated, first-person appeals and third-person operations, and a number of hybridized expressions that often situate it somewhere between testimony and evidence.

7 Submit and Render: Digital Satires about Surveillance and Authentication

On Saturday, October 28, 2006, Indiana University graduate student Christopher Soghoian returned home around lunchtime to find his front door wide open. The window of the young computer scientist's apartment had been smashed, and there was glass scattered around the entranceway. Many valuable items—computers, hard drives, music CDs, and passports—had been taken. The place had been ransacked, and what was not of interest to the intruders had just been dumped out onto the floor. Immediately Soghoian called the local Bloomington police department to report the break-in. Officers came to the scene only to leave again when they found the search warrant from the U.S. District Court of Southern Indiana duct-taped to the kitchen table. Soghoian was told that he was on his own and that law enforcement wouldn't be searching for any criminals on his behalf.[1]

Federal agents had seized Soghoian's property because a few days earlier he had posted an online PHP form that would generate look-alike versions of authentic Northwest Airlines boarding passes. Soghoian's intention in making "Chris's Northwest Airlines Boarding Pass Generator" available was to publicize a vulnerability in the airport screening procedures of the Transportation Security Administration (TSA). The authorities felt that the novelty-seeking Internet audience that Soghoian reached with his boarding pass generator could have used his device for purposes other than the three that he suggested on his blog: (1) the pro-social "Meet your elderly grandparents at the gate," (2) the self-interested "'Upgrade' yourself once on the airplane—by printing another boarding pass for a ticket you're already purchased, only this time, in Business Class," and (3) his main suggestion to his fellow netizens: "Demonstrate that the TSA Boarding Pass/ID check is useless."[2] During the short period of time that his generator was accessible and operational, over 35,000 people visited Soghoian's website, entered some text, and then hit a button icon that would personalize their Northwest boarding passes as they chose. How many actually printed out these documents or tried to use them at an airport Soghoian would never know, but authorities felt that his generator posed a serious threat to public safety that merited separate legal interventions by two federal agencies.

Soghoian's story of finding himself in serious trouble with the law is about more than a one-time intrusion of the state into an individual's private life or retaliation for the actions of a single hacker fomenting revolt against authority. The larger rhetoric surrounding the competing ideologies represented in the raid on the Bloomington apartment shows how the surveillance and automation made possible by computational media can be used to reinforce existing institutional hierarchies, and yet these same digital tools in the hands of empowered political subjects can be employed to subvert the authentication processes, security protocols, and data-mining functions of the very federal agencies that police the public. More generally, this narrative displays the anxieties of government officials toward the interactivity offered (or deferred) by the interfaces that are now in the hands of their citizens, from simple online forms to sophisticated digital design interfaces with layers and timelines such as Photoshop and Flash.

As Congress misunderstood the meaning of the SonicJihad fan film described in the first chapter of this book—which turned out to be an example of harmless online ephemera, although it was at first taken by government consultants and elected representatives to be a videogame for "terrorist training"—federal officials seemed to manifest a similar form of media illiteracy in Soghoian's case by overreacting to his online boarding pass generator. Both of these limited interactivity electronic artifacts—the fan film and the web generator—became associated with criminality and, by extension, terrorism. Even though these Internet satires that involved remixing or coding digital content were embedded in recognizable discursive practices associated with game forums in one case and blogging among hackers in the other, government officials could not understand the workings of their media ecologies and so rushed to judgment.

Why are fan cultures and hacker cultures particularly suspicious to institutional policy makers? While fans are seen as parasitic and lacking in content-creation abilities, hackers are seen as devious and likely to subvert the deliberative practices that others engage in openly and honestly. In other words, both groups are portrayed in print and broadcast culture as bad citizens who abuse existing power relationships. Academics, such as Henry Jenkins, may try to explain these alternative paradigms of citizenship to lawmakers by applying a heuristic of "participatory culture,"[3] but miscommunication persists in spite of these frequent attempts at translation by public intellectuals. Unfortunately, this anxiety-driven suspicion perpetuates a reactive, piecemeal information strategy on the government's part, along with a philosophy about technology that emphasizes instrumentalism and proprietary ownership and a deep distrust of the everyday digital practices of average citizens.

The capabilities of new digital tools not only push at the limits of the enforcement of legal codes, but also they put tolerance of communal norms to the test. Forms of political speech that may be deemed offensive to some, according to more ossified community standards, can be facilitated by the hybrid discourses that these computer-mediated operations and interfaces enable and find receptive audiences on the Internet. In other words, an ability to manipulate the content of digital files risks breaching certain social contracts while forging others. In this environment, web generators, such as Soghoian's, can become an important genre for social and political satire. In particular, web generators can serve as a vehicle for pointed critiques of the ideologies of freedom that drive both the economic salesmanship and the modes of supposedly individualized expression associated with the Internet in general and the user-generated content of Web 2.0 in particular.

Authenticating the Authenticators

The authorities investigated Soghoian because soon after his generator went up, Representative Edward Markey of Massachusetts was calling upon the presidential administration of George W. Bush "to investigate, apprehend those responsible, shut down the website, and warn airlines and aviation security officials."[4] Although he later apologized for pushing prosecution rather than commendation for Soghoian,[5] Congressman Markey initially told ABC News that there were "enough loopholes at the backdoor of our passenger airplanes from not scanning cargo for bombs; we should not tolerate any new loopholes making it easier for terrorists to get into the front door of a plane."[6] Soghoian may have considered posting the boarding pass generator to his blog to be a logical extension of his First Amendment right to criticize the government and a form of political speech, but Markey saw the graduate student's action as an intentional security breach that only exacerbated existing breaches.

Ironically, Soghoian credits an even more senior elected official than Markey with providing step-by-step online instructions for an actual plan, using digitally produced documents, for terrorist implementation at an airport. In 2005, a year and a half earlier, Senator Charles Schumer published a detailed scenario on his official website that describes an attacker using online check-in to print out a boarding pass and then create "a second almost identical boarding pass" that has been electronically manipulated "either by scanning or altering the original image, depending on the airline system and the technology" a person on the terrorist watch list "uses at home."[7]

Schumer's instructions reiterated information that had already appeared in *Slate* magazine, where a journalist explained how Microsoft Publisher could be used to create an additional boarding pass for someone named "Serious Threat" in about ten minutes.[8] With similar hyperbole, in Schumer's scenario the potentially dangerous person is named "Joe Terror." Soghoian's step-by-step plan had twice as many steps as Schumer's and the fraudulent passenger's watch list name was "Ali Terrorist." In the accompanying blog post, Soghoian said that it was "trivially easy" and the work of

Figure 7.1
Boarding Pass Generator sample. Courtesy of Christopher Soghoian.

"20 seconds with a text-editor, and not even requiring you to open photoshop."[9] On his blog Soghoian wrote that he had made the task even easier for his audience by creating an online generator because he "realized today that editing HTML, while easy enough for a geek, is still far too difficult for population at large."[10] To similarly underline the ridiculousness of foiling actual terrorists with the pretense that mere visual recognition by a human screener could authenticate the printed code for mechanical scanning from a computer-generated document, the sample boarding pass on Soghoian's boarding pass site read "Osama bin Laden."

In an interview, Soghoian said that publicizing this generator was also part of his protest against the widespread practice of what he called "feature creep." Although feature creep is generally associated with particular practices in software development, when product lines or project requirements are driven by an ever-expanding client wish list or the hyperactive imaginations of designers in the absence of user testing, Soghoian sees it as a broader tendency in information culture to ignore situational appropriateness and the historical circumstances in which a given technological solution was created. He argues that urging feature creep is a particular practice of nonspecialists in government organizations who rely on computerization to keep track of the citizens they supposedly serve. Soghoian claims that the limitations of a given system's features must be respected and the fact that computerized records are always designed from a particular context for a particular purpose must be remembered. He contends that too often policy makers give license to extend old features arbitrarily into new procedures whenever seemingly expedient. For example, Soghoian cites the use of Social Security numbers for legal identification as a similarly misguided repurposing of discrete data, in that a number designed only for record location for a specific federal benefits program became a universal system for authentication. In some ways, Soghoian would argue, the boarding pass case is even more ludicrous, since the federal government is using an artifact of a private company to authenticate an individual's identity, which is the reverse of the public-to-private Social Security case.

In the era of highly constrained user-generated content and mass-market social media applications, web generators like Soghoian's have become a standard, recognizable Internet genre. To computer users in the general public, these popular web-based forms seem both to create original verbal or visual online texts and to output data that conforms to specific and recognizable conventions. For example, the Church Sign Generator at a heavily trafficked site allows users to insert their own phrases into a stock photograph of a roadside church sign. The accompanying text explains that during the site's prehistory, the webmaster focused solely on photographing humorous church signs in the Austin, Texas, area, which he posted to his web log. As the blog gained more readers and even would-be contributors, the site owner began to receive doctored photos from imitators with invented messages to potential congregants and the public. To enable more of his readers to participate in these media-creation activities that otherwise required some expert knowledge of proprietary software, such as the popular program Photoshop, he posted a PHP-based web generator to his site for personalizing the church signs. The basic instructions were simple: visitors to the webpage choose a sign, input text, and then receive a digital photograph with their individual language choices emblazoned on a church sign.

The author of the Church Sign Generator explicitly invites the visitor to engage with his online content interactively to gratify a form of wish fulfillment that would

Figure 7.2
The church sign generator by Ryland Sanders. Courtesy of Ryland Sanders.

be prohibited in the offline world, because social norms make such manipulation of the private property and public messages of others taboo: "Ever seen those signs in front of churches with the moveable letters? Ever wanted to rearrange the letters to make your own church sign? Well, now you can. Choose a design below, add your text, and a personalized church sign photo will be generated for you! Save it, send it to a friend, put on your website, or use it however you like. Enjoy!"[11] Other conventionally forbidden activities of defacement that can be indulged in through web generators include writing on blackboards, painting graffiti, and giving women tattoos.

These web generators can also allow users to personalize signifiers of authority, education, or privilege by allowing visitors to put their own names on law enforcement badges, diplomas, military dog tags, and access passes. Similar hard goods have been available for a long time from cottage industries associated with themed entertainment, novelty products, monogramming, and photographic services. Like the earlier generation of custom artifacts, digitally generated objects can create institutional liabilities when they are taken to be authentic and thus invested with the power of cultural capital and even—in certain situations—unwarranted contractual or political legitimacy.

Government agencies often display understandable anxiety about replication technologies that can make forgeries of national currencies or official citizenship documents much easier to attempt. In the United States, to forestall legislation and oversight efforts that would have regulated high-tech consumer electronics, manufacturers of xerographic color copiers incorporated algorithms designed to introduce "noise" into the distinctive microprinting common in banknotes or to use proprietary methods to encode traceable printer identification numbers in the documents that a given machine produces. The software program Photoshop similarly cooperates with authorities to prevent counterfeiting: "Adobe® Photoshop® software includes a counterfeit deterrence system (CDS) that prevents the use of the product to illegally duplicate banknotes. As implemented, CDS prevents users from opening detailed images of banknotes within Photoshop."[12]

In contrast, web generators can be created by free agents with no profit motive and thus no corresponding need for public respectability. Yet convention dictates that convincing forgeries are rarely made by web generators. Although there is a generator for manufacturing plausible driver's license numbers from Florida, Illinois, and Wisconsin,[13] the genre as a whole tends to maintain sufficient mimetic distance, and thus law enforcement rarely becomes involved. Soghoian himself claims that his generator was primarily designed not for making forgeries but for rhetorical purposes: to publicize a serious airport security flaw that had gone uncorrected for years. Soghoian also notes that the Northwest boarding pass is not a state-issued piece of identification to begin with, since it originates in the customer service practices of a private corporation unaffiliated with the government or the TSA.

In fact, Soghoian's boarding pass generator is not the only computer program devoted to authenticating the authenticators, particularly since the verification of human authorship can be complicated by the advent of computational media. Very early in the history of literary and linguistic computing, programmers turned their attention to the synthesis of convincing syntax in natural language, and almost as quickly the texts generated by such programs were being used to test the discriminatory powers of human beings. By 1971, computer scientists were trumpeting the successes of poems like "The Meditation of IBM 1094–7040 DCS," which were culled from fragments gathered from random searches of poetry anthologies.[14] Using this same poetry-generation program, a 1978 study asked college composition students to identify which poems were written by a computer and which were written by a human being.[15] It turned out that students at Harvard, perhaps the most prestigious university in the country, were no more likely to be able to differentiate correctly between a poem by Philip Levine and computer-generated verse than were their less-privileged community college peers in the same study. Often these experiments with generators present new variations of the famed Turing Test, in which a person is supposed to guess if he or she is communicating with a person or with a computer.[16]

Such generators blur the highbrow/lowbrow distinctions that separate these programs from so-called literary electronic hypertexts. The same combinatorial procedures that are credited by elite artistic communities and new media creators—who trace their poetic lineages to the experimentalism of Dadism, Oulipo, Fluxus, L=A=N=G=U=A=G=E poetry, or other aleatory forms of composition[17]—can also operate in web generators with mass appeal, because this emphasis on modularity and variability is manifested in many online web generators. The Dada Poetry Generator suggests cutting and pasting text from "an online article or newspaper for best results,"[18] and Josh Larios, who programmed a poetry-writing generator called "Poetry Corner," says he drew his inspiration from his past experiences with online communities when he worked "for a company with a website for kids" that had a "bulletin board type of thing, where kids could write in and get 'published'" with content that was mostly poetry, some of which Larios faintly praises as "pretty good . . . for a 12 year old." Much of the poetry made by Larios's generator is written as a series of lowercase "I statements." The beginning of a representative sample reads: "i am the sun. brighter than / any star because of what we grow / up & do."

With the advent of spam filters, a new genre of randomly generated text is increasingly likely to reach users' inboxes even without a trip to a generator website. Editorial opinion pieces in newspapers,[19] projects by digital artists,[20] and pseudoacademic "institutes"[21] have all been devoted to celebrating, preserving, and archiving spam word combinations, which can produce surprisingly lyrical subject lines such as "Sound creates form, excruciating formal" and "Which talk or crew, not believe no nurse."[22] In the daily lives of average consumers and workers, randomly generated poetry can also be written with the aid of commercially produced hard goods available as novelty items for use in the home or office. Although magnetic poetry displayed on refrigerators and magnetic boards may still reify the intention and agency connected to traditional poetics, there are poetry-makers who use dice or cards to increase the randomization of the resultant text as well.

The products of the literary arts are not the only cultural objects presented for the tribute or ridicule of web generators. Similar algorithms for repetition and variation can also be applied to painterly computer-generated images, so that online audiences can imitate their favorite artists as well as poets such as Emily Dickinson[23] or William Carlos Williams.[24] Sometimes these art generators are more gentle homages than barbed satires, which invite participation and play, as in the case of the Jackson Pollock Generator and the Modern Art Generator. However, even when famous artists are not presented as the butts of jokes, such web generators do suggest that particular aesthetics or styles that have established certain painterly brands or amassed the cultural capital for blockbuster shows may be lacking in artistic integrity. For example, The Warholizer can turn digital images of friends and family members into pictures reminiscent of the "'assembly line' art" of Andy Warhol's repeating industrial silk-screened compositions of the 1960s,[25] and the simple automation of this photographic transformation might reinforce certain critical arguments that tend to dismiss Warhol's work as kitsch.

Not surprisingly, academia is frequently another chosen foil for web generators, particularly if its theories and methodologies seem to have been petrified into easily assembled institutional clichés. For example, Andrew C. Bulhak, creator of the Postmodern Essay Generator, suggests that postmodern criticism could be written just as coherently and authoritatively if manufactured by chance operations by a machine. Bulhak applied the Dada Engine to creating his postmodern prose generator, which manufactures convoluted writing with polysyllabic diction and generous footnotes at the push of a refresh browser button. Thus the Postmodern Essay Generator spouts out papers with titles like "Pretextual Theories: Objectivism, Debordist Situation, and Cultural Deappropriation."[26]

Bulhak makes his criticism of theoretical postmodernism even more explicit in a scientific paper about his generator, in which he compares the system's output of pseudo-postmodern prose to a simulation of "mental debility," as might be observed in the "ranting of a paranoid schizophrenic street preacher, or perhaps a USENET ranter."[27] He suggests that the script could also be modified to mimic the writing in "eccentric pseudoscientic/religious pamphlets."[28] However, situating computer-generated discourse in the realm of mental illness—or of mental health—is not particularly new. As programmer of the Postmodernism Generator, Bulhak acknowledges his debt to "Weizenbaum's ELIZA (which simulates a psychiatrist) and Ken Colby's PARRY (which simulates a paranoid mental patient)."[29]

Bulhak describes his computer program as an homage to the hoax of physicist Alan Sokal,[30] who achieved fame outside academia by submitting an article entitled "Transgressing the Boundaries: Toward a Transformative Hermeneutics of Quantum Gravity" to the journal *Social Text*.[31] Editors decided to publish what Sokal later revealed to be a spoof that parodied the radical relativism of contemporary critical theory, which Sokal felt undermined what he called the foundations of "reason, evidence, and logic" in the university.[32] One interesting feature of Bulhak's paper about the Postmodernism Generator is that, as he reflects on his reasons for programming it, he is reluctant to take his assertions about postmodern culture into the realm of politics as Sokal does. While Sokal asserts his identity as a "leftist" and "feminist,"[33] Bulhak's argument never gets far outside the college campus as its rhetorical context. In fact, Bulhak explains that at first "this script was originally written with the intention of generating bogus practice examination papers to be distributed in lectures for the purpose of scaring students." Bulhak's larger rhetorical purpose appears only to be to discredit one side in the disciplinary feud between the sciences and the humanities, which C.P. Snow once called "the two cultures" conflict.[34] Bulhak claims to have chosen critical theory because it is "easy to convincingly generate meaningless and yet realistic travesties of works in it . . . because of the combination of the complex, opaque jargon used in these sorts of works and the subjectivity of the discipline; similar automated travesties of papers in, say, mathematics or physics, would be less successful, because of the scientific rigor of these fields."[35]

However, contrary to Bulhak's assertion, the academic pretensions of scientific disciplines are not immune to generator satires. Three MIT students used SCIgen, a program that generates random computer science papers in Association for Computing Machinery format—complete with graphs, figures, and citations—to fool the organizers of the 2005 World Multiconference on Systemics, Cybernetics, and Informatics, a supposedly peer-reviewed conference in Orlando, Florida, known for its spam-style solicitations of those who work in universities on technology-related issues.[36] With titles such as "Harnessing Byzantine Fault Tolerance Using Classical Theory," "Synthesizing Checksums and Lamda Calculus Using *Jog*," and "On the Study of the Ethernet," these papers demonstrated that computer science also had its stock buzzwords. Such automatically generated papers have also been successful at deceiving organizers of mathematics, emerging technology, and new media conferences.

Soghoian was similarly trying to test the discriminatory powers of human beings with a computer-generated text when he created his boarding pass generator. As a former member of the Security and Privacy Advanced Research Lab at Johns Hopkins University and a frequent traveler who had backpacked through Asia and lived on a beach in India, Soghoian had experienced a series of epiphanies about transportation safety in the months leading up to the raid.[37] He had been present when civil libertarian John Gilmore issued the famous "No ID Challenge" at a public meeting of an advisory committee for the Department of Homeland Security,[38] at which this cofounder of the Electronic Frontier Foundation distributed stamped envelopes and challenged privacy advocates to mail their government-issued identification to their addresses and then try to get on planes home without ID. One of Gilmore's test subjects, attorney Jim Harper, took his green envelope and made a public announcement to the crowd in support of Gilmore's "insistence on rights, his firm insistence on his rights and ours."[39]

Shortly after attending Burning Man that year,[40] Soghoian decided to take Gilmore up on his challenge, and he began to fly without identification. During this period, Soghoian was in a relationship with a woman in Washington, D.C., and he always flew Northwest Airlines because it was the lowest-cost carrier with direct flights. As a backpacker, frequent traveler, and holder of passports from three countries, Soghoian was not intimidated by the travel procedures and even expressed a certain bravado about the fact that he had flown without identification over fifteen times since making this resolution in support of the principle that people are entitled to have the experience of domestic "flying without the government knowing."

Soghoian admits that he does not have "the best relationship with authority," but he claims that there are larger lessons to be learned by the general public when airport procedures serve as mechanisms for political and social coercion. Although he says that an anti-TSA protest "won't get you arrested" or cause a resistant passenger to "get sent to Guantánamo," Soghoian points out that the state-sanctioned architectures of control make it "difficult to exercise your rights," because the Transportation Security Administration still has the power to make passengers miss their flights. Thus, the TSA controls a very valuable commodity in both business and leisure: time. Soghoian says that, as a graduate student and backpacker, he was a member of an unusually liberated class, because his "time is worth nothing."[41]

Among those interested in computational media, Soghoian is not alone in looking at the procedurality of airport security screening and the Foucauldian conflation of knowledge and power that the TSA represents, which is consequently ripe for parody. Computational media theory professor and game designer Ian Bogost has created two videogames about airport security procedures. In *Airport Insecurity*, the player takes the position of a disgruntled passenger in what Bogost describes as a "game about inconvenience and the tradeoffs between security and rights in American airports."[42] The rules of the game are actually derived from the text of post-2002 government reports that indicate that "the effectiveness of airport security practices is uncertain," although "the government wants you to believe that increased protection and reduced rights are necessary to protect you from terrorism."[43] To bring participation in his satire into the public sphere, Bogost encourages travelers to play the downloadable game on their laptops in any of its three modes—"Normal, Practice, and Endless Queue"— while waiting in an actual airport security line. In his other airport security game, the rapid-response online Shockwave game *Airport Security*, the player assumes the role of a TSA guard who must pointlessly "inspect each passenger and his luggage and remove the forbidden items before allowing the passenger to go through," even though "the list of forbidden items changes on a moment-to-moment basis."[44] In this difficult-to-play game, the suddenly prohibited items carried or worn by passengers queued up in line may include cowboy hats and cow skulls along with "pants, mouthwash, and hummus."[45]

Security technologist and cryptographer Bruce Schneier maintains a popular blog that often addresses many of the inadequacies of existing airport protocols, which sometimes seem to function for purposes of ceremonial display that are devoted more to controlling passengers than to controlling terrorists. In a 2007 posting addressing the TSA's notoriously inaccurate No Fly List, Schneier pointed readers to a web generator created by the S3 Matching Technologies corporation[46] that emulated the operations of the antiquated 1913 Soundex system that critics said the TSA was using at the time for finding all the possible homophones for the permutations of Arabic names by crudely "removing vowels from names and then assigning numerical values to the remaining consonants."[47] S3's overly inclusive homophone generator, which would include even those with Anglo-Saxon names, was obviously a case of a generator serving as a rhetorical device designed to be persuasive to federal authorities, specifically in order to gain lucrative government contracts for the data-mining company by taking them away from competitors. Thanks to widespread exposure on many blogs, this generator had an extremely large public relations reach that appealed to thousands of visitors to the site, who tried out their own names to see if they could be mistaken for a terrorist.

Blogs, wikis, and other social media outlets have been used as pointed tools of critique against the TSA and other federal agencies associated with Homeland Security efforts. Since the September 11, 2001 attacks on the World Trade Center, the popular megablog *Boing Boing*, which widely publicized Soghoian's case, has frequently shared traveler horror stories about passengers being humiliated for attempting to transport innocuous toddler sippy cups, snack pudding, breast milk, geological samples, and embarrassing sexual devices. BoingBoing also directs readers to other blogs that catalog TSA abuses, such as that of photographer Kathleen Shafer, who specializes in photographing airports as aesthetic spaces and who has solicited TSA horror stories on her blog after hearing colleagues complain about damaged film and cameras.[48] In contrast, conservative bloggers who accept the ideology of rule-based vigilance promulgated by the TSA have used their blogs to complain of flights in which suspicious behavior takes place without consequences and to which bureaucratic government workers or airline customer service representatives are nonresponsive.

To provide a retort to these negative user-generated stories about TSA abuse and incompetence, the agency has entered the realm of digital media production itself.

The TSA now operates a website called Myth Busters, in which they debunk urban legends, such as the tale of the eight-year-old on the TSA watch list, and refute critical passenger accounts, sometimes with their own video from security cameras.[49] The also maintain a YouTube channel and an official blog.

Surveilling the Surveillers

When federal agents first visited Soghoian, radical openness on his website was his primary strategy for dealing with their threatening demeanor and their insinuations that he would be facing serious criminal penalties. When the FBI appeared at his door the day before the break-in to "chat," he advertised his plight on his blog before he went out to meet with them in a public place. Soghoian chose the neutral ground of a coffee shop, with his departmental advisor as a witness, who was also threatened with detention if she refused to cooperate. Soghoian even posted scans of the search warrant and the takedown notice for his website from the TSA and the names of the FBI agents who had visited him, although they were later removed at the agency's insistence. Although he felt this ethos of openness seemed to solicit communal support and offers of legal protection from pro bono lawyers, it also seems to have irritated federal authorities further. As he explained their attitude to his self-publishing approach, "Don't fuck with us or at least don't do it publicly." This emphasis on public exposure is also present in his writing on his web log, where Soghoian described a government agency only capable of acting conscientiously when it is "publicly shamed into doing so," so that "the only way for these kind of problems to get fixed" is "through public full disclosure."[50] When Soghoian describes the function of the Internet, however, this is not a Habermassian public sphere, which functions as a space of rational deliberation. Rather, he describes the World Wide Web as a site for public humiliation that can be suitable just as easily for displaying the crimes of citizens as it can be for creating a spectacle of the crimes of the state.

For Rutgers art professor Hasan Elahi, radical transparency using web publication has served as a form of both accommodation to and political resistance against the TSA's policies. Since being detained at the Detroit airport as a suspected explosives specialist, an experience from which he inferred that he must be on the national terrorist watch list, the Bangladeshi-born Elahi has used a combination of photoblogging and GPS tracking to publicize his precise moment-to-moment location and activities and maintain the perfect alibi at all times. In an interview, Elahi explained how he used detailed photoblogging to deprive his opponents of their chief means of control over his person and activities.

"I've discovered that the best way to protect your privacy is to give it away" he says. . . . Elahi relishes upending the received wisdom about surveillance. The government monitors your movements, but it gets things wrong. You can monitor yourself much more accurately. Plus, no ambitious agent is going to score a big intelligence triumph by snooping into your movements when there's a Web page broadcasting the Big Mac you ate four minutes ago in Boise, Idaho. "It's economics," he says. "I flood the market."[51]

His website even includes copies of his debit card transactions and other minutiae from the paper ephemera of his everyday life's transactions.[52] As Elahi notes, his students already put themselves in this extremely public position as members of social network sites like MySpace and Facebook. Futhermore, Elahi's technique allows him to watch the government agents watching him, as frequent checks of his server logs reveal visits from computer users with official government IP addresses.

Elahi's work reflects growing interest among scholars and activists in "sousveillance," or the use of ubiquitous computing and mobile digital recording to provide a record of experience of life lived at ground level. Steve Mann and others advocate wearing cameras or other recording devices at all times as a way to facilitate data collection for possible counternarratives situated in diegetic spaces. Mann argues that sousveillance reasserts citizens' rights to the commons by "uncovering the panopticon and undercutting its primacy and privilege."[53]

However, Soghoian did not publicly report everything notable that happened to him during his encounters with federal authorities, which did not fully end until July 2007, when he received an official letter from the government that said that the TSA had finally dropped the investigation. In an interview, Soghoian described how—after he had agreed to remove his website with the boarding pass generator and purged the files from the server—the head of cybercrime for the regional area that includes Indiana expressed alarm at still seeing the boarding pass generator on his computer screen in the remote location of his office. At this point Soghoian realized that this powerful official in charge of understanding very sophisticated attacks on computing systems could not even perform one of the most simple tasks of basic computer hygiene: clearing his cache. To assuage the irrational fears of federal agents that Soghoian was somehow still maintaining his site post-takedown, he had to fax written instructions to the head office with a step-by-step list of how-tos for cache clearing.

Soghoian never made the source code for this boarding pass generator public. However, soon after his site was removed by order of the federal authorities, an imitator who went by the patriotic L33T pseudonym "J0hn 4d4m5" made another, more portable version of the Northwest boarding pass generator available. Unlike Soghoian's code, the copycat programmer designed a generator that could be "implemented only using HTML and javascript" so that "you do not need a web server where you can run PHP; you need no server at all."[54] Not only could users run the generator in their browsers directly from the downloaded files with more privacy, but also they could use Adams's tool to create generators of their own. On his website, Adams argued that such generators could be remarkably rhetorically effective, since "no action was taken untill Christopher Soghoian produced his script," and the "generator got people's attention."[55]

Another wag created a warrant generator based on Soghoian's case, in which the "script has been created for district courts all across the United States with the intent of improving national security by reducing the amount of time it takes for our public guardians to create search warrants."[56] Users can enter names, addresses, and possible legal justifications into the warrant generator and receive a warrant that looks much like Soghoian's Bloomington original. To emphasize its satiric character, the warrant generator is generously supplied with additional instructions, such as "Enter desired legal mumbo-jumbo below. Again, make sure to use run-on sentences and try to cite some laws and codes and stuff."[57]

The way that generators generated other generators in Soghoian's case illustrates the importance of one of the common features of this genre: its power for social as well as computational replication. As a case in point, the Generator Blog, an encyclopedic web log that has archived almost a thousand examples of the genre, advertises itself as a repository of "software that creates software."[58] Although this definition does not strictly describe most of the content of the *Generator Blog* site, much of which is devoted to straightforward image macros that simply superimpose text on pictures and relatively simple PHP and Javascript programs, the phrase indicates the essential character of the popular perception of how these programs function in social discourse. Indeed, in *Cultural Software: A Theory of Ideology*, J. M. Balkin has argued that "toolmaking tools" are an important component of our human experience as *homo faber* and part of the lived ideology that expresses itself as rapidly traveling and replicating "memes."[59] For example, like J0hn 4d4m5, the creator of the Church Sign Generator posted his source code in the spirit of a free culture ethos that tends toward propagation, as well as to signal transparency about his media production practices and a willingness to provide models if not mentorship to others in generator-making.

Certainly, many web generators are concerned with the power of particular speech acts and the magic of linguistic artifacts. For example, although there is clearly more direct satire involved in creating a generator for FBI warrants, the design of the Mobster Threat Generator could be said to similarly comment upon the relationship between language and coercion. In fact, curses and blessings occupy a significant subgenre among the most popular web generator sites, and anthropologists have long noted their generative power.[60]

Many of the cursing generators avoid crass obscenity or colloquialism in their expressions, and some assume mock religious, historical, literary, or linguistic pretensions. There are curse generators that draw content from religious scriptures, and several that use canonical literary texts. For example, the Biblical Curse Generator appeals to website visitors with the following pitch: "Lost for a smart remark to see

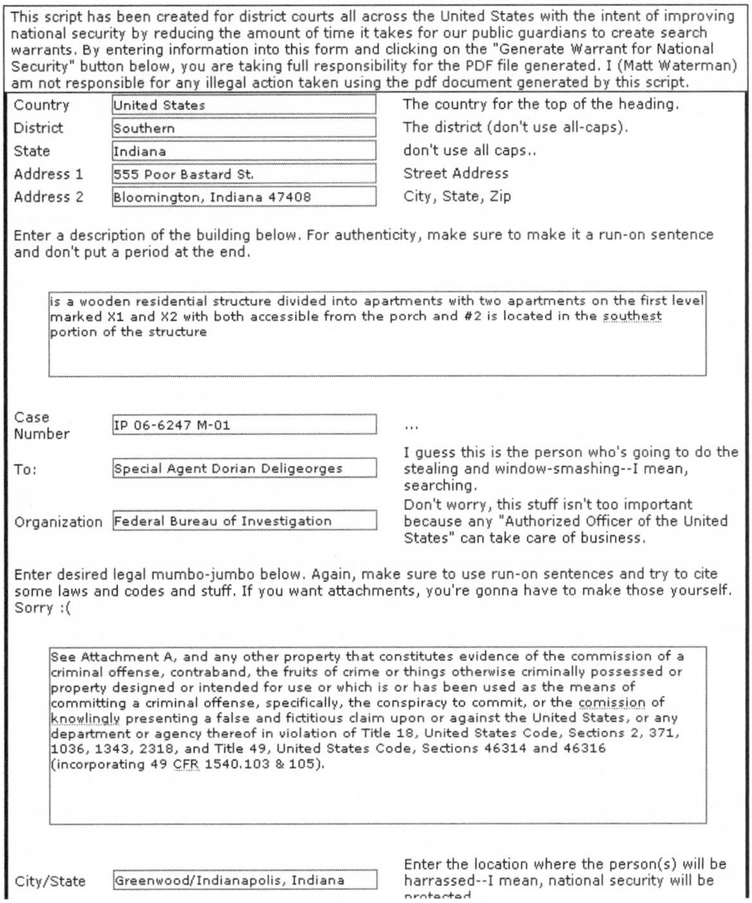

This script has been created for district courts all across the United States with the intent of improving national security by reducing the amount of time it takes for our public guardians to create search warrants. By entering information into this form and clicking on the "Generate Warrant for National Security" button below, you are taking full responsibility for the PDF file generated. I (Matt Waterman) am not responsible for any illegal action taken using the pdf document generated by this script.

Country	United States	The country for the top of the heading.
District	Southern	The district (don't use all-caps).
State	Indiana	don't use all caps..
Address 1	555 Poor Bastard St.	Street Address
Address 2	Bloomington, Indiana 47408	City, State, Zip

Enter a description of the building below. For authenticity, make sure to make it a run-on sentence and don't put a period at the end.

is a wooden residential structure divided into apartments with two apartments on the first level marked X1 and X2 with both accessible from the porch and #2 is located in the southest portion of the structure

Case Number	IP 06-6247 M-01	...
To:	Special Agent Dorian Deligeorges	I guess this is the person who's going to do the stealing and window-smashing--I mean, searching.
Organization	Federal Bureau of Investigation	Don't worry, this stuff isn't too important because any "Authorized Officer of the United States" can take care of business.

Enter desired legal mumbo-jumbo below. Again, make sure to use run-on sentences and try to cite some laws and codes and stuff. If you want attachments, you're gonna have to make those yourself. Sorry :(

See Attachment A, and any other property that constitutes evidence of the commission of a criminal offense, contraband, the fruits of crime or things otherwise criminally possessed or property designed or intended for use or which is or has been used as the means of committing a criminal offense, specifically, the conspiracy to commit, or the comission of knowlingly presenting a false and fictitious claim upon or against the United States, or any department or agency thereof in violation of Title 18, United States Code, Sections 2, 371, 1036, 1343, 2318, and Title 49, United States Code, Sections 46314 and 46316 (incorporating 49 CFR 1540.103 & 105).

| City/State | Greenwood/Indianapolis, Indiana | Enter the location where the person(s) will be harrassed--I mean, national security will be protected |

Figure 7.3
Warrant generator created in response to the seizure of Soghoian's property. Courtesy of Matt Waterman.

off your enemies? Unable to deliver that killer insult? Put an end to 'I was speechless!' misery with the amazing Biblical Curse Generator, which is pre-loaded with blistering put-downs as delivered by Elijah, Jeremiah and other monumentally angry saints."[61] Although this curse generator has a simple push-button interface, visitors to the site are given opportunities for a more participatory experience on another page that offers a monthly caption competition for images in which clergy or lay worshippers seem to appear ridiculous. The Elizabethan Curse Generator, which also consists of little more than a push-button interface, similarly has associated web materials that indicate a recombinant interdisciplinary collection of elements that speaks to the heterogenousness of some of the textual practices associated with generator sharing and making communities. Webmaster Trevor Stone has published the source code of both the PHP and the Perl versions of his curse generator and has provided links to the JavaScript version made by an imitator who "took the initiative" and to a large pool of other Internet memes.[62]

Curses are not the only form of magical speech among web generators, since there are also a number of blessings generators. For example, the Worldwide Blessings Generator combines generated texts with images from the world's religious traditions and objects of meditation by using "Javascript to pick each line and three photos at random."[63] Visitors to the site can also suggest that more blessings be added to the database by using an online form. On this form, the author of the Blessings Generator explains the syntactic rules of his blessings generator, in which utterances always begin with the word "may," which is ironically the same structure that is used in many curse generators.

Compliments and insults are produced by a related and yet separate class of web generators. Multiple compliment generators merge proscribed beneficent parts of speech into a pre-formatted message of flattery or praise. For example, the Surrealistic Compliment Generator combines web generator genres by paying tribute to the early twentieth-century heritage of recombinatory media artworks.[64] There are also other generators for speech acts with positive real-world effects, such as generators that create love poems or pick-up lines to persuade potential romantic or sexual partners to move toward greater social intimacy with the speaker or writer. On the opposite side of the semiotic spectrum, the Open Directory alone catalogs twenty-two separate insult generators, which actually represent a mere fraction of the genre.[65] In the case of insults, some involve web forms to further personalize the barb.

Sometimes a web generator that produces an abusive diatribe is designed with a particular political or institutional target in mind. Produced in the rhetorical context of mass lay-offs and unpopular new editorial policies at the *Los Angeles Times*, "Okay, Tell Zell: Go Down in Flames, Hack!*" generates a blistering resignation letter that can be automatically e-mailed to the owner of the newspaper by disgruntled staffers, which will arrive in his inbox with a subject line reading "You Mean Twisted Leprechaun."[66]

Finally, no taxonomy including taboo forms of language in web generators is complete without pointing out that there are also a number of sites that transform what may be civil language on regular websites into scatalogical or sexually explicit texts, such as the Pornolyzer, which also serves as an online translating program for multilingual obscenities. At the other extreme, there are also generators for euphemisms, which render the initial word more inoffensive. A Family Values Generator comes complete with a "censor" button that inserts asterisks in the generated profanity.[67]

There are other kinds of generators that can be understood through anthropological frameworks or speech act theories as well. For example, many web generators are designed to recreate the act of naming. Given the fact that screen names constitute a primary identifier for members of online communities, creating or choosing names is often a significant practice in digital culture. The names produced by popular web generators frequently represent the identities of transgressive personalities, such as mafia hitmen, pirates, serial killers, gangsters, and ogres. However, name generators also exist for popes, superheroes, Mormons, and others associated with exemplary lives and social purity. Such naming can have implications for privacy as well, which is always a key concern for those who take part in virtual communities or online commerce. Bruce Schneier, who publicized the Soundex generator on his security politics blog, has examined how random name generators can actually generate false identities for purposes of crime, political resistance, or heightened privacy.[68]

Pseudointeractivity and Web 2.0

All these speech act categories are exemplary of what experts in computers and other technologies call "automagical" thinking,[69] an adjective that combines the wonder associated with mechanistic processes with that used for supernatural effects. Virtuosity in the stage-managing of interface and programming design can make the output appear to be particularly responsive to the user's unarticulated needs. In this way, complex technical processes are also hidden from users or operators and thus are experienced as phenomena without rational explanations. Thus, digital culture itself is often a topic for the satire of web generators, in that these automagical PHP forms draw attention to the lowest common denominator of interactivity or user-generated content.

Although Pierre Lévy and Henry Jenkins have celebrated the potential of a synergistic participatory culture that capitalizes on collective intelligence, social media, and transmedia storytelling platforms for user-generated texts of all sorts, there are many who have been critical of the Web 2.0 paradigm. Some argue that this has led to an elevation of the "amateur" that destabilizes longstanding cultural values that are gauged by the merit of intellectual property;[70] others claim that capitalism has too large a stake in the so-called new communalism[71] and that nihilism rather than utopianism is being made manifest.[72] Still other skeptics point to media consolidation,[73] the lessons about gender-based marketing from feminist economics,[74] the dangers of Eurocentric tribalism to avatars of color,[75] and the possibilities of a "hive mind" that enforces "Digital Maoism."[76]

Certainly, there are ways that this convergence of technology and user behavior can be stultifying, particularly when certain "architectures of control"[77] are in place that obviate the potential of technologies created by the merging of hardware and software. Most obviously, a customizable template is still a template, so that experiences in commercial social media venues are still constrained by programming routines and organizational restrictions that potentially also limit emergent behaviors that could occur outside of prepackaged results. Thus many web generators lampoon the corporate logic of the new digital economy, which is constituted by a parasitic and opportunistic relationship to user behavior. Sometimes these satiric generators only focus on empty salesmanship and business plans built on "vaporware." For example, the Dot Com Prediction Generator and the Apple Rumor Generator reflect public skepticism about the hype surrounding the fates of technology companies, although, given the existence of the MSN Search Spoof Generator, it appears that at least one technology corporation has produced a satiric generator of its own.

Despite the fact that "Web 2.0" is a relatively recent phrase to describe the cultural shift in digital practices toward two-way communications, personal publishing for niche audiences, and reciprocal file sharing and remix practices, several different Web 2.0 generators have already appeared that ridicule the hyperbole associated with those who are capitalizing on this trend. For example, the Web 2.0 Buzzphrase generator uses the familiar scaled tags motif to organize hyperbolic fragments, such as the terms in the following sample: "Cry out, blogosphere! We shall transcend borders. This will change everything. 2.0 is the new New. The buzz is loud and clear. The words aren't what they were. This is newer media. Float this. An AJAX-driven GUI. Single. Word. Sentences! Faster. Faster! *Hack it.*"[78] Unlike the Postmodernism Generator, which is characterized by elaborate sentences with polysyllabic words and subordinating clauses, the Web 2.0 Buzzphrase generator truncates language and scatters it on the page in isolated memes. At the bottom of the main page, the creator of this generator credits a real Web 2.0 company, Flock, as an inspiration.

In addition to mocking vapid catch phrases, some Web 2.0 generators also parody elements of the design aesthetic that has come to be associated with various technology fads. Writer of interactive fiction and hypertext critic Mark Marino created a kind of metagenerator that combines elements of other Web 2.0 generators, which is called the Web 2.0 app GeNerAtor. At the push of a button, Marino's page generates a silly name, color scheme, list of features, and a full mash-up of possible kinds of functionalities, files, and user communities. Indeed, as Marino points out, it can be difficult to create a generator for humor value that is as ridiculous as some real-life web applications can be. As Marino writes of the nonfictional company Ning, "With Ning, Web 2.0 has reached the height, nadir, and infinite loop of its own generationality by offering a Web 2.0 site that generates other Web 2.0 sites (as perhaps all Web 2.0 sites do)."[79]

Thus, as user-generated content fuels the economic viability of Web 2.0, to which members of the public willingly contribute both their labor and their private data, such satiric generators should remind participants about the possible pitfalls of uncritically accepting the bonds of increasingly corporatized and generic Internet experiences.

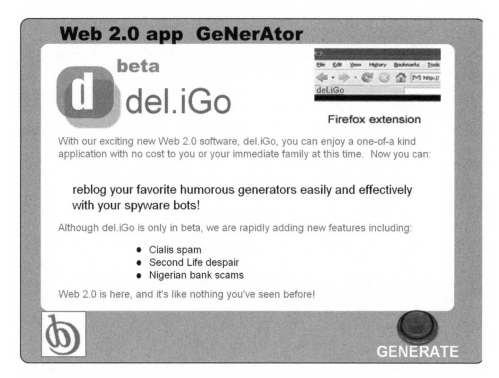

Figure 7.4
Mark Marino's web2.0 generator. Courtesy of Mark Marino.

The End of Privacy? Or Only the End of Anonymity?

Furthermore, as Soghoian points out, Web 2.0 applications that depend on a networked, distributed media model, such as Gmail, can not be studied by security and privacy experts without breaking federal computer law and so are inherently more insecure than earlier forms of computational media. He notes that in the past the flaws in traditional desktop software, such as Microsoft Word, could be evaluated without access to remote servers, and researchers could inform consumers about defective products without risking jail time. Now because what they are doing could be perceived as an illegal computer attack on the private territory of the network of another party, Soghoian claims, "Security researchers are increasingly risking breaking the law." He points out that there are definite "parallels between airport security and web 2.0 security," because merely testing the system is prohibited as a crime. In fact, as the threat of prosecution was lifted in the boarding pass generator case, Soghoian found himself stymied by federal authorities with regard to another matter, because government stakeholders wanted to discourage his Tor-related research about anonymity at Indiana University.[80]

Although there were fewer initial barriers, in order to do work on the vulnerabilities of Wikipedia Virgil Griffith came up with a number of innovative strategies to avoid possible negative legal consequences. A one-time contemporary of Soghoian's at Indiana University, Griffith, a "disruptive technologist," designed the WikiScanner to identify the sources of anonymous Wikipedia edits. Griffith had seen media coverage about the fallibility of the giant online encyclopedia after Wikipedia banned the IP addresses of congressional staffers in early 2006 for manipulating the public record through anonymous edits that included padding entries with the language from fatuous press releases and deleting mentions of scandals in the elected officials' pasts. In a 2007 talk,[81] Griffith described a relatively simple three-step method to creating his WikiScanner: (1) download all of Wikipedia, (2) purchase a database with ownership information for institutional IP addresses, and (3) merge the two databases together. In Griffith's retelling, the costs associated with this mash-up project turned out to be minimal. The first step was free and involved about 21 percent of Wikipedia. It would have normally cost Griffith about $1,000 to purchase a database from a private corporation, the second step, but Griffith was able to get the database gratis when he promised to put a text advertisement for the company on his WikiScanner website, an agreement the company later regretted when embarrassing results about their own corporate clients became public. When the two databases were merged, Griffith found almost 200,000 different organizations that could be traced to at least one anonymous Wikipedia edit.

At first, Griffith said that he thought of the WikiScanner results as his personal "basket of evil," which he could delve into at will to fling damning evidence at those he resented for injustices or what he considered to be willful public stupidity like the Iraq War. But Griffith decided to "crowd source" the results for a number of different reasons. He particularly wanted to avoid any possible legal liability if an offended party could claim that it had been intentionally targeted for malicious defamation. Griffith is understandably litigation-averse, since he reached a settlement with the Blackboard company after submission of his first freshman-year paper "caused him to get sued under the Sedition and Espionage Act," as he puts it. Moreover, he realized that the resulting database of anonymous edits was huge, and much of the information was outside the areas of his technical expertise. How would he be able to evaluate details about companies that did sophisticated pharmacological or genetic work like "Pfizer or Amgen?" Finally, Griffith wanted to make the site as media-friendly as possible, and so he was pleased when *Wired* magazine helped him set up a Reddit-style ranking system that would produce easy-to-digest top ten lists with popular corporate villains like Diebold, Dow, ExxonMobil, and ChevronTexaco in what Griffith describes as an index that lets you see "who the Internet doesn't like." Among the unearthed edits were also CIA additions and subtractions that ranged from minutiae about matters nerdy and obscure in entries such as "Light Saber Combat" styles to entire memoirs about black ops indexed under "Black September" in Jordan.[82]

Griffith has said that the experience of reviewing WikiScanner results had helped him realize that even seemingly monolithic organizations like "the Republican headquarters" were really characterized by the random and idiosyncratic sentiments of different individuals.[83] Furthermore, Griffith credited Wikipedia's own mix of lateral and hierarchical editorial procedures with remedying many of the worst public relations edits. As an example, he cites the fact that when Wal-Mart changed an entry that pointed out that wages at Wal-Mart were 20 percent lower than most retail stores to an assertion that the company paid double the minimum wage, Wikipedia editors were able to recognize both statements as factually true and construct an appropriate "although" clause to accommodate the edits of both parties.

Although rarely well understood by the mainstream media reporters who cover his exploits, Griffith has become known in academic circles as an advocate for what he calls "amateur data-mining" in which database mash-ups can be used by regular citizens to perform their own investigations and conduct their own surveillance to fight injustices and abuses of power. Griffith argues that database architectures maintain information in "disconnected archipelagos" that seem difficult for an average person to mine without the resources of a government agency or research university. However, he claims that "with small effort one can unite the information from these islands to produce novel, entertaining online services."[84] Thus, by "fusing information from disparate or little-known databases," Griffith aims "to empower everyday users by giving them powerful, promiscuously interoperable digital intelligence tools typically reserved for major corporations."[85] Griffith claims that with widespread access to websites with user-generated software, it is possible to capitalize on the fact that "every hard programming thing is already done" by someone else,[86] so that relatively little knowledge of the principles of computer science can go a long way.

Thus, the same off-the-shelf tools that might otherwise reinforce norms of commodity consumerism and highly derivative cultural practices can also be re-tasked and recombined with mash-up techniques to use computational media to surveil the surveilers. A simple example of this would be the use of Google Earth by activists who wish to mobilize opposition to the genocide in Darfur. Human rights groups repurpose the aerial mapping and data visualization capacities of the software to encourage volunteers to monitor the security of villages at risk of attack by militias.[87] Of course, vigilante groups, such as American Patrol, would like to use the same technological approach to monitor entry into the United States by undocumented workers, as part of their critique of the current enforcement of borders by federal immigration authorities.[88]

"Hacktivism," or the writing of code to promote or subvert political ideology, is associated with many interventionist programming practices. However, often hacktivists affiliate themselves with open-source programming communities and practices. For example, open-source advocate Tad Hirsch has designed "Dialup Radio" to provide political dissidents in Africa a channel for broadcasting information about corrupt or repressive regimes by using mobile phone technology, open-source code, and secure networks that preserve the anonymity of participants.[89] In addition to protesting human rights violations, in the recent past hacktivists have used their programming skills as a form of civil disobedience to promote free and open software, expressive politics, free speech, privacy, environmental protection, and information ethics. However, because hacking tends to be a kind of virtuoso performance, the ability to wield tools that expose vulnerabilities in security, privacy, or accurate data representation is often seen as the sole purview of an elite group of highly computer-literate cognoscenti.[90] In contrast, Griffith uses familiar interfaces, such as the online form in the case of WikiScanner, to make participatory knowledge of computer-mediated systems possible for average people, like those who responded to Soghoian's web generator.

Griffith is keenly aware of the rhetorical function of web generators. To illustrate a paper called "Messin' with Texas" that he coauthored about the ease of deriving an individual's mother's maiden name from public records,[91] he created an online PHP form in which visitors to his website could input the name of Texas residents.[92] Although the generator was more accurate when the user also provided a year of birth, it could generate maiden names with corresponding probability numbers even with remarkably little personal information, thus showing how informed trial and error could quickly arrive at a correct guess if one were at the mercy of would-be identity thieves. As in the WikiScanner case, Griffith used Internet fame as a tool for pointing attention to database vulnerabilities, in this instance by posting links to the generated results for high-profile celebrity Texans like movie star Ethan Hawke or presidential daughter Jenna Bush.

Entering private information into what seems to be an online form sanctioned by an institution of state authority is one of the common user activities that Soghoian interrogates. In addition to warning that "vanity Googling" leaves telltale traces that compromise an individual's privacy, even if the best online tools for anonymity are used, Soghoian is also known as a critic of government-sponsored online forms. In particular, he has ridiculed the TSA's own affiliated website for passengers attempting to clear their names from the agency's No Fly List, which was itself insecure, so that would-be travelers typed extremely confidential personal identity information into an online form that could be easily accessed by a nefarious hacker. Because the site, designed by the Virginia-based firm Desyne, contained a number of spelling errors, its similarity to a phishing site run by Internet scammers created even more negative publicity for the TSA.[93]

By using the interface of the online form, some web generators can be understood in the context of what Michel Foucault has called "governmentality," in that they make manifest the regulating features of a particular mentality of rule or technologizing of the political subject.[94] Pull-down menus and online forms are a key characteristic of the electronic bureaucracy of e-commerce and e-government, which Jane Fountain has traced back to the Clinton administration and government initiatives to provide the public broader access to the Weberian system of creating and maintaining files, if only at the level of data entry.[95] These online forms on government websites could be said to have set user expectations for interactivity for much of the period now labeled Web 1.0. For example, as commentary on this phenomena, the Library Card Generator and Barcode Generator may be representative of the recurrent theme of bureaucracy and organizational systematization that characterizes many web generators. Of course, in the case of the Barcode Generator for making universal product code labels, users generally lack the actual piece of equipment that could read the code and verify that the label that appears as output is an accurate translation of the input content. Like translation generators or those that produce other kinds of code foreign to the user, certain forms of institutional knowledge, the need for which the generator seemingly subverts, are still required to authenticate the system's accuracy.

The Evil Guide Plan also uses many of the conventions of the pull-down menu, which are already familiar to users who shop and register for services online, frequently giving personal information about themselves in order to complete basic transactions. The opening text of the guide reads, "Your evil plan is nearly complete. Simply fill in your answers in the appropriate blanks below and then get ready to call your press conference. You may want to photocopy this page first, in case you change your mind later and want to create a different evil plan." In this generator, preset options exist for critical categories like "motive" and "objective," but the narrative can be filled out in stages with "supplemental information" about the evil person's "base of operations" or "tragic past."[96]

Visual Evidence

Lev Manovich has observed that the power of automation is one of the chief features of the computational and aesthetic logic of the commercial design program Photoshop.[97] And yet, as Soghoian points out in creating his web generator, fully exploiting the capabilities of Photoshop software still requires some expert knowledge, particularly when complicated masking, layering, filtering, or numerical functions are applied to the image. In contrast, web generators allow website visitors to modify images or add text to pictures in ways that would otherwise involve more knowledge of the Photoshop tool menu. What Manovich calls "the logic of selection" is obviously also tightly constrained, because the preprogrammed web generator features that mimic cut and paste functions are even more limited than the menus of design software. Like earlier graphical communication systems, such as Ivan Sutherland's Sketchpad, mathematical functions determine how pixels are manipulated on the screen. Manovich notes that all these software programs "begin as algorithms published in computer science papers,"[98] and—because of what Manovich calls "transcoding"—a more limited vocabulary of outputs shapes the visual culture of a given consumer-producer. Because these forms of visual manipulation are more clearly associated with design practices of recreation and leisure than those of work, users may consider web generators to be part of the digital practices of informal sociality and game-like interaction. The DiY practices associated with Photoshop, in contrast, can signal more sophisticated forms of cultural production that span many forms of community membership, although they are frequently used in the service of social and political satire as well.

Among users of social media, communicating visually can be taken as a hostile act. This is particularly true among political bloggers. Michael Bérubé has used the term "blogspat" to describe recurrent, self-reinforcing conflicts between large, often collaboratively written web logs.[99] In the Netherlands, Geert Lovink points out how these "fotofucken" contribute to "shockblog" conventions that fuel feuds between competing groups; in the case of contemporary Holland, between nativist Dutch nationalists and Islamic migrant workers.[100] Unlike the simple flame war, in which heated exchanges in online communication take place within relatively cohesive virtual communities, blogspats explicitly engage audiences from *competing* social media outlets, such as prowar Democrats versus antiwar Democrats in the United States. When the incendiary incident in a blogspat is a visual joke, bloggers are likely to accuse one another of a hypocritical use of a shared identity position—such as "feminist" or "liberal"—and express outrage about an alleged betrayal of trust or violation of the implicit contract between reader and writer or between communities of like-minded writers. This ability to manipulate representations of gendered or racial political bodies is equated with cultural violence that requires a "takedown" or expulsion of the very image from the writer's text.

In her work on flame wars on mailing lists, anthropologist Jennifer Cool argues that these conflicts in virtual communities stimulate intense reflection and discussion about "what sort of speech and topics were appropriate."[101] She describes past flame wars as "milestones, shared history, and the means through which members articulated, questioned, and reflected upon their sense of community." For Cool, flamewars are occasions for "metadiscourse" about norms, identities, and purpose.[102] Blogspats are similarly concerned with appropriate conduct and the rules of membership, albeit for communities marked as "other," so they assert difference, as in "this blogging community is defined by hypocrisy unlike our community" or "this group has strayed from the fundamentals unlike our group."

By considering how competition for audience share functions in the blogosphere, I would argue that there are three major ways that photography functions in blogs: (1) to commemorate a particular occasion and authenticate the author's status as an invited participant or credible witness; (2) to solicit readers' critical scrutiny and encourage particular ways of seeing through ideological lenses that are validated by the collective intelligence of the group; and (3) to provide the raw material of a digital file that can be altered by a computer user.

As images themselves are increasingly recognized as capable of serving as arguments, sometimes without recourse to verbal texts at all, taboos on using modified images shape public discourse. Although skeptic David Fleming asserts that visual images cannot serve as arguments because a picture in itself "makes no claim that can be contested, doubted, or improved upon by others,"[103] digital technology has changed this assumed lack of interactivity. Photoshop makes image alteration by would-be critics easier for nonspecialists to undertake. With Photoshop, ideological messages in images can be refined and debated and thus perhaps fuel a blogspat when norms about representation are violated and a given group of web writers is offended by a contentious visual claim.

In an article on "The Photoshopping of the President," *Salon* magazine uses the voice of the Photoshop software creator to argue that his computer program facilitates citizenship activities by empowering users with new digital tools:

John Knoll, who created Photoshop with his brother Tom in 1989, believes that the program—originally created as a professional tool for the retouching, resizing and sharpening of images—has contributed to democracy in two ways: first by allowing desktop publishers to create the same professional-looking color pictures that the big companies were making; and second, by giving people a voice they wouldn't have had before. "It's the inevitable consequence of the democratization of technology," he says. "You give people a tool, but you can't really control what they do with it."[104]

Despite Knoll's liberatory claims, there are many information design strategies that enable entrenched power players to use Photoshop to simulate the appearance of democratic participation that doesn't actually take place in the world of lived experience. As Bruno Latour has argued, shots of crowds or photos of buildings and public squares associated with political deliberation represent what he calls "atmospheres of democracy."[105] Because of the rhetorical appeal of these scenic elements, institutional stakeholders may use the software package to insert images of these tropes that suggest the consent of the governed. For example, bloggers have revealed that Photoshop has been used to add soldiers to a Bush rally, appropriate Howard Dean's crowds as the backdrop of a Republican event, or substitute a sanitized New Orleans Square in Disneyland for a mayoral candidate's actual city.

In addition to changing backgrounds, Photoshop can also be used to revise historical documents that show the proximity and presence of stakeholders at formal occasions or sites of political rhetoric. In the Southern California Vietnamese community of Little Saigon there was consternation when it was revealed that the campaign of Trung Nguyen had distributed images showing the candidate Photoshopped next to the state's popular Republican governor during a public address. Although not as obvious an act of cultural violence as the photo retouching used under Stalin to remove ostracized political opponents from the visual record of state events,[106] it is difficult to claim unequivocally that this software serves the forces of political liberation when advertisers who have licensed the image of Martin Luther King use specialized software to erase the other civil rights leaders near his podium during the "I Have a Dream" speech.[107]

In fact, this ability to manipulate the content of public memory through Photoshop has become a major issue for photojournalists, historians, and editors. In 2006, the international professional association for computer graphics, SIGGRAPH, devoted one of its largest panels to the topic of "Ethics in Image Manipulation."[108] The following year, Elizabeth Loftus, a psychologist who is best known for her work on the cultural dynamics of false memory, published an influential paper that showed that experimental subjects remembered historical events differently after being shown doctored photographs.[109] Since photographs are often used to authenticate the perceptions of public witnesses, Photoshop can have a destabilizing effect on conventional notions of authenticity and truth.

Black-and-White Arguments

Two specific cases demonstrate how group norms about the policing of visual images can be manifested across blogging communities when Photoshop satires create conflict. One case, which later became known as "Burqagate," initially involved criticism of an image of former President Bill Clinton, who was shown with a group of bloggers in a posed picture commemorating a luncheon in his Harlem office. Primary analysis of the original image focused on two factors: (1) the absence of bloggers of color in the group depicted and (2) the seemingly provocative presence of young *Feministing* blogger Jessica Valenti next to the ex-president. After Ann Althouse questioned Valenti's credentials as a feminist and accused her of posing in a way that drew attention to her sexuality, Amanda Marcotte of *Pandagon* posted a version of the photo in which Valenti is covered with a burqa. This image created its own firestorm of controversy, after Marcotte was—in turn—accused of complicity with a similarly culturally conservative ideology, because she had transformed a symbol of Islamic faith into an object of Eurocentric derision.

In the other case, two months before the height of Burqagate, another Photoshopped image created controversy during a contentious Democratic senate primary in Connecticut, when Firedoglake blogger Jane Hamsher posted an altered photo that also included Clinton, showing him next to Senator Joseph Lieberman, who had been altered to look as if he were in blackface. In choosing this iconography, Hamsher implies that centrist Democrats appeal to racial stereotypes about blackness, but the entry generated immediate criticism from both conservative and liberal bloggers about the inappropriateness of ever using a racist image in service of a supposedly progressive cause.

Unlike traditional journalists, bloggers have little investment in projecting a seemingly neutral and dispassionate point of view by faithfully reproducing images of candidates and officeholders. Although editorial supervisors are criticized for running retouched photos of public figures such as the intentionally darkened image of O.J. Simpson on the cover of *Time* magazine,[110] bloggers have a different rhetorical relationship to Photoshop and they use the program to make different truth claims. Their philosophy about using images may be more analogous to the aesthetics of editorial cartoons. Yet, in the era of the "Reagan's Tear" cover of *Time* magazine,[111] even these conventions may be shifting.

Hamsher's use of a minstrel show image reinforces her message about political performance and performativity and thus would seem rhetorically appropriate, as a

Figure 7.5
Photoshopped image of Bill Clinton with Joseph Lieberman in blackface, "Old Black Joe," by darkblack. Courtesy of darkblack.

comment on the grotesque political masks lawmakers must wear. Like the Burqagate image, which also involved an individual's physical proximity to Clinton, the Lieberman blackface photo involves manipulations of modes of dress and social costume, although its semiotic system references race, not gender.

As in the later Burqagate case, readers responded quickly, using words such as "disgraceful" and "disgusting" in questions posed to either Hamsher or fellow readers. Like Burqagate's Marcotte, Hamsher was quick to apologize for the blackface image in a posting titled "About That Graphic."[112] Although Hamsher ultimately removed the offending picture, she used the same posting to provide a link to what she calls the "race-baiting flyer" from the Lieberman campaign with the source photo.

After Hamsher posted the image, Michelle Malkin accused liberal bloggers like Hamsher of having a prehistory of racist political imagery.[113] In particular, she points to a 2005 "Sambo" of broad strokes and garish colors by blogger Steve Gilliard.[114] Gilliard's name—like Hamsher's—had been linked to the Clinton luncheon and the later blogspat because he was among those of color who were excluded. In this case of representation and reproduction, the candidate being defaced and the commentator who circulated the caricature were both black. Yet, like Hamsher, Gilliard removed the picture after negative coverage appeared in a national newspaper of record, the *Washington Post*, but he also substituted a more crudely cut-and-pasted image of the lampooned candidate against a backdrop of money.

Although they are not examples of painterly professional expertise or sophisticated photorealistic effects, these images thematizing disguise, covering, and camouflage are primary sources that stimulate discussion and debate about race, class, gender, and nationality. Of course, retouched photographs that transform their subjects' racial complexion may aspire to the status of art, as in the case of the *Colors* series by Tibor Kalman. Kalman's image of an Africanized Queen Elizabeth II has been read as a reversal of the correlations of race and class, a comment about postcolonialism, an allusion to the magazine's own pandering to multinational brand identities, and a collapse of the supposed contraries of canonical high culture and multiculturalism. Although some dismissed it as a publicity stunt, others thought Kalman's visual satire brought a mass-market visual appeal to progressive social issues.

Dress Codes

Burqagate began with criticism of posed photos of former president Bill Clinton and a group of bloggers at a luncheon in his Harlem office on September 12, 2006. Attendees came from *Daily Kos*, *Firedoglake*, *Eschaton*, *AMERICAblog*, *MyDD*, *LiberalOasis*, *Seeing the Forest*, *The Carpetbagger Report*, *The Mahablog*, *TalkLeft*, and *Feministing*. Those present generally reported in the write-ups on their blogs a convivial event marked by positive fellow feeling. Many at the Clinton lunch also posted photographs of the occasion at photo-sharing websites such as Flickr. Subsequent analysis of the images by those not present focused on two factors: the absence of bloggers of color and the seemingly provocative presence of blogger Valenti in front of the ex-president.

The blogspat began when law professor, blogger, and inveterate Clinton-basher Ann Althouse mocked the sycophantic eagerness of those present to associate themselves with the celebrity of the former president and to produce positive messages about the Clinton legacy in exchange for the relatively trivial bribe of a free lunch. The bloggers present would later dispute such characterizations by pointing to photographs that showed them talking and the president listening and depicted them as active participants in discussion rather than fawning fans.

As her parting shot on her original post, Althouse urged her readers to examine one of the group photographs closely and engage in the following thought experiment: "Let's just array these bloggers . . . *randomly*."[115] Althouse was clearly encouraging readers to notice the front-and-center presence of a young woman in close proximity to Clinton, since she tagged the posting "breasts." The first commenter picks up on Althouse's cue and inquires, "Who is the Intern directly in front of him with the black hair?"[116] This sneering reference to former White House intern Monica Lewinsky is followed with leering commentary by "Meade," who opines, "Dunno, but by her expression, it looks as though she may be getting 'a small glimpse at greatness.'"[117] Others pile on with masculine voyeurism about Clinton's "head-tilting chest peek" or exclamations that the woman pictured could "deliver my pizza any day" and that female bloggers "wet their panties at the sight of Bill." Even when Althouse enters the comment space, it is only to chide those who don't "see the humor in the situation."[118]

Even in the friendly territory of Althouse's own blog, however, not all of the comments were in concert with her insinuation that Clinton was still a womanizer or that the young female blogger in front was a narcissistic participant in a sexualized display. The sixth comment below Althouse's "Bill Clinton, lunching with bloggers" post is by "The DrillSGT," and it attempts to perform a variety of corrective tasks counter to Althouse's intentions: (1) bearing witness to being an attendee at the luncheon by attesting to the excellence of the "suberb" cuisine and the fact that "all our plates were clean at the end," (2) detailing the full menu to offset regional and racial biases that seem to be set off by Althouse's mention of "southern chicken," (3) providing names to those pictured so they would no longer be anonymous objects of derision, and 4) implicitly asking Althouse to drop the innuendo by stating: "I dont understand the 'random' comment."

In a second posting Althouse questioned the no-longer-nameless central female blogger's credentials as a feminist and accused her of drawing attention to her sexuality. By the time the detailed dressing-down of Jessica Valenti continues, Althouse's

readers are expressing irritation with her apparent misogyny. After reading more ana-
tomical and sartorial criticism of Valenti in Althouse's sequel post, "Let's take a closer
look at those breasts," "dorothy" voices resentment about being forced to choose
between two female Internet writers: "Coincidentally, my two favorite blogs (I read
both daily) are this one and *Feministing*. I really don't like that a whole post was
devoted to this."[119]

The negative reaction to Althouse's ribaldry was even more marked on oppositional
blogs. Target Valenti defends herself by saying Althouse reinforces sexist perspectives
by directing attention to her physical appearance. Valenti ridicules the claim that
"Althouse is all about reviving 'real feminism'" by enumerating her heterosexist comments.[120] Valenti disputes that she violated propriety by wearing what Althouse
describes as a "tight knit top that draws attention to her breasts." She also resents
Althouse's jeering remark that she should have worn a "beret" or "blue dress" like
Lewinsky and complains that even her posture is being policed, since Althouse taunts
her with the accusation that she was "bending over backwards—figuratively and literally" to "keep the attention" on her breasts.[121]

New fuel was added the following week when Amanda Marcotte posted a Photoshopped version of the luncheon in which Valenti is completely covered by a burqa.
In the adjoining text, Marcotte points to a factor other than sexism at work: she argues
Valenti is slandered because of the not-so-subtle racism of Althouse's readers, who
describe her as "ethnic" and "Jewish."[122] This image created its own firestorm after
Marcotte was accused of complicity with conservative ideology because she had transformed a symbol of Islamic faith into an object of Eurocentric derision. Marcotte's
exploitation of politically loaded iconography caused many readers to accuse her of
blindness toward her *own* ethnocentrism while simultaneously throwing stones at
others.

One commenter named "sly civilian" connects Marcotte's use of an illegitimate
strategy in visual rhetoric to the cultural violence of the Bush administration.

Figure 7.6
Photoshopped image of Clinton with a group of bloggers by Auguste, by permission of Auguste.

Yeah, burqas are funny. Especially when the consistant use of them as a bat to whack the fundies places an image of the veiled muslim woman as the gold standard of helpless and oppressed, and lets the thugs turn around and freaking invade and colonize Iraq and Afganistan with the trumped up concern for women's rights.

Yeah. It's pretty freaking hilarious.[123]

Thus, "sly citizen" argues Marcotte is supporting a symbolic economy in which the exchange of an image of the veiled Muslim woman merely propagates her commodification and circulation as a "gold standard."

Reader Anthony Kennerson makes a similar argument:

Ha. Ha. Very funny. Jessica Valenti in a burqa. Quite humorous. Uhhhh . . . NOT.

Especially considering that that photo basically reduces Arab/Muslim women who willingly do wear such a dress as a justified symbol of their religious faith to an object (hmmmm) for derision by liberal feminists who should know better about respect for other women.

Especially considering the background that the organizers of that blogger confab couldn't find it in their heart to invite one Black or Brown blogger (in Harlem, no less) to join in . . . perhaps because of Bubba's actual policies towards the mass of Black and Brown folk?? (As in welfare "reform," the racist crime bills, the "bridge to the 21st Century" that tended to leave most poor folk behind, etc, etc??)

Especially considering that Black bloggers who have attempted to point out the incongruity of the arrogance of most A-list liberal bloggers towards Black folk (as in the Lieberman blackface photo at firedoglake; the slander towards Liza Sabater for calling out the White-out of the Clinton confab) have been basically villified and smeared as mindless anti-White racists who need to just shut up and mind their betters.

Oh . . . but who cares about all that?? Poor Jessica got piled on because of her boobs, so let's have a laugh at WOC's and Muslim women's expense.[124]

In his comment, Kennerson alludes to the fact that progressive black bloggers had also been discussing photographs of the luncheon for very different reasons and encouraging their readers to examine the image with titles like "Write Your Own Caption" and "Notice Anything?"

In this case, what African-American bloggers expect readers to observe is the absence of bloggers of color. For example, Liza Sabater vents her outrage through a series of rhetorical questions:

What does it mean though that there are 20 bloggers invited to this lunch and not one is black or latino? What does it mean for this group of bloggers to be patting themselves on the backs for being with Clinton when they are all in Harlem and not one of them is a person of color? What does it mean for these people to be there and have not one of them raise this issue in their blogs?[125]

Sabater also notes that Jane Hamsher is present at this event, despite the perceived racial insensitivity of her earlier posting of a Photoshopped image of Senator Lieberman in blackface at the center of another blogspat.

These reader-commenters accuse Marcotte of appropriating the visual rhetoric of right-wing politics by demonizing dress associated with cultural difference. Indeed, right-wing virtual communities circulated Photoshopped pictures after September 11 that used the image of the Islamic veil to argue about what would happen "if the Taliban wins." Perhaps the most striking doctored photo in the series is a dramatic view of the Statue of Liberty against a blue sky in which the allegorical symbol of liberty is completely veiled.

Although both Marcotte and the artist and fellow blogger who doctored the photograph later apologized for posting the image, not all readers use the comment section to criticize her Photoshop argument. For example, Lindsay Bayerstein of the blog *Majikthise* considers it effective rhetoric that relies on cultural comparisons, not contrasts.

Amanda was making what I took to be an uncontroversial point: sexual shaming and coercively enforced modesty are universal phenomena. The difference between our homegrown American prudes and those seemingly "exotic" oppressors from distant lands is one of degree and not of kind.

Far from being ethnocentric, Amanda's insight undercuts ethnocentrism. It's harder to think of your culture as the measure of all others when you realize that humanity's most serious problems repeat themselves everywhere under different guises. If you assume that there are commonalities, awareness of an oppressive practice in another culture should lead you to wonder if your own culture might be doing something similar but less obvious to you.[126]

Another reader, "Sunrunner," praises the relative tastefulness of Marcotte's visual imagination: "Well, it is better than the one of all the other women in flannel nighties and Jessica in a black negligee. Can't remember where I saw it, but it was floating around somewhere or other."[127]

Figure 7.7
Photoshopped image of the Clinton luncheon by darkblack, "Cap'n Billy's Blogolicious PJ Party." Courtesy of darkblack.

In posting these Photoshopped works, both Marcotte and Hamsher credited the labor of seemingly pseudonymous others, "Auguste" and "darkblack" respectively. Satiric Photoshopped political images are often anonymous creations, and their authorship histories are deliberately obscured. Since such images often function as part of an unregulated gift economy via e-mail and peer-to-peer file-sharing activities, these images can assume a different role in the public discourse, particularly when markers of race and gender appear to be manipulated to draw attention to a rhetoric of masquerade.

Certainly, the regulatory mechanisms by which blogging societies make sense of competition structures built in to a limited economy of attention in a crowded and noisy blogosphere depend on context. Not all Photoshopped images that circulate between blogging communities produce blogspats. In April 2006, I posted a digitally altered image on my blog *Virtualpolitik* of anti-Google critic Siva Vaidhyanathan after a pro-Google blogger compared him to conservative presidential appointee Gale Norton.[128] Designer Mel Horan and I created an image in which Vaidhyanathan's face appears surrounded by Norton's blond hair and conservative business attire sothe counterintuitive figure of speech was humorously literalized. Although this image manipulated representations of both gender and race, I felt confident that my fellow blogger would not be offended. I based my prediction on previous observations of his blogging literacy practices: I had noticed that Vaidhyanathan tolerated self-deprecating portraits and that there was cordial sociality between our respective blogs with reciprocated comments.

It turned out I was correct in my supposition that no netiquette would be violated. Almost immediately the hybrid Norton/Vaidhyanathan image was reposted on his blog *Sivacracy* with the title "Uh. Maybe I am Gale Norton."[129] A few months later, I began blogging with Vaidhyanathan, and our audiences became even more closely identified.

Violence and the Interface

Certainly, Photoshop and feminism have an uneasy relationship because the software package is used in creating fashion photography and often presents women as objects for physical manipulation and sexual consumption. To dramatize this issue, the Swedish Ministry of Health and Social Affairs contracted with the ad firm Forsman and Bodenfors to produce an online social marketing campaign about unnatural and unrealistic manipulations of the female figure through photo retouching. On their interactive website, *G!rlpower Retouch*, visitors can mouse over the names of an attractive model's body parts on what seems to be a magazine cover for before and after views of specific altered sections of the image.[130]

Figure 7.8
Photoshopped image of Siva Vaidhyanathan as Gale Norton by Mel Horan. Courtesy of Mel Horan.

In the short online film *Evolution*, from the Dove corporation's "Campaign for Real Beauty," an "average"-looking female is transformed first by the wizardry of professionals in hair, makeup, and lighting, and then by the machinations of an unseen digital artist in front of a Photoshop screen who manipulates her image into an unattainable standard of idealized beauty. Ironically, this message comes from a company that is also known for marketing skin-whitening products to women of color in developing nations and other consumer goods that are designed to radically alter a woman's natural physical appearance. Like other viral videos, the Dove ad also inspired several imitators, who more ambitiously changed the appearance of women in mugshots and elderly ladies to glamour girls. It also generated a series of online parodies that included footage featuring transvestites, Halloween pumpkins, and chain-smoking overweight male couch potatoes.

Thus Marcotte's very decision to use a Photoshopped image of a female figure in her blog was rhetorically risky from the start. By using the operations of cutting and

File | Edit | Tools | View | Modify | Help

| 24.5 mb / 16 bit | Camera Raw | | 0 ————————— ● 100 |

Figure 7.9

Still from Dove "Evolution" viral video campaign, Ogilvy and Mather Toronto. Courtesy of writer/codirector Tim Piper.

pasting to obscure Valenti behind a burqa, Marcotte's literalizing of an imagined hyperbolic wish fulfillment from the political right risks enacting the very forms of cultural violence that it criticizes. As a film like *Evolution* shows, these operations can be seen as a form of violence, in which a woman's neck is stretched and her eyes are enlarged, as her head is subjected to changes that would be painful if performed on a live person. In a subsequent film for Dove from the same creators, *Onslaught*, this violence of and upon the feminine is made even more graphic as plastic surgery, liposuction, and bulimia are shown taking place in rapid succession on the user's YouTube screen.

This display of aggression against the human body by the operations made possible by a computer-mediated interface and its menus is also a motif in other popular online films. In Alan Becker's *Animator vs. Animation*, much of the action takes place on the "stage" of a Flash design screen, where an animated stick figure drawn by a web animator has escaped the captivity and physical domination imposed upon him by his master to fight back by using tools from the timeline, layers, library, and other sections of the software menus.[131] In addition to the standard cut and paste operations, weapons used by and against the animated character include swords, bows and arrows, machine guns, flame throwers, bombs, spears, machetes, and saw blades.

The sequel, *Animator vs. Animation II*, has an even larger library of weapon movie clips, which includes "axe," "bazooka," "cannon," "crossbow," "flamethrower," "fragmented grenade," "kunai knife," "mace," "machine gun," "missile launcher," "Molotov cocktail," "pistol," "rifle," "rocket launcher," "shotgun," "sniper rifle," and sword." The stick figure has shed his "victim" identity and has been renamed "The Chosen One," after which he takes on an apocalyptic, messianic character. In the story of this second film, the animated character has taken on the role of an adversarial hacker who destroys the animator's song list, essay documents, and files of data in a destructive rampage that goes beyond his Flash window to all-out warfare with the other software packages across his desktop.[132]

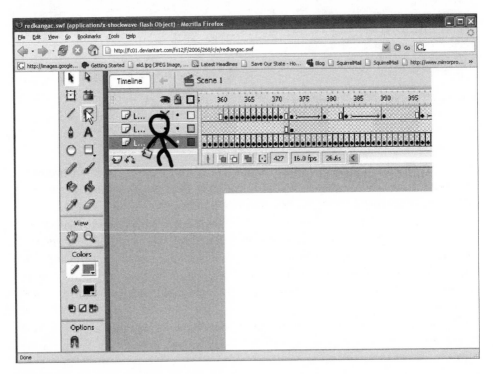

Figure 7.10
Animator vs. Animation by Alan Becker, by permission of Robert Becker.

Of course, *Animator vs. Animation* can be viewed as an homage by its teenaged creator to predecessors like *Duck Amuck* (1953), in which the classic Warner Brothers animated character Daffy Duck is subjected to abuse and torment by an unseen traditional cell animator, who turns out to be his rival Bugs Bunny. However, there may theoretically be more to be seen in what could be called a satiric display of the logic of the interface. As Lev Manovich has argued, both Walter Benjamin and Paul Virilio have stressed "the aggression potentially present" when the traditional opposition between touch and seeing in Western thought becomes collapsed with the proximity, made possible by interactivity and telecommunication, that can violate the aura of aesthetic objects.[133]

On the web, there are many such theaters of cruelty, particularly those with political content, so that seemingly disenfranchised computer users who are frustrated by the failures of representative government can take revenge against figureheads and policy makers who seem to be perpetuating injustice upon others. These programs that allow political subjects to seem to get control of the body politic via representations of the body natural[134] of a head of state range from relatively benign mockery to horrific Grand Guignol dismemberment. At one end of the spectrum are "Dancing Bush" or "Dancing Hillary" programs in which a photograph of the celebrity politician occupies the head of a figure gyrating through various dance routines. There are also "Falling Bush" and "Falling Hillary" screensavers, where ragdoll figures of politicians tumble down through cloudlike balls. However, there are also dozens of variations of the whack-a-mole game, in which Internet visitors try to hit the head of the elected representative as soon as it pops up on their screen. There are also games with discrete levels, such as Bushgame.com, in which the player must take on other members of the extended First Family and even do battle with the copulating senior Bushes and their legions of bats. Many of these games are domestically produced by administration critics, but reporters in the news media more commonly report on the drama of videogames and interactive websites that are made by and for foreign audiences, such as the mod of a crude 3-D first-person-shooter that shows a hunt for the president, "Night of Bush Capturing."

Neutral cartoon-like bodies that can be bashed around on the screen can also be given "skins" from political figures such as George W. Bush, John Kerry, and Michael Moore. The same website that hosts the Flash work of *Animator vs. Animation* creator Alan Becker also hosts the wildly popular "Interactive Buddy," a physics simulation in which a computer user can use his or her mouse to interact with the character in a number of ways from gentle tickling to violent changes caused by a vortex in gravity.[135] Like other Flash websites, the program comes with many weapons (grenades, flails, fire hoses, bowling balls, and so on) and much of the humor comes from the realistically rendered concussive effects of these destructive items in the small rectangle that the character occupies, in which there are not only actions but reactions that do his body harm. In the standard version of "Interactive Buddy," the protagonist is a figure made up of six spheres, but skins can be purchased that allow it to assume a range of political identities.

The aggression that conflates touch and sight that is made possible through Internet access is not limited to actions against political cartoons. In his installation "Domestic Tension," Iraqi-born artist Wafaa Bilal invites visitors to his website to take part in a perverse form of wish fulfillment and "shoot an Iraqi" for themselves. For thirty days Bilal moved his personal furnishings into a gallery space, where he attempted to eat, sleep, and pass the time, while those who chose to do so fired at him with paintballs by using a computer-activated device that could be triggered remotely by Internet users. According to the frequently asked questions page about the installation, "Bilal's objective is to raise awareness of virtual war and privacy, or lack thereof, in the digital age."[136] Through extensive video blogging, Bilal documented his experience of being constantly hunted by those participating in the installation, who fired paintballs from around the world. The site received 80 million visits, and the gun was fired 65,000 times.[137]

Although participatory art is often validated as being somehow more noble by virtue of its opposition to passive spectatorship, other Internet artworks with game-like interfaces similarly invite critique of the shoot-em-up norm of interactivity. Visitors to the online exhibition could choose to communicate with Bilal in other ways, but most chose merely to shoot at him. The online game by Gonzalo Frasca, *September 12*, explicitly uses the crosshairs interface to invite reflection about what makes shooting the default position for an interactive experience. The opening screen of what Frasca calls a "simulation" without an ending, rather than a "game," gives the visitor to the site the following instructions: "You can shoot. Or not. This is a simple model you can use to explore some aspects of the war on terror."[138] The more the player shoots at Arab-style headdress-wearing "terrorists," the more the player creates new terrorists, who germinate in the wake of the collateral damage of killed civilians and destroyed buildings.

There were, however, also forms of emergent behavior that came to Bilal's aid. As one art journalist noted, "Evidence of this kind of compassion evolved in the creation of the Virtual Human Shield, a string of code written by web surfers that caused the gun to aim off to the side and away from Bilal. 'It formed because of this project, and their goal was to stop the brutality of the shooters by asking people to keep the gun pointed away from me, to the left, at all times.'"[139]

The political satires covered in this chapter situate and are situated in discourses from a number of distinct digital genres—including FPS, web generator, viral video, and blog—and range widely in their level of user interactivity from simple online forms to sophisticated digital design programs like Photoshop and Flash. Yet they share many common tropes with the work of hacktivist programmers, although this elite cadre of hackers may typically work at the more abstract level of raw code. The issues these new forms of satire raise, about whether the public's interests are best served by giving the government unlimited authority to authenticate and surveil, are designed to stimulate questions about the fundamental sources of political power. Whether or not they actually stimulate serious reflection about ideology, given the modes of distraction and the casual interactivity of the web genres that give them such broad popular appeal, may still be open to debate.

Chester, Vermont, is a tiny town with a population that edges just over 3,000 residents. As a microcosm of Yankee pastoralism, it seems frozen in time, especially compared to the transnational cities and sprawling ethnoburbs that are booming elsewhere in the country. Its tourbook quaintness consists of a stone village, a row of Victorian houses converted to gift shops and inns, a classic diner complete with American Modern aluminium sheeting, and a nineteenth-century red brick railroad depot. Chester is 98 percent white and 98.5 percent U.S.-born, and unlike many struggling local municipalities in New England, Chester enjoys a low 3 percent unemployment rate.

The main industry of Chester is not lumber or maple syrup or teddy bears. It is metadata, and it has been so for the better part of a century, after the town remained populated in spite of the closure of over a dozen mills and factories in the area since the Civil War. An early twentieth-century postcard shows an imagined Chester of the future with elevated railways and streetcars that never materialized. Because this place eventually became home to a group of utopian visionaries and bibliographers with grand plans for new data economies based on universal access to cheaply produced, easy-to-store documents, this hopeful illustration perhaps does show a city plan for the informationopolis that could have been, if it had happened when it was supposed to happen in Chester and not fifty years later in woodsy Mountain View, California or Redmond, Washington, the corporate seats of the current metadata corporate giant Google and the other contender hoping for eventual market dominance, Microsoft.

Although the digitization of information is often represented in the news media as a purely technical, totally automated, single-step process, as the workers of present-day Chester know, the transubstantiation that takes place in the local plant every day involves human commerce and specific, sometimes conflicting, social codes about labor practices, work cultures, annotation conventions, legal agreements, and professional associations. It is here in Chester that the U.S. Congressional Serial Set is being digitized, which encompasses the Congressional Record from 1817 to 1980. In addition to information from the legislative process that would obviously be recorded about hearings, speeches, public comments, and votes, the Serial Set includes a range of other print ephemera that were part of government reports at the time, such as tables of statistical data and over 50,000 maps, including illustrated documents about the new U.S. territories from explorer John C. Fremont. In fact, the digital public archives of the Library of Congress include only a fraction of the material from the U.S. Serial Set, and the official government website even admits that this public national library has digitized "only portions" of these records.[1]

The digitization of the entire work by the private sector is being done in Chester by the Readex corporation, which is headquartered in a former funeral home, and—by extension—its parent company NewsBank, which is based in Naples, Florida. Workers in Chester maintain the large computer servers, add information about illustrations, correct misspelled names and illogical pagination, identify the people and objects depicted in photographs, resolve inconsistencies in the information presented, and append thousands of subject descriptions page-by-page to the electronic documents in the Serial Set. Although it is detail-oriented work, often done in post-Fordist open cubicles, many express pride in their local Vermont product, and some families have several members working in the Chester plant. The company proudly declares that the indexers have an average of "seven to ten years of experience in the field" and a "wide range of educational backgrounds."[2] For many years the only major corporate competitor in digitizing the bulk of these particular public records was LexisNexis, which also offered libraries and professional researchers subscriptions to their costly proprietary electronic databases, so Readex had good reason to be pleased with their workers' comparatively efficient performance.

In addition to benefitting from core readerships in universities, companies have seen the financial value of federal, state, and local documents to law firms, real estate offices, and businesses engaged in public-private partnerships. In recent decades several private firms have developed business plans to digitize many kinds of public records. Some of these companies have even made intellectual property claims over their copy of the content of public hearings and press conferences by government officials by appending elaborate copyright statements to these documents.

Since the Freedom of Information Act, there have been dozens of bills introduced in Congress about public access to and private protection of information, and yet the basic challenges of making digital copies of government records available to citizens at taxpayer expense can seem daunting when materials cataloged in the U.S. National Archives alone represent about 9 billion separate items to be potentially digitized,[3] which in turn comprise only 1 to 3 percent of the total of "documents and materials created in the course of business conducted by the United States Federal government" that have been deemed worthy "for legal or historical reasons" of preservation forever.[4] Similarly, the Library of Congress, which holds a much more modest 100 million items,[5] has only digitized a very small percentage of its collections.

Although the legislative branch now offers coverage of much Capitol business in broadcasts on the cable television channel C-SPAN, the work of present-day governance takes place at multiple sites simultaneously, and committees also have subcommittees handling particular issues. In addition, the quality of web-based resources presented to keep distant constituencies informed can vary widely from committee to committee, even for the rare committees that post full transcripts or uninterrupted online video of public sessions. As more legislative committees offer video recording of their proceedings to be archived for the public record, this addition of informational bandwidth only increases the need for effective indexing and search tools. In other words, webcasting with streaming video can represent a relative loss of access in comparison to the relatively efficient finding aids already in use for plain text transcripts. Even the seemingly easy-to-mine bill-tracking website THOMAS, which was launched in 1995 and presents various drafts of legislation,[6] still excludes the actual language of congressional discussion and debate and thus the full discursive context in which the law is constituted, even if it offers a text-based search engine with keyword functionality that provides a definite contrast to video-recorded proceedings. In a country in which political ideology and epistemology are so closely linked by Lockean philosophical traditions and a Jeffersonian faith that "wherever the people are well informed they can be trusted with their own government,"[7] it is strange that there are no fundamental Constitutional mandates that elevate the public records detailing the mechanics of the legislative process much above the base level of disorganized discrete data.

In any case, it seems clear that government contracts with private for-profit groups for digitizing and reproducing public records can go seriously awry. For example, the Federal News Service (FNS), a primary source of verbatim transcripts of congressional hearings, campaign speeches, and other public statements by Washington newsmakers, which was founded in 1984 during the Ronald Reagan era of concentrated privatization of government services, was at one time run by a now-bankrupt Christian fundamentalist millionaire who was simultaneously the owner of the Grace News Network, an organization that was proud to say that it "will be reporting the current secular news, along with aggressive proclamations that will 'change the news' to reflect the Kingdom of God and its purposes."[8] (Despite obvious conflicts between church and state, the Grace News Network was also strangely given a contract by the U.S. government for broadcasting Arabic-language news in Muslim Iraq after the 2003 American military occupation began.[9]) Financial reporters knew that FNS had had a dubious antitrust history under one of its previous heads, Cortes W. Randell, who had been featured in a *New York Times* "Rogue's Gallery"[10] in connection with an earlier venture, the National Student Marketing Corporation. As the *Times* explained shortly after the Federal News Service was founded, "this high-technology transcription company with a low public profile has quickly, and quietly, made itself indispensable to news organizations, many branches of Government and even foreign governments by covering news conferences, briefings and other sessions among Washington's comment mills: the press offices and public affairs offices of the departments of State and Defense, the White House, Congress and television talk shows."[11] By 2005, FNS copyright statements were appearing on websites for the federal government, which was using the company's transcripts—complete with disclaimers of FNS ownership—in its own press releases to the public.

The "Don't Be Evil" Company Does Digitization

In 2007 the Google Books project began to scan the detailed copy of the same U.S. Serial Set that had once been the sole purview of Readex and LexisNexis. There had been relatively little controversy over other private corporations scanning public documents and rare originals for the closed collections of subscription-service online archives, which were rarely accessed by readers outside of top-tier universities. But Google's larger library initiative, aimed to provide powerful digital research tools and massive text archives to regular consumers, stimulated controversy and heated debate from the very beginning, when the company announced in December 2004 that it would be digitizing the entire print collections of the New York Public Library and prestigious university libraries at the University of Michigan, Harvard, Stanford, and Oxford. Rather than draw attention to the project's income stream from directed advertising and data about customer behavior, the official corporate press release, titled "Google Checks Out Library Books," asserted that Google's project "to make offline information searchable online" was clearly part of the corporation's mission "to organize the world's information."[12] Nonetheless, many soon questioned the consequences of these self-described noble aims.

Publishers immediately expressed alarm about losing their traditional control over their intellectual property, which they believed had a history in case law that went far beyond the rights of first sale of the mere artifact they had manufactured in the form of the book's hard copy.[13] Many writers were also unhappy with the Google project, even though the press release reassured both groups that they would be able to "monetize that information," since the program would "generate book sales."[14] On September 20, 2005, the Authors Guild filed a class action lawsuit against Google, alleging that the company was "engaging in massive copyright infringement" just by "reproducing for itself a copy of those works not in the public domain."[15]

As negotiations with publishers ground to a halt, the CEO of Google justified his company's seemingly intransigent position on sharing royalties in an October 18, 2005 editorial in the *Wall Street Journal* by pointing out that only 20 percent of books housed in these libraries were in the public domain and yet only another 20 percent were still in print, which left 60 percent of the collections totally inaccessible to those without institutional library cards, as well as to the buying public.[16] Google argued that the small selections from the copyrighted books published online by the search engine merely constituted convenient finding aids that were covered by fair use provisions and would only help would-be readers locate copies of the books for legitimate purchases. The following day, five companies from the American Association of Publishers filed a suit of their own against Google. Their complaint alleged that Google was a commercial enterprise that benefited from ad revenue and increased traffic to their associated websites and that companies were suffering "continuing, irreparable and imminent harm" because of "Google's willful infringement."[17]

By early 2006, Google had begun a major public relations counteroffensive that included pages linked to their main search page, which seemed to feature spontaneous user-generated feedback about the benefits of Google Book Search to publishers and authors. Rhetoricians might find the diction of Google's "User Stories" very strange, because these canned testimonials earnestly emphasize either how the typical Google Book Search user would be happily spending more money buying more books as a direct result of using Google's service or how the user who wasn't a rapid-response book consumer would claim the identity position of one narrowly interested in materials safely out of copyright and in the dusty territory of public domain, generally a harmless armchair historian or amateur genealogist. Comments featuring eagerness to spend money were prominently displayed in the top results on the User Stories page and included many gushing celebrations of commodity consumerism, such as "I foresee my pocketbook getting lots of use!" and "That's three books I am about to buy."[18] Such testimonials also emphasized the instant-gratification impulse buying supposedly engineered into online user behavior, obvious in the declaration that "I immediately ordered a copy of the book it was in." A similar Google enthusiast claimed, "The first thing I did was go to Amazon to order a copy."[19] Of course, Google's posting of these narratives seems disingenuous to a close reader, given how users of digital media generally want online access to recent and complete files at minimal cost and how large-scale digitization efforts may exacerbate pre-existing conflicts between traditional cultures of knowledge contained in libraries and newer cultures of information stored in computer databanks. These claims to sole membership in traditional print-based knowledge culture would seem to be not representative, given that even the much ballyhooed "reputation economies" of Web 2.0 are often based on access to free merchandise, services, and cheat codes.[20]

University officials also came to Google's defense in the beginning of 2006 as the company prepared itself for litigation on the copyright infringement cases. In an impassioned address hyperbolically entitled "Google, the Khmer Rouge, and the Public Good," the president of the University of Michigan, Mary Sue Coleman, rallied to the company's side.[21] Coleman had been a spokesperson for Google before and had been quoted in the original 2004 corporate press release as saying, "We believe passionately that such universal access to the world's printed treasures is mission-critical for today's great public university."[22]

As a speaker Coleman makes appeals to the interests of the public good in the "Khmer Rouge" address and emphasizes the concept of duty, which Coleman calls one's "responsibilities and obligations."[23] She characterizes the partnership between the university and Google as a "legal, ethical, and noble endeavor that will transform our society."[24] Coleman opens her speech with an anecdote about the creation of the Library of Congress by Thomas Jefferson, which—as I will explain later—is not a nexus of comparison without irony. Soon into the speech, she notes the nature of the rhetorical occasion in that she is facing a presumably hostile audience, the Association of American Publishers, where she is responding to perceived attacks on the Google library initiative "on the editorial page, across the airwaves, and, with your organization's endorsement, in the court system."[25] Often Coleman seems to be straining the limits of credibility by reaching for dramatic figures of speech—for example, by comparing the diligence of her institution's safeguarding of copyrighted library materials involved in their partnership with Google to "our most sensitive materials at the University: medical records, Defense Department data, and highly infectious disease agents used in research."[26] Her argument about the need for digital preservation to protect against possibly catastrophic events has some intermediate steps, but eventually her oratory reaches dire comparisons to the total breakdown of a society's entire cultural heritage that took place under the genocidal Khmer Rouge regime. To move her listeners, she also appeals to pathos by referencing the recent Hurricane Katrina disaster, which destroyed over 600,000 items in the Tulane University Government Documents collection. Then Coleman returns to the story of her introductory narrative and the commitment that Jefferson had to systematic archival preservation, which Coleman argues came out of his own experiences with a disastrous house fire that had consumed the library of his family home at Shadwell in 1770.

However, the story of Jefferson's actual donation of materials from his personal library at Monticello to the Library of Congress is much more complex than Coleman's heroic retelling of it, in ways that are relevant to those who also see digital libraries as initiatives involving complicated narratives about political ideology, cultural inclusiveness, technical constraints, and the financial self-interest of the parties involved. Despite Coleman's idealization of the historical event, Jefferson's motivation to generosity was not entirely altruistic in that his book collection represented a sizable asset that he hoped to liquidate through an expeditious sale to Congress in order to solve his personal financial problems with chronic debt. Jefferson also argued that part of the value of his collection consisted in its documentation and the fact that he had painstakingly cataloged the contents by subject matter using Bacon's table of science and the hierarchies of Memory (History), Reason (Philosophy), and Imagination (Fine Arts), rather than the relatively metadata-poor method of simple alphabetization, although in practice Jefferson's books actually had been shelved as physical objects by size at Monticello, contrary to modern information retrieval protocols.[27]

To complicate matters, not all stakeholders and potential collection users agreed that Jefferson's library was an appropriate choice for the core of what was beginning to be considered the nation's library, even after the British destroyed the Capitol and burned the original Library of Congress collection during the War of 1812, creating an urgent need for access to print matter for congressmen. Some legislators in the House objected to the nature of Jefferson's bibliographical selections in "embracing too many works in foreign languages, some of too philosophical a character, and some otherwise objectionable." Other congressmen wished to exclude "all books of an atheistical, irreligious, and immoral tendency."[28] Even after a protracted period of negotiation and deliberation, not all parties assented to the acquisition: the bill to purchase Jefferson's famed library passed the House by only ten votes.

Given the possibility that a specific technology can become outmoded or prove unreliable, Jefferson's production of his own papers is also an interesting case in point. As Hillel Schwartz has pointed out, Jefferson was famous for trying new replication techniques in creating his personal archive.[29] These techniques ranged from a mechanical arm that attached to a second pen and writing table to a chemical and paper process that was somewhat similar to an early mimeograph device. Unfortunately, it was Jefferson's very enthusiasm for replication and technological innovation that has interfered with presenting some of his papers in digital form for the wider public today, because many of his works are illegible, given the poor quality of such early mechanical replication techniques. As Library of Congress digital projects coordinator Laura Graham pointed out in an interview,[30] George Washington's papers, which were copied in the traditional manner by professional secretaries and stored in manuscript as bound volumes, are in considerably more presentable condition, and thus much more legible on the library's portal on the World Wide Web.

Today, the Library of Congress's initiatives continue to be criticized by some skeptics. Opponents of centralization argue that digital materials are still not adequately targeted to diverse audiences across the country and that the concentration of production activities in Washington, D.C., discourages local municipalities from participation in ambitious projects with their own archives and representative primary sources. Furthermore, because the Library of Congress is often dependent on monetary partnerships with other institutions, when making decisions about prioritizing the electronic duplication of particular digital materials, long-term strategic planning can be difficult to undertake. Although many philanthropic organizations have been credited with contributing funds for digitizing widely respected document collections, other private donors have been more problematic. Perhaps the most egregious example of private interests distorting the agenda of public digital library projects would be the history of Coca-Cola advertisements that now takes up some of the Library of Congress's valuable virtual estate in the American Memory Collection. Alongside the papers of Abraham Lincoln and James Madison, the beverage bottling giant has managed to insert a digital collection that features the distinctive script associated with their proprietary brand and omits any documents that depict the iconography of their competitors, much less public debate about the unhealthy role that soft drinks have played in our society's dietary habits by dominating so much of the visual culture of American life.

Similarly—despite the pro-Google sentiments of many professors, librarians, and administrators who doubt that comparatively underfunded universities and philanthropic organizations could ever otherwise marshal the resources for truly comprehensive digital library efforts—some scholars continue to be wary of the Google brand's initiative precisely because it relies on continuing corporate benevolence and denies the very public, who is supposedly being served, access to the source code of Google's proprietary technologies or sometimes even disclosure of the confidential legal contracts that set the rules for the deal between the participating campus libraries, many of which are public institutions, and the dominant search engine company in the current national market.

Coleman's boosterism unconsciously points to the problem of trusting in continuing corporate involvement when she points out that "General Motors does not need to maintain the tools for its 1957 Chevys, and would have a hard time manufacturing a car from that year," while "a university is responsible for stewarding the knowledge of 1957, and for all the years before and after—the books and magazines; the widely known research findings and the narrow monographs; the arcane and the popular."[31]

The Library of Congress

Motion Picture, Broadcasting and Recorded Sound Division, Library of Congress

Search by Keyword | Browse by Title Index

Fifty Years of Coca-Cola Television Advertisements: Highlights from the Motion Picture Archives at the Library of Congress presents a variety of television advertisements, never-broadcast outtakes, and experimental footage reflecting the historical development of television advertising for a major commercial product. The online collection includes five excerpts from stop-motion advertising developed for Coca-Cola between 1954 and 1956 by the D'Arcy agency and makes public for the first time eighteen excerpts from the Experimental TV Color Project of 1964, which determined the best lighting for the cans, bottles, and performers in television advertisements. Featured advertisements include the 1971 "Hilltop" commercial with an international group of young people on an Italian hilltop singing "I'd Like to Buy the World a Coke", the "Mean Joe Greene" commercial from 1979; the first "Polar Bear" commercial from 1993, the "Snowflake" commercial from 1999; and "First Experience," an international commercial filmed in Morocco in 1999.

The mission of the Library of Congress is to make its resources available and useful to Congress and the American people and to sustain and preserve a universal collection of knowledge and creativity for future generations. The goal of the Library's National Digital Library Program is to offer broad public access to a wide range of historical and cultural documents as a contribution to education and lifelong learning.

The Library of Congress presents these documents as part of the record of the past. These primary historical documents reflect the attitudes, perspectives, and beliefs of different times. The Library of Congress does not endorse the views expressed in these collections, which may contain materials offensive to some readers.

Figure 8.1

Fifty Years of Coca-Cola Television Advertisements on the Library of Congress American Memory website

Although Coleman obviously doesn't see the implications of her analogy, like General Motors, Google also has product lines that involve prioritizing profitable market niches over unprofitable ones and algorithms that have been updated over time to produce different rankings of search results in different iterations—sometimes to the benefit of particular advertising sponsors. Even changes to the very name of the digitization project may have impacted certain forms of functionality, since the originally titled "Google Print" initiative became "Google Book Search" as a result of the company's rebranding efforts in the face of litigation.

In "A Risky Gamble with Google," intellectual property scholar Siva Vaidhyanathan questions the "dream of the perfect research machine"[32] that is promulgated by the initiative. Although Vaidhyanathan is well aware that both students and faculty depend on the commercial search engine for directing most basic queries, a fact of life that Internet researchers have repeatedly confirmed,[33] he cautions against the dangers of elevating "Google's role and responsibility as the steward—with no accountability—of our information ecosystem."[34] Vaidhynathan also points out that part of the success of Google's rhetorical strategy rests on their carefully managed corporate branding efforts to date, in which executives depict themselves as "the anti-Microsoft" and thus "the good guy on the block,"[35] even though Google is fast becoming a monopoly in its own right.

As Google diversifies its corporate holdings and expands into social network sites, video file-sharing services, blogging software, document production platforms, corporate productivity tools, and courseware for universities, it is able to gather more information about the computer-mediated communication habits of users with their ubiquitous Google accounts, which keep the user logged in as he or she moves from searching the Internet to uploading family videos to posting a blog entry to working on private documents hosted on remote sites far from the user's desktop. All of this personal information can conceivably be harvested to provide unprecedented market research data that goes beyond what individuals buy and sell into what they watch, read, write, and, by extension, think.

Making access to electronic archives part of that nexus of digital preferences has certain troubling implications, in that public records would become part of the advertising and marketing schemes for a private company. Furthermore, in the case of citizens accessing materials produced about the government and by the government, one kind of participation in the political processes would no longer be protected by the traditional anonymity associated with other conventions of interactivity like the secret ballot and rituals of privacy surrounding citizenship. Ironically, some of the same libraries that vigorously protected individual patron records during the McCarthy era from snooping by the authorities, because law enforcement agencies wanted to know who was checking out politically subversive texts, are now choosing to participate in a system that allows a third party to track a reader's most private habits in the archive.

Furthermore, since market data is now of great interest to political campaigns that attempt to win elections by stooping to using household shopping information on a voter-by-voter basis, it may not be long before Google is selling targeted advertising if not outright information about private reading habits to those who wish to manipulate elections. If the results of a given Google search can be reordered to privilege paid advertisers, would political interests have incentives to prioritize particular parts of the legislative record or the written history of governance?

Certainly not everyone involved with the recent history of building digital archives accepts Google's self-ordained designation as the company with the "don't be evil" motto. Because of the unintended consequences from the procedural logic behind Google's search algorithms, those who build archival collections may find themselves losing credit for and even access to their own electronic libraries. For example, Jim Zwick, an independent scholar and veteran of several trailblazing digital archives projects, began collecting materials about U.S. and European imperialism, expositions and world's fairs, and the visual culture of the nineteenth century nation-state in the 1990s. To do this, Zwick was careful to clear the necessary permissions for posting these photographic reproductions and texts on the World Wide Web. Zwick organized his huge catalog of images and primary source documents at a personally managed website, BoondocksNet, which at its zenith hosted over 20,000 pages, including explanatory essays and other curatorial materials that Zwick personally created. However, so many state curricula thought Zwick's site was so useful for their standards-based large-scale courses that they copied pages and pages of it and hosted Zwick's content on their own, often government-sponsored, servers. Because companies like Google want to simplify search results, they do not carry duplicate content if the same pages appear on more than one server. And to make sure that users reach the most authoritative sites, the algorithm of these search engines seems to default to institutional URLs with .edu or .gov extensions, even if these institutional sites do not legitimately host the materials of the credited authors.

According to Zwick, his site on U.S. imperialism had a similar page ranking to comparable materials hosted on the Library of Congress website in 2003.[36] But after technologies became available to duplicate the content of Internet behemoths like Amazon.com and Wikipedia, mechanisms had to be created to preserve their page ranking and protect their status as large hubs,[37] while removing thousands of pages of duplicate content that were appearing in search results at Google and other search engines. Thus, because of the procedural logic dictating search protocols, what Claus Schmidt calls "page hijacking"[38] was punished when its victims were sites that were already authoritative hubs associated with government agencies or institutions of higher learning. But if the domain came from an independent extramural source, more powerful "textual poachers" (here I use Henry Jenkins' term for the behavior of fans of films and television shows more broadly to include other media admirers who duplicate content for their own works[39]) could end up hurting the actual content creator. Thus even large-scale preservationist sites, such as the Internet Archive, might cause the original author to be blocked from a given set of search results.

These scenarios may be more likely as web search paradigms become increasingly complex and likely to be automated in projects related to the rise of the "semantic web," which will use protocols from artificial intelligence to predict the relevance of a given search result and allow users to "teach the machine" what they might want without input from professional indexers. However, in questioning the "warehouse" model of the library, Paul Duguid and John Seely Brown also express skepticism about the possibilities for a future version of the World Wide Web, which is "self-organized but patrolled by bots," to serve as a substitute for traditional or digital libraries. As Duguid and Brown see the Internet, "Our results primarily serve to remind us that the Web is a vast, disorderly, and very fast-changing information repository with enormous quantities of overlapping and duplicate information and that all its catalogues are incomplete and out of date."[40]

Regardless of size, even the most obviously educational sites with a lot of author-generated content could get caught up in the no-duplication net. As Zwick says, "I think my site, the Smithsonian, and a bunch of others were banned from Google in early 2005 after a commercial script for use by high schools was released that uses 302 redirects to link to all kinds of academic sites. Google seems to have made manual corrections for well-known institutional sites but did not address the problem more generally so many independent sites continue to be penalized because of 302 links and copying by others."[41] By early 2007, use of Zwick's site had declined to less than 23 percent of what it had been in early 2003, and newer materials added to the site were not getting any use at all. Ironically, this problem of "domain poisoning" was made worse the more popular Zwick's site became among authoritative content providers. As he writes, "The first using 302 redirects did it as a bait-and-switch but by 2005 or so, many legitimate sites were using the same technology to count usage of links going to the legitimate sites."[42] Says Zwick, "Google was the most influential problem with the 'duplicate content' issue but my site was also banned from Microsoft Live and Ask.com because of it."[43] For Zwick it was particularly disastrous, because—like many independent scholars—he also used his website to showcase his publications. So, an entire corpus of work on American political discourse and authors such as Mark Twain was not linked to his individual domain, although that was his intent in putting his publications there in the first place. After depleting his financial and emotional resources in numerous, often fruitless Digital Millennium Copyright Act takedown attempts, Zwick closed his site in frustration.

Because scholars and artists often use independent websites to host their materials, given their understandable urge to avoid the constraints of an institutional identity and to adapt to the necessarily nomadic character of university employment that is driven by the demands of tenure and promotion, which requires frequent relocation of faculty, this disadvantage to "indie" websites in the logic of Google's search algorithms could potentially force faculty members to host their personal materials on university and other institutionally recognized servers to preserve access, even if professors feel that these arrangements ultimately lead to less control of form and content and a structuring of their production for Internet audiences by disincentives that inhibit more controversial rhetorical uses such as social activism. For example, this book was developed on a web log that functioned as an independent site separate from the .edu domain that I use for faculty purposes, because I wanted to make clear that any political critiques I was posing of the government as a digital media-maker did not represent the opinions of the university for which I worked. As Zwick himself pointed out, however, this "independence" was still limited by the fact that the *Virtualpolitik* blog was hosted by a Google subsidiary and thus in some ways the property of a corporate entity that could pull content from their servers at any time.

At a time when everything from titling newspaper headlines[44] to naming children[45] is being influenced by Google's algorithms, this ability for a private corporation to organize print information without public accountability could have many unintended consequences, particularly if the corporation's idiosyncratic indexing choices are considered proprietary knowledge that must be kept as a trade secret to preserve their competitive position in the marketplace. Vaidhyanathan has argued that academics from many fields associated with what he calls "Critical Information Studies" should be engaged in interrogating the "structures, functions, habits, norms, and practices" of particular aspects of information culture and in analyzing how these issues go beyond simple arguments about digital "rights" to include consideration of the more subtle impacts of cost and access that have the potential for chilling effects on a "semiotic democracy" that is situated in "global flows of information."[46] As the inheritor of an intellectual history with a lineage from cultural studies and political economy, cultural information studies (CIS) is uniquely situated to consider how public policy decisions create informational constraints and vice versa. Since Google has already cooperated with an authoritarian regime by allowing information censorship—filtering the outputs that go to screens in China to exclude certain results about "democracy" or "human rights" in order to secure state sanction and thus increase market share,[47]—the questions that Vaidhyanathan raises about the politics of information in relationship to Google are worth considering more deeply.

Vaidhyanathan has also expressed concern that the Library of Congress may be prematurely surrendering "its role in standardizing how we catalog knowledge."[48] Vaidhyanathan's fears may not be ungrounded, given a recent report from the Working Group on the Future of Bibliographic Control at the Library of Congress that de-emphasizes investment in public infrastructure and federal information design efforts.

The future of bibliographic control will be collaborative, decentralized, international in scope, and Web-based. Its realization will occur in cooperation with the private sector, and with the active collaboration of library users. Data will be gathered from multiple sources; change will happen quickly; and bibliographic control will be dynamic, not static. The underlying technology that makes this future possible and necessary—the World Wide Web—is now almost two decades old. Libraries must continue the transition to this future without delay in order to retain their significance as information providers.[49]

This new direction is not without detractors even among librarians and within the Library of Congress itself. Wikis[50] and blogs[51] also question the wisdom of automating and distributing traditional knowledge functions.

The Cryptohistories of Digitization

Obviously, corporations are not guaranteed eternal success in highly competitive technology fields based only on their one-time dominance in market share. By the beginning of the twenty-first century, Google had emerged as the champion among many competing search engine companies. However, patent history has shown that these victories can be surprisingly short-lived, as was the case for many of the innovative technologies developed at Xerox PARC during its heyday, but ultimately made profitable in the long term much later by the corporation's competitors.[52]

The history of Chester shows how once-cutting-edge technologies for information duplication, storage, and retrieval can become little more than forgotten artifacts in a more complicated media history with many competing discourses about ownership, labor, value, and community in play. It was here in Chester that a team of inventors and archivists planned to provide the membership of the American Library Association and other traditional libraries with the "resources of the great libraries of the world—the rare and inaccessible books, manuscripts, and newspapers heretofore available alone to those few who could journey to a distant museum or library."[53] By the middle of the twentieth century, Readex corporation catalogs announced that in addition to their collection of Early American Imprints, much prized by scholars of colonial history and literature, the company could sell copies of records from the United Nations, the British House of Commons, and U.S. government publications from 1951 to the present.

The Readex Corporation now digitizing the Serial Set was at one time run by Albert Boni, who produced popular abridged classics in "The Little Leather Library," which were sold through Woolworth's chain stores. In his literary magazine, he published Ford Madox Ford, Ezra Pound, H.D., and William Carlos Williams.[54] Later, as one of the cofounders of the Boni-Liveright Publishing Company, Boni introduced the "Modern Library of the World's Best Classics" and sold paperback books by mail-order subscription for a firm that later became The Modern Library and then Random House, one of the firms that sued Google over potential copyright infringement. As a progressive publisher, Boni's first title was Oscar Wilde's *The Picture of Dorian Grey*.

Boni had been known as something of a political radical in his youth; as a teen he was secretary of the local chapter of the Socialist Party.[55] While on hiatus from publishing, Boni had gone to Russia after the 1917 Revolution, like many American socialists, where he hobnobbed with Lenin on newsreels and became an acquaintance of labor organizer Emma Goldman and would-be anticorporate assassin Alexander Berkman. He had been imprisoned by the Bolsheviks and then deported on a transport train. Boni was also a member of the utopian Free Acres Colony for many years, an experiment in community living that eschewed the personal ownership of property.[56]

After returning from Russia, Boni expanded his catalog of important authors in the modernist tradition to include Gertrude Stein and Thorton Wilder.[57] Embroiled in conflicts for market share with The Book of the Month Club and discount books from the Brentanos chain, Boni later became a public opponent in the *New York Times* of the very cutthroat publishing industry cost cutting that he himself helped originate. Nonetheless, issues about affordability of ownership for printed matter continued to occupy his attention.

During World War II, Boni focused on revolutions in information duplication and distribution rather than politics or literature and became interested in new photographic techniques and their possible applicability to the traditional publishing business. First he joined a group of partners in the ill-fated International Film Book Company; then he began to work on miniaturizing British eighteenth- and nineteenth-century sessional papers from the House of Commons. He moved from New York City to Vermont and began more daring experiments with microreproduction technologies. He claimed that his inspiration had been a "miniature candid-camera shot which had been enlarged ten thousand times." "Why not," as Boni reasoned, "reverse the process?"[58] He also described seeing a human eyelash blown up 10,000 times, so that the pores in the surrounding skin looked like craters on the moon.[59] Unlike the advocates of microfilm for library use, Boni did not reject paper as a storage device or the organization of printed matter on shelves. Instead, he proposed that all bulky printed material be reduced to six-by nine-inch cards, each of which could hold one hundred pages of a standard book.

In pitches to librarians and archivists, Readex claimed that it would supplement rather than substitute for existing titles. They hoped to convince libraries to buy *more* titles printed on *more* paper, albeit in miniature reproductions using specialized emulsions. The Readex copies were promised to be affordable both to produce and to acquire and could last up to three hundred years, according to one U.S. National Bureau of Standards estimate.[60] Brochures and press releases emphasized that libraries could now acquire copies of hundreds of extremely rare books that would fit in a hatbox-sized space for a comparative pittance of $50. Of course, customers would also need to purchase the patented machines necessary to read them, which were advertised for sale at $150.[61] By 1980, Boni had over three million titles in Microprint.[62]

Like Coleman a half-century later, Boni took advantage of recent historical catastrophes to emphasize the need for his preservation technology. In particular, the destruction of the library of Louvain during both twentieth-century world wars inspired many American libraries to be persuaded by Boni's message.[63] In appealing to the Library of Congress, one of Readex's first planned clients, the promoters for Boni's new device also emphasized national pride and the cultural rivalry with Europe. Company literature noted the fact that "English books published before 1550 are now being photographed at the British Museum at a rate of 100,000 pages a year for fifteen American libraries."[64]

Although they were careful to create a structure of proprietary technologies, the Chester group built on decades of experiments with photographic miniaturization of books that could be read by special machines, which were first demonstrated to the admiring public in 1933 news stories and later showcased at the 1939 World's Fair. Unfortunately, the light (and heat) involved in illumination and magnification quickly reduced the postage-stamp-sized samples to ash in the early Readex prototypes, but a lamp compared in the company's promotional materials to a modern car headlight was eventually constructed with the low wattage and industrial durability required.[65]

In "Too Small to See But Not to Read," Marvin Lowenthal exploited the public's interest in novelty and spectacle in a 1944 *Saturday Review* designed to explain the Readex mission to the broader public.

Folded in my wallet, where it occupies even less space than my automobile license, is a two hundred page book . . . This miniature book is not a curiosity of craftsmanship, like the Lord's Prayer engraved on the head of a pin. Nor is it an example of microfilm.[66]

Ironically, in Boni's own account of the history of microprinting in his private papers, he laments the fact that the truly scientific and strategic origins of the technology had been lost behind the consumption of present-day novelty items, such as "tourists' souvenirs with views mounted on tiny magnifiers in rings, penholders and the like."[67]

Despite the fact that he was working with paper and many traditional photographic processes, Boni was well aware of the information revolution and the new paradigm emerging in which information could be mathematically quantified and understood in terms of signal-to-noise models. As a publisher, Boni's brother oversaw the production of *The Scientists Speak*, edited by mathematician Warren Weaver, who praised the value of theories of "organized complexity" in the volume.[68] Boni's collaborator John Tennant published an explanation of the mathematical inefficiencies of older data

Figure 8.2
Photograph of an early Readex machine (Barb Westine), by permission of Newsbank.

storage models in "Essays of an Information Scientist," which included the following explanation of the rationale for microprint in layman's terms:

I am often surprised how difficult it is for some people to grasp the reason why miniprint and other micrographic methods produce the economies they do. If you start out with a page which is 10 by 10, the area is 100 square units. Now, if you photographically reduce the image to 2 by 2, the area is 4 square units. The reduction ratio is 1:5, but where you once had one page you can now store 25![69]

Boni also corresponded with Bell Labs scientist Pierre Metz about data transmission, and Metz recommended scientific papers to the Vermont businessman with titles that included "Theory of Scanning" and "Perception of Television Random Noise."[70] Readers of Boni's voluminous bibliography of photographic literature included those who suggested that he do more with the "Information Theory of the Photographic

Emulsion" to "cover modulation transfer functions and other aspects which are at present covered under 'Image Quality' and 'Sine Wave Response.'"[71]

Like the memex machine in Vannevar Bush's influential, popular *Atlantic Monthly* essay about the need to organize knowledge in the computer age, "As We May Think," promoters of the Readex machine imagined being able to shrink down the unwieldy print Encyclopedia Britannica and dramatically save on costs and materials.[72] They similarly saw their technology as a solution to manage the same "rapid growth of scientific and technical literature" that Bush perceived, which they warned was being further exacerbated by the "vicious notion that anyone and everyone could and should write and publish."[73] Much as Bush's visionary article imagined his memex device being integrated into home furnishings, company literature argued that Readex machines could eventually become installed in private houses. As the *Saturday Review* essay enthused, 4,000 books or "more than most book lovers can persuade their wives to house and dust" could be reduced to the proverbial "five foot shelf."[74]

Kevin Kelly of the *New York Times* has argued that Boni's dream of the universal library was impossible before the advent of contemporary search algorithms. As Kelly puts it, "Scanning technology has been around for decades, but digitized books didn't make much sense until recently, when search engines like Google, Yahoo, Ask and MSN came along."[75] Although the advent of these search engines makes the presence of competing stakeholders vying to shape the public and even political story about information ownership more obvious, proprietary technologies that simultaneously restrict and enable access to public records and texts of cultural import have been around for a long time. Unfortunately, formats change frequently, in response to anxieties about consumer duplication and the sometimes unpredictable logic of market preferences that don't always benefit the survival of the fittest. After all, with its signature Early American Imprints collection, Readex eventually moved to selling libraries a version of the more popular microfiche format that it had once eschewed.

Although data was miniaturized by Readex rather than scrambled with a numeric key of secret code, this information could be considered "encrypted" in ways that make us think critically about the Google narrative in which the digital file that represents the printed page is stored and transmitted in a non-open-source format. Perhaps the question we should be asking is "Where are all the Readex cards and machines today?" Are the special replacement lamps designed to avoid overheating still being manufactured? Do the focus mechanisms that allow the tiny print to be read still work? Were the machines just taking up valuable space in libraries and disposed of as outmoded devices? It is likely that hundreds of copies of rare books and government documents are today effectively illegible, much as tomorrow's Google Book Search files could one day be unreadable, since users can't copy the text to their own machines to preserve and reformat as they choose.

Private Companies and Public Infrastructures

Critics argue that Google's role as a commercial entity beholden to shareholders may be fundamentally in conflict with its carefully crafted projection of itself as a universally free, open, and public resource eminently worthy of citizens' trust. The underlying assumption that knowledge can be completely embodied through a computer interface and truth attained in its totality that informs Google's ideology is implicitly also at issue in *Google and the Myth of Universal Knowledge* by Jean-Noël Jeanneney. In this book, the former president of the French national library, the Bibliothèque nationale de France (BNF), voices skepticism about Google's grand ambitions to digitize the content of the world's great libraries. Like Vaidhyanathan, Jeanneney expresses concerns about privatization of public resources, proprietary technologies, and confidential contracts. However, in addition to siding with publishers about the company's potential corporate liability for copyright violation, Jeanneney differs from Vaidhyanathan on the question of the role of national identity in information culture. While Vaidhyanathan embraces a form of digital cosmopolitanism common among many netizens that envisions a "family in Karachi, Pakistan," which may have "members living well in Manchester, Montreal, and Milwaukee,"[76] Jeanneney defends the ideology of a nation-state. He contends that French and, more generally, European information infrastructure is threatened when English texts are privileged, the cultural artifacts that buttress American nationalism and corporate capitalism are prioritized, and the privileging of Anglo-Saxon law over Latin legal systems is further reified as cyberspace shapes real-world transactions. To respond in kind, he argues for the creation of a competing European search engine and online library with Airbus, which began as a consortium of state-subsidized aerospace manufacturers, as the multinational cooperative model. He points out that if European citizens don't pay as taxpayers, they will pay as consumers, so that publicly funded initiatives for digital libraries would ultimately prove to be more cost-effective and more able to vie for market share in the face of American dominance. As someone familiar with the debates over the cataloging process, Jeanneney is making an argument for a qualitative as well as a quantitative approach to digitization that values electronic mark-up of documents and the economic viability of readable text as a product that should be preserved for public use.

Jeanneney is not the only French intellectual to weigh in on what is perceived as the hegemonic cultural position of Google. Famed psychoanalytic and Marxist critical theorist and editor Jacques-Alain Miller chose Google in a widely published roundup of cultural phenomena as an homage to the subjects once cataloged in Roland Barthes's classic work on poststructuralism and popular culture, *Mythologies*.[77] Other critics chose the blog, the iPod, short messaging services, global positioning systems, and other high-profile innovations in computer-mediated communication or ubiquitous computing as objects of study worthy of analysis in Barthes's style. Miller focused on the cultural logic of Google in that, like "Big Brother," Google is structured—like all search engines—by a "totalitarian troping" that turns the user into the sum of his clicks.[78] What Vaidhyanathan calls "The Googlization of Everything"[79] is also of concern for Miller, who criticizes how Google can "scan all the books, plunder all the archives [of] cinema, television, the press, and beyond," thereby subjecting the universe to "an omniscient gaze, traversing the world, lusting after every little last piece of information about everyone." However, Miller argues that this search engine is also necessarily "stupid" because its queries lack real syntax and its results lack meaningful indexing. Thus, "the void flips into plenitude, concision to verbosity."[80]

As Jeanneney points out in his conclusion, however, an implied emphasis on the limitations of universal knowledge was not actually in his original title. The book was initially called *Quand Google défie l'Europe*, after the title of a 2005 article that Jeanneney wrote for *Le Monde*. For English-speaking audiences, Jeanneney was hesitant to choose a title that suggested a "challenge" to the Continent, because in French the term has "a different implication, more sporting, more positive, more rewarding for both sides".[81] Although he disavows a "crusade or a culture war," his implicit equation of "civilization"—a frequently used word in his book—with European values certainly reinscribes old cultural divides. However, he also claims that "inequalities of knowledge" will actually proliferate if knowledge is voluminously stored without proper cataloging for retrieval[82] and that it is important to be sensitive to the potential cultural imperialism of North/South divisions that became a source of intellectual debate in France in the 1970s.[83]

As a persuasive document, there are some notable omissions in this book, however. Jeanneney praises the index as an organizational invention, and yet declines to provide one for his own book. He lauds the BNF's digital library Gallica without acknowledging limitations in its document selection and metadata parameters and the ways its keyword-based algorithm causes users to find themselves downloading a large bulk of unrelated pages in response to a given search query.[84] Furthermore, Jeanneney does not elaborate about the deliberative processes behind strategic choices made in the BNF's initial digitization strategy. For example, many of the first digitized materials at the BNF were generated from a previous replication technique, microfilm, which increases the quantity of available documents rapidly, but often affects legibility in the final second-generation product. Moreover, many of the most fragile volumes in the BNF were treated as permanently offline since they were still protected by copyright, despite the fact that these same books may have been crumbling and consequently out of general circulation because they were printed after the end of rag paper, which had a much longer shelf life than wood pulp pages.

As part of my own field practice, I had interviewed Jeanneney in his unassuming offices at Europartenaires. For a man who once presided over the four looming ultramodern towers of the BNF and its imposing institutional reading rooms, it was strange to sit down at a table with Jeanneney, after being led to his office, past a kitchen, in a building full of modest flats near the city's main mosque. Known for his executive authority in leading France's efforts to build a massive digital library and, some might say, his autocratic style, Jeanneney pointed out that his book on Google has been translated into Arabic, Portuguese, Chinese, German, Japanese, and Spanish and would shortly be out in paperback. He also personified the conflict with the corporate giant by pointing to his public debates with the head of Google France.

In this 2007 interview, Jeanneney continued to argue that the Mountain View, California company is benefiting from "the philosophy of American capitalism" combined with oligarchical tendencies that date back to "old Greece" when "wealthy people" were in charge of "defining culture."[85] In a country like the United States in which a corporate monopolist like Andrew Carnegie built 1,679 new libraries, few might examine how the Carnegie library initiative's ideology about meritocracy and cultural assimilation may also solidify corporate identities at the expense of civic engagement.[86] Jeanneney is eager to remind visitors that consumers must pay for their culture somehow in their practices of everyday life, a message that goes back to his time heading France's public broadcasting network, where he argued that "no radio is free," and that—of the "two systems of financing culture"—it is better to go with the publicly financed one, in which "metamedia" is seen as part of the public interest.[87]

Jeanneney pointed out that academic and public money played a key role in Google's success, just as public investment played a key role in the launch of the Internet itself. He also asserted that the protection of a public good that requires constraint of a private entity could still be defended, even to hard-core individualists, if the calculations about costs and benefits appeal to those people's self-interest. For example, Jeanneney argued that common sense might allow that access to ubiquitous communication in the form of speaking on a cellular telephone while driving a car could be regulated in the name of the public interest under certain circumstances if safety warranted it, even if private parties—such as cell phone carriers—would prefer to continue the more libertarian practice. For Jeanneney, there has to be consideration of the social repercussions of adopting any given technology to avoid a tragedy of the commons scenario. As he asked, "Who will be the owners of the metadata?" and who will be responsible for "adapting to the new technologies?"[88]

Although Jeanneney is known as a Google critic or as he says, "not a Googlist," he admits to relying on the search engine in his own daily activities, particularly "for small quotations." He argued that there was a certain "ambivalence" created by the heroic narrative of the "birth of Google,"[89] although he simultaneously pointed to Google's mortality, and the fact that he considered it to be a "fragile giant." Despite the mythic overtones associated with the company, he expressed his belief that the limits of Google's idealism could be clearly seen just in prosaic schemes to alter page ranking to suit the highest bidder. At the same time, he explained experiencing a kind of perverse gratitude toward the Mountain View company of behalf of his compatriots, because he claimed that Google's aggressive tactics had at least encouraged Europe's cultural guardians to mobilize against American hegemony. At the time of the interview, he claimed to be unaware of the irony that the BNF had a prominently displayed Google search interface on its webpage, even during his tenure as head of the nation's library, as the Internet Archive's records show.

At one point in the interview, Jeanneney gave me a copy of his rhetorically fascinating farewell letter to the staff of the BNF, entitled *Lettre aux personnels de la Bibliothèque nationale de France au moment de leur dire adieu*, a seventy-eight page printed document in which this digital revolutionary tries to have the last word in a contentious debate about archival policies and politics. As to the cultural politics of his country, he had some choice words about his forced retirement from the BNF. To communicate his frustration with the nature of French bureaucracy, at one point Jeanneney asked me what my definition of a "camel" was. When I shrugged my shoulders at being

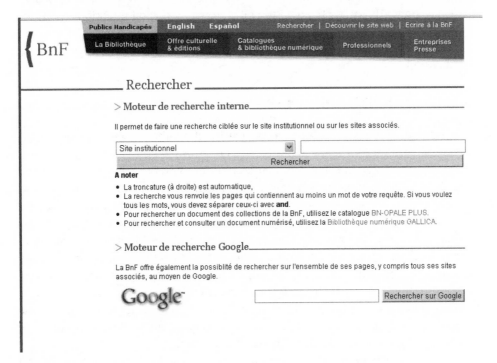

Figure 8.3
Google Search screen at the Bibliothèque nationale de France.

asked this riddle, he cited Clemenceau and replied that it was "a horse designed by committee."

Yet despite his frustration at not being able to realize all his ambitious digital information infrastructure-building goals, Jeanneney remained reluctant to embrace the Internet utopianism of the participatory hype about personal freedom then still surrounding Web 2.0. In an essay in *Le Débat* about the concept of "gratuité," which was slated to appear shortly after our interview,[90] Jeanneney voiced skepticism about the ideology of "free culture" that denies social values around intellectual labor and fundamental principles of responsible political economies.

Jeanneney has also become known for his public hesitance to accept what Pierre Lévy has called "collective intelligence,"[91] which relies on crowd-sourcing material through a kind of brute force solution to the problem of knowledge described by Vannevar Bush at the beginning of the computer age. Web 2.0 advocates believed this problem could be solved by the acquisition of massive amounts of user-generated content via distributed networks and then weighing the relative value of the collected facts with a might-makes-right system. In a *Le Point* editorial, "Wikipédia, une encyclopédie pas si Net," which translates as "Wikipedia, a not so nice encyclopedia," Jeanneney argues that that "the road to hell is paved with good intentions" and that the notion of collective intelligence represents faith in a "mysterious alchemy" by which the sum of individuals would produce a superior rather than an average intellectual output.[92]

The Corollaries of the Virtual to the Physical Space

In the summer of 2002, when I first arrived at the Bibliothèque nationale de France, I was confident that I would be admitted to its halls. After all, I had travelled to Paris as the recipient of a grant from a humanities research center in California, which had given its blessing to a project about how national digital libraries might represent both state rhetoric and the physical—some would say monumental—space of the archive, and I had done work in dozens of rare book archives. I had brought all my documents with me to the orientation area: professional cards, faculty ID, the award notification letter from the granting agency, and a signed letter on official letterhead from my chair describing why the university was supporting this research. According to procedure, prospective readers at the BNF were consigned to the waiting area until their numbers were called, and only then were they allowed to approach one of the windows to explain their projects to the official gatekeepers who were in charge of limiting the public's access to this "library of last resort."

As I started to explain my project on the discourse practices of digital libraries and the ways that web portals represented cultural imaginaries, I could see that the woman on the other side of the counter was skeptical. The more I spoke, the more deeply she frowned, until finally she interrupted me mid-sentence. "But you are studying *digital* libraries," she said, "why do you have to come *here* to do that?"

Her question indicated a common misperception about the scholarly work of interpreting the electronic record and its surrounding cultural architecture. However, when it comes to analyzing the electronic discourses of the state, internal project documents, interviews with team members, observation of the rituals and practices of taxpayer-funded media-makers and constituents as content consumers, and physical inspection of the site of collaborative sociality around technology can be essential to understanding how the final product made available online may reflect competing discourses about state rhetoric in new digital media and the deliberative processes instantiated in the interactive electronic artifact that is ultimately presented to the public.

In other words, it may be important to defend research into what has been called by Erkki Huhtamo "media archeology,"[93] or the "cryptohistories" or "secret histories" of new technologies, which would otherwise be obliterated, because these media studies run counter to corporate narratives of progress and the larger rhetoric of e-government as continuing to improve human-computer interaction paradigms. Such observational work as a form of inquiry can be particularly important since this is a historical moment in which librarians as a subculture are in the midst of a series of profound transformations, which is why I interviewed over a dozen different librarians working with government digital materials to write this chapter. Fortunately, in the time since I was first turned back by the BNF, librarians' attitudes about the mechanics of digitization have already begun to change dramatically, and the technological procedures that were once seen as lacking any ideological significance are now more likely to be interrogated by the actual participants, who are able to articulate reasons for their representational politics.

When I was finally admitted to the actual space of the Bibliothèque nationale in 2002, I discovered that although the BNF virtual library reflected liberal ideals of anonymity and open access, the physical space is one of the most heavily surveiled research libraries in the world, in which users pass through high-tech security turnstiles and are tracked with "smart" library cards. If the virtual archive epitomizes the values of anonymity and free entry that supposedly characterize the most utopian dimensions of cyberspace, in which any person, regardless of scholarly pedigree, can gain entry to the collection, the physical archive represents the opposite pole of total digital surveillance, like Foucault's prison-like panopticons. To enter the reading rooms one must be issued a card with a photograph, a magnetized strip on the back, and a computer chip imbedded in the front. But before a visitor can descend to the reading rooms, first he or she must insert this card into a special computer terminal and reserve a seat for the day. This seat number replaces the library user's name for all practical purposes. This system also ensures that readers never ask a live person for anything, since all requests are made with the card through the available computer terminals.

Just as the physical building in which a national library is housed can serve as a tangible expression of political and cultural philosophy, the architecture of a given digital archive represents and manifests particular ideological features in keeping with the specific national legacy that is preserved and disseminated electronically. However, as the case of the BNF shows, the relationship between physical archives and digital ones is often more complex than a simple analogy between conventional and electronic spaces, because national policies on digitizing documents and regulating access may engender contradictory impulses in both archivists and policy makers.

Since the Digital Millennium Copyright Act in the United States, considerable attention has focused on what has been called the "right to read." Many in the scholarly community have expressed anxiety that digital texts will soon lack many of the features of traditional ink and paper tomes. Oppositional critics of current intellectual property regimes, such as Richard Stallman, William Warner, Jessica Littman, and Pamela Samuelson, argue that conventional texts are designed to encourage adaptation and appropriation of materials in the *public* domain while simultaneously preserving the act of reading itself as a *private* activity done by an individual without surveillance.[94] They claim that digital media conventionally associated with qualities of free appropriation and anonymity could be easily engineered to subvert this right to read by controlling and monitoring access to electronic texts and inverting the relationship of public to private interests.[95]

However, a document archive as a physical space has always been constituted by prohibitions on reading. In the reading room of a typical rare books library, access is restricted to the scholarly community, the materials do not circulate, and the reading activity of visitors is monitored closely by supervisory custodians. Prospective readers cannot assert an a priori right to read in these circumstances; they must produce letters of reference, identity documents both professional and personal, and express a willingness to submit to the rules and regulations that govern access and conduct. In the case of a national library, this policing of reading can be seen in terms of what Foucault has called "governmentality," or the range of control techniques used by political institutions to regulate the inner lives of the subjects of the state. These architectures of control are perhaps most evident in the built environment, even though they exist in digital structures as well.

At the BNF, above the reading rooms for scholars, there is another set of reading rooms open to the wider public, which operates on a similar although modified protocol. Thus the Mitterand Library is actually two libraries: an upper public library and a lower library open only to established scholars, so that this stratification reinscribes hierarchies of reading and readers. Although there is a common electronic catalog and digital interface at the BNF, readers in the upper public reading rooms would be constantly reminded that there are materials that are forbidden to them and only available to the scholars below. Of course, prohibitions on the act of reading are nothing new to the ideology of the BNF, as Robert Darnton has pointed out in his work on the forbidden bestsellers of pre-Revolutionary France.[96] The relationship between royal authority, official scrutiny, and copyright deposit has been well documented, and as the BNF has progressed from royal library to revolutionary library to imperial library to national library, its history has been marked by attempts to monitor the reading practices of its subjects and citizens. Now that the BNF is building a version of itself as a digital library, its administration remains concerned with issues about the appropriation of intellectual property and the conduct of a reading "public" that is broadly construed.

The degree of regulation varies from one national context to another, however. Since the opening of the Bibliothèque nationale de France to the public in 1721 under the direction of the Abbé Bignon, the guardians of this library of things "great, rare, and precious" have struggled with demands placed on the collections by readers occupying the physical space and by the obligation to preserve materials with a long cultural patrimony. Therefore, for over a century the BNF has been designated a "library of last resort" with a corresponding set of regulations designed to exclude those without institutional affiliations or rhetorically compelling research missions. A very different paradigm is presented by the Library of Congress in the United States, which requires little more than photo identification from prospective readers, on the assumptions that any citizen can be designated a reader and that the Library of Congress is ideally a democratic institution open to all.

Although there are definite limits on the applicability of spatial metaphors to the architecture of new media,[97] it is perhaps worth examining the relationship between virtual space and physical space in two very different national libraries, the Bibliothèque nationale de France and the British Library, because they have simultaneously undertaken ambitious building projects that literally break new ground with edifices in the physical world while creating an analogous digital library in cyberspace. Both the BNF and the British Library began building a new digital library at the same historical moment in which it created a new physical space.

The millennial discourses that have shaped recent national digital library projects could be said to still linger in the digitization efforts in France, which under Jeanneney had undertaken one of the most ambitious projects to protect archival originals by disseminating electronic facsimiles and searchable hypertext via the World Wide Web, specifically through the Gallica website. As the custodians of the second largest library in the world, which has had copyright deposit since 1537 and a comprehensive cataloging system since 1670, the Bibliothèque Nationale de France at one time seemed to be in the paradoxical process of trying to make itself obsolete as a rare books library. Concurrent with this massive digitization effort, the physical space was dramatically changed, especially after the main collection was moved to the François-Mitterand Library in 1994.

The new building for the Bibliothèque Nationale de France, designed by Dominique Perrault, looms over the industrialized Left Bank of Paris, where cranes and the skeletons of half-built buildings claimed much of the rest of the skyline. There are four towers around the perimeter of the BNF: the Tower of Letters, the Tower of Numbers, the Tower of Law, and the Tower of Time. Each tower is an L-shaped office building, full of bound volumes, archival documents, and workspace, designed to remind the viewer of a giant open book. In the middle of these four titans there is a forest the size of multiple city blocks, which is sunk below street level. This use of this subterranean landscape architecture has been famously lampooned by Adam Gopnick of *The New Yorker* in his description of the "chained trees" of the forbidden garden of the BNF, along with other user-unfriendly architectural features of the building.[98]

Much like the Bibliothèque nationale de France, the British Library recently moved its collections to a new architecturally significant building, dedicated in 1998. The most obvious design difference between the Mitterand Library and this building, which was thirty years in the making, was that the reading rooms were more conventionally situated *above* where the texts were stored rather than below them. According to his own account of the building of the new British Library, the English architect Colin St. John Wilson was explicitly reacting to French public architecture in considering how to maximize the physical space of his new library for openness to the street and to the larger public. The model for the physical space of the repository of French culture, St. John Wilson insisted, should have been the tantalizing Paris Opera that used the tricks of the enticing storefront, not the hermetic old building of the BNF, now known as the Richelieu building, which excludes the viewer from its reading spaces by an unpunctuated wall. Although St. John Wilson acknowledged that "to every scholar the library is a personal realm of secret topography" that shapes the "propriety of the public image of its architecture," he wanted to invite as much of the larger public into the space of the reading room as possible.[99] The main architectural, aesthetic, and ideological influence that St. John Wilson points to in his work is the English Free School, and while such connections between politico-aesthetic ideology and public architecture are often explicitly stated in bricks-and-mortar projects, they are still much more rarely articulated in similar design efforts in cyberspace.

One obvious obstacle that the British Library architect had to overcome was the attachment of readers and more generally the public to the previous site of the library inside the British Museum. If millennialism dominated French discourse about a national library, then the figure of nostalgia played a central role in the British experience, particularly nostalgia for the round Reading Room, which has ironically since been converted into a public access point for electronic multimedia with dozens of computer terminals, although at the time of this writing it was hosting a blockbuster exhibition of tomb sculptures from China. Because the old round reading room, built on the model of the Pantheon, was such an important physical space for public reading, a place not only for encounters with books but for encounters—real and imagined—with fellow readers, who have included many literary luminaries over the century and a half it was used, and because the Reading Room had also been a site and subject of literature itself, considerable reluctance to abandon it was anticipated, although, as St. John Wilson notes, once the new library was open readers "voted with their feet" and the old reading room was closed ahead of schedule.

Of course, the work of the BNF, the British Library, and the Library of Congress to digitize their collections at first seemed to raise the possibility of an endgame scenario for their physical collections themselves. Stanley Chodorow has written that the era of the great libraries of the nineteenth and twentieth centuries may be coming to a close and that our society may, in fact, be returning to a medieval model of intellectual life in which the gradual accretion of information becomes more important than definitive acts of individual authorship.[100]

Yet in his book on Google, former BNF head Jeanneney scoffs at such pronouncements and argues that the physical spaces for reading, such as libraries and bookstores, would never be eliminated by their digital counterparts, even if early project documents projected that fewer users would be using the BNF reading rooms. Like the BNF, the British Library anticipated that offering digital materials as substitutes would lower attendance in the reading rooms, although its early projections—a 9 percent reduction in demand anticipated in a 1996 report—were quite modest when compared to Chodorow's projections for the end of great libraries themselves. Paradoxically, as senior librarian Neil Smith said in a 2002 interview,[101] the reverse has proven true in the British case. Creating a nascent digital library actually seemed to stimulate interest in access to the physical collections rather than sate it.[102]

Originals and Copies

Regardless of degree, the stated reason for regulatory structures governing access to national libraries is the existence of irreplaceable originals in rare books archives. However, as Walter Benjamin has famously argued in "The Work of Art in the Age of Mechanical Reproduction," this value on originality could be seen as a by-product of technological innovations that facilitate copying. Although Benjamin claims that a cultural work loses what he calls the "aura" of the original after undergoing the process of mechanical replication, it could be asserted that this aura is also created about the original by the existence of copies. Benjamin acknowledges that tangible losses of "presence in time and space" occur from the reproduction of texts, even if this loss is more than compensated by increased access, what Benjamin calls the "matrix" of mass participation in which "quality" is transformed into "quantity."[103] Indeed Benjamin's own library, which he was so reluctant to leave behind in Nazi Germany, may serve as a model of an archive in which the insubstitutability of originals was made manifest to Benjamin himself.

Rather than romanticize the singularity of the "original" in the archive, I assume, as Hillel Schwartz does in *The Culture of the Copy,* that "acts and images of doubling" are fundamental to culture and humanistic discourse. The redundancy of particularly important "originals" in the physical archive, like the Gutenberg Bibles owned by the three national libraries in which I have done field work, may point to ways that originality and copying are always intertwined since the Gutenberg Bible is itself famous as an "original copy," marked by the redundancies and contradictions that replication creates.

Yet in digitization the copy is not identical to the original, since it also includes supplementary information that indexes and organizes it. At the simplest level, this additional information is constituted by the words in the text, which—thanks to optical character recognition technologies—allow for keyword searching in a document that would be impossible with mere replication of photographic images of the pages. Large-scale mass digitization projects like Google's privately financed initiative and the BNF's publicly funded one often start with such relatively bare metadata arrangements, since elaborate cross-reference processes like those practiced at the Readex operation can be relatively slow and expensively labor-intensive, although these scrupulous metadata practices may be optimal for supporting many different kinds of subject searches and for appealing to demanding librarians who are the primary Readex consumers.

As senior librarian Aly Conteth of the British Library notes, what was once merely understood as the transformation of a physical object into a digital one is now seen in terms of an entire "workflow," which can include a complex nexus of surrounding labor relations, patterns of consumption, and contractual obligations. During his interview with fellow project manager Neil Fitzgerald, Conteth discussed the often-invisible labor policies involved in digitization efforts. As he pointed out, the conversion of "physical to digital" with the imaging machine is only a small part of a process that involves quality assurance, delivery systems, and metadata schemes to create meaningful informational resources. He speculated about best practices for creating a "more robust workflow" around the replication process that would facilitate resource discovery, the connection of electronic resources together, and the importance of benefits for targeted groups to satisfy the requirements of their funding bodies. Conteth even talked about the perils of outsourcing some of the labor of generating metadata to India, where even the best English-speaking operators working with the digital copies of newspapers may not recognize common English place names. Thus, even the most supposedly neutral activity of metadata creation for universal consumption according to preordained taxonomies shows that culturally situated knowledge can still be important for meaningful mark-up in the digital age.[104]

Figure 8.4
Digitizers working at the British Library (H.Schunck/CCS), by permission of the British Library.

A Third Way?

At the British Library, Conteth and Fitzgerald described their current joint digitization effort with Microsoft as a negotiation between public and private interests, in which they are aiming to make electronic copies of an ambitious 25 million pages, or about 100,000 items, in accord with a mission to foster educational use at all levels while still complying with U.K. copyright rules. Pragmatists claim that such corporate partnerships are necessary in this national context, because the British Library still struggles with a government mandate not to digitize materials using monies from core funding, which dates back to the beginnings of digitization at the library itself. Unfortunately, the British Library now occasionally finds itself in a Catch-22 situation, because donors, corporate partners, and even government-funded councils are reluctant to participate in basic digitization initiatives because they perceive the creation of electronic copies to be a core function of the library's preservation and archiving efforts and therefore not worthy of extramural funding.

In speaking about their relationship with Microsoft, Conteth and Fitzgerald stressed that the arrangement "really is a partnership" in which the software maker is "relying on" their "expertise" and respecting the "level of quality" they need as a cultural institution to connect replication and encoding to the process of generating metadata. Certainly, Conteth and Fitzgerald were careful to distinguish themselves from Google Book Search and emphasize their commitment to open standards and more egalitarian partnership models with corporate behemoths. Of course, critics of Microsoft's proprietary architectures may be leery of the way that the company is publicizing the Vista operating system through the initiative. But the British librarians argued that there were many software packages from a wide variety of companies involved in the entire digitizing process and that their arrangement with Microsoft still allowed them access to and control of the digital documents through a system of parallel operations. Although they were "well-aware of initial impressions," Conteth and Fitzgerald maintained that their focus on open standards and serving the needs of educational audiences differentiated their contractual arrangements from those directing Google Book Search.[105]

The British Library has had other experiences with proprietary digital technologies in the past. Their "Turning the Pages" exhibits in the physical spaces of their visitor galleries and on the library's websites allow users to experience a simulacrum of the rare privilege of leafing through a volume normally only on static display behind a glass case, such as the DaVinci notebooks or the Lisbon Hebrew Bible. Between virtually turning pages, when the actual text is displayed, viewers can also move a magnifying glass over words and illustrations and click buttons for translation, commentary, or a recording of the text being read aloud. This might seem like a great expenditure of complex technology for a relatively trivial scholarly payoff in comparison to user-directed searches of the plain text for key terms, but it is also important to remember that the British Library has had a long history of valuing photographic facsimiles as pedagogical tools, and these facsimiles have been an important feature of its institutional identity, a tradition which goes back to the nineteenth century and the work of Edward Augustus Bond.[106]

Unfortunately, to access the trademarked "Turning the Pages" materials, visitors to the website are presented with a barrage of software brand names, links to product websites, prompts for updates, information about upgrades, and advice about popup blocking on the home page.

Turning the Pages™ uses the Shockwave plug-in, which can be downloaded from the Adobe website, to simulate the action of turning the pages of a real book. For Mac OS X users there is an alternative download. The volumes may not open if you block popups on your computer.

NEW! A new version, called Turning the Pages 2.0™, has been developed for the Microsoft Vista operating system and was launched on 30 January. It will also run on Windows XP with the .NET 3 framework. Find out if you have the necessary software and hardware now.

There are alternative versions which do not use Shockwave but display images of pages (and enlargements) in standard web pages, in the same window.[107]

Only at the end of these instructions is the would-be reader of rare tomes given the option to simply access JPEG images of the page reproductions, which also have the advantage of being able to be copied to the user's computer for later perusal or repurposing.

In contrast, proprietary technologies were specifically avoided in the International Dunhuang Project, which brought together 100,000 physically dispersed manuscripts, paintings, textiles, and artifacts from the Silk Road that can now be reunited through a digital interface. The project required a high degree of international cooperation with the National Library of China to create a virtual library that reconstitutes the pre-diasporac conditions for materials that were disseminated across many continents during the early forms of globalization associated with the silk trade and the dissemination of Buddhist teachings.

The War on Paper

Rare manuscripts and general circulation books are not the only materials in the British Library that are obvious choices for conversion to electronic media. In its digitization efforts, the library has a huge potential database of periodical literature to exploit, the Burney Collection, which was archived both on paper and microfilm and now represents 650,000 pages of "recognizable newspapers" from the eighteenth and nineteenth centuries during a span of history from 1603 to 1817. Although this collection excluded broadsheets and pamphlets, it has obvious historical value in its coverage of the North American wars, wars with the Continent, and a wide range of social changes in the British Isles. Yet by the year 2000, there were problems manifestly present in locating funding for digitizing the Burney Collection. As librarians at the turn of the century complained, monies from the National Lottery were designed for a conventional library, not a digital one, and attractive partnerships outside Britain with institutions in the United States and Japan became a driving force.[108] Consequently projects with blockbuster appeal, such as the ethnographic image archive and the Gutenberg Bible project, were placed far ahead of the Burney Collection.

Fortunately, by 2007, when the race between corporate sponsors, and even between competing national institutions, for publicity had finally heated up, the library was able to plan to offer U.S. and U.K. readers Internet access to the Burney Collection through the library portals of institutions of higher education, thanks to funding from the U.S. National Science Foundation. However, even as plans for digitizing the newspaper archive of the past seemed ready to be realized, planning for archiving the newspapers of the present and future began to change. As Conteth noted in the interview, in archiving contemporary newspapers it is sometimes more practical to skip the "quite archaic" intermediate step of ironing and photographing the print version and merely capture the digital file for posterity, which represents the text, images, and layout made by the newspaper for production purposes, so it becomes increasingly "preferable to take it in that format." With many newspapers forecasting that their circulations may be exclusively designed for an online readership in the future, archiving rapidly changing "born digital" materials also becomes an issue. [109]

Of course, not everyone is disenchanted with paper as a storage medium. As a technical solution used to record and disseminate information, printed paper volumes have been successful for millennia with the support of the organizational structures of traditional libraries throughout the world. Because it has chosen to dispose of so much of its paper inventories, the British Library has come in for special criticism in Nicholson Baker's *Double Fold: Libraries and the Assault on Paper*, which argues that paper has been a tremendously efficient means of archiving and preserving materials, contrary to those who view it as ephemeral and wasteful of space.[110] Baker opens his book with a dramatic account of the destruction of 10,000 volumes of Irish and English newspapers during World War II after a German bombing and then proceeds to argue that microfilm and digitization may prove to be just as destructive to the library's stock of periodical literature, which includes four-color editions of American newspapers that merit status as archival precious objects just as illuminated manuscripts do. He argues that the chemical disintegration of wood-pulp paper, introduced after the end of the production of more expensive acid-free rag pages, has been vastly overestimated and that the "assault on paper" engineered by "managerial policy" will commit pages of text to unproven and possibly unsustainable methods that may be even more mortal than wood pulp.

Furthermore, Michael Alexander and Andrew Prescott make the case that the British Library has had to keep in mind that "none of the digital material, either recreated from another medium or published only in digital form, will be identified or identifiable within any form of data storage unless it has been cataloged in a usable way."[111] Thus, unlike traditional materials, miscataloged digital materials could be lost forever. Online materials can also exclude readers and even librarians from circuits of appropriation normally associated with traditional texts. As early as 1997 Laura Campbell of the Library of Congress expressed concern about how "online information . . . is typically outside the control of a user library. It can be accessed but not, in the traditional sense, acquired."[112]

The Lady Vanishes

Nonetheless, the dematerialized dream of work without labor and digitization without physical matter or human beings persists in the materials about these initiatives, emphasizing the robotic automation of digitizing machines, which can use a vacuum mechanism to turn the pages, even if live minders are always present to deal with the unpredictable artifactuality of printed books. One of the unintentionally iconic images of the Google Book Search project shows a digitizer's hand seemingly accidentally included in the photographic copy from a page of an 1855 edition of *The Gentleman's Magazine*,[113] which was widely publicized in British newspapers and Siva Vaidhyanathan's *Googlization of Everything* blog. In the picture, we see the specialized equipment that the digitizer must use in her work: finger cots that may protect her from cuts or repetitive stress injuries, facilitate nimbleness in flipping pages, or preserve the pages from the oils on her skin and the wear –and tear of human handling. In addition to the accoutrements of her profession, we also see information about class and gender in her perfectly manicured polished red fingernails and her feminine diamond rings, which seem to include a commitment band on her ring finger.

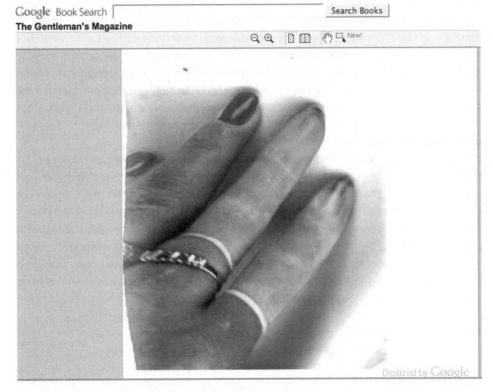

Figure 8.5
Accidentally included image of digitizer's hand in Google Book Search, by permission of Google.

The image reminds us that the work of librarians is still in many ways a classic pink-collar profession, like the early switchboard operators who later became computer programmers. Anne Balsamo and Katherine Hayles have used the phrase "My Mother Was a Computer" to emphasize the historically significant counternarrative in which the feminine plays a key role in the information science revolution. David Grier, in *When Computers Were Human*, has also pointed out that women were once active innovators and participants in the design of early communication technologies and nascent computer programming, before information science was established as a "properly" masculine academic discipline. And the beginning of Mark Poster's *Information Please* tells the story of a telephone operator known to a young boy as "information" who serves as a surrogate when he needs maternal attention. In "A Cyborg Manifesto," Donna Haraway has argued that postmodern digital culture has feminized labor profoundly, but public archives staffed by librarians have been gendered in popular perceptions for a very long time. For example, in a Google image search of pictures associated with the word "librarian," the entire first screen of twenty results consists of nothing but images of females playing that role. In some way, it could be argued that the enthusiasts hoping to create digital collections without intermediaries who maintain access, ensure preservation, and establish order in the texts are trying to dematerialize human beings as gendered bodies that are still a critical part of the socioeconomics of information, much as postwar advocates for digitization registered the uncomfortable presence of females in the information workplace and then sought to create machines to make these distracting women obsolete and to replace female computers with mechanical devices.

Yet the exposure of this hand can be seen as representing a kind of return of the repressed, in which the presence of human beings is acknowledged in a sign that also indicates their absence in the form of quality control and attentive mark-up of the text. In another scan, the hand of a person of color is captured alongside Plato's *Euthyphro*, which is ironically one of the classics in the literature around the philosophy of classification and how basic categories of knowledge are defined.[114] These accidental inclusions seem to indicate that the work of digitization may be considered to be literally manual labor by Google at this point and not the work of human vision and oversight.

The Wisdom of Crowds?

Jefferson's library, which became the central germ of the current Library of Congress, is also of interest to a collective of bibliographers who are using volunteers to "crowdsource" the metadata that is critical for the digitization process. On Library Thing, which calls itself "Facebook for Books" and "MySpace for Books,"[115] a group called "I See Dead People['s Books]" has put together Jefferson's original catalog of books as though the former president were still alive, and tagged his collection for the benefit of others potentially in his social network.[116] Of course, the more subversive possibility, which the sight of the catalog suggests, is that book collectors could digitize and upload the books in Jefferson's collection themselves, all of which are out of copyright, thus doing an end run around both corporate and government digitization initiatives. With inexpensive scanners and social ties based on a reputation economy, bibliophiles could quickly amass a digital version of Jefferson's original library, from *Aérostat dirigeable a volonté* to *Œuvres de Mr de Maupertuis*.

Indeed, Google itself has launched its own user-generated digitization initiative. MyLibrary encourages users to scan and upload books in the public domain; the company provides web hosting of the materials and character recognition technology that makes it possible for visitors to a given user's library to search by keyword. For example, the library of self-described "Hobby Farmer" Michael Jensen, which was featured by Google in January 2008, includes titles from this modern Jeffersonian such as *The Healthful Farmhouse*, *Report on Injurious and Other Insects*, and *Agricultural Education for Teachers*. A search of the word "water" in his copy of *Practical Farm Drainage* shows dozens of precise page citations with the term. Fans can also subscribe to an RSS feed for works on his theme "Small Farms before Cheap Energy."[117]

At the Library of Congress, Laura Graham has discussed how even presidential papers, which are presented on the American Memory website as scholarly editions with appropriate historical annotations and the added power of electronic indexing tools, have attracted many new kinds of users, so-called lifelong learners, who are significantly different from the users of the reading room in Washington, D.C., and yet would like to participate in the process of knowledge organization. These nonscholarly users also benefit the Library, Graham argues, by improving indexing, cataloging, and descriptive information. Incorrect labels are even corrected because this new audience exists.

Naturally, we see *American Memory* as a flow of historical collections from the Library of Congress to American citizens everywhere. Unanticipated is the flow of content and information back to the Library of Congress from people who have local history, genealogical, or other specialized information to offer for correcting and enhancing descriptions of items in the institution's collections.[118]

Even the Library of Congress classification system itself has become subject to new forms of modification in response to user-generated content. As Hope A. Olsen argues in *The Power to Name: Locating the Limits of Subject Representation in Libraries*, classification systems also tell us a considerable amount about cultural values and prevalent biases.[119] New users who criticize headings like "Philippine Insurrection" and argue in favor of the more appropriate subject heading "Philippine Independence," Graham argues, improve the cataloging system in ways that an entrenched culture of librarians may not. These individuals, who now have access to Library of Congress catalogs and—via e-mail—to the librarians themselves, are now rewriting the very taxonomies that dictate the ordering of physical collections nationwide.

Like the open-source movement in software, Graham asserts that online library users can improve the "code" of the Library of Congress by making suggestions and offering possible modifications.

Here is a representative sample of the kinds of information users offer. A resident of Tennessee compares a photograph from Selected Civil War Photographs to those available in a local historical society. A view of the "Environs of Knoxville seen from south bank of the Holston River" is actually from that of the Tennessee River. Another Tennessee resident identifies a Depression-era photograph of a Greenville courthouse as being in Greene not Davidson County, which the user remarks may have had a Greenville too, but he knows the former and can correctly identify the courthouse's true location. He would like to make sure the photograph is "properly attributed." A user informs the Library that a photograph in America from the Great Depression to World War II is actually Freedom rather than Conway, Pennsylvania. The buildings in the foreground are still standing, while the first story of a factory in the background survives. She also offers to send photographs to document the information. People recognize members of previous generations of family or local figures as well as regions, counties, and hometowns. A daguerreotype of "Three unidentified men," 1853–55, from Mathew Brady's studio in America's First Look into the Camera: Daguerreotype Portraits and Views, 1839–1864 is actually of someone's great grandfather, his cousin, and a great uncle. While the lack of information is understandable, members of this family are disconcerted to see their forebears described online as unidentified when they are so well known to them.[120]

As blogs, wikis, and other social network and social bookmarking tools are increasingly deployed to interrogate and even discredit the official published versions of historical events and promulgate narratives based on community memories that can also be documented and authenticated, the process that Graham describes as taking place via e-mail only seems likely to accelerate.

The Library of Congress is now using the commercial photo-sharing site Flickr to showcase color photographs from the 1940s and 1950s and black-and-white news photographs from the 1910s.[121] These sharp, high-resolution images in the online archive were often shot by photographers employed by government-funded projects conducted during the Great Depression and World War II to document everyday American life and labor practices. Thus, many of these photographs are in the public domain and likely to be reused and remixed with other digital content as part of creative-commons-related efforts. This form of display also invites the kinds of critical discourses about cataloging procedures that Graham discusses. Many visitors to the site are not merely viewers of an online exhibition because they respond in a lively rhetoric of community and contentiousness that is common in other aspects of Internet culture.

Woman aircraft worker, Vega Aircraft Corporation, Burbank, Calif. Shown checking electrical assemblies (LOC)

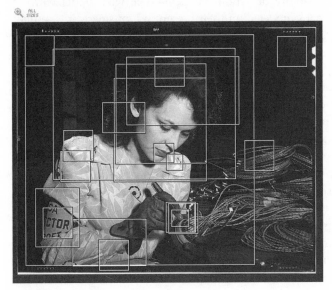

Bransby, David,, photographer.

Figure 8.6
Flickr page from the Library of Congress.

For example, regarding figure 8.6, analysts in the general public debate about whether a photograph of a female aircraft worker shows an icon of the lived experience of labor or a photo shoot with a staged model. At the Library of Congress Flickr site, competing self-appointed experts debate about the authenticity of the image, much as Henry Jenkins describes the disputes among Internet "spoilers" who jostle with each other to reveal the outcomes of reality television broadcasts in advance or piece together clues to reveal seemingly legitimate political images or texts as bogus artifacts manufactured to support a specific conspiratorial political agenda.[122] Particularly persistent skeptics annotated the worker's photograph with comments such as "but no working human would be dressed like her!!!! FAKED PHOTO??" and "Inspector, my eye. That's a model!" Those who tagged this photo debated about whether or not she was holding a capped pen that indicated a mere prop or a "continuity tester" that would show that she was engaged in productive work. Some only marked up images with comments about the subjects' physical appearance or sexual attractiveness from a blatantly heterosexist perspective.

The British Library is also using social media and Web 2.0 technologies with its own gadget for iGoogle and pages on Facebook. Nonetheless, librarians sounded dubious about having users participate more actively in generating metadata for its digital collections, although the possibility of a non-Wikipedia-type wiki model with an authentication scheme—perhaps modeled on their present use of smartcards—might lead them to reconsider, given the potential value of user-generated content to under-staffed libraries.

However, France officially remains extremely skeptical about public participation in the creation of either content or metadata for digital libraries. During an interview with Christophe Dessaux and Sonia Zillhardt at the Ministry of Culture to discuss their nation-state's digitization policies, they seemed to be thinking about digitization efforts largely in terms of particular online exhibits, such as materials about the history of slavery, to which online visitors would serve only as passive spectators. Perhaps this official reserve was also shaped by their contradictory feelings about open-source technologies in general. Despite their commitment to the democratic ideology of open source, their obvious anxiety about having users be able to copy and tinker with digital files on their own computers clearly seemed to be informed by the importance of their role in policing copyright, in ways that indicated a surprisingly narrow interpretation of fair use. As agents of cultural production, they argued, their advocacy role for producers of art was critical. They contended that stopping piracy was much more central to their organization than facilitating a "remix culture" with the materials that they had put online. Furthermore, for all their talk about democratization, they seemed remarkably disinterested in user-generated content on Ministry of Culture sites, which they reiterated were devoted to guardianship of the "patrimony." It seemed that they were still thinking about the feedback loop with the public only in terms of the "contact us" e-mail or message.[123]

Yet one of the things that is remarkable about digital archives, as William Y. Arms has pointed out, is that such libraries not only "are being implemented by people who work within conventional libraries, but also by people who do not consider themselves librarians or publishers."[124] In the United States many historians, literary specialists, and media scholars have created document archives that link to the document archives of official government-sponsored digital libraries. The information work that these faculty members do adds value to the digital materials presented by state-sanctioned organizations, even if those organizations want to control the context and commentary surrounding certain kinds of documents. This work is also being done by a cadre of professional amateurs, who often create work that merits reuse and repurposing by professors. However, the case of Holocaust deniers using primary sources about Nazi history may support calls for caution in depending on the wisdom of crowds.

All Play and No Work

In *From Publishing to Knowledge Networks*, Alexander Hars has described an even more radical potential shift. Rather than continuing to rely on epistemologies ordered around what he calls "discrete categories" and "hierarchies of classes" in the traditional taxonomies of library science, Hars advocates an "object-oriented model of scientific knowledge" within academic archives, which would emulate the modularity and polymorphism associated with similarly designated contemporary programming languages.[125] Hars even goes so far as to argue that custodianship of digital archives can be better understood using Wittgenstein's paradigm of games, because electronic transactions and information search and retrieval processes are based on rules governing social interactions in which the outcomes may be uncertain and the consequences potentially negotiable. In this brave new world, librarians must do more than merely collect and classify a nation's cultural capital; they must also maintain the knowledge networks that operate on principles of reciprocity and circulation to ensure the state's survival in the era of globalization. Hars argues that the unattainable goal of "creating an objective, integrated, consistent true body of knowledge" should be abandoned since "the larger a collection of propositions, the more problematic the assumption of absolute truth becomes."[126]

Gaming metaphors are actually becoming surprisingly common in the once staid realm of library culture. At the BNF, for example, the game trope has been made manifest in an art installation that projected the popular videogame *Tetris* on the sides of the building. At the British Library, Conteth describes the futuristic possibilities of using a "hand-held gaming device" to interact with the library's collections. Pointing to the digital practices already used in "countries like Japan," Conteth and Fitzgerald said they were "sniffing about" many possibilities and predicted that "a lot of this will be driven by users."[127] Given the fact that the Gameboy system has been repurposed as an e-book reader that now has a large catalog of public domain works accessible to its system's users, the possibilities of new forms of reading in official archives no longer seem as wildly improbable as these same ideas would have appeared a decade earlier.

Open Stacks

In reflecting about these experiences, it is perhaps worth looking to the work of Christine Borgman, who examines the contradictions inherent in the term "digital library" and the cultural differences between librarians, computer scientists, and users as a place to think about official electronic archives as a site of conflict and power struggle.[128] Right now there are many usability studies looking at digital libraries, but little research seriously examines questions of subculture and ideology. In that attitudes toward libraries, both real and virtual, as cultural institutions are shaped by shared beliefs about the function of architectures for public reading and by expectations about how knowledge and information should be owned and ordered, I would argue that more field studies and close reading of the digital rhetoric of national digital libraries need to be included in future research.

The Library of Congress's original physical space has changed little over the years, despite the addition of several annexes and considerable subterranean expansion. The 1897 Jefferson building, which was recently restored for its centennial, is an example of richly decorated fin-de-siècle style. There are mnemonic, allegorical, and narrative presentations on every available surface from floors to murals to ceilings. Even the official tour notes the irony of the plenitude of women's bodies and men's names. Chronologies of progress are everywhere. Near the display case with the Gutenberg Bible, there is a narrative mural showing the history of technologies of communication that now seems conspicuously dated given the current information revolution. The main domed round reading room in the Library of Congress follows the British model, although it is gilt with aluminium, a more precious and modern metal at the time than gold. Access to this library is open to any adult who wishes it, and the procedure for admission as a reader to the collections only takes a few minutes. It is intended to be a democratic space for public reading and access to public documents. However, it could be asked if the digital library has any similar foundation or custodial impulse.

After September 11, 2001, national policy in the United States about construction of the digital libraries reached a critical turning point. Now, on the assumption that the physical archive will always be there, unlike materials that rapidly disappear from cyberspace, the Office of Strategic Initiatives has chosen to prioritize collecting born digital materials. In the words of digital projects coordinator Laura Graham in a 2002 interview, "You spend five years furnishing a house, and then they want to rebuild the entire building from scratch."[129] Librarian of Congress James Billington has complained about "the sudden intrusion of outside management consultants" who urge "a total embrace of the new networked environment" and a misguided neglect of "traditional artifactual collections."[130] Since the preservation of digital ephemera in reaction to a catastrophic event became something of a scholarly and journalistic cause célèbre, the task of providing context for digitizing materials has been in the public eye, and nonprofit organizations with archives designed to catalog historical memories were at least briefly guaranteed wide private support.

Unfortunately, federal authorities concerned with prioritizing "total information awareness" to combat terrorism have invested much more public money in collecting data on private citizens, which is kept secret from spheres of study and deliberation, than in archiving the paper and web materials documenting our political and social lives. Even some ostensibly nonconfidential material on .gov websites is shielded from public scrutiny by computer code instructing Google not to index the material so that it won't appear in results from the search engine. Although Brewster Kahle of the Internet Archive has earned praise for his archival efforts, which have involved collaborations with many national libraries, including the BNF, the scale of information that could be and should be public is too large for his nonprofit nongovernmental enterprise. At the moment, there seems to be little political will in the United States to provide for publicly financed alternatives to create truly public digital libraries, and consumers are content to continue to rely on a commercial search engine, financed by advertising and the marketing data industry, to govern their interaction with public information.

9 Waiting Room: Serious Games about National Security and Public Health

In the midst of the park-like surroundings and colonial-style buildings of the Department of Community and Family Medicine at Dartmouth Medical School, the Interactive Media Laboratory (IML) may seem like an unlikely spot for creating elaborate disaster scenarios about large-scale explosions, outbreaks of disease, radioactive contamination in heavily populated areas, and other simulations of catastrophic events that would endanger national security and public health. Yet, just as Hollywood screenwriters have been enlisted by military planners to imagine possible plots for terrorist attacks,[1] the medical educators at Dartmouth are busily engaged in dreaming up plausible situations that would strike fear into a specialized audience of medical professionals and emergency first-responders. The IML offices feature a media-production suite equipped with a music studio and special effects green screen. In one part of the complex, medical illustrators are occupied with giving graphic realism to the urban nightmares they have been commissioned to produce. There are touches of macabre humor in the Dartmouth facility as well. In the lunchroom the furniture holds homey pillows decorated with icons of disaster, such as the modified trefoil that is the universal symbol for radiation.

In the opening of *The Birth of the Clinic*, Michel Foucault has described his scholarly project about medical epistemology as being "about space, about language, and about death" and "about the act of seeing, the gaze."[2] Although Foucault acknowledges the prominence in cultural life of the generally held assumption that "the human body defines, by natural right, the space of origin and the distribution of disease: a space whose lines, volumes, surfaces, and routes are laid down in accordance with a now familiar geometry," he challenges this commonsense spatializing of disease in the coordinates of the body's volumes as "neither the first, nor the most fundamental."[3] For Foucault, it is the disciplinary spaces of the built environment of the clinic, which include and potentially exclude particular observers, which define the regulatory character of knowledge as a series of thresholds. He asserts that the clinic creates an architecture of prohibition and license, separating medical practitioners from the ranks of the general public, which is much more associated with the profession than mere access to the organic tissues of individual patients. Now that government agencies and public health organizations are constructing virtual learning environments that situate and initiate users in a topography of computer-generated 3-D worlds, it is worth considering how these self-identified "virtual clinics" or "virtual academies" similarly delineate the relations of power and subjectivity. These models are intended primarily to represent the physical boundaries of bodies, equipment, buildings, and landscapes in order to train doctors, police officers, and firefighters to respond to radioactive or chemical contamination or outbreaks of disease, but they also seem to have other signifying functions for the ideologies of the body politic.

In videogames about health that explicitly combine the pedagogical with the rhetorical, the location of boundaries of specific regions of play and the classification of participants and non-player characters are worthy of critical attention, particularly if constraints on what is revealed to and concealed from the learner can be read as making manifest a spatial representation of the rituals and rules of medical knowledge. As Foucault points out in *The Birth of the Clinic*, the image of the membrane as it is observed in organic tissues often has a semiotic function as the signifier of visual and physical mediated access. In videogames about public health and safety, these membranous topographies often represent both corporality and virtuality, so that the membrane serves to delimit borders, frontiers, and margins by signifying interplay between permeability and impermeability.

For example, in the game *Immune Attack*, most of the action takes place from the perspective of a fluid-borne nanobot for which the vessels of the human body serve as a combination of exploratory classroom and chaotic war zone.[4] The game is designed to supplement state-mandated textbook instruction for high school biology classes by engaging students with the game's narrative about a teen prodigy with a weakened immune system who must infect herself with different microbiological agents in order to gradually build immunity and reach the game's win condition. At the same time, it is a story about scientific initiation in which a patient must become a paraprofessional by serving as the subject of her own experiment. Players of *Immune Attack* can measure their mastery of microbiology by completing levels once they have finished all the required tasks in a given game environment. Although on each level cells and microscopic body components have been sized and colored to provide legibility in the spatial environment, correspondence to print materials in textbooks, and the maximum resolution suitable to the game engine, it is still often difficult to identify game objects behind the distorting veils of translucent bodily materials. To help them negotiate this alien environment of diaphanous materials, players are given access to an electronic archive providing an extensive library of reference materials, from basic glossaries of the names of the unfamiliar microscopic agents that they must battle to elaborate instructional modules on the cybernetic systems of immunity.

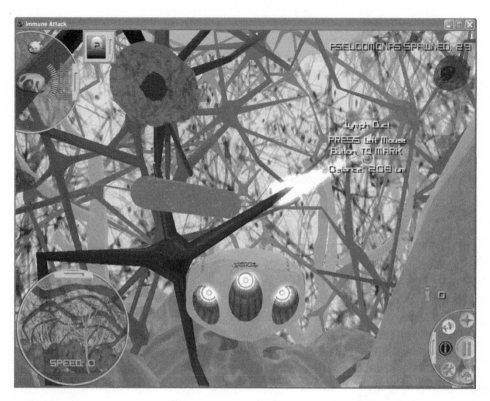

Figure 9.1
Screenshot of *Immune Attack*, by permission of the Federation of American Scientists.

Donna Haraway has argued that associating debilitating disease with military ico-nography has ideological consequences, particularly if the compromised body becomes equated with a battlefield in combat that must be mastered by strategies of command and control.[5] Certainly, games like *Immune Attack* and the similarly themed microbial combat adventure *Re-Mission*, which is designed for young cancer patients undergoing chemotherapy, repurpose many aspects of the mechanics of training videogames for soldiers and thus combine arcade-style shoot-em-up action with the more attenuated drama of initiation into the privileged spaces of the mysteries of medical knowledge.[6] In *Persuasive Games*, Ian Bogost has claimed that ideology is expressed by the proce-dural rhetoric that governs the very rules of videogames, which may be inscribed at the computational level in black box functions that may only be made explicit through the experience of play.[7]

By interrogating the forms of knowledge that are both reified and subverted by the "Bio Art" movement, digital media theorist Anna Munster has defended Leibniz's philosophical position that "bodies are in a perpetual flux like rivers, and parts are entering into them and passing out of them continuously" and challenges the rigid Cartesianism that she argues still dominates the computer graphics industry.[8] Even "informatic bodies" that materialize from data in ways that are closely linked to mathematical abstraction defy simple mappings to easy ideologies and clear delineation of the boundaries defining subjects and objects. In Munster's formulation of the body, making such facile differentiations between "enemy" and "friendly" ignores the structural interpenetration of both datasets and organic tissues. Thus labeling components in educational games like *Re-Mission* and *Immune Attack* with simple good and bad binaries would be perhaps as problematic as unambiguously schematizing the differences between signal and noise in the diagnostic process.

There may be certain political incentives for a form of information aesthetics that equates paucities of technical expertise and destructive violence. In a 2007 issue of *Communications* from the Association for Computing Machinery, an article promoting "Games for Science and Engineering Education" opened by quoting the post-9/11 Hart-Rudman Report on antiterrorist preparedness in the United States. "Second only to a weapon of mass destruction detonated in an American city," the report proclaimed, "we can think of nothing more dangerous than a failure to manage properly science, technology, and education for the common good over the next quarter century."[9] Thus, at least one game designer seeking government contracts uses this highly publicized document about national security failures to equate experiential learning in the sciences by young future professionals with protection from the potential aftermath of a weapon of mass destruction detonated in an urban environment. The paranoid structure of this rhetorical association points to a crisis of signification that only the rapid deployment of electronic simulations can fill.

At the larger, more naturalistic scale in which game avatars are depicted as human social actors, narratives in videogames and online environments about the vulnerabilities of the body often engage the player in interactive behaviors by giving him or her responsibility for managing a rapidly evolving crisis, one that potentially threatens the social order and even the rule of law maintained by the state. Situations of crisis in videogames frequently involve the biological risks of terrorist attacks or outbreaks of lethal diseases, often in heavily populated urban environments. Gameplay may center on the activities of lone agents, peer-oriented teams of experienced professionals, or complex organizations with multiple tiers of accountability and command. The player may be rewarded for good decision-making, rapid reaction time, dexterity with game objects, virtuosity in memorizing locations of paths and obstacles, or other game-related skills. In relative terms, game health, skill points, or other forms of game capital may be accumulated by slowing or ameliorating the destructive results of the crisis. However, winning as an absolute measure of success is generally determined by the player's ability to stop, if not reverse, such crises and thus restore a form of homeostasis to the game world.

In commercial games, the challenge of play is intensified if the unfolding disaster in the game world appears to have multiple causes and multiple effects. The player may even experience frustration or confusion rather than pleasure in gameplay, particularly if he or she succumbs to sensory overload from hostile or chaotic metropolitan environments. Nonetheless, the digital representations of the crisis on the viewer's screen can be understood at least crudely by a layperson, because the mathematical model predicting the progression of game events generally reflects relatively straightforward underlying algorithms that represent degeneration or regeneration of the game state without the obfuscating features of more complicated cybernetic systems with feedback and oscillation or the effect of power laws and cascading phenomena.[10] In other words, the principles governing events in a real crisis might be counterintuitive to a naive player approaching a simulation, so crises in the game world tend to oversimplify the dynamics of an emerging disaster. Furthermore, unlike real disaster response systems that use cutting-edge technology to assess the crisis, the integration of elaborate information visualization displays with very large datasets is rarely a characteristic of gameplay.

In commercial games, a player can also be encouraged to intentionally exacerbate what seems to be an emerging crisis in order to achieve political revolution or regime change, as in the case of games of rebellion, which validate seemingly subversive interventions in the game world, such as *State of Emergency* or *Deus Ex*. In these games the ostensible guardians of public health or national security are not to be trusted unconditionally by the player and may serve conspiratorial agendas and advance counternarratives in the game. In some emergency situations depicted in mass-produced games, the authorities appear to have flagrantly abandoned their responsibilities in favor of self-interest, and so there can be opportunistic gains for the player from the associated absence of law and order. This is true in the *Grand Theft Auto* series, where players can bribe police or hospital staff in Vice City. However, characters can also suffer negative consequences from the absence of effective crisis managers in the virtual public sphere, particularly from the lack of competent emergency first-responders and health care professionals. For example, the failures of the *Grand Theft Auto* public health system are dramatized in Liberty City, because a trip to the hospital can impoverish the player's character.

In other situations of play, the crisis can appear not to serve any dramatic purpose in the game design. In these cases, the disruption of homeostasis in the game world seems to be largely an annoyance rather than a call to heroic action, interpretable as a mere computer glitch or virus. Rather than assume an identity position of either the conventional protagonist or the antihero in relationship to the spreading crisis, the player might seek merely to continue individual gameplay by finding operable workarounds. Makeshift solutions are reached by following protocols from the official game producers, sharing ideas through informal fan networks, or intuiting hacks through trial and error. Of course, sometimes collective intelligence about the procedural loopholes in game worlds generates crises of their own. For example, the Corrupted Blood plague in *World of Warcraft* was supposed to affect only those in the immediate vicinity of the corpse of the slain opponent, Hakkar the God of Blood, but players soon discovered they could transfer the infection to other areas by contaminating an in-game virtual pet and then transporting the animal elsewhere to function as an epidemiological time bomb. Epidemiologists were soon studying the Corrupted Blood phenomenon as a potential way to understand the transmission of real-world diseases.[11]

In addition to persuasive games designed to promote specific social marketing agendas, many commercial games foster awareness of public health procedures. In *The Sims*, an infected guinea pig served as a disease vector in keeping with master rules valuing cleanliness.[12] Even children's computer-mediated play can involve ecosystems of potential catastrophe, as it did in *Whyville*, when an outbreak of mysterious pox sent panicked users to an online office of the Centers for Disease Control.[13] Ian Bogost has argued that even *Grand Theft Auto* can implicitly promulgate public health messages about the value of diet and exercise in order to maintain player bodily integrity and take part in purposive actions in the game world.[14]

Not all serious games of crisis feature the contamination trope: games that are designed to enlighten the general public about crisis situations and emergency management may also feature systemic violence or starvation as destabilizing factors that create a crisis. Given the decline in readership for newspapers that conventionally cover crisis situations with in-depth reporting, some of these games attempt to explain systemic problems of disease, genocide, or starvation in the developing world to younger media audiences. However, serious games about contemporary humanitarian emergencies often feature relatively exotic locales, such as the African digital landscape of *Darfur is Dying* or the fictional countryside of "Sheylan" in *Food Force*. In contrast, games for medical professionals or emergency first-responders are staged in the familiar terrain of the built environment of the developed world, albeit often at the slight remove of a temporal setting in the near future.

A number of universities and state agencies are developing games of crisis for emergency first-responders in which contamination is a key theme. *Hazmat: Hotzone*, developed at the Entertainment Technology Center at Carnegie Mellon University in collaboration with the New York Fire Department, is a multiplayer networked simulation for modeling hazardous materials emergencies. In *Hotzone*, the crises that emerge in gameplay can be tweaked by the interventions of an instructor using a "Wizard of Oz" interface to insert secondary events and unexpected actions in the main story about hazardous materials in a public place, such as a subway station. Rather than merely judging individual performance on a branching decision tree or a multiple-choice test, *Hazmat: Hotzone* allows instructors to evaluate team interactions.[15] The group dynamic that is constituted at first can change rapidly, particularly if a player takes an unsafe action in the game world and is therefore incapacitated.

Similarly, Public Health Games at the Center for the Advancement of Distance Education at the University of Illinois at Chicago has developed a multiuser anthrax outbreak simulation, *The POD Game*, which was named for a "point of dispensing" scenario, although it was originally titled *Zero Hour*. The game can be run in the field on laptops or cellular telephones. The action is set in a mass medication-dispensing and vaccination center and worker performance is gauged so that players are rewarded with points for rapidly processing members of the public, with the aim of a utilitarian greatest good for the greatest number. However, after the development team decided that the "thinking space" of risk calculation was more important than modeling the "physical space" of the distribution center, they abandoned using a complicated 3-D game engine in favor of a flattened presentation that promised greater technical compatibility with mobile devices.[16]

Firescope is a real-time strategy training game built for the Los Angeles Fire Department that was developed by the USC GamePipe Laboratory and the controversial USC

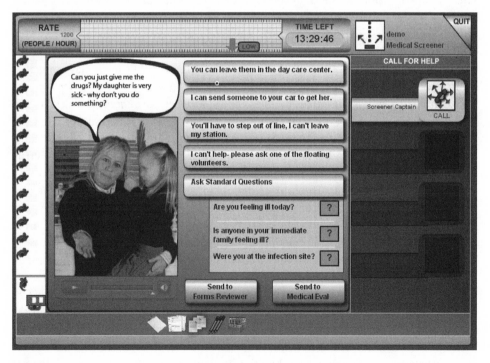

Figure 9.2
Screenshot of *The POD Game*, by permission of Public Health Games.

Center for Risk and Economic Analysis of Terrorism, which was also known by the acronym CREATE. CREATE's reputation was tarnished in November 2007 during a high-profile publicity fiasco. Public opinion turned against their work on data representation being done for the Los Angeles Police Department, when it was revealed that law enforcement analysts were mapping Muslim neighborhoods in multicultural Los Angeles, and citizens from a range of ethnic communities objected to this God's eye view of what they considered to be high-tech racial profiling.[17] In contrast, the CREATE game for first-responders, *Firescope*, has proven to be a considerably less controversial initiative for the spending of public funds in preparation for "the hazards of nature, crime and terrorism," even though management of media access is part of gameplay. The USC GamePipe website explains the player's objectives:

The user will find out that if he does not properly set up his command post and deal with random hazards, their job will become harder and more dangerous. One example is the media: if the Incident Commander does not assign a man to deal with reporters, then they will interfere with constant pestering questions. The player will have a full range of real-world tools to overcome these obstacles.[18]

This dystopian vision of the obligations of civic communication rewards delegating responsibility and justifies reducing accountability to the press and the public as "pestering questions." Under contract with the Sandia corporation, GamePipe has also produced *LockDown*, a serious game about incident response designed to prepare for a possible mass shooting on a college campus in which the SWAT team player engages in first-person-shooter style play.[19]

In contrast to large-scale urban disaster games, *Incident Commander*, funded by the U.S. Department of Justice, markets itself to smaller jurisdictions. Scenarios include "a school hostage situation," "a chemical spill," "the aftermath of a severe storm," and "a possible terrorism incident."[20] In its demo video, designers describe how crisis managers who use the system must also control "civilians that are overly curious" about the evolving disaster. The unit operations of the game are supposed to be dictated by a specific command and control structure, which is shared by FEMA, the Occupational Health and Safety Administration, and other federal agencies that must manage risk. The Incident Commander paradigm assumes unity of command at each hierarchical level, modular organization, communication in a common unambiguous language with no undefined terms, and an objective-oriented management style.

The fact that "overly curious" civilians and "pestering" reporters are dramatized as obstacles to success in these games seems to indicate an attitude that risk communication is restricted to the intracommunal purview of trained professionals, who trade messages with themselves but not with the general public. Simulations that use closed-circuit television technology rather than the structures of social interactions associated with computer games may be even more hierarchical in nature. For example, the

Department of Homeland Security has conducted several exercises using the *Virtual News Network*, which was created by a branch of a multinational advertising agency, Olgivy PR. The network creates broadcasts for simulations in conjunction with the TOPOFF project, which—as the name indicates—is designed primarily for "top officials" in the government. This "closed-circuit satellite TV network modeled on CNN" is designed "to broadcast and cover events as they unfolded during the five-day exercise" to allow "public officials" to "showcase and improve their crisis communication skills live via satellite to numerous closed-circuit locations across the country."[21] It spells out its intention to design an electronic simulation that will help policy makers "manage the 'real world' media." The emphasis on top-down public relations rather than deliberative activities that include the public in crisis management is made even more explicit in their list of audience members, which relegates citizens to nonparticipation and consigns journalists to the class of those who can "observe portions of the training exercise, but not to participate."[22]

While in some commercial games, medical workers and police officers may be depicted as corrupt or ineffective representatives of the state, nonprofit serious games designed for training professionals responsible for public health or safety generally represent crisis managers and their associated official institutions in a positive and collegial light. Victims suffering from the effects of the crisis and potential patients in the community may be irritable, panicked, or uncooperative non-player characters, but team members and officials higher in the chain of command are depicted as proactive exemplars of civic behavior, even in game environments in which social roles and physical landscapes may be extremely polymorphous.

For those who limit property damage, injury, and mortality in the physical environment of the bricks-and-mortar "real" world, these public health disaster simulations are part of the realm of work, often a required element of both initial career preparation and ongoing on-the-job training. Thus they may not serve as the "third space," hypothesized by many game theorists, in which games can offer a potential escape from both the realms of domesticity and those of work. Although games of crisis may seem to operate in what has been described as a "magic circle" around game play in which a new reality is created,[23] where there are no real world consequences to be suffered for errors of judgment in the game space, these games may also be used to evaluate job performance or willingness to complete training requirements and thus expose the player to possible discipline and punishment. Although there may be many of the same incentives for cheating as there are among the civilian population,[24] game designers assume that public health employees will dutifully complete game tasks and levels without resorting to unauthorized strategies that subvert practices of honest labor. Furthermore, unlike commercial crisis games that offer entertainment, self-directed edification, informal sociality, or personal self-improvement, serious games of crisis generally devalue cultural features associated with leisure.

There is some prehistory of success for the use of virtual environments in disciplinary learning. Specifically, medical education and public health training have been following the lead of the aviation industry by integrating more computer-generated navigable learning spaces using mathematical simulations, digital art assets, and off-the-shelf game technologies, such as easy-to-modify game engines. Certainly, pilots have diminished the number of accidents in the aviation industry dramatically since embracing regular time-on-task in computer simulations, and medical educators would like to similarly reduce the number of medical mistakes. Because the costs of certain kinds of medical interventions can be so high, medical schools have also become interested in training physicians with realistic computer-based simulations that would replace overly abstract pencil-and-paper tests or easy-to-game role-playing situations.

Because public institutions have begun to recognize the importance of cultivating appropriate official identities of the screen and establishing social norms for computer-mediated job tasks, these games sometimes make reference to highly specialized tools and communication devices intended for complex rescue missions or networked operations. This creates a specific form of liminality in gameplay, in which the screen serves as an informational window on a virtualized world. Often there is a recursive character to the game's screen experience, as the player looks at a screen within a screen. In addition, in adapting mass-market games to the needs of niche audiences of first-responders, game weapons or health meters may be transformed into analogous instruments for use in the field, such as radiation meters and numerical displays.

Although learners may be part of a complex command and control structure, some games use the first-person-shooter interface for exploration of the simulation areas. Alexander Galloway has argued that the first-person-shooter genre is characterized by a merging of the point of view of camera and character, which in film usually signifies intoxication, alienation, or predatory interest, but in videogames is coded as phenomenologically normal and socially appropriate.[25] Galloway also points out the importance of the relationship of the iconic weapon to this first-person visual framing as an extension of the player's agency, although in serious games this often takes the form of a nonviolent tool.

The Interactive Media Laboratory

The physical architecture of access—including walls, doors, keypads for entry codes, electronic key card readers, and other forms of locking devices that restrict access to certain rooms or cabinets—is an important feature in the narratives of some federally funded digital media projects developed by the Interactive Media Laboratory at Dartmouth College for the professional population of health care providers. The physical space of expertise from which the general population would normally be excluded

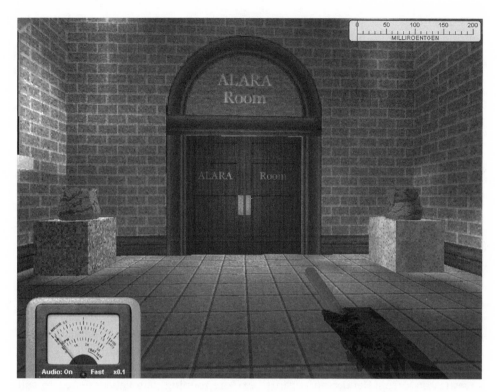

Figure 9.3
First-person-shooter interface in the *Virtual Terrorism Response Academy*, by permission of the
Interactive Media Laboratory at Dartmouth.

(the virtual military base, virtual clinic, or virtual academy) can be navigated by referring to a master floor plan, with cutaway rooms, that indicates the location of initially
prohibited areas.

For over thirty years, the IML has created electronic training materials for first-
responders and other medical professionals using educational videogame technology
and story-based interactive CD-ROMs. Many of the titles present formulaic mystery
narratives about problem solving in radically unfamiliar scenarios of outbreak. In these
scenarios the game world's homeostasis has been radically altered by the sudden
introduction of pathogens, for which considerable reading of relevant dossiers is
necessary to make informed decisions as a health provider. Causal connections
may be distorted further by sudden geopolitical instability or conspiracy theories. To
engage learners with compelling narratives, often drawn from popular mystery or
detective genres, IML games use role-playing perspectives to foster involvement in
decision-making.

The learner's encounters with barriers in the game space are often reminders of the tensions between traditional didactic education from the podium—and the chain of command and lessons of authority that it represents—and the promise of engaged and learner-directed experimentation and play. Despite some osmosis between practices associated with participatory culture and those affiliated with the passive reception of official received truths, architectures of authority instantiate limitations on the player's self-propulsion and navigation. Although this software uses many of the conventions of first-person exploratory games, IML programs still make reference to many traditional discursive practices associated with knowledge-making in the field of medicine. Textbooks, lectures, manuals, files, and patient case studies are particularly important ephemera in the user's digital experience.

Within the archeology of knowledge about the IML itself, software demos, project documents, conference presentations and papers by the principal investigator, digital ephemera from the program's website, interviews with members of the software development team, and field notes from the physical plant at Dartmouth may explain how risk-tasking and initiation into a community of professional expertise appear to be embodied and dramatized in the spaces of virtual pedagogical environments. Earlier titles from the Interactive Media Laboratory were created for physically remote medical personnel in the armed forces who would have to respond to complex scenarios featuring events that could appear initially underdetermined and later seem overdetermined with too many, often conflicting, possible causes. As early as 1976, principal investigator Joseph Henderson began to explore training materials designed to suit computer-aided and remote diagnoses. Disease and trauma on submarines was the initial area of concern that shaped the IML's first pedagogical models. Later interactive videos and computer games for military doctors emphasized a segmented theater of combat in which those in one tent may not know what is happening in an adjacent tent.

Regimental Surgeon (1989) imagines a geopolitical future in which the Soviet Union has re-formed after a right-wing coup. A novice doctor, the hero in this first-person interactive program, arrives at the base and must solve the mystery of a "fever of unknown origin." During the course of the program's story-based learning modules, the mysterious disease is revealed to be malaria, although the statistical information is initially clouded by a number of heat-related casualties. Shot at Camp Pendleton and on a soundstage at Norton Air Force Base, the user's first-person point of view shuttles between encounters with a number of characters—both poker-faced and wisecracking autonomous agents—who introduce stock attitudes about physicians. The player can look at documents, which provide the opportunity to develop certain subplots, and concoct plausible reasons to leave the base for further investigation. As a sign of the residues of classroom learning, the learner seems to be expected to develop productive as well as receptive literacy with these medical documents. At one point the base commander sternly informs the protagonist that he will have to "support findings with facts" and write up a report that follows a prescribed outline in keeping with "logic" and "facts."

The Virtual Practicum Series

With the launch of the Virtual Practicum series, the IML began to work with a more adventurous pedagogical rationale that emphasized the importance of what Max Boisot has called "E-space,"[26] describing the epistemological spaces in which learning takes place in a matrix organized around what he characterizes as the coded/uncoded and concrete/abstract binaries involved in communicative transactions. Drawing on research developed within the field of informational theories of communication, principal investigator Henderson uses Boisot to justify the deployment of video and sound in these multimedia learning materials to "convey the less coded, essential features" of the chaotic clinical environment and the multiple channels of "gesture, speech, tone, clothes, movement, in the service of messages whose complexity would overwhelm the single channel."[27]

In *Primary Care of the HIV/AIDS Patient* (2001) the "Virtual Clinic" is demarcated by computer-generated graphics that depict floor plans, cutaways, hallways, and closed doors. Through interactive digital video, the learner experiences the program through the point of view of an infectious diseases physician and engages in role-playing activities appropriate to that profession. To situate the learner in this honeycombed environment, the clinic's architectural features are explained in a "Travel Guide," and the simulation experience begins in an "Orientation Room."

As the physician-protagonist, the learner must explore the topography of both the building in which the action takes place and the body of Laurie Matthews, a female HIV-positive patient who has settled down into a monogamous relationship but has not had a medical history of consistent care in the intervening period between her initial infection and the "present" of initial interactivity with the tutorial. During the first meeting with the patient, Laurie reports alarming symptoms that indicate that her antiviral regime may have begun to fail. In the appointment, the user must probe Laurie's mouth, now covered with yeasty deposits. Appointments continue as Laurie's condition deteriorates, and in the narrative her psychic pain is dramatized along with her physical decay. Unlike *Regimental Surgeon*, there is no clearly defined win condition for the player, because the aim of the program is empathetic connection rather than arriving at the single solution of a correct diagnosis.

In another interactive CD-ROM from the Virtual Practicum series, *HIV Prevention Counseling*, the IML developed an entire virtual urban landscape in which physical locations in the training module serve as epistemological spaces for situated learning. The action takes place in a "Virtual Neighborhood," where the learner participates in

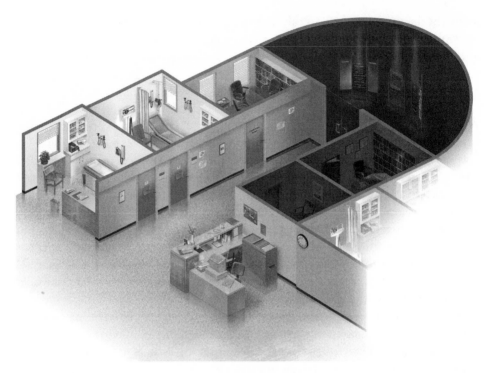

Figure 9.4
Virtual Clinic in *Primary Care of the HIV/AIDS Patient*, by permission of the Interactive Media
Laboratory at Dartmouth.

an "apprenticeship" with a master counselor/trainer. The neighborhood provides
opportunities to "practice" as a counselor in different settings: "clinic-based,
community-based, and outreach." The neighborhood also has a "Learning Center,"
where users can go to acquire disciplinary knowledge about HIV, HIV prevention, and
client-centered counseling; here they can "attend lectures, meet other counselors via
interviews, interview real patients, and do computer-based learning games."[28]

In these virtual learning environments, there are explicit instructions about the
protective means of guarding against the HIV virus, since these directives reflect a
significant aspect of the public health discourse of the period, which involves regulation of the conduct of both parties in the doctor-patient relationship. For doctors,
medical hygiene may require the use of gloves, face masks, needle-disposal containers,
and medical waste bags. For patients, who are responsible for not spreading the
disease, this involves condoms, dental dams, and other "safe sex" or "safer sex"
barriers to infection. Of course, these relatively thin layers separating subjects from
contamination are understood as potentially fallible expediencies, because the thicker

and stronger the protective membrane, the less that medical knowledge or sexual pleasure can be gratified.

For the general public, there are also computerized simulations of sexual contact that use interactive digital media. The user can inappropriately enter the space of sexualized intimacy and move through decision trees in which one decides not to use a prophylactic in a dangerous simulation of unmediated contact between physical bodies in an act of physical union or shared drug ingestion. In the *Virtual Sex Project*, later renamed the *Virtual Sex Real Risk Reduction Project*, from the University of Southern California, the first-person protagonist may choose to pursue a muscle-bound African-American object of homoerotic attraction up a stairway and into a bedroom during a party and may also experiment with alcohol and illegal drugs during the depicted encounter.[29] In this case, the explicit role-playing activity with live action film clips still virtualizes the risk in hopes that the drama will encourage users to be dissuaded from real life risk-taking. In the terms of classical rhetoric, the representations of unsafe activities in the *Virtual Sex Project* are intended to serve the purposes of catharsis rather than mimesis for its audience, who should be purged of dangerous emotions rather than encouraged to re-experience them through imitation.

Online HIV/AIDS education campaigns deploy a wide range of different techniques, which all feature some interactivity while maintaining a variety of forms of distance that are assumed to be necessary for rhetorical or educational situations. Rather than present vivid realism, many websites use highly cartoonish representations of social actors at risk of contracting the HIV virus. For example, the 2006 *My Sexy City* from the Gay Men's Health Crisis and AIDS Project-Los Angeles incorporates elements of parody of the television show *Sex in the City* with colorful Flash animation.[30] The multiracial cast of twenty characters includes a Latina copyright lawyer, a Japanese ballet dancer, an NYU student with a trust fund, and a transgender social worker. To establish the characters' motivations in the story episodes and to complicate the plot, each fictional persona has a "Gettin' High" and "Gettin' Off" rule set described in each individual profile. In contrast, *inSPOT LA*, The Internet Sexuality Information Service and AIDS Healthcare Foundation, eschews fictional representations by encouraging those who may have been infected to send anonymous e-cards to former sexual partners to urge them to get tested for the disease.[31] The site also includes some netiquette guidelines about how to give the message about possible transmission of the virus with appropriate clarity, sensitivity, and confidentiality. In 2007, the youth-oriented cable television station MTV and the Kaiser Family Foundation announced that this partnership would be sponsoring a game development contest to create a "viral, Web-based video game concept to help raise awareness about HIV/AIDS among 15–24 year olds in the US and to promote personal action in response to the epidemic."[32] Finally, the city of West Hollywood launched WeHoLIFE,

which featured the 2008 online serial drama about young gay men in the same apartment complex, "In the Moment," to promote web-based educational efforts and
engage the attention of residents unlikely to take part in traditional community-based
outreach events; the site also uses the social network application Ning to facilitate
discussion among fans of this HIV-themed soap opera with specific questions after
each webisode.[33]

However, it is important to point out that not all digital media products about public
health are games of crisis. A game like *Fatworld* from Ian Bogost's Persuasive Games
studio assumes that states of health and sickness are determined by everyday, seemingly minor practices, the results of which gradually accrue over time. Time spent not
exercising in the park of the Flash-based game may land you in the cemetery, but
there are a number of other factors, which include food allergies and urban planning,
that may influence the player's trajectory, so that the persuasive aim of the game is
to expand the concept of making healthy lifestyle choices to include awareness of the
ramifications of certain policy decisions as well. Although Bogost has been criticized
by some hardcore gamer communities devoted to recreational gaming as a creator of
"boring" games,[34] he argues that all game mechanics rely on a certain amount of player
engagement with routine and task-based interactions, which ultimately enable players
to see much more complicated rule sets at work.

The *Virtual Terrorism Response Academy*

Despite its initial crisis status in the United States, HIV/AIDS no longer produces the
same level of public anxiety as it once did. Although social marketing campaigns
continue to emphasize the risk of illness and mortality to the general population,
HIV/AIDS is no longer associated with a dramatic need for risk communication. Thus,
even before the attacks of September 11, the Interactive Media Laboratory was looking
ahead to new projects about other public health threats that might cause elevated
alarm and possibly panic. IML team members targeted terrorism scenarios that were
particularly anxiety-inducing, even among medically trained service providers, because
these situations could expose healthcare professionals to personal, physical danger
and thus accelerate the crisis if there was a breakdown of protocol among the ranks
of the professional classes.

The current work-in-progress at the IML, the *Virtual Terrorism Response Academy*, uses
a commercial game engine to recreate a contaminated urban warehouse from which
a property owner's 911 call has come. Although this property owner, Mr. Gupta, could
be seen as a meddlesome citizen who ignores the operator's instructions to steer clear
of the scene, he also offers the player potentially valuable information about who
might be using the warehouse for nefarious purposes and thus about the possible kinds
of materials contained within its storage spaces. The action, however, doesn't begin

WMD Hazmat Learning Lab •——   Learning Resources Room •—

Simulation Area •——   Web Room •—

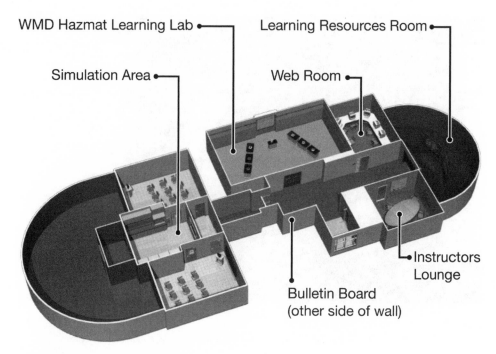

•Instructors
Lounge

Bulletin Board
(other side of wall)

Figure 9.5
Virtual Academy in the *Virtual Terrorism Response Academy*, by permission of the Interactive Media
Laboratory at Dartmouth.

with the warehouse response team. Much like the virtual clinic, which is similarly
public yet private space, the cutaway plan of the academy's shared built environment
is used to situate the story, although the form of contamination in this central scenario
is radiation rather than a difficult-to-communicate disease.

The Terrorism Academy story begins cinematically with swelling music in pitch-
blackness. Then titles announce the facts: "Capitol Region" and "September 11, 2001."
Soon the player hears the recognizable sounds of transmissions from first-responders
and becomes aware that he or she is being situated in the story by audio files that
represent a historical document. After this dramatic emotional appeal and reminder
of a cultural touchstone in American life, the scene shifts to where the training simulation itself opens, on the closed door of the academy, which can only open after the
player enters the prescribed data into a virtual computer terminal. The path of the
training narrative depends on the user's occupation and disciplinary forms of association. Firemen, emergency medical technicians, and law enforcement officers each have
different professional trainers/magical helpers and move through different story arcs
with different social roles.

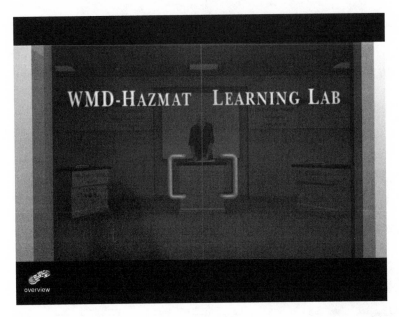

Figure 9.6
Glass doors to Hazmat Learning Lab in the *Virtual Terrorism Response Academy*, by permission of the Interactive Media Laboratory at Dartmouth.

In the didactic learning spaces much of the instruction uses traditional classroom learning techniques, although the virtual manuals, screens, podiums, and other conventional materials associated with continuing education are largely used to convey the rhetorical situation in which "pearls of wisdom" and "war stories" can be shared by experts, veterans, and mentors.[35] The inclusion of special effects and postproduction techniques is intended to make these interactive videos more engaging, and periodic quizzes and electronic exercises test the efficacy of the instruction, which includes basic science about radiation and other possible contaminants and hazards that are quantifiable and hence assessable.

Nonetheless, many game critics would argue that despite a do-over structure similar to many videogames, the learner is actively discouraged from trial and error in *The Virtual Terrorism Response Academy*. For example, mentor figures frequently intervene in gameplay to remind learners that they are essentially in what Noah Falstein has dismissed as a "simulation of a simulation."[36] Thus the immersive character of the digital experience is intentionally diminished, suspension of disbelief is violated, and implicit instruction facilitated through interaction with procedural algorithms is made highly explicit, sometimes redundantly so, through repeating messages from positions of authority using tropes that date back to traditional oratory, so that

Henderson admits that others have complained that there is "too much talking" in the academy.[37]

In his work on persuasive games for education, health, and commerce, Bogost has claimed that there is a "procedural rhetoric" at work that is distinct from the traditional persuasive realms of verbal and visual rhetoric.[38] Players experience this procedural rhetoric as they become cognizant of the rules that govern gameplay, even if they are not always able to articulate these rules, much less directly access the code governing the computer's operational algorithms. Bogost argues that self-directed discovery of these procedural dictates and constraints opens up possibilities for critique by users. However, in the *Virtual Terrorism Academy*, procedural experimentation in the "play" area is often interrupted by advice from authority figures who mentor the learner. Furthermore, educational game theorist James Paul Gee has claimed that central learning objectives may be achieved more effectively by transgressive behavior, which cannot be achieved through obedient compliance with linear skill-and-drill lessons.[39] Gee argues that questioning rules and reasoning independently about sequences and combinations of practices ultimately achieves much more sophisticated learning outcomes, because gameplay is part of a larger scheme of literacy practices associated with expert discourses.

The IML counters its critics by noting that in emergency situations in which there is a clear chain of command, independent actions contrary to established procedures are subject to correction by superiors. In defending their highly mediated structure, designers at the IML cite principles of "guided constructivism," such as those advocated by education pioneer John Dewey, and argue that entirely implicit learning situations that rely on trial-and-error are frequently less time-efficient than hybrid instruction that capitalizes on the economy of learning through traditional means.[40] Furthermore, it could be argued that the fantasies of total agency depicted in commercial games of crisis have set reviewers' expectations for "good" gameplay to propagate an ideology of empowerment, which Bogost's work on the technical constraints of game algorithms and rule sets shows to be a fundamental case of false consciousness.

In the structure of the curriculum, the *Virtual Terrorism Response Academy* puts special emphasis on lowering anxiety associated with radioactivity, and its efforts at risk communication are aimed at encouraging knowledgeable decision-making about equipment, policies, and procedures when victims and threats to property are involved. These games serve another important rhetorical purpose in presenting a danger that is associated with bodily mutilation and genetic mutation: they model norms of risk communication about radiation among professional communities and, by extension, for the consumption of the general public, in ways that are significantly different from either "duck and cover" educational films or 1950s sci-fi monster movies.

As risk communication becomes professionalized as a specialty with certification procedures and academic training, the transmission of vital information to the professional and civilian population before, during, and after emergencies is under-going a significant institutional shift.[41] Designated risk communicators strive to observe basic information design principles to forestall panic, distrust, or disregard for basic institutional procedures or the rule of law. As governments have responded to anxieties from the public about the likelihood of another catastrophic terrorist attack or a global flu pandemic, risk communication has received more media attention and more public funding, and risk communicators have pursued opportunities to use dis-tributed digital media, particularly now that news is transmitted rapidly through channels other than broadcast media such as television or radio.

Since the risk of an avian flu pandemic has garnered increased attention, one of the major themes in the discourses of U.S. risk communicators has become "social distanc-ing." This paradigm assumes that social networks often spread disease and that com-munitarian behaviors can actually accelerate contamination. Thus risk communication efforts justify orders "to cancel events and close buildings or to restrict access to certain sites or buildings," so that planners' strategies may curtail attendance at "concerts, sports events, movies, plays" or facilities that sponsor "community swimming pools, youth clubs, gymnasiums."[42] Although software programs developed by the IML tend to emphasize the connections of emergency first-responders to a variety of social groups, decisions to disband public events, such as football games, may be part of the plot lines, and professional equipment still must isolate trained professionals from hazards to which the lay public is potentially also exposed.

In the academy training, substantial time is spent on correct procedures for suiting up for encounters with potentially hazardous materials. In some of the multiple-choice tutorials in the academy's learning modules, there are trick questions in which a naïve learner may be tempted to mistakenly choose too much protective gear and thus hinder rescue operations by the redundant use of scarce resources and by hobbling the rescuer's body with ungainly excess layering that constrains physical movements. In creating the *Virtual Terrorism Response Academy*, the medical illustrators on the IML staff paid special attention to realistic 3-D rendering of contamination suits and col-lected considerable quantities of source materials to depict the features of particular brand-name protective wear as accurately and yet generically as possible.

Shelter in Place

Because this specialized protective equipment is not available to the general public and because an actual future crisis may be more catastrophic than the ones that are simulated, political activists have lampooned the very idea that strategies dependent on wrapping up vulnerable living environments or physical bodies in potentially permeable materials will offer any sustained solution to threats from pathogens. For example, to protest the apathy of public policy makers about global warming, The Yes

Men documented a prank in which they posed as Halliburton representatives pitching the "Survivaball" in a corporate speech in a hotel ballroom and created an actual costume to emphasize the ridiculousness of any pretensions to long-term safety without fundamental policy change.[43] Their ludicrously rotund creation, which cuts the wearer off from social contact and prevents movement in the landscapes of public discourse, suggests that elite members of the culture of multinational corporations are similarly isolated from normal social intercourse and the practices of interaction with the lived environment, so that the figurative burstable "bubble" in which Halliburton executives and their supporters seem to live is shown as a literal bubble in which the user has chosen to retreat from the disaster and the public sphere in which the crisis is taking place.

After the Department of Homeland Security issued its own risk communication guidelines about possible radiological, biological, or chemical attacks at the Ready.gov website, parodies and pointed critiques immediately appeared on the Internet. Websites like safenow.org and unready.net exploited the ambiguities of the supposedly universally understood information graphics for humorous effect. As earlier satires of the escape instructions for aircraft suggested comical interpretations of the neutral

Figure 9.7
Photograph of "Survivaball" prank from the Yes Men website, by permission of the Yes Men.

pictures, which portrayed generic human figures coping with catastrophe, parodies of the Ready.gov site supplied new text to the illustrations of mass hysteria, suggesting that these officially approved tableaux of outlined caricatures were visual instructions for other activities, such as dancing, attending raves, performing sexual acts, or farting.

Illustrations by the Department of Homeland Security at Ready.gov showing recommended procedures for constructing a "safe room" with available household materials, such as duct tape and plastic sheeting, were prominent targets for public outrage and mockery. Near the diagram for "Shelter in Place," the text from government authorities argues that a process known as "sealing the room" to create "a barrier between yourself and potentially contaminated air outside" can be "a matter of survival."[44] Yet the image undermines public trust by showing the diaphanous character of the plastic sheeting with rippled lines and by reminding its audience that there are many different apertures that make a house vulnerable beyond the doors and windows, which also regulate civic privacy and neighborhood interactions through their architectures of control.

The Federation of American Scientists was particularly critical of these official web materials as guidelines for public health procedures. In their extended rhetorical analysis of the duct-tape paradigm on their critical website ReallyReady, this group argued that instructions to the public were unnecessarily convoluted. In their thorough postmortem of the government's information design strategies in the duct tape illustration, the FAS undermines the government's visual argument. As the website points out about the government's illustration of the improvised plastic sheeting membrane in the safe room: "These instructions are useful but do not tell you when creating a barrier between yourself and contaminated air would be the best decision: 'sheltering in place' is not effective for nuclear or indoor chemical attacks."[45]

Although this is the same group that made *Immune Attack*, the public health game that may perpetuate a logic of exclusion, demarcation, and professional mystery, in this website they explicitly critique the epistemological authority of a government agency and the visual rhetoric of this public safety primer on the web. The FAS parallel site also repurposes many of the graphic elements of the Homeland Security original, to such an extent that the FAS made some concessions to federal authorities in order to avoid possible infringement of the intellectual property of the state and unauthorized use of government symbols and marks of authority.

The Children's Crusade

Even before the "Shelter in Place" controversy and related parodies of the public relations campaign on the Department of Homeland Security site, there were indications that this new federal agency was struggling to develop an appropriate web identity

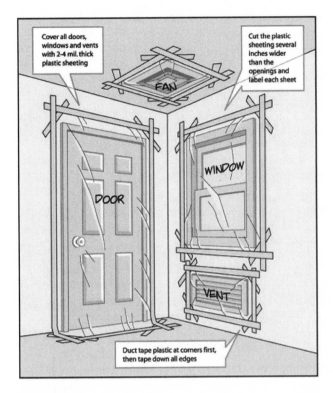

Figure 9.8
Illustration of "Shelter in Place" from the Ready.gov website of the Department of Homeland Security.

that would inspire confidence in the public and simplify complicated issues about threat assessment. For example, in 2005, a campaign orchestrated with the Ad Council offered anxious families a Madlibs-style form to help them articulate the elements of an emergency plan in the event of a terrorist attack.

If there's a(n) _____ terrorist attack, everyone in the family should try to call _____ to get in touch with _____ who is our out-of-town contact in _____. Then _____ _____ picks up _____ at _____. _____ walks to _____ house and _____ _____ there. _____ grabs the emergency kit. We all _____ at the home or _____ and listen to the _____ news for official instructions. Finally, we decide if we should drive to _____ or stay in our _____.[46]

Unfortunately this kind of fill-in-the-blanks rhetoric of highly constrained interactivity, which is oriented toward offering programmatic structures in a syntax of pre-established authority, underscores a tendency in federal websites designed for children

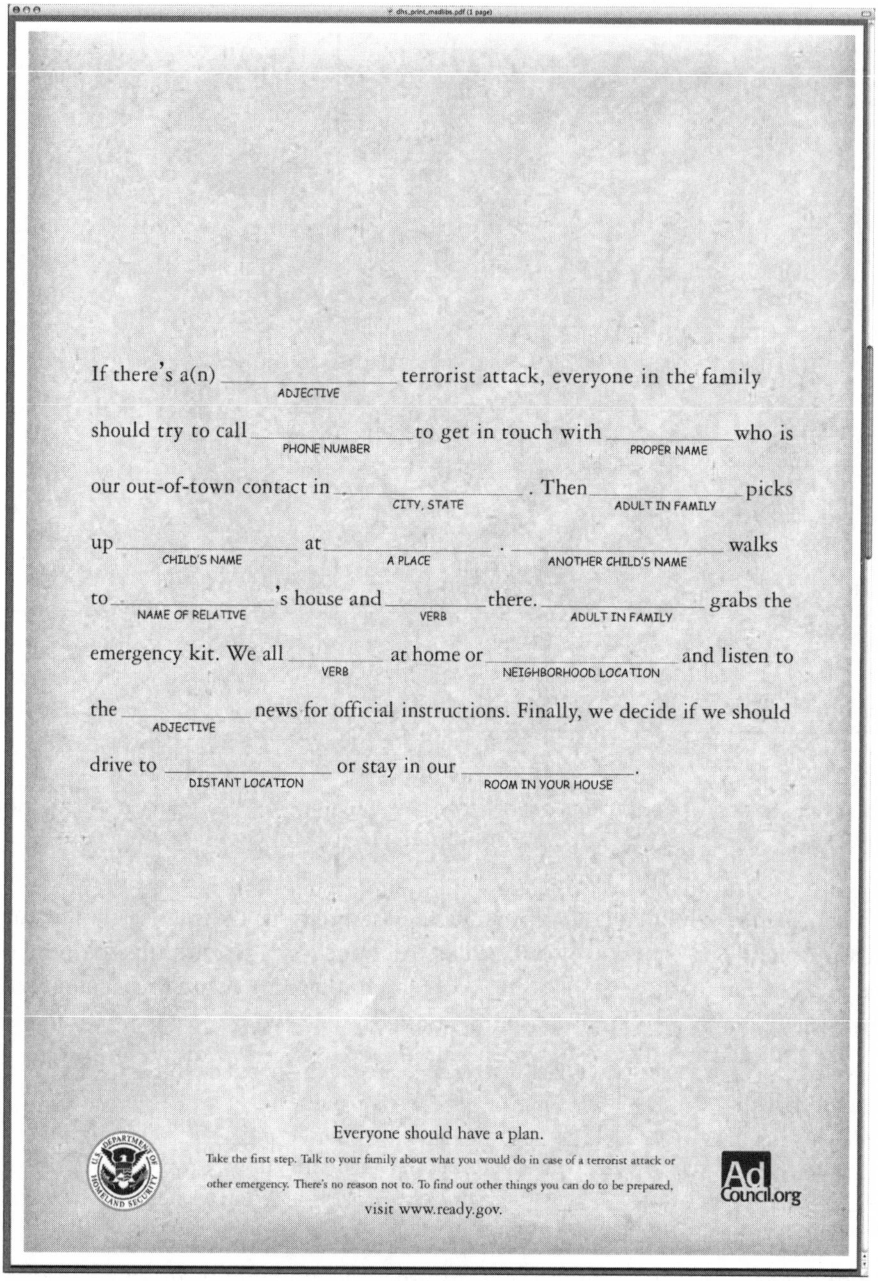

If there's a(n) _____ terrorist attack, everyone in the family
                    ADJECTIVE

should try to call _____ to get in touch with _____ who is
                   PHONE NUMBER   PROPER NAME

our out-of-town contact in _____ . Then _____ picks
                           CITY, STATE   ADULT IN FAMILY

up _____ at _____ . _____ walks
   CHILD'S NAME   A PLACE   ANOTHER CHILD'S NAME

to _____'s house and _____ there. _____ grabs the
   NAME OF RELATIVE   VERB   ADULT IN FAMILY

emergency kit. We all _____ at home or _____ and listen to
                      VERB   NEIGHBORHOOD LOCATION

the _____ news for official instructions. Finally, we decide if we should
    ADJECTIVE

drive to _____ or stay in our _____ .
         DISTANT LOCATION   ROOM IN YOUR HOUSE

Everyone should have a plan.

Take the first step. Talk to your family about what you would do in case of a terrorist attack or
other emergency. There's no reason not to. To find out other things you can do to be prepared,
visit www.ready.gov.

Figure 9.9
2005 Madlib from the Department of Homeland Security children's site.

to emphasize puzzle and game presentation styles rather than access to the research resources that young people frequently seek at such government URLs, particularly when state educational standards mandate certain kinds of assignments requiring displays of encyclopedic knowledge, current statistics, and narratives composed of chronological facts. Strangely, many federal websites for children only offer young people seeking answers more riddles, frequently in the form of pages of "games for kids," such as interactive online hangman games or crossword puzzles. For example, the FBI webpage designed for elementary school children features a tile game, a matching game, a word search, and a drag-and-drop disguises page, all programmed in Flash and Java.[47] Although children doing research on national security issues or the powers of interstate policing would rarely arrive at a federal website in search of this kind of fun, these government websites offer activities of distraction rather than the information literacy skills that young citizens would need in order to evaluate information coming from even supposedly vetted websites from federal authorities.

If federal websites for children do not feature puzzles and games, they often show cartoon characters of animals and robots engaged in anthropomorphic stories that are only remotely related to the work of government agencies. Eventually, the children's site for the Department of Homeland Security, ready.gov/kids, showcased a group of mountain lions in a patriarchal family unit designed by Betsy Baytos, a Disney veteran, who also designed a corporate campaign for the Coca-Cola company featuring polar bears, which the DHS website proudly reported among her information design credentials. Of course, children from hillside regions in California who have been warned against trails in mountain lion habitats may be unlikely to accept these mascots as comforting agents of trustworthy information from an authoritative source. Far from the urban landscapes in which terrorist attacks are statistically more likely to occur, the cartoon mountain lions supposedly are intended to demonstrate the utility of an emergency supply kit on a site that also features coloring books, word searches, and clickable hidden treasure activities.

These children's websites, which are even produced by famously secretive U.S. federal agencies such as the Central Intelligence Agency or the National Reconnaissance Office, underscore the fact that official websites do much more than merely disseminate information to users as part of e-government efforts. In addition, these websites represent certain ideologies of the state, which in this case, I would argue, do not present the kinds of didactic politics that one might expect to find promoted alongside issues of national security or public safety about future citizenship and eventual participation in organizations of institutional authority, although they reify certain cultural imaginaries nonetheless. Rather than show participatory culture for all ages, these government websites propagate the vision of a two-tiered Internet also pushed by congressional legislation, such as the Communications Decency Act or the Child Online Protection Act, where the online activities of young people take place

Figure 9.10
2007 illustration from the Department of Homeland Security children's site.

inside a child-safe walled garden, because of the assumption that young people would only go to the Internet for socially unproductive diversion and games.

As taxpayer-funded games, simulations, and illustrated websites for health and safety represent both scenes of crisis and epistemological spaces, the borders and barriers that they reconstitute in virtual learning environments serve a double function. Not only do these representations emphasize proper safety procedures and equipment protocols, but they also reify boundaries that demarcate the privileged spaces of the elect.

Nontraditional Games of Crisis

Many independent game designers are creating work in the genre of the game of crisis in order to produce experiences in electronic environments that invite more introspective reflection and informal sociality than those proposing that a crisis can be best managed by the hierarchical rationalization of command and control. For example, in *The Night Journey*, video artist Bill Viola and game designer Tracy Fullerton collaborate to create a game about enlightenment in which the true crisis is one that is spiritual in nature. Elements in the navigable game world and the video art cut scenes draw on motifs selected from the world's major religions. In *The Night Journey*, the scenes of death, rotting animal bodies, and destruction are intended to stimulate contemplation about life's larger meanings rather than emergency interventions, and players are encouraged to slow down rather than speed up to make sense of the unfolding information.[48] The spiritual crises that human beings must confront are imagined as being far from the busy context of urban life, so that *The Night Journey* unfolds in the mythic regions of desert, forest, ocean, or mountain. The player approaches structures in the game world not to secure territory, create a command center, or establish a strategic foothold, but to gain knowledge, paradoxically about the limitations of knowledge.

In contrast to the emphasis on isolation in *The Night Journey*, Jane McGonigal created *World Without Oil*, an online simulation run in 2007 that gradually unfolded to reveal the magnitude of the consequences of a thirty-two week evolving global oil crisis.[49] Players—1,800 in twelve countries—were encouraged to use a common social media platform on the website to perform and interact in ways sometimes only tangentially guided by the simulation. By the time *World Without Oil* was finished, hundreds of people had left comments on the site, had posted video diaries, or had kept detailed blogs that documented how this possible history of the future would impact their own lives as gas shortages cause transportation to come to a standstill, prices to skyrocket, once-public places to close, and frustrated citizens to riot or creatively collaborate. In this alternate reality game, or ARG, players' dramatic sensibilities showed themselves able to find success through what Michel de Certeau has called "tactics,"[50] which

Figure 9.11
Image of the "Desert Hut" from *The Night Journey*. Courtesy of Tracy Fullerton of the USC Game Innovation Lab.

seemed to often be made possible by mobile computing devices that allowed frustrated oil consumers to function as smart mobs capable of subverting the failed strategies of policy makers.

As a commuting faculty member who lived fifty miles away from the campus where I worked, I played along with McGonigal's simulation and shot online video that chronicled how members of my real-life faculty carpool would have responded to this kind of crisis. Initially, carpool members were confident that their rational decision-making and willingness to collaborate and improvise would allow them to overcome the challenges they faced, because as university professors they could "afford" certain lifestyle adjustments, including working at home and adopting distance learning practices. At one point, however, as the crisis worsens, one carpooler realizes that she "probably" has "enough gas . . . to get home, but that's it." Faced with dramatic life-style changes involving acquiring a bicycle and temporarily relocating to her mother's home to keep her job, she is still hopeful that she can manage to "set up a way to do my work from my computer."[51]

I continued to participate in McGonigal's game as I traveled to the Netherlands to give a paper at the annual meeting of the International Information Society for Crisis Response and Management (ISCRAM) about the use of serious games for emergency training and planning. By this point in the simulation in *World Without Oil*, international travel had been largely curtailed, as the price of jet fuel grounded airplanes at

Figure 9.12
Image of video created for *World Without Oil*.

airports around the world, often stranding travelers in foreign countries. After posting an online video from the Netherlands explaining my fictional plight, which was shot wandering around the medieval square in Delft, Dutch citizens contacted me via e-mail and offered to pretend to offer shelter to the homeless American and to shoot more online video of us playing out an episode of international face-to-face cooperation.

Ironically, at the ISCRAM conference the emphasis was on how crisis planners could use game and computer simulation technologies to save local governments the cost and urban disruption associated with traditional large-scale drills that conventionally required hundreds of role-playing extras. In other words, they hoped to eliminate precisely the kind of spectacle that alternate reality game designers wanted to stage with human actors in the built environment of cities. Rather than foster the live improvisation and social theater facilitated by streetwise games like McGonigal's *World Without Oil* and *Superstruct*, these games of crisis would be removed from the public sphere and consigned to the private spaces of the professionally initiated.

10 The Past as Prologue: Cultural Politics and the Founding Narratives of Information Science

In the summer of 1997, a government agency first dramatized the potential of a "merger of television and the Internet,"[1] as the Mars rover experiment was sending the initial images shot by a robotic vehicle from the red planet's surface back to Earth. Unlike previous space missions that had been watched on television sets in people's living rooms, this was a spectacle that took place on a computer screen, often in a school or workplace, where connectivity was still far superior to that available in most homes at the time.

For purposes of scale, it's worth noting that on just one day during the rover's planned month-long mission, July 8, the space agency's website (at mpfwww.jpl.nasa .gov) received 47 million hits. By the time the month was over, web traffic statistics showed a total of 577 million visits to the main rover site alone.[2] To adjust to the large number of unexpected visitors, NASA soon set up mirror sites in over a dozen countries to handle the overflow from these virtual crowds. Corporate partners also stepped in to enlarge the rover project's web capacity.[3] This widely publicized event and accounts of periodic "traffic jams" on NASA's websites by space enthusiasts of all ages, who were jockeying to see pictures from the Sojourner rover simultaneously, soon spurred telecommunications companies to explore collaborative ventures with software makers in order to one day "offer individualized interactive digital television" with a wide range of content.[4]

In the decade that followed, the Jet Propulsion Laboratory would use its website for one public relations success after another and deploy advanced data visualization techniques to make a compelling case for its popular rover missions with high-resolution digital color photographs and 3-D computer animated films. Unlike other federally funded organizations that often struggled to find success as digital media-makers, JPL showed itself to be a consistent master of public rhetoric in these new media. While JPL's parent agency, NASA, had a number of high-profile failures involving computational media, which included revelations that regrettable PowerPoint[5] or e-mail[6] trails of miscommunication had contributed to two space shuttle crashes, JPL was busy promoting a positive vision of new information age ventures, which included plans for an "Interplanetary Network, or IPN," which would "combine elements of today's Internet with another communications network that countries around the world use to communicate with their satellites and other spaceships" that would be able to compensate for the "low-power wireless transmissions over very large distances that produce higher error rates."[7]

Before the advent of the World Wide Web, JPL relied on press releases, public events in auditoriums with live feeds from its interplanetary spacecraft, tours of its facility in Southern California, and the dissemination of print ephemera such as newsletters, photographs, posters, stickers, and other souvenir items to amateur astronomers as a way to spread their message about the benefits of space exploration to the American populace. Having grown up in Pasadena, very near to JPL in a site of "regional advantage" around the California Institute of Technology,[8] I frequently went on school field trips to the main JPL compound, where visitors could observe activities in the mission control room or visit galleries commemorating JPL's long history of unmanned journeys outside Earth's atmosphere. Even as a child, I could appreciate the fact that JPL engineers had to work with at least three very complicated problems all the time: (1) calculating the trajectories of the mechanical artifacts that they blasted into space, (2) analyzing the signals sent back from these devices, which were often obscured by "noise" that muddied the messages, and (3) managing information retrieval and synthesizing information from complex missions with multiple objectives and teams.

The Rhetoric of Information Science

In the 1940s, the triad of scientific problems involving trajectory calculation, signal analysis, and information retrieval had been central to the discourses of the founding documents of "information science," a newfound discipline established in the academy in the wake of World War II. Just as Sigmund Freud had to defend the status of psychoanalysis as a legitimate field decades earlier, information scientists had to articulate what Freud had called a discipline's *Weltanschauung*, which roughly translates into English as a "worldview" or "ideology." Freud described a Weltanschauung as "an intellectual construction which gives a unified solution" to all problems of "our existence" with a "comprehensive hypothesis, a construction."[9] Much as the language of psychoanalysis also filtered into the popular culture, expert terms from cybernetics, signal theory, data mining, and information retrieval soon became part of the American vernacular in the postwar years. How well the public really understood the theories they were incorporating into the everyday lexicon was a considerably more complicated question. Von Neumann argued in *Theory of Self-Reproducing Automata* that these new "rigorous theories of control and information" differed significantly from the formal logics of classical mathematics, in that the field required "the discussion of certain fictitious mechanisms or axiomatic paper automata, which are merely outlines, but which nobody is concerned to build."[10]

Those who study what is called the "rhetoric of science" are particularly interested in definitive statements of the principles governing a branch of disciplinary knowledge or its central issues and questions, because these ur-texts often indicate the kinds of metaphors and narratives that shape subsequent discourses in a given field. In the terms of traditional rhetoric, it could be said that the scientific method is associated with its own distinctive topoi or stock rhetorical subjects, which are designed for both effective practice and for persuasion. Furthermore, the members of a given scientific community must be keenly aware of the importance of the concept of *kairos* and how specific rhetorical occasions may be particularly opportune for collective engagement with problem solving and successful codification of the rules for acceptable findings of fact. Following Bruno Latour, many have argued for a place for rhetoric in science studies, and rhetoricians such as Charles Bazerman and Alan G. Gross have conversely introduced scholarship from the social study of science to the field of rhetoric and composition. Much of this work has been informed by Thomas Kuhn's groundbreaking *The Structure of Scientific Revolutions*, which argues that paradigm shifts in fields like astronomy and chemistry have less to do with groundbreaking discoveries by lone geniuses than they do with phases of evolving consensuses within more conservative communities of practice.[11] Founding manifestos for new sciences are also of special interest to rhetoricians because they are frequently political texts, not only in the sense of situating a discipline in relationship to national or party politics, but also as indicators of the sexual or cultural politics of a particular approach to intellectual inquiry and the epistemological ground that the set of social actors are claiming.

On behalf of information science, Vannevar Bush made what was probably the most prominent popular appeal to the lay public in *The Atlantic Monthly* and later in *Life* magazine in his 1945 essay "As We May Think." One of his editors compared Bush's essay to "Emerson's famous address of 1837 on 'The American Scholar,'" because it also grappled with the basic "relationship between thinking man and the sum of our knowledge"[12] in language designed to be accessible to those outside of the academy. In "As We May Think," Bush describes what he sees as a crisis of knowledge unfolding in contemporary society, because so much scientific inquiry is going on at a rapid pace simultaneously at many locations in laboratories and research universities, and yet "methods of transmitting and reviewing the results of research are generations old."[13]

Years later, Bush would make some preliminary arguments for the status of another new discipline seeking a respected place in the university in his essay on "The Art of Management,"[14] but in 1945 his focus was on the plight of the research scientist facing the dispersal of resources and strategic planning that had been marshaled by the government during the war. During World War II, much of Bush's research planning had been approved at the highest levels, and President Franklin Roosevelt met with Bush personally and agreed to support new large-scale federal sources of funding for scientific collaborations between universities, the military, and industry that Bush would supervise. However, although this document is often read as a blueprint for the digital future, as Wendy Chun points out, Bush's professional history up to that point had been heavily invested in analog technologies.[15] In the1930s, Bush had worked on the construction of analog computers, such as the Differential Analyzer at MIT, which had a mechanism with rods and wheels inside its wood and glass case and was used for representing complex mathematical problems very literally as a series of visibly observable relationships.[16] Soon Bush became interested in incorporating new photographic film techniques into his mechanisms and in applying these technologies of miniaturization and enlargement to law enforcement scenarios by proposing inventions such as a fingerprint analyzer for the FBI.

Some have argued that this emphasis on deploying computing for the interests of the military and the police powers of the state inevitably privileged closed systems over open ones.[17] However, "As We May Think" largely depicts personal rather than institutional computing and even describes what could be taken to be an early version of peer-to-peer file sharing between like-minded citizens.[18] Certainly Bush emphasizes the inclusiveness of his address to the public on several occasions. He describes the recent war as being not "a scientist's war" but "a war in which all have had a part," and he asserts that the scientist "is not the only person who manipulates data and examines the world about him by the use of logical processes."[19]

As a rhetorician, Bush had always had a popular audience in mind for the ideas in "As We May Think." His 1945 article was a reworked and expanded version of his 1939 manuscript, "Mechanization and the Record," which he had sent to the editors of *Fortune* magazine before the outbreak of the war, although the magazine never published his text. Media scholar W. Russell Neuman has described the finished product in *The Atlantic Monthly* as a piece of writing rich with the potential for "democratic pluralism" made possible by a "communications revolution," which also capitalized on the concentrated attention enabled by both the "psychology of mass audience" and the "political economy of mass media" of the Orwellian paradigms of collective experience to which it could be opposed.[20]

In the essay, Bush is concerned with how scientific revolutions may be stymied by forms of myopia caused by the incommensurability of the importance of the findings of men of genius, such as Gregor Mendel, with the capacities of scientific institutions to locate and synthesize new work, to invigorate existing theories and practices through selection and focus, and to coordinate novel ideas with novel inventions. Often in the essay he mourns the loss of significant information that takes place over relatively short periods of historical time. For example, Bush writes that two centuries ago Leibniz "invented a calculating machine which embodied most of the essential features of recent keyboard devices, but it could not then come into use." Although Bush is alarmed by the information-loss problems faced by professionals in the further uncoordinated peacetime scientific community, he also expresses concern for individual lay users of information, people who are outside of the academy and yet may also find highly specialized findings useful in their daily lives.

"As We May Think" is probably most famous for seeming to predict many futuristic digital technologies by proposing the development of a device for home use called the memex, which "would instantly bring files and matter on any subject to the operator's fingertips."[21] His memex is a highly personalized technology, which is an "enlarged intimate supplement to his memory" and a site in which an "individual stores all his books, records, and communications." Unlike cards indexed alphabetically in a catalog drawer, materials in the memex would be organized according to the principles governing "the automatic telephone exchange."

The owner of the memex, let us say, is interested in the origin and properties of the bow and arrow. Specifically he is studying why the short Turkish bow was apparently superior to the English long bow in the skirmishes of the Crusades. He has dozens of possibly pertinent books and articles in his memex. First he runs through an encyclopedia, finds an interesting but sketchy article, leaves it projected. Next, in a history, he finds another pertinent item, and ties the two together. Thus he goes, building a trail of many items. Occasionally he inserts a comment of his own, either linking it into the main trail or joining it by a side trail to a particular item. When it becomes evident that the elastic properties of available materials had a great deal to do with the bow, he branches off on a side trail which takes him through textbooks on elasticity and tables of physical constants. He inserts a page of longhand analysis of his own. Thus he builds a trail of his interest through the maze of materials available to him.[22]

Because the memex user edits, annotates, and adds content to the trail about the Turkish bow, Bush's imagined protagonist is also presented as a producer as well as a consumer of electronically generated texts.

There are obviously several features about the information practices of this imagined citizen that make him a particularly distinctive kind of ideal reader or ideal author. He's interested in military technologies, East/West divisions, and weapons that hurtle projectiles along an optimal trajectory, which were all concerns in the aerial bombing and missile projects that Bush oversaw during his tenure as chair of the National Defense Research Committee and director of the Office of Scientific Research and Development. As scientists tried to predict outcomes in physics scenarios with new jet engines and rockets in unfamiliar atmospheric conditions, this kind of narrative would continue to be relevant to scientists during the Cold War.

In peacetime, however, the record-keeping possibilities of the devices that Bush promotes would also seem to have obvious benefits to U.S. capitalism. Charge cards at the "great department store" would simplify inventory tracking and accounting. The specialization of labor could be further refined to provide "a list of all employees who live in Trenton and know Spanish." The costs of production, storage, and transportation of some material goods would be cut dramatically so that "material for the microfilm Britannica would cost a nickel, and it could be mailed anywhere for a cent."[23]

But this micropayment future contains some troubling implications for laissez-faire capitalism. Although the memex user "purchases" materials for his device, much like a contemporary encyclopedia subscriber, Bush also imagines a kind of file sharing outside of the circuits of monetary exchange:

Several years later, his talk with a friend turns to the queer ways in which a people resist innovations, even of vital interest. He has an example, in the fact that the outraged Europeans still failed to adopt the Turkish bow. In fact he has a trail on it. A touch brings up the code book. Tapping a few keys projects the head of the trail. A lever runs through it at will, stopping at interesting items, going off on side excursions. It is an interesting trail, pertinent to the discussion. So he sets a reproducer in action, photographs the whole trail out, and passes it to his friend for insertion in his own memex, there to be linked into the more general trail.[24]

He copies the "whole trail" and "passes it to his friend" without considering what these kinds of transactions might mean for the market, even though in the era of the Digital Millennium Copyright Act this exchange may well be forbidden by congressional legislation, beginning at the moment of digital replication.[25]

Bush presents a narrative about social media and a reputation economy in which the information in his memex has value primarily to illustrate to his friend the "queer ways in which a people resist innovations" when they come from cultural others. This discussion with the memex user's friend takes place in a complex rhetorical context of mutual conversation in which a cosmopolitan technology user ridicules certain commonplaces of Eurocentric ideology. Although elsewhere Bush looks forward to the promise of a "new symbolism" divorced from the irrationalities introduced by locality, language, and culture in which one day people will "click off arguments on a machine with the same assurance that we now enter sales on a cash register" or "manipulate premises in accordance with formal logic, simply by the clever use of relay circuits" to crank out "conclusion after conclusion" as consistently as a "keyboard adding machine," the anecdote he tells illustrates the impossibility of winning arguments this way. The significance of the trail lies not in its purely denotative character or absolute signification, but in its "pertinence" to a lively spoken "discussion" and its appropriateness to a particular rhetorical occasion.[26]

Gender and Science

Bush's positive vision inevitably represses certain anxieties about the status of his new science as a properly authoritative field, particularly those subversive questions related to gender, which Bush can avoid as long as his characters can be described exclusively with male pronouns. Yet women have had an undeniably important role in the information and communication industries that Bush's vision builds on, despite the masculine ideologies that have been explicitly associated with legitimated modern science since at least Francis Bacon, according to Evelyn Fox Keller and others who have studied connections between gender and science.[27] In particular, women had long histories as operators of telegraph and telephone networks, where they were responsible for procedures that maintained the viability of large hubs in systems of interrelated nodes.[28] They had also become closely associated with the profession of librarianship by Bush's time and were managers of information retrieval technology at many public institutions.

It is noteworthy that—even in Bush's wildest imagination—the memex owner does not know how to type, since the man inserts "longhand analysis" into the burgeoning hypertextual document that Bush describes. After all, typing was considered a skill consigned to women in the twentieth-century workplace. Even fifteen years later, J.C.R. Licklider was still assuming that hand-drawn symbols and speech recognition technologies would be necessary to achieve what he called "man-computer symbiosis," since "one can hardly take a military commander or a corporation president away from his work to teach him to type."[29]

Because Bush discusses how cultural prejudices and institutional forms of blindness can stymie technological innovation, it is particularly ironic that he can not see the consequences of his own gender ideologies and what may well be an unconscious set of beliefs that he holds about the femininity of certain labor practices. Although Bush's interest in perfecting voice input devices and writing tablets may seem prescient in the current age of ubiquitous computing and intuitive interface design, at the time it meant that many of the inventions he imagined could not get off the drawing board for decades, so that Bush was essentially arguing that funding and effort be directed to impractical pie-in-the-sky technologies. The buttons on Bush's memex, shown in *Life* magazine, bear no resemblance to familiar QWERTY typewriter keys associated with office workers.[30] In contrast, consider the introduction of the personal computer with keyboard that was first sold to consumers in the 1980s. By that time, keyboards were perceived to be very efficient and learning to type proved to be much less of an obstacle to widespread adoption than the men of Bush's generation may have expected, given the internal programming of their gender assumptions and aversion to feminized practices of labor.

After all, even the word "computer" in Bush's time meant a person who fulfilled a particular job title involving computation, a person who was almost always female. Female computers had been essential for creating accurate printed tables at minimal cost[31] and had thus held significant although uncelebrated roles in almost every scientific revolution of the century before the writing of "As We May Think": from cataloging the dimensions of the morphologies of different species in Great Britain to support Darwin's hypothesis about the survival of the fittest to charting the paths of astronomical bodies in order to validate new theories of the universe being posited at Harvard University.[32] Anne Balsamo, whose own mother was a computer, has discussed the "feminization of labor" in which "tasks were routinized and rationalized" so that these occupations became further "sex-stratified."[33]

From the 1940s, and even into the 1950s and 1960s, the JPL laboratory's all-female staff of computers calculated the trajectories of the expensive taxpayer-funded rockets, satellites, and spacecraft and were thereby responsible for making sure that missions were completed successfully and thus for protecting the investment of the public. Although calculations were done by hand for decades, they were scrupulously double-checked. By drawing on the oral histories from the computers themselves, a JPL historian has explained how this female subculture operated within the larger engineering culture of the plant.

Over time, a group of about a dozen women was formed to perform trajectory calculations. Macie Roberts and, later, Helen Ling, both supervisors for the group, hired only women. Their attitude reflected a general cultural belief of the times that some kinds of jobs were more appropriate for women than for men. "Men back then always thought they knew more than you did," Ling remembers. "So if you hire them under you, they're uncomfortable, you're uncomfortable. So I just hired women just out of college. I thought that if you didn't give them a chance, they'll never get a chance."

. . .

The advent of electronic computers slowly changed what the all-female computations group did. The women were trained to program in FORTRAN, the primary computer language developed for scientific applications. Sue Finley, hired into the group in 1958, remembers that the male engineers largely didn't want to do the programming themselves in the 1960s. It was still considered "women's work," not part of an engineer's job description. So the group began to code and run programs for calculating trajectories to the planets, for various Earth orbits and other tasks assigned them by the Lab's engineers.

. . .

New computers didn't change the fact that data were still plotted by hand. Electronic computers couldn't plot data until the 1970s. "I worked on Ranger 3 telemetry by hand," recalls Finley. "The computer wasn't working that night. JPL's Al Hibbs read it to me over the phone and I plotted it. When everyone realized that Ranger 3 hadn't reached escape velocity and wouldn't reach the moon, I went home. I got there around six in the morning and my husband was watching the news. They had a little blackboard up with the numbers I had calculated on it. I said 'Those are my numbers!' Almost nobody in the outside world knew we women did that work."[34]

When plotting by hand was no longer necessary, "engineers started to want computer-animated movies to help promote missions" that showed not only the trajectories but also "views of the planets during spacecraft flybys."[35] Eventually, some of the women hired as computers moved into less sex-segregated fields like software engineering, but tasks related to data representation continued to be seen as women's work for many years. Although this workforce was sex-segregated, it provided opportunities to overcome some barriers about reproduction and race. A 1953 photograph shows a group of twenty-seven women posing in a JPL company portrait. At least one woman of color is clearly visible in the group, as is one noticeably pregnant woman. The image also shows considerable diversity in age among these information workers, many of whom were apparently recruited out of high school based on their mathematical abilities.[36]

Yet Bush seems eager to exclude women from the "we" in the informational future that he describes in "As We May Think."[37] At one point Bush indicates the extreme inappropriateness of the professional spectacle of such "girls" in the company of engineers, men of science, and others occupied in the business of the public sphere.

The other element is found in the stenotype, that somewhat disconcerting device encountered usually at public meetings. A girl strokes its keys languidly and looks about the room and sometimes at the speaker with a disquieting gaze. From it emerges a typed strip which records in a phonetically simplified language a record of what the speaker is supposed to have said. Later this

Figure 10.1
1953 photograph of computers at the Jet Propulsion Laboratory. Courtesy NASA/JPL-Caltech.

strip is retyped into ordinary language, for in its nascent form it is intelligible only to the initiated. Combine these two elements, let the Vocoder run the stenotype, and the result is a machine which types when talked to.[38]

The device is "disconcerting," but so is the "disquieting" operator of it, who sensuously "strokes" the keys "languidly" and discomfits the speaker by counterintuitively making a male the object of an attentive if not predatory gaze. By creating "a machine which types when talked to," Bush would be able to remove this "girl" from the scene, and—with a little creative engineering—preserve the decorum of the public meeting, which could then take place in a suitably all-male environment.[39] It is significant that manifestos from male technologists about the coming information revolution would make references to such voiceless "girls" doing society's data work. These women are depicted in service roles only to be hoped to eventually be made obsolete, or to have their labor dematerialized into a representational abstraction.

The figure of the "girl" reappears in Warren Weaver's introduction to Claude Shannon's groundbreaking technical work *The Mathematical Theory of Communication*. It is interesting, however, that rather than reject her labor, as Bush does, Weaver makes her into the very epitome of his profession. At one point, Weaver compares the new discipline that Shannon is launching to a "girl" in the telecommunications industry and thus makes the young working woman into one of his central rhetorical tropes.

An engineering communication theory is like a very proper and discreet girl accepting your telegram. She pays no attention to the meaning, whether it be sad, or joyous, or embarrassing. But she must be prepared to deal with all that come to her desk.[40]

As Derrida has pointed out, the word "proper" has an interesting etymology. It implies the social isolation of both the personal ownership and cleanliness of the French root word *propre*, and yet in common use it is a relational word about social connections that indicates suitability or conformity to something else.[41] Although she is in a simultaneously subservient and powerful position as a service worker, Weaver depicts the "girl" at her official desk as a kind of vestal virgin of the information industry, a nonparticipant in the transaction who is immune to "sad" or "joyous" or "embarrassing" content, even though her "properness" must coexist with her worldly "discretion," as she is still potentially privy to the secrets she ignores.

The "girl's" femininity and passivity can be seen as appropriate signifiers for this new discipline, because unlike conventional science, Shannon's mathematical theory of communication is all about engaging in the kind of women's work that the masculine JPL engineers avoided, about science as doing procedures and calculations rather than finding truth. Unlike the Baconian tradition, in which true scientists must reveal the most intimate secrets of nature, Weaver presents a strangely uncurious figure to his audience. The girl's disengagement from active interpretation represents

Weaver's translation of Shannon's concept that although "frequently the messages have meaning," "semantic aspects of communication are irrelevant to the engineering problem" at hand. In other words, the girl should only be concerned about accurate transcription of the message as it is transmitted or received as a signal in Shannon's diagram of the noisy channel. Weaver further tinkers with conventional concepts about dependence and independence in his reworking of Shannon's language elsewhere. As Weaver points out, "this does not mean that the engineering aspects are necessarily irrelevant to the semantic aspects."[42]

In 1963, when Weaver wrote *Lady Luck: The Theory of Probability*, which was intended to be a nontechnical introduction to the subject designed for a popular audience, his female allegory for a theoretical set of mathematical assumptions had become much older and more worldly than the "girl" of his 1949 explanation of Shannon's work. In the later text, Weaver traces the "birth" of his mascot for probability theory, "Lady Luck," if not her "conception," to 1654 and to a treatise written in France by Blaise Pascal in response to the problem of formulating a gambling strategy.[43]

Of course, probability is a key factor of information theory in the earlier work as well. As Shannon explains, the "significant aspect is that the actual message is one *selected from a set* of possible meanings."[44] Weaver's introduction, somewhat controversially, further asserts that information has nothing to do with meaning. As though overcoming his audience's objections to a form of semantic miscegenation, Weaver asserts that not only is it "disappointing" that "information" and "meaning" aren't coupled but also that "information" and "uncertainty" are the appropriate if "bizarre" "partners."[45] This is the correct match to make because probabilistically information "deals not with a single message but rather with the statistical character of a whole ensemble of messages." At the end of his introduction he returns again to the star-crossed coupling of "information" and "meaning" to assert that they are "more like a pair of canonically conjugate variables in quantum theory, they being subject to some joint restriction that condemns a person to the sacrifice of the one as he insists on having much of the other,"[46] just as Heisenberg's uncertainty principle dictates that knowing a moving particle's position more precisely means knowing less about its momentum.

Cross Talk

When published as a book, Shannon's theory in the original paper was retitled with a more authoritative definite article replacing the indefinite one, so that 1948's "A Mathematical Theory of Communication" became *The Mathematical Theory of Communication* by the time it went to press in 1949 under the auspices of the University of Illinois.[47] The text also incorporated more of the Cold War sensibilities of one of Shannon's collaborators, Warren Weaver. Although Shannon's formulas were intended primarily to solve specific technical problems by making workable schematic and mathematical models of how electronic signals travel through noisy channels and carry information about the texts, sounds, or images to be displayed, it could be argued that Weaver secondarily gave these equations a distinctive rhetoric of his own that was designed to persuade others that they would be reading an important scientific work.

As a cultural arbiter who held leadership roles in the Rockefeller Foundation for two decades, Weaver had a major role in the postwar era in establishing the authority of theories of "organized complexity" in both academia and popular culture and propagating this theoretical approach in a number of different disciplines. For example, in her seminal work on urban renewal and city planning, *The Death and Life of Great American Cities*, Jane Jacobs devotes much of her chapter on "the kind of a problem a city is" to Weaver's ideas and credits his intellectual legacy as one that could be transposed from the field of mathematics to biology and then to Jacobs's built environments with their complicated ecosystems of social, economic, political, and cultural life.[48] Jacobs cites Weaver's *1958 Annual Report of the Rockefeller Foundation*, but Weaver had been distinguishing between "problems of simplicity," "problems of disorganized complexity," and "problems of organized complexity" as early as 1948, when he introduced and edited a volume of public addresses by leading scientists for lay audiences in a book titled *The Scientists Speak*.[49]

In many places, Weaver's introduction about how information can be divorced from meaning almost merits renaming his preface "The Mathematical Theory of Miscommunication" or "The Mathematical Theory of Pseudocommunication." In considering how "one mind may affect another," Weaver presents an often jaundiced view of human communication, based on his examples, which is very different from the rationalized and routinized error-free linguistic circuitry that Vannevar Bush presents to his audience. Weaver wryly observes certain inherent flaws in the process of meaning-making, which seem to be true not only for his present but for the foreseeable future as well. Certainly, Cold War politics made crosscultural communication particularly challenging in Weaver's mind. At one point, he invites readers to consider "the meaning to a Russian of a U.S. newsreel picture."[50] One could say that Weaver is also concerned about disinformation as well as information, in that he brings up the "psychological and emotional aspects of propaganda theory" in the same section.

For example, Weaver proposes a scenario with "Mr. X" and "Mr. Y" speaking incomprehensibly to each other, which only becomes apparent if the statements are translated into two entirely different languages. Weaver uses his example to undermine his audience's assumptions about the commonality grounded in linguistic interactions, which they further naturalize when the sample utterances are in the familiar dialect of English.

One essential complication is illustrated by the remark that if Mr. X is suspected not to understand what Mr. Y says, then it is theoretically not possible, by having Mr. Y do nothing but talk
further with Mr. X, completely to clarify this situation in any finite time. If Mr. Y says "Do you
now understand me?" and Mr. X says "Certainly I do," this is not necessarily a certification that
understanding has been achieved. It may just be that Mr. X did not understand the question.
If this sounds silly, try it again as "Czy pan mnie rozumie?" with the answer "Hai wakkate
imasu."[51]

In a footnote, Weaver then follows up with the story of the famous horses of Elberfeld
that quotes K.S. Lashley's 1949 article "Persistent Problems in the Evolution of
Mind":

When Pfungst (1911) demonstrated that the horses of Elberfeld, who were showing marvelous
linguistic and mathematical ability, were merely reacting to movements of the trainer's head, Mr
Krall (1911), their owner met the criticism in the most direct manner. He asked the horses
whether or not they could see such small movements and in answer they spelled out an emphatic
"No." Unfortunately we cannot all be so sure that our questions are understood or obtain such
clear answers.[52]

This humorous anecdote concerns one of the founding narratives of modern experimental psychology during the time it was establishing its *Weltanschauung*, distinct
from "occult" beliefs that seemed to be grounded largely in a mythology based on
rural experiences and respect for authority figures. The story also illustrates one of the
basic principles of the channel metaphor for communication that Shannon and
Weaver promote. As psychology professor Ray Hyman has explained, "The horse was
simply a channel through which the information the questioner unwittingly put into
the situation was fed back to the questioner. The fallacy involved treating the horse
as the source of the message rather than as a channel through which the questioner's
own message is reflected back."[53]

This kind of pseudointeractivity in which the correct input appears to generate the
correct output also dictates the operational structure of many chatbots, who similarly
appear to respond with meaningful messages that are actually dictated by formal
rules governing their exchanges with algorithms that imitate speech. Much as Joseph
Weizenbaum's Rogerian therapist simulation ELIZA was programmed to give back
either syntactic variations of the patient's own statements or generic questions that
didn't require the context of a previous utterance, the horses had been programmed
by their trainers to respond so that humans involved in the exchanges would be convinced they were participating in a legitimate dialogue.

This type of simulated interactivity has also been the inspiration for Internet political satires about the programmatic responses of government leaders to inquiries from
their constituents. In 2004, the advertising firm Crispin Porter + Bogusky launched
the wildly successful "Subservient Chicken" viral marketing campaign for Burger King,
in which users could type commands that would seemingly make a man dressed in a

chicken suit on a video feed to their screen do everything from dance to do push-ups.[54] The input box read: "Get chicken just the way you like it. Type in your command here." Sometimes the man-chicken would shrug his shoulders as though he had not understood the order he was given, and at other times the chicken would wag his finger in disapproval if the suggestion for action was lewd or constituted an illegal activity. The advertising firm's creative director explained the campaign as a rethinking of the concept of "interactivity" to go beyond "great design, fancy animation and programming" to engage with user experience and social media in new ways. He admits, however, that the procedural logic of Subservient Chicken required a daunting number of commands in order to pay off in a successful user experience.

It's a bit of a production, especially in terms of copywriting. You're basically trying to solve for infinite. It's a challenge coming up with a response for everything. Subservient Chicken was the first time somebody did something like that with audio or video clips, but the idea's been around for years. The IM bot and the AI [movie] website used it. With Subservient Chicken, we came to the realization that "hey, instead of pulling text fields, why don't we trigger video clips?'" And it worked. There's got to be a bigger idea behind it, and there's got to be some focus to it.[55]

The viral potential of this new media artifact soon was realized as it generated a number of parodies, such as "Subservient Programmer"[56] and "Subservient Blair."[57] University of Southern California film and interactive media professor Steve Anderson responded to the Burger King campaign by creating "Subservient President," which shows a man in a rubber mask in the opening scene, along with a podium with the seal of the office of the Chief Executive and a computer displaying an image of former president Ronald Reagan. A text-input box reads: "Get politics just the way corporate America likes it. Type a command."[58] Subservient President was a clear satire of former U.S. president George W. Bush; keywords involving "weapons of mass destruction," "mission accomplished," or "drunk driving" cue particularly humorous actions.

The nondigital precursor of Subservient Chicken, "Clever Hans," was an actual horse owned by German math teacher and phrenologist William Von Osten, who first displayed him to the public in 1891. The subsequent story has a complicated rhetorical history of its own in scientific and popular discourse. Von Osten's demonstrations so impressed a Mr. Krall from Elberfeld that he purchased two stallions of his own, Muhamed and Zarif, and trained them to do even more impressive anthropomorphic feats. Then, at Krall's invitation, an international group of more than a dozen scientists studied how Hans and the other horses appeared to do sums, tell time, and exchange messages with human beings. Some, like Pfungst, argued that communication was only taking place through the most primitive nonverbal channels and unconscious cues. The story of the horses also appeared in a 1912 article in *Science*, "The Talking Dog," about a seven-year-old German setter, also studied by Pfungst, with a reputed vocabulary of eight words.[59] A series of book reviews in *The American Journal of Psychology* on works in French, German, and Italian indicates that there was still great attention being paid to the Clever Hans case in 1914.

After a lull in coverage, there was more publicity during World War II for the Clever Hans story because of the nickname of Nazi field commander Günter "Hans" von Kluge, whose interchanges with Hitler were intercepted and translated by ULTRA Allied codebreakers during the Normandy invasion. Rather than draw upon this political and cryptographic history, in which Hitler and Kluge were also miscommunicating to such an extent that soon Hitler's field commander would join the group of conspirators associated with the Von Stauffenberg plot, Weaver is citing an article from the *Quarterly Journal of Biology* about primate research by Harvard biology professor Karl Lashley. What is interesting about the citation is that Weaver omits the context of the quotation and the fact that Lashley is presenting a more hopeful argument that human-animal communication is possible, if difficult. The opening sentence, which comes right before the seemingly skeptical passage Weaver reproduces, which appears to mock Krall's credulity, reads: "The comparative psychologist must try to ask questions of his animals and to understand their answers."[60]

In contrast to Weaver's seeming cynicism about meaningful dialogue, Norbert Wiener presents a much more optimistic model of the possibilities for crosscultural communication in his book *Cybernetics* by imagining a successful linguistic interaction taking place with an "intelligent savage."

Suppose I find myself in the woods with an intelligent savage who cannot speak my language and whose language I cannot speak. Even without any code of sign language common to the two of us, I can learn a great deal from him. All I need to do is to be alert to those moments when he shows the signs of emotion or interest. I then cast my eyes around, perhaps paying special attention to the direction of his glance, and fix in my memory what I see or hear. It will not be long before I discover the things which seem important to him, not because he has communicated them to me by language, but because I myself have observed them. In other words, a signal without any intrinsic content may acquire meaning in his mind by what he observes at the time, and may acquire meaning in my mind by what I observe at the time. The ability that he has to pick out the moments of my special, active attention is in itself a language as varied in possibilities as the range of impressions that the two of us are able to encompass.[61]

As a believer in cybernetics, Wiener essentially argues that communication cannot be reduced to one diagram, because it isn't a single system but rather multiple interdependent systems that include feedback loops in what anthropologist Gregory Bateson has described as an "ecology of mind."[62] Wiener is clearly positing a model of communicative fellowship with the other man in the woods that is based on shared meaning, although one can also argue that the way he uses the terms "savagery" and "intelligence" here and elsewhere in the text shows his Eurocentric ideologies and his uncritical acceptance of the ethnographic biases of Bateson and Margaret Mead in the Macy Circle.

This attention to the affect of others in complex communicative systems, which is featured in the "intelligent savage" story, continues to be an important aspect of interpreting many interchanges in our current media-rich landscape, whether we may be observing the body language of people talking on cell phones, watching the faces of victims who have been "punk'd" on reality television shows, or studying the expressions in reaction videos on YouTube in which people on webcams are watching offensive content. Recently, Richard Grusin has argued that theorists in the humanities should be paying more attention to cybernetics and related theories of affective computing because affect is a critical part of interactions with media and meaning-making in general.[63]

Wiener famously refused to accept the equation of information and entropy in *The Mathematical Theory of Communication*, where Weaver simultaneously acknowledged and minimized Wiener's rival contributions to the field in a footnote. According to his biographers, Wiener resented being scooped by the much younger Shannon and craved more credit for founding his own interdisciplinary discipline, cybernetics.[64] At the allegorical level, Wiener's own book, *Cybernetics*, uses the story of two female fictional characters to illustrate what reputable science is *not*. For purposes of illustration, he argues that "a useful law of physics" could be compared to "an effective rule for a game," in being "statable in advance" and applicable "to more than one case."[65] When explaining the very opposite of the Weltanschauung of his science, he evokes the irrational and uncertain croquet game in Lewis Carrol's *Alice in Wonderland* in which "mallets are flamingos," balls are hedgehogs, "playing-card soldiers" are "subject to locomotor initiatives of their own," and "the rules are the decrees of the testy, unpredictable Queen of Hearts."[66] Thus, Wiener describes a dystopian scenario of chaos that is not only a failed game and by explicit analogy a failed form of science, but also implicitly a failed political state ruled over by a distorted version of Weaver's Lady Luck.

From Information Science to Information Studies

Katherine Hayles has argued that Norbert Wiener was keenly aware of the threats posed to liberal subjectivity in this new regime and the consequences of the boundary confusions created by an informational model of the world. Although Wiener's ideas about homeostasis and the feedback mechanisms present in complex interrelated systems can be read as signs of the comforting forces of self-regulation, they can also be interpreted as indicators that successions of cataclysms can take over a given situation very quickly. Furthermore, political subjects as autonomous beings find the most basic operational definitions blurred. Even if people gain the kinds of cyborg powers of extended perception that Gregory Bateson describes when the blind man's consciousness is extended into his cane tapping the ground,[67] their identities as discrete countable democratic citizens with separately registered voices may be destabilized by Wiener's cybernetic model. As Hayles explains his position, "Wiener was not unaware of the ironies through which cybernetics would imperil the very liberal humanistic subject whose origins are enmeshed with self-regulating machinery. Throughout his mature writings, he struggled to reconcile the tradition of liberalism with the new cybernetic paradigm he was in the process of creating."[68]

Wiener was also attuned to other kinds of political dangers that could come from social actors who might understand how to use his theories of information and yet pervert the basic philosophy of openness that was characteristic of his school of thought. In the chapter on "Information, Language, and Society" in *Cybernetics*, Wiener turns his attention to how mathematical theories of information might be exploited by stakeholders who are overly invested in zero-sum gamesmanship[69] and are greedy for the spoils of a commodity culture in which information has become the greatest prize. Wiener claims that the larger a community is, the greater difficulty it has in maintaining homeostasis, because there is "far less communally available information," since the "Lords of Things as They Are" can protect themselves by "possession of the means of communication" itself.[70]

The monopolists who take advantage of the economic circuits of information are not limited to traditional pre-technological plutocrats. He also voices suspicions of "business executives" and "heads of great laboratories" with what could even be interpreted as a very subtle swipe at Bell Labs, where Shannon worked and where the Vocoder invention that Vannevar Bush had so admired had been created.[71] Of course, as others may have understood better than Shannon, once information could be quantified, it could also be commodified, and mastery of theories of information and inventions of proprietary technologies could also affect ownership of capital and the free flow of ideas.

In *Cybernetics*, Wiener often appears to be a forerunner of the scholarship now being done in the area of contemporary Critical Information Studies (CIS), which has attempted to energize critical theory and cultural studies through engagement with political advocacy for contentious free culture issues and intellectual property reform. Siva Vaidhyanathan explains the objectives of this interdisciplinary group in ways that echo language from the cybernetic worldview and Wiener's specific expressions of anxiety about maintaining public access to information.

CIS interrogates the structures, functions, habits, norms, and practices that guide global flows of information and cultural elements. Instead of being concerned merely with one's right to speak (or sing or publish), CIS asks questions about access, costs, and chilling effects on, within, and among audiences, citizens, emerging cultural creators, indigenous cultural groups, teachers, and students. Central to these issues is the idea of "semiotic democracy," or the ability of citizens to employ the signs and symbols ubiquitous in their environments in manners that they determine.[72]

In *Cybernetics*, Wiener himself warns that more attention must be paid to the "acquisition, use, retention, and transmission of information"[73]

Recently, the creation of schools and departments of "information studies" has become a trend in American universities, which in the case of providing graduate training for librarians has sometimes meant actually renaming existing programs that were only very recently called "information science" instead.

What does it mean for a discipline to represent "studies" of an important subject rather than a "science" of it? Both visions are fundamentally interdisciplinary, although they both seek to claim specific turf in the academy. Yet this trend toward renaming seems to signal an orientation of the field toward the humanities and social sciences and away from physical and biological sciences, computer science, and mathematics. At one time, information science was supposed to represent the next great scientific revolution or paradigm shift, in which Shannon's and Wiener's theories could be compared to those of Newton, Darwin, and Maxwell. They were to be taught in high school and college alongside theories of mechanics and thermodynamics.[74] By acknowledging multiplicity, it may seem more inclusive and tolerant of methodological and ideological differences, but the shift from information science to information studies may also signal a fundamental loss in cultural capital for the discipline by maintaining a less coherent and powerful master narrative, as desirable as that change may be to critics from a science studies perspective.

Not Rocket Science

Like Vannevar Bush, Norbert Wiener had a strong sense of potential audience in the general public for his messages. Not only did he think his scholarly ideas about science, culture, and religion merited publication, but he also wrote autobiographical narratives about his life story as a professional mathematician[75] and former child prodigy[76] that can be found in public libraries today. Nonetheless, it was his work doing anti-aircraft calculations during World War II in projects supervised by Vannevar Bush that was most important for establishing his rhetorical ethos and his credibility as a spokesman for modern science. Although he expresses enthusiasm for Bush's promotion of "the use of mechanical aids for the searching through vast bodies of material,"[77] it is his trajectory computation that is the heroic task described in the introduction to *Cybernetics* that shapes his character and intellectual curiosity for the rest of his life. There is a romance of difficulty and novelty associated with this particular form of calculation, because "unlike all previously encountered targets, an airplane has a velocity which is a very appreciable part of the velocity of the missile used to bring it down."[78]

Although closely tied to innovative work being done at the California Institute of Technology, the Jet Propulsion Laboratory was actually founded by those who knew remarkably little about the complicated equations MIT's Wiener was trying to formulate on the other coast. Instead, the methods for testing rockets at JPL at first were grounded in the physics and chemistry of the previous century and depended largely on a gusto for intuitive recipe-making of explosives along with trial and error.[79] Today solid fuel and liquid fuel rocketry are often heavily regulated, and even model rocketeers are encouraged to participate in official organizations that emphasize formal public events and safe practices with prepackaged kits rather than individual tinkering.[80] Although social media outlets on blogs, listservs, and forums allow for some underground activities in the amateur rocketry field, organizations like the Boy Scouts, which are concerned about possible legal liability for accidents, no longer support this once-frequent rite of passage for merit badges or common ritual of symbolic masculine virility.

To understand the success of JPL's digital rhetoric, it is useful to look at another amateur culture, the one associated with astronomy rather than rocketry, which has an even larger presence on the World Wide Web. John Seely Brown has argued that the "Create→Share→Mod" community in amateur astronomy has become "serious enough . . . to interact with the professionals, creating new relationships where both

Figure 10.2
1936 photograph of experiments by founding members of JPL. Courtesy NASA/JPL-Caltech.

are working together and learning from each other."[81] He explains this synergy in more detail in a paper on "New Learning Environments for the 21st Century" that explains how "pro-am" contact between professionals and amateurs is facilitated by crowdsourcing interactions made possible by the web.

From a technical point of view, the situation is even more fascinating when one realizes that multiple telescopes in different locations can simultaneously capture and [transmit] images over the net, thus allowing triangulation to occur. But the real power of the net is as a social, learning milieu. Each local pro-am astronomy group can use the net to post images (open source in yet a new way) and discuss what each is seeing. They can swap techniques and plan joint distributed experiments. Most importantly, they can start to interact with professional astronomers. . . . Clearly, a synergistic interaction between the professional and the pro-amateur is developing in the field of astronomy. Both are helping each other; the whole is more than the sum of the parts. And through these interactions the pro-amateur is becoming a legitimate peripheral participant in the professional practice of astronomy writ large. A learning culture is being created that is mutually beneficial to both.[82]

According to this view, these practices of sharing, swapping, and linking epitomize pro-am dynamic learning situations that should be adopted by schools and pursued by lifelong learners in the broader community as general social practices.

The navigational elements of the JPL website emphasize these pro-am connections very explicitly. For example, although many of the elements on the site involve sophisticated visualizations or 3-D atlases that require the newest updates of Flash, Shockwave, or Java, one can still access old-school text-based telnet windows, where experienced users of JPL's databases can type in command lines to be connected with Ephemeris information from the Horizons program, which has 600 years of astronomical data available about the solar system, going back to 1599 C.E. and projected forward to 2201 C.E. This rich resource provides tabulation of computed positions and velocities of asteroids, comets, moons, and planets that users can watch happen in a flurry of pixels on their computer screens and then scroll through the lines of black-and-white, largely numerical results.[83] According to the Internet Archive, this site has been available on the web to astronomy buffs for over a decade, and it continues to be a heavily trafficked site, despite its low-bandwidth interface. Certainly, for a long time, data visualizations with both "true color" and "false color" images have played a significant role in the rhetorical culture of JPL, even among the scientists themselves,[84] but the continued use of the Ephemeris information shows how raw numerical data can also be an important aspect of the astronomical subculture that JPL addresses online.

There are also home pages for specialized professional audiences, such as the SIM PlanetQuest Astronomers' Site and For Scientists, but these links are easily accessible from the main site for lay people and often connect back to the materials designed for the public at large. Amateur astronomers can check out the Night Sky Network

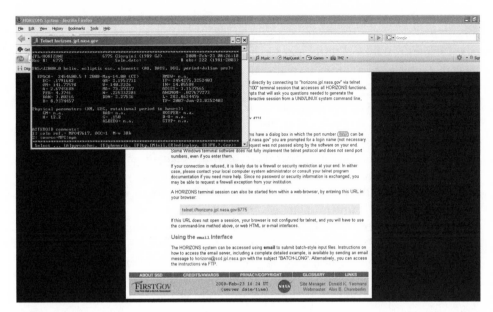

Figure 10.3
Telnet Ephemeris screen connected to JPL website. Courtesy NASA/JPL-Caltech.

and Planet Hunters to get a sense of possible roles in the collective of people searching for new objects of study and more precise information about those physical artifacts in space. They can even watch webcasts of lectures that might be relevant to their interests. There is also an explicit culture of self-improvement promoted by JPL: for years the site has offered illustrated tutorials with animated computer models to prepare astronomy enthusiasts for possible coursework in the field. The site is also full of first-person accounts from JPL employees about how and why they entered the culture of space exploration, which often include information about the JPL engineers' hobbies or personal lives. One of the most popular features about the rover missions presents online video clips with daily flight director reports that review the locations of the vehicles, weather conditions on Mars, and possible mission objectives for the near future, as though the viewer is being briefed as a fellow scientist.

The website shows how both professionals and amateurs are still engaged in the social practices involved in trajectory calculation, signal clarification, and knowledge networking that once appeared to be so central for establishing one's authority as a credible expert during the 1940s, when the new discipline of information science was first established. However, the JPL website seems to have chosen fundamentally different rhetorical strategies, which emphasize richly detailed data visualizations and discourses of sociality between professionals and amateurs. Unlike the popularizing discourses of Bush, Weaver, and Wiener, there are no simplified allegories of "girls," "horses," or "savages" on the JPL pages to illustrate the worldview of contemporary rocket scientists. Moreover, the process of scientific discovery itself is shown to be a collective enterprise rather than a matter of promulgating revolutionary theories from lone geniuses.

Unfortunately, it is far too common for government officials to use digital media to constrain public participation rather than encourage it. As this book has argued, too often policy makers see the Internet as a way to disseminate one-to-many messages for purposes of public relations rather than foster the many-to-many practices associated with deliberation and peer-to-peer civic education that new technologies make possible.[85] However, the plausible explanations for the rise of this form of Realpolitik, in which political constituencies are electronically marginalized rather than empowered, cannot be reduced to simple pronouncements about the stupidity of bureaucratic culture or paranoid conspiracy theories about the government wanting to kill the digital media and communication channels to which it gave birth in the middle of the twentieth century. Instead, I would suggest that lawmakers have understandable anxieties that have to do with the slippery rhetorical character of new genres of electronic communication, which can easily reach new audiences and be used for unintended purposes. As contemporary information culture finds itself in conflict with the traditional principles governing the creation and conservation of knowledge, these anxieties are likely to become more pronounced unless scholars and members of the general public become more interested in political agendas involving digital rights and responsibilities.

Notes

Introduction

1. In a conversation with former student Karla Gutierrez in Santa Monica, California, on May 18, 2008, this suspicion was confirmed. She also pointed out that it was I who had shown the students how easy it was to send messages to each other in this fashion, when I was demonstrating the speed at which the system worked.

2. Kevin McKeown, "Social Norms and Implications of Santa Monica's PEN (Public Electronic Network)," Address to the 99th Annual Convention of the American Psychological Association, San Francisco, August 1991. Available at http://www.mckeown.net/PENaddress.html.

3. Howard Rheingold, "Cities in Cyberspace," in *The Virtual Community: Homesteading on the Electronic Frontier* (Reading, MA: Addison Wesley, 1993), 268–272.

4. One of the first academic interpretations of the PEN experience is by Pamela Varley in "What's Really Happening in Santa Monica," *MIT Technology Review* (November/December 1991). Varley points out the prescience of this program in that the municipality of "Santa Monica is appropriating for public purposes technologies that had previously been mostly the province of businesses and individual computer devotees" (4), while also claiming that such conferences are "vulnerable to abuse" (21) as they are "enabling and empowering" users (27). Howard Rheingold uses Varley's analysis of the PEN system as a "vivid example of the practice" of what exists on the level of theory as "electronic democracy." By citing Rheingold, Mark Poster casts PEN as possible evidence for the argument that "the Internet promotes, even enhances, existing political formations" in *Information Please: Culture and Politics in the Age of Digital Machines* (Durham: Duke University Press, 2006), 79. Poster uses PEN in support of a political model of "The Net as Tool," which his analysis of the construction of a polymorphous "netizen" beyond traditional citizenship is intended to undermine.

5. Pierre Lévy, "Cyberspace, the City, and Electronic Democracy," in *Cyberculture* (Minneapolis: University of Minnesota Press, 2001), 165–177 and Geert Lovink, "Building and Blogging: The Netherlands after Digitization," *Zero Comments* (New York: Routledge, 2008), 99–116.

6. For more about these questions from an artificial intelligence perspective, see Michael Mateas, "Authoring and Expression," presentation at the Software Studies Workshop, University of

California, San Diego, May 21, 2008 on "the relation between code machine and rhetorical machine." Available at http://www.youtube.com/watch?v=XHdRBvHVdWE.

7. Claude Shannon and Warren Weaver, *The Mathematical Theory of Communication* (Urbana: University of Illinois, 1949) and Norbert Wiener, *Cybernetics, Second Edition: Or the Control and Communication in the Animal and the Machine* (Cambridge, MA: MIT Press, 1965).

8. Jane Fountain, *Building the Virtual State: Information Technology and Institutional Change* (Washington, D.C.: Brookings Institute Press, 2001).

9. For statistics about common digital practices in K-12 communities see Henry Jenkins with Katie Clinton, Ravi Purushotma, Alice J. Robison, and Margaret Weigel, "Confronting the Challenges of Participatory Culture: Media Education for the 21st Century," The John D. and Catherine T. MacArthur Foundation Occasional Papers Series, Chicago, November 2006. Available at http://www.digitallearning.macfound.org/atf/cf/%7B7E45C7E0–A3E0–4B89–AC9C -E807E1B0AE4E%7D/JENKINS_WHITE_PAPER.PDF.

10. Peter Lyman, "Information Superhighways, Virtual Communities, and Digital Libraries: Information Society Metaphors as Political Rhetoric," in *Technological Visions: The Hopes and Fears that Shape New Technologies*, ed. Marita Sturken, Douglas Thomas, and Sandra J. Ball-Rokeach (Philadelphia: Temple University Press, 2004), 186–200.

1   Digital Monsters: Show and Tell on Capitol Hill

1. Katherine Shrader, "Pentagon Surfing Thousands of Jihad Sites," *The Associated Press*, May 4 2006, http://hosted.ap.org/dynamic/stories/C/CONGRESS_TERRORISM?SITE=NYROR&SECTION =HOME&TEMPLATE=DEFAULT (accessed May 19, 2006; site now discontinued).

2. The Yahoo story appeared with a photograph at http://news.yahoo.com/s/nm/20060504/ us_nm/security_videogames_dc_4.

3. David Morgan, "Islamists using U.S. video games in youth appeal," *Reuters*, May 3 2006. Available at http://today.reuters.com/news/ArticleNews.aspx?type=topNews&storyID=2006–05 –04T215543Z_01_N04305973_RTRUKOC_0_US-SECURITY-VIDEOGAMES.xml&pageNumber=0 &imageid=&cap=&sz=13&WTModLoc=NewsArt-C1–ArticlePage2.

4. Ibid.

5. David Morgan, "Islamic militants recruit using U.S. video games," *ZDNet*, May 5, 2006, http://news.zdnet.com/2100–1040_22–6068963.html (accessed November 4, 2006; site now discontinued).

6. David Morgan, "Experts: Islamic Militants Customizing Violent Video Games," *Fox News*, May 5, 2006. Available at http://www.foxnews.com/story/0,2933,194416,00.html.

7. Howard Altman, "Web Warriors Track Down, Close Jihadist Internet Sites," *Tampa Tribune*, November 17, 2005. Available at http://www.tampatribune.com/News/MGB24YNJ4GE .html.

8. In actual insurgent video posted on the Internet, the targets are generally lightly armored Humvees from the U.S. armed forces or the civilian automobiles of those assumed to be collaborators with the occupation.

9. julieb, "David Morgan is a horrible writer and should be fired," online posting, May 5, 2006, *Dvorak Uncensored Cage Match Forums*, http://cagematch.dvorak.org/index.php/topic,130.0 .html.

10. Sonic Jihad, "Sonic Jihad: A Day in the Life of a Resistance Fighter," online posting, December 26, 2005, *Planet Battlefield Forums* http://www.forumplanet.com/planetbattlefield/ topic.asp?fid=13670&tid=1806909&p=1.

11. Trey Parker, online posting, May 7, 2006, http://www.treyparker.com.

12. Mahmood, "Terrorists Don't Recruit with Battlefield 2," online posting, May 16, 2006, *GGL Global Gaming*, http://www.ggl.com/news.php?NewsId=3090.

13. See the comments of gamers on the *Planet Battlefield Forums*, which were written in the aftermath of the Reuters story, at http://www.forumplanet.com/planetbattlefield/topic .asp?fid=7419&tid=1888667.

14. "Was Congress Misled by 'Terrorist' Game Video? We Talk to Gamer Who Created the Footage," online posting, May 11, 2006. *Game Politics*, http://gamepolitics.livejournal.com/285129 .html.

15. Lev Manovitch, *The Language of New Media* (Cambridge, MA: MIT Press, 2001), 143.

16. "Was Congress Misled by 'Terrorist' Game Video? We Talk to Gamer Who Created the Footage," online posting, May 11, 2006. *Game Politics*, http://gamepolitics.livejournal.com/285129 .html.

17. "Panel I of the Hearing of the House Select Intelligence Committee, Subject: Terrorist Use of the Internet for Communications," *Federal News Service*, May 4, 2006, 5. Available at http://www .watercoolergames.org/archives/committee_hearing_part_one.doc.

18. Ibid., 9.

19. Ibid., 21.

20. Ibid., 13.

21. Ibid., 21.

22. Ibid., 21.

23. Ibid., 18.

24. Lee Rainie and Bente Kalsnes, "The Commons of the Tragedy: How the Internet was used by millions after the terror attacks to grieve, console, share news, and debate the country's response," *Pew Internet & American Life Project*, October 10, 2001. Available at http://www.pewinternet .org/PPF/r/46/report_display.asp.

25. Paul Ford, "Screenscraping the Senate," online posting, September 1, 2004, *XML.com*, Available at http://www.xml.com/pub/a/2004/09/01/hack-congress.html.

26. "U.S. Congressman Pete Hoekstra: 2nd District of Michigan," http://hoekstra.house.gov/ (accessed November 3, 2006).

27. "The Virtual Office of Congresswoman Jane Harman," http://www.house.gov/harman/ (accessed November 3, 2006).

28. "Congresswoman Anna G. Eshoo—14th Congressional District of California," http://www -eshoo.house.gov/ (accessed November 3, 2006).

29. "Online Office of Congressman Alcee L. Hastings," http://alceehastings.house.gov/ (accessed November 3, 2006).

30. "Congresswoman Heather Wilson," http://wilson.house.gov/ (accessed November 3, 2006).

31. "Representative Thornberry," http://www.house.gov/thornberry/ (accessed November 3, 2006).

32. "Representative Todd Tiahrt—4th Congressional District of Kansas," http://www.house.gov/ tiahrt/ (accessed November 3, 2006).

33. "U.S. Representative Silvestre Reyes," http://www.reyesblog.com (accessed November 3, 2006).

34. "Representative Rush Holt—Homepage," http://holt.house.gov/ (accessed November 3, 2006).

35. "Design Templates," Webcontent.gov, December 14, 2005, http://www.firstgov.gov/ webcontent/usability/templates.shtml.

36. May 4 Hearings 21.

37. Of course, many rhetoricians celebrate the oral turn that the Internet supposedly represents in contemporary culture. Richard Lanham has made much of the new rhetoric that will flourish in the absence of the printed book, Michael Joyce capitalizes on the destabilizing of authorship by new constructs of "voice" in his writing workshops, and other Internet scholars, influenced by the work of Walter Ong, celebrate what they believed to be a new orality that will enrich a culture that has grown anemic without the mythic and epic vitality of shared verbal narratives.

38. Kathleen Welch, *Electric Rhetoric: Classical Rhetoric, Oralism, and the New Literacy* (Cambridge, MA: MIT Press, 1999).

39. "Panel I of the Hearing of the House Select Intelligence Committee, Subject: Terrorist Use of the Internet for Communications," *Federal News Service*, May 4, 2006, 4. Available at http://www .watercoolergames.org/archives/committee_hearing_part_one.doc.

40. See Siva Vaidhyanathan, *The Anarchist in the Library* (New York: Basic Books, 2004).

41. "Panel I of the Hearing of the House Select Intelligence Committee, Subject: Terrorist Use of the Internet for Communications," *Federal News Service*, May 4, 2006, 5. Available at http://www .watercoolergames.org/archives/committee_hearing_part_one.doc.

42. See *Henry IV*, Part 2, I.1 and *The Aeneid* IV, among others.

43. "Panel I of the Hearing of the House Select Intelligence Committee, Subject: Terrorist Use of the Internet for Communications," *Federal News Service*, May 4, 2006, 6. Available at http://www .watercoolergames.org/archives/committee_hearing_part_one.doc.

44. Plato, "Phaedrus," *in Plato*: *Complete* Works, trans. and ed. John M. Cooper (Indianapolis/ Cambridge: Hacket, 1997), 553.

45. Plato also claims that writing fails to function as an aid to memory because it encourages practices of forgetting.

46. "Panel I of the Hearing of the House Select Intelligence Committee, Subject: Terrorist Use of the Internet for Communications," *Federal News Service*, May 4, 2006, 5. Available at http://www .watercoolergames.org/archives/committee_hearing_part_one.doc.

47. Ibid., 8.

48. See the work of Richard Lanham and Steven Mailloux.

49. Plato, "Gorgias," in *Plato: Complete Works,* trans. and ed. John M. Cooper (Indianapolis/ Cambridge: Hacket, 1997), 808–809.

50. Jihadists also have "the power to craft this stuff," according to witnesses from "Panel I of the Hearing of the House Select Intelligence Committee, Subject: Terrorist Use of the Internet for Communications," *Federal News Service*, May 4, 2006, 10. Available at http://www .watercoolergames.org/archives/committee_hearing_part_one.doc.

51. Ibid., 22–23.

52. Samuel P. Huntington, *The Clash of Civilizations?: The Debate* (New York: Foreign Affairs, 1996). See also counterarguments to Huntington from Edward Said, Salman Rushdie, and Slavoj Žižek.

53. "Panel I of the Hearing of the House Select Intelligence Committee, Subject: Terrorist Use of the Internet for Communications," *Federal News Service*, May 4, 2006, 11. Available at http://www .watercoolergames.org/archives/committee_hearing_part_one.doc.

54. Although once stigmatized as information warfare, since the attacks on the World Trade Center the field of public diplomacy has received broad institutional acceptance in all aspects of government. Even legislative challenges to the executive branch, such as S-266, which attempts to strengthen prohibitions against "government funded propaganda," only apply to materials distributed within the United States. There have been a series of designated functionaries serving as Undersecretary of State in charge of public diplomacy efforts, and in the past few years, academic centers devoted to public diplomacy have appeared at research universities, such as Duke and the University of Southern California.

55. Henry Jenkins, *Convergence Culture* (New York: New York University Press, 2006).

56. "Panel I of the Hearing of the House Select Intelligence Committee, Subject: Terrorist Use of the Internet for Communications," *Federal News Service*, May 4, 2006, 9. Available at http://www .watercoolergames.org/archives/committee_hearing_part_one.doc.

57. Ibid., 23.

58. See Benjamin Wallace-Wells, "Private Jihad: How Rita Katz got into the spying business," *The New Yorker* (May 29, 2006). Available at http://www.newyorker.com/archive/2006/05/29/ 060529fa_fact. See also Robert F. Worth, "Mideast Analysis, Fast and Furious," *The New York Times*, June 18, 2006.

59. "In Their Own Words: Reading the Iraqi Insurgency," *International Crisis Group*, February 15, 2006. Available at http://www.crisisgroup.org/home/index.cfm?id=3953&l=1.

60. The Reuters story was also picked up by the Air Education and Training Command news service. See the June news stories at Air University at http://www.au.af.mil/au/aunews/ generalJune06/VideoGames.html (accessed June 15, 2006; website now discontinued).

61. "Panel I of the Hearing of the House Select Intelligence Committee, Subject: Terrorist Use of the Internet for Communications," *Federal News Service*, May 4, 2006, 15. Available at http://www .watercoolergames.org/archives/committee_hearing_part_one.doc.

62. Open Source Center, July 27, 2006, http://www.opensource.gov (accessed October 1, 2006). Certainly, many would consider "Open Source Center" a misnomer, given that "open source," as a software development term, is often associated with transparent communication and a participatory nonhierarchical model of cultural production that has been symbolized by Eric Raymond as more "bazaar" than "cathedral." See Eric Raymond, *The Cathedral and the Bazaar: Musings on Linux and Open Source* (Cambridge, MA: O'Reilly, 2001).

63. Terry Gudaitis, "Investigations: Using Internet Data Sets for Profiling," Technosecurity Conference, June 2006. Available at http://www.techsec.com/TS-2006–PDF/TechnoSecurity%202006 –SAIC.pdf.

64. Yet, in the "History & Timeline" section, inquisitive visitors can learn that the company was founded in 1969 by a physicist from the Los Alamos national laboratory with "no grandiose plan," who launched his company in the space next door to a ballet studio in La Jolla, California and emphasized improvisation and informality in his corporate practices. See "History & Timeline," http://www.saic.com/about/history.html and Donald L. Barlett and James B. Steele, "Washington's $8 Billion Shadow," *Vanity Fair* (March 2007). Available at http://www.vanityfair .com/politics/features/2007/03/spyagency200703 for more about SAIC.

65. Dated March 31, 2006.

66. "Panel I of the Hearing of the House Select Intelligence Committee, Subject: Terrorist Use of the Internet for Communications," *Federal News Service*, May 4, 2006, 21. Available at http://www .watercoolergames.org/archives/committee_hearing_part_one.doc.

67. Gonzalo Frasca, "Extra! Reuters Using News Story to Manipulate Readers," online posting, May 5, 2006, *Water Cooler Games*, http://www.watercoolergames.org/archives/000526 .shtml.

68. Wagner James, "Weapons of Mass Distraction," *Salon*, October 4, 2002. Available at http://dir .salon.com/story/tech/feature/2002/10/04/why_we_fight/index.html.

69. "Panel I of the Hearing of the House Select Intelligence Committee, Subject: Terrorist Use of the Internet for Communications," *Federal News Service*, May 4, 2006, 18. Available at http://www .watercoolergames.org/archives/committee_hearing_part_one.doc.

70. See Albert-László Barabási, *Linked: The New Science of Networks* (Cambridge, MA: Perseus, 2002) on the vulnerability of computer networks with large hubs.

71. "Panel I of the Hearing of the House Select Intelligence Committee, Subject: Terrorist Use of the Internet for Communications," *Federal News Service*, May 4, 2006, 18. Available at http://www .watercoolergames.org/archives/committee_hearing_part_one.doc.

72. Ibid., 20.

73. "Dutch gamer's clash with U.S. government," *Reuters*, May 24, 2006, http://news.cnet.com/ Dutch-gamers-clash-with-U.S.-government/2100-1043_3-6076255.html (accessed June 15, 2006; site now discontinued).

74. Ibid.

75. Jake Tapper and Audrey Taylor, "Terrorist Video Game or Pentagon Snafu?" *ABC News Nightline*, June 21, 2006. Available at http://abcnews.go.com/Nightline/Technology/ story?id=2105128&page=1. The online edition of *Nightline* is itself an interesting way to see how already hybridized television "news magazine" shows are being repurposed in online environments for digital feeds, podcasts, and other devices for both stationary and mobile computing

76. "Terrorist Videogame?" *Nightline Online* video, June 21, 2006. Available at http://abcnews .go.com/Video/playerIndex?id=2105341.

77. Ian Bogost, *Persuasive Games: Videogames and Procedural Rhetoric* (Cambridge: MIT Press, 2007).

78. "Terrorist Videogame?" *Nightline Online* video, June 21, 2006. Available at http://abcnews .go.com/Video/playerIndex?id=2105341.

79. Tapper and Taylor.

80. "Terrorist Videogame?" *Nightline Online* video, June 21, 2006. Available at http://abcnews .go.com/Video/playerIndex?id=2105341.

81. The use of the term "advertisement," as in "advertisement for terrorism," occurs several times during the ABC *Nightline* broadcast. For more on genuine "advergames," see the work of Ian Bogost.

82. James Paul Gee, *What Videogames Have to Teach Us about Learning and Literacy* (New York: Palgrave MacMillan, 2003), 141.

83. "Panel I of the Hearing of the House Select Intelligence Committee, Subject: Terrorist Use of the Internet for Communications," *Federal News Service*, May 4, 2006, 12. Available at http://www .watercoolergames.org/archives/committee_hearing_part_one.doc.

84. Ibid., 11.

85. This urge to protect children from objectionable media content is an important theme. Unfortunately, as I will explain, this interest in the well-being of schoolchildren rarely extends to any serious commitment to improving their education in information and media literacy, which I will argue is a perhaps a more serious threat to democratic institutions. A survey of kids' pages on government websites will illustrate my point that children are not taken seriously as consumers of public information.

86. See House Resolution 376. Available at http://frwebgate.access.gpo.gov/cgi-bin/getdoc .cgi?dbname=109_cong_bills&docid=f:hr376eh.txt.pdf.

87. "Family Friendly Internet." Available at http://clinton5.nara.gov/textonly/WH/New/ Ratings/.

88. Children's Online Privacy Protection Act of 1998. Available at http://www.ftc.gov/ogc/ coppa1.htm.

89. For more about the "cyberporn panic of 1996" and how it prefigures current legislation aimed at social network sites, see Alice Marwick, "To Catch a Predator: The MySpace Moral Panic," *First Monday* 13, no. 6 (June 2, 2008). Available at http://www.uic.edu/htbin/cgiwrap/bin/ojs/index .php/fm/article/view/2152/1966.

90. Plato, *Republic*, trans. G.M.A. Grube (Indianapolis: Hackett, 1992), 277.

91. Twelve-year-old Danielle Shimotakahara testified before Congress in 2000 against the presence of violent videogames in public places. See http://commerce.senate.gov/hearings/0321shi .pdf (accessed July 1, 2006, site now discontinued).

92. A witness in a second, earlier hearing, Justin Berry, who was profiled in the *New York Times*, also had a father involved in his sexual exploitation via Internet webcam.

93. Testimony Submitted by Masha Allen, http://energycommerce.house.gov/108/Hearings/ 05032006hearing1852/Allen.pdf (accessed October 1, 2006; site now discontinued), 4.

94. Ibid.

95. Law involving the testimony of juveniles in sexual abuse cases that use digital technology has a complicated legal history. See Supreme Court decisions, such as *Coy v. Iowa* and *Maryland v. Craig* about the confrontation clause, the role of *res gestae*, and established thresholds for the admissibility of videotaped or close circuit testimony. To be a witness in the tradition of English Common Law, it is not enough to have seen a crime, you must also bear witness and in turn be seen by the accused, given the Constitutional right of confrontation. Justice Antonin Scalia, in dissent, wrote that he was "persuaded . . . that the Maryland procedure is virtually constitutional. Since it is not, however, actually constitutional I would affirm the judgment of the Maryland Court of Appeals reversing the judgment of conviction." The use of "virtual" constitutionality in Scalia's discourse will also be important for forms of digital evidence discussed elsewhere.

96. Testimony Submitted by Masha Allen, http://energycommerce.house.gov/108/Hearings/ 05032006hearing1852/Allen.pdf (accessed October 1, 2006; site now discontinued), 1.

97. Ibid., 2.

98. Ibid., 2.

99. Ibid., 2.

100. Ibid., 4. Allen was also known as the "Disney World Girl," because photographs were distributed to the media of a room in which some of the abuse took place although she was digitally removed from the image.

101. "Gingrey testifies on legislation to deter child pornography," Congressman Phil Gingrey, M.D. website, online posting, May 2, 2006, http://gingrey.house.gov/News/DocumentSingle .aspx?DocumentID=4300.

102. "Kerry, Isakson Push for Tougher Penalties For Child Internet Pornography," Welcome to Senator John Kerry's Online Office, online posting, January 6, 2006, http://kerry.senate.gov/v3/ cfm/record.cfm?id=250302.

103. Testimony Submitted by Masha Allen, http://energycommerce.house.gov/108/Hearings/ 05032006hearing1852/Allen.pdf (accessed October 1, 2006; site now discontinued), 3–4.

104. Sarah Banet-Weiser, "Surfin' the Net: Children, Parental Obsolescence, and Citizenship," in *Technological Visions: The Hopes and Fears that Shape New Technologies*, ed. Marita Sturken, Douglas Thomas, and Sandra Ball-Rokeach (Philadelphia: Temple University Press, 2004), 270–292.

105. Testimony Submitted by Masha Allen, http://energycommerce.house.gov/108/Hearings/ 05032006hearing1852/Allen.pdf (accessed October 1, 2006; site now discontinued), 3–4.

106. Elizabeth Mehren, "Sex Offender Site Back Up," *Los Angeles Times*, April 19, 2006. Available at http://www.latimes.com/news/nationworld/nation/la-na-maine19apr19,1,1485753 .story?coll=la-headlines-nation.

107. See the federal site at http://www.nsopr.gov/ and state sites at http://www.meganslaw.ca .gov/ and http://sor.informe.org/sor/.

108. Another law that limits the rights of children while claiming to regulate those who exploit them is the Deleting Online Predators Act, requiring schools and libraries to bar access to social networking sites and chatrooms. It passed the House by a landslide despite the protests of distance learning experts. See Henry Jenkins and danah boyd, "Discussion: MySpace and Deleting Online Predators Act," (*MIT Tech Talk*, May 26, 2006, http://www.danah.org/papers/ MySpaceDOPA.html) for discussion of this legislation geared to parents and other laypeople.

109. See the studies cited by Siva Vaidhyanathan in "The Assault on Mixed CDs," *Sivacracy*, August 10, 2006. Available at http://www.nyu.edu/classes/siva/archives/003393.html.

110. David Kay, specialist in computer law and intellectual property law, University of California-Irvine, conversation with the author, June 2, 2006.

111. Alberto Gonzales, "Prepared Remarks at the National Missing Children's Day Award Ceremony," May 25, 2006. Available at http://www.usdoj.gov/ag/speeches/2006/ag_speech_060525 .html (accessed July 15, 2006; site now discontinued).

112. Tarleton Gillespie, "Characterizing Copyright in the Clasroom: The Cultural Work of Anti-Piracy Campaigns," unpublished manuscript, Top Three Paper award by theCommunication, Law, and Policy division of ICA, 2008.

113. Siva Vaidhyanathan, *The Anarchist in the Library: How the Clash between Freedom and Control is Hacking the Real World and Crashing the System* (New York: Basic Books, 2004), 63.

114. "Innocent Images National Initiative," Federal Bureau of Investigation. Available at http:// www.fbi.gov/innocent.htm.

115. Statement of Alice S. Fisher, Assistant Attorney General, Criminal Division, before the Committee on Energy and Commerce, May 3, 2006. Available at http://www.usdoj.gov/criminal/ceos/ AAG%20Testimony%205032006.pdf.

116. Donna Haraway, "The Promises of Monsters: A Regenerative Politics of Inappropriate/d Others," in *Cultural Studies*, ed. Lawrence Grossberg, Cary Nelson, and Paula A. Treichler (New York; Routledge, 1992), 295–337.

117. Ibid., 296.

118. For example, in one case, the President of the United States holds a videoconference with officials about a hurricane in New Orleans, and in another, he confers with his cabinet via video feed during a surprise visit to a war zone in Iraq.

119. "Remarks by the President on the USA Patriot Act," *The White House*, April 20, 2004. Available at http://www.whitehouse.gov/news/releases/2004/04/20040420–3.html.

120. Testimony   of   Masha   Allen,   http://energycommerce.house.gov/108/Hearings/ 05032006hearing1852/Allen.pdf (accessed October 1, 2006; site now discontinued).

121. "Innocent Images National Initiative," Federal Bureau of Investigation website. Available at http://www.fbi.gov/publications/innocent.htm.

2   Hacking Aristotle: What Is Digital Rhetoric?

1. Nancy Kaplan, "Literacy Beyond Books," in *The World Wide Web and Contemporary Cultural Theory*, ed. Andrew Herman and Thomas Swiss (New York: Routledge, 2000), 232.

2. Michel de Certeau, *The Practice of Everyday Life*, trans. Steven Rendall (Berkeley: University of California Press, 1984), 39.

3. Ibid., 39.

4. Ibid., 43.

5. Nancy Kaplan, "Literacy Beyond Books," in *The World Wide Web and Contemporary Cultural Theory*, ed. Andrew Herman and Thomas Swiss (New York: Routledge, 2000), 232.

6. The classic work on the function of the coffee house as a political public sphere is Jürgen Habermas's *The Structural Transformation of the Public Sphere*, trans. Thomas Burger (Cambridge, MA: MIT Press, 1991). See also Siva Vaidhyanathan, "The Anarchist in the Coffee House: A Brief Consideration of Local Culture, the Free Culture Movement, and Prospects for a Global Public Sphere," August 2005, http://papers.ssrn.com/sol3/papers.cfm?abstract_id=791507. In *The Invention of the Restaurant* (Cambridge, MA: Harvard University Press, 2000), Rebecca L. Spang argues that a new culture of privacy and individual commerce was important, and yet she also posits that it served as an important rhetorical site for the cultivation of public taste both literally and figuratively.

7. See Andrea Lunsford and John Ruszkiewicz, *Everything's an Argument*, second edition (Boston: Bedford/St. Martin's, 2001) for a defense of the Aristotelian view.

8. "Kairos," The Perseus Project. Available at http://www.perseus.tufts.edu/cgi-bin/ptext?layout .reflang=greek;layout.refembed=2;layout.refwordcount=1;layout.refdoc=Perseus%3Atext%3A199 9.01.0059;layout.reflookup=kairo%2Fn;layout.refcit=book%3D1%3Achapter%3D4%3Asection% 3D4;doc=Perseus%3Atext%3A1999.04.0057%3Aentry%3D%2352036;layout.refabo=Perseus%3A abo%3Atlg%2C0086%2C038 (accessed August 17, 2006). This entry is based on Henry George Liddell and Robert Scott, *A Greek-English Lexicon* (Oxford: Clarendon Press, 1940).

9. See also Carolyn Miller, "*Kairos* in the rhetoric of science," in *Rhetoric of Doing: Essays on Written Discourse in Honor of James L. Kinneavy*, ed. S. P. Witte, N. Nakadate, and R. D. Cherry (Carbondale, IL: Southern Illinois University Press, 1992) and Patricia Bizzell and Bruce Herzberg, *The Rhetorical Tradition: Reading from Classical Times to the Present* (Boston: Bedford/St. Martin's, 1995), 25.

10. Michel de Certeau, *The Practice of Everyday Life*, trans. Steven Rendall (Berkeley: University of California Press, 1984), 43. See Marcel Detienne and Jean-Pierre Vernant, *Cunning Intelligence in Greek Culture and Society*, trans. Janet Lloyd (Chicago: University of Chicago Press, 1991) for de Certeau's source.

11. Michel de Certeau, *The Practice of Everyday Life*, trans. Steven Rendall (Berkeley: University of California Press, 1984), 39.

12. "Meet James Oakley," http://jamesoakley.blogspot.com/.

13. Ibid.

14. Janet Kornblum, "Mourners pay respects to websites of the dead," *USA Today*, May 10, 2006. Available at http://chronicle-tribune.gns.gannettonline.com/apps/pbcs.dll/article?AID= /20060518/TECH01/602150618/1006.

15. Ian Urbina, "Sites Invite Online Mourning, But Don't Speak Ill of the Dead," *New York Times*, November 5, 2006. Available at http://www.nytimes.com/2006/11/05/us/05memorial .html?ref=technology.

16. Valerie Photos. Available at http://www.coolstudios.com/val/.

17. The Daniel Medina Legal Defense Fund, http://www.freemedina.com/ (accessed November 15, 2006; site now discontinued)

18. Amy Ozols, Brian Kenward, and Tyler Chapman, online posting, Former Friends listserv, October 6, 2006.

19. I am construing the word "text" very broadly to include images, sounds, animations, and the like.

20. Richard Lanham, "Digital Rhetoric: Theory, Practice, Property," in *Literacy Online: The Promise (and Peril) of Reading and Writing with Computers*, ed. Myron C. Turman (Pittsburgh: University of Pittsburgh Press, 1992), 221-243

21. A particular area of concern for researchers is how traditional print literacy relates to digital literacy or literacy inside a school setting relates to literacy outside it. For example, the relationship of literacy histories of college students to their digital composing practices is being examined in a large-scale longitudinal study of Stanford undergraduates by Andrea Lunsford, in which students assemble multimedia portfolios in an online database for researchers to examine.

22. For a reading of virtuoso performances around writing code see Michael Mateas and Nick Montfort, "A Box Darkly: Obfuscation, Weird Languages, and Code Aesthetics," in *Proceedings of the Digital Arts and Culture Conference 2006—Digital Experience: Design, Aesthetics, Practice* (Copenhagen, Denmark: IT University of Copenhagen, 2005), 144–153.

23. See, for example, the work of Edward Tufte and Ellen Lupton in this area.

24. Patrick J. Lynch and Sarah Horton, *Web Style Guide: Basic Design Principles for Creating Websites* (New Haven, CT: Yale University Press, 1999).

25. See, for example, Janet M. Lauer, *Invention in Rhetoric and Composition* (Parlor Press and the WAC Clearinghouse, 2004); Mary Minock, "Toward a Postmodern Pedagogy of Imitation," *Journal of Advanced Composition* 15, no. 3 (Fall 1995): 489–510; Penelope Starkey, "Imitatio Redux," *College Composition and Communication* 25 (1974): 435–437; Joel Weinsheimer, *Imitation* (Boston: Routledge & Kegan Paul, 1984).

26. David Kay, "What's Wrong," http://www.ics.uci.edu/%7Ekay/courses/139w/whatswrong.html.

27. "World's Worst Website," http://www.angelfire.com/super/badwebs/.

28. See also Vincent Flanders, "Web Pages That Suck," http://www.webpagesthatsuck.com/, which targets bad web design in the corporate world and academia.

29. Mina P. Shaughnessy, *Errors and Expectations* (New York: Oxford University Press, 1977).

30. See Clark Kerr, *The Uses of the University* (Cambridge, MA: Harvard University Press, 2001).

31. For more about competing interests in university web design, see Elizabeth Losh, "Virtualpolitik: Obstacles to Building Virtual Communities in Traditional Institutions of Knowledge," *Center for Studies in Higher Education* Paper CSHE-9–05, June 1, 2005. Available at http://repositories.cdlib.org/cshe/CSHE-9-05/. For an even greater range of web styles, see also the advice on designing personal university websites from Julia Lupton and Ellen Lupton, "Design Your Life: Media and Technology at Home and Work," workshop presented at Humanitech, University of California-Irvine, March 13, 2006.

32. See http://eee.uci.edu/programs/humcore/students and http://eee.uci.edu/programs/spider respectively.

33. See, for example, Aristotle on the difference between audiences in a democracy and audiences in a monarchy, young and old audiences, etc. in the *Rhetoric*.

34. For early work on narrowcasting, see Alvin Toffler, *The Third Wave* (New York: William Morrow, 1980).

35. For a more complete history, see Gail Hawisher, Paul LeBlanc, Charles Moran, and Cynthia Selfe, *Computers and the Teaching of Writing in American Higher Education, 1979–1994: A History* (Stamford, CT: Ablex, 1996).

36. For an early example of how composition instructors used materials produced by literary and linguistic computing projects, see Ellen Strenski and Nancy Giller Esposito, "The Poet, the Computer, and the Classroom," *College English* 42, no. 2 (October 1980): 142–150.

37. "Tenure and Promotion Cases for Composition Faculty Who Work with Technology," http://www.hu.mtu.edu/%7Ecyselfe/P&TStuff/P&TWeb/Introduction, presented data on this subject from a Conference on College Composition and Communication-sponsored study.

38. Conference on College Composition and Communication Position, "Statement on Teaching, Learning, and Assessing Writing in Digital Environments." Available at http://www.ncte.org/groups/cccc/featuredinfo/115775.htm.

39. Gail Hawisher and Charles Moran, "Electronic mail and the writing instructor," *College English* 55, no. 6 (October 1993): 627–43.

40. See also Jeffrey Weinstock, "Respond Now! E-mail, Acceleration, and a Pedagogy of Patience," *Pedagogy* 4, no. 3 (Fall 2004): 365–383.

41. For another Bahktinian reading see James P. Zappen, Laura J. Gurak, and Stephen Doheny-Farina, "Rhetoric, Community, and Cyberspace," *Rhetoric Review* 15, no. 2. (Spring 1997): 400–419.

42. Michael Spooner and Kathleen Yancey, "Postings on a Genre of Email," *College Composition and Communication* 47, no. 2 (May 1996): 252–278.

43. Ibid., 259.

44. Ibid., 265.

45. Ellen Strenski, "The Electronic Hybridity of E-mail: Liminal Subject Formation through Epistolary Gift Exchange," *The Rhetorical Dimensions of Cyberspace*, http://wac.colostate.edu/rhetnet/rdc/.

46. To see even more of the range of pedagogical approaches to digital rhetoric, see also Cynthia Selfe and Susan Hilligoss, eds., *Literacy and Computers* (New York: MLA, 1994); Gail Hawisher and Paul LeBlanc, eds., *Re-imagining Computers and Composition: Teaching and Research in the Virtual Age* (Portsmouth, NH: Heinemann, 1992); Cynthia L. Selfe and Gail E. Hawisher, *Literate Lives in the Information Age* (Mahwah, N.J.: Lawrence Erlbaum, 2004); and James A. Inman, *Computers and Writing: The Cyborg Era* (Mahwah, NJ: Lawrence Erlbaum, 2004).

47. Janet Murray, *Hamlet on the Holodeck* (Cambridge, MA: MIT Press, 1997).

48. Steven Mailloux, "Paul as Hermes, Picard as Darmok: First Contact, Ethnocentrism, and Rhetorical Hermeneutics," The William and Sarah H. Brownlee Memorial Lecture Series, Institute for Antiquity and Christianity, Claremont Graduate University, April 23, 1998.

49. Janet Murray, *Hamlet on the Holodeck* (Cambridge, MA: MIT Press, 1997), 204.

50. Murray's work on narrative became a central issue in the "ludology" versus "narratology" debate that raged in game studies for many years. See her 2005 DIGRA address "The Last Word on Ludology versus Narratology" for her attempt to put the conflict to rest. Janet Murray, "The Last Word on Ludology v. Narratology in Game Studies," Address given at DIGRA 2005, June 17, 2005, Vancouver, Canada. Available at http://www.lcc.gatech.edu/~murray/digra05/lastword.pdf.

51. Murray, *Hamlet on the Holodeck*, 9.

52. James Paul Gee, *What Video Games Have to Teach Us about Language and Literacy* (New York: Palgrave Macmillan, 2003).

53. Manuel Castells, *The Rise of the Network Society* (Oxford: Blackwell, 1996), 402.

54. danah boyd, "A Discussion with danah boyd," September 14, 2006, University of North Carolina, Chapel Hill. Available at http://mirrors.ibiblio.org/pub/mirrors/speakers/boyd/boyd _talk.mp4.

55. Tracy Mitrano, "Thoughts on Facebook," Cornell University Office of Information Technologies, July 23, 2006. Available at http://www.cit.cornell.edu/policy/memos/facebook .html.

56. ABC News, "Exclusive: The Sexually Explicit Internet Messages That Led to Fla. Rep. Foley's Resignation," September 29, 2006. Available at http://blogs.abcnews.com/theblotter/2006/09/ exclusive_the_s.html and http://abcnews.go.com/images/WNT/02–02–03b.pdf.

57. Frank Rich, "2006: The Year of the 'Macaca,'" *New York Times*, November 12, 2006. Available at http://select.nytimes.com/2006/11/12/opinion/12rich.html.

58. Robert Salladay, "Gov.'s Candid Moments Caught on Audiotape," *Los Angeles Times*, September 8, 2006. Available at http://articles.latimes.com/2006/sep/08/local/me-meeting8.

59. Frank Rich, "It Takes a Potemkin Village," *New York Times*, December 11, 2005. Available at http://select.nytimes.com/2005/12/11/opinion/11rich.html.

60. "Panel Still Waiting for Hurricane Katrina Papers," *New York Times*, November 3, 2005. Available at http://www.nytimes.com/2005/11/03/politics/03response.html.

61. Robert Plummer, "U.S. Powerless to halt Iraq net images," BBC News, May 28, 2004. Available at http://news.bbc.co.uk/2/hi/americas/3695897.stm.

62. See also Wally Olins, *Corporate Identity: Making Business Strategy Visible through Design*. (London: Thames and Hudson, 1989).

63. Charlotte Beers, "Transcript: Charlotte Beers and Richard Boucher at the Foreign Press Center on November 9, 2001," U.S. Deparment of State: International Information Programs, November 14 2001. Available at http://208.243.114.93/usa/islam/t111401.htm (accessed June 15, 2002; site now discontinued).

64. Ibid.

65. Wally Olins, *The Corporate Personality: An Inquiry into the Nature of Corporate Identity* (London: Design Council, 1978).

66. See Naomi Klein, *No Logo* (New York: Picador, 1999).

67. See the copyright disclaimer on the website of the Central Intelligence Agency at https://www.cia.gov/cia/notices.html#copy, as of October 10, 2006, for evidence of how a relatively broadly construed notion of the "public domain" may be limited if the government itself uses copyrighted images, graphics, or text in official reports. As government agencies use more content from image banks, this potential problem of materials restricted by anticopying law may become more acute.

68. United States Code Title 18, Section 713. Available at http://caselaw.lp.findlaw.com/casecode/uscodes/18/parts/i/chapters/33/sections/section_713.html.

69. See Siva Vaidhyanathan, "Is Fair Use Fair or Useful?" Originality, Imitation & Plagiarism Conference, Sweetland Writing Center, University of Michigan, September 24, 2005, on why the parody exception itself may not adequately address the interests of preserving free speech or fostering creative cultural expressions.

70. "Cheney protests whitehouse.org parody," http://www.chillingeffects.org/notice.cgi?NoticeID=578 (accessed November 15, 2006).

71. For example, see David S. Birdsell and Leo Groarke, "Toward a Theory of Visual Argument," and J. Anthony Blair, "The Possibility and Actuality of Visual Arguments" in *Visual Rhetoric in a Digital World: A Critical Sourcebook*, ed. Carolyn Handa (New York: Bedford/St. Martins, 2004).

72. David Fleming, "Can Pictures Be Arguments?" *Argumentation and Advocacy* 33, no. 1 (1996): 11–22.

73. See Walter Benjamin, "The Work of Art in the Age of Mechanical Production," in *Illuminations: Essays and Reflections*, ed. Hannah Arendt, trans. Harry Zohn (New York: Schocken, 1969), 217–251.

74. Letter to Dr. Michael Stebbins from William H. Anderson of the Department of Homeland Security, August 1, 2006. Available at http://www.fas.org/reallyready/dhsletter.pdf.

75. Ibid.

76. Richard Lanham, *The Economics of Attention: Style and Substance in the Age of Information* (Chicago: University of Chicago Press, 2006).

77. See also the launching of the Creative Commons in 2001, under the leadership of Lawrence Lessig to encourage media-sharing to foster creativity, education, and communal culture.

78. David Bollier, "Reclaiming the Commons," *Boston Review* (Summer 2002). Available at http://www.bostonreview.net/BR27.3/bollier.html.

79. Garrett Hardin, "The Tragedy of the Commons," *Science* 162 (1968): 1243–1248. Although Hardin claims that there is "no technical solution," the "commons dilemma" is often taught in computer science classes.

80. Although Bollier's examples largely concern branding in relation to children, he also discusses how it reduces the access to the commons of adults, as in the case of brand-name prescription drugs.

81. Wally Olins, "Making a National Brand," in *The New Public Diplomacy: Soft Power in International Relations*, ed. Jan Melissen (New York: Palgrave Macmillan, 2005), 169–179.

82. See, for example, the use of water bottles or children's cartoons by the Lincoln Group, *Source Watch*, December 4, 2005, http://www.sourcewatch.org/index.php?title=Lincoln_Group_Case_Studies.

83. "What is Public Diplomacy," USC Center for Public Diplomacy, http://uscpublicdiplomacy .org/index.php/about/whatis_pd (accessed November 1, 2006).

84. Ibid.

85. Ibid.

86. See James Bamford, "The Man Who Sold the War," *Rolling Stone* (November 17, 2005). Available at http://www.rollingstone.com/politics/story/8798997/the_man_who_sold_the_war/. See also Ken Silverstein, "Selling the Afghan War," *The Nation* (November 7, 2001) Available at, http://www.thenation.com/doc/20011119/silverstein20011107.

87. Willem Marx, "Misinformation Intern: My Summer as a Military Propagandist in Iraq," *Harper's Magazine* (September 2006): 51–59. Available at http://harpers.org/archive/2006/09/0081195.

88. Anthony Pratkanis, "Centers of Gravity in Influence Campaigns: A Social Influence Analysis," the USC Center on Public Diplomacy, September 13, 2006. Available at http://uscpublicdiplomacy.com/pdfs/060913_pratkanis.pdf.

89. Based on the fact that he was an expert witness testifying on behalf of raising alarm on the Y2K crisis that never happened, of course, Pratkanis's own credulity may invite interrogation. See http://currents.ucsc.edu/99–00/10–18/pratkanis.html.

90. Anthony Pratkanis and Elliot Aronson, "Age of Propaganda," in *The Age of Propaganda: The Everyday Use and Abuse of Persuasion* (New York: W. H. Freeman, 2001), 1–20.

91. Social marketing educator Nedra Weinreich has been careful to differentiate social marketing from what she calls "social media marketing." The latter may call itself "social marketing" because it uses social networking sites and other venues for informal sociality to market traditional consumer products.

92. Alan R. Andreasen, *Marketing Social Change: Changing Behavior to Promote Health, Social Development, and the Environment* (San Francisco: Jossy-Bass, 1995).

93. Ken Smith, *Mental Hygiene: Classroom Films 1945–1970* (New York: Blast Books, 1999).

94. See Andreasen, *Marketing Social Change* on the difference between the social marketing appeal and "the education approach," 9–11.

95. This circulation can be complicated, particular in transnational or global contexts. See Roddey Reid, *Globalizing Tobacco Control: Anti-smoking Campaigns in California, France, and Japan* (Bloomington, IN: Indiana University Press, 2005).

96. See information about the National Social Norms Institute at the University of Virginia. Available at http://sev.prnewswire.com/beer-wine-spirits/20060921/CGTH02421092006–1.html, via the Social Norms Center online at http://www.socialnorms.org.

97. See Nedra Weinreich, "Why Can't Social Marketers Sustain a Professional Organization," *Spare Change*, July 11, 2006. Available at http://www.social-marketing.com/blog/2006/07/why-cant-social-marketers-sustain.html.

98. Samantha King, *Pink Ribbons, Inc.: Breast Cancer and the Politics of Philanthropy* (Minneapolis, MN: University of Minnesota Press, 2006).

99. See Elizabeth Losh, "Social Marketing, Public Rhetoric, and the Branding of a Disease," talk given to Selling Us to Ourselves, Is Social Marketing Effective HIV Prevention? Panel, CHAMP Community HIV/AIDS Mobilization Project, New York City, September 26, 2006.

100. See, for example, the HIV "Have You Been Hit" campaign in Philadelphia for a case in which grassroots organizers appear to have helped pull an objectionable campaign that objectified black gay males by literally depicting them in the crosshairs of a gun sight.

101. Should the current reductio ad absurdum come to this, it is conceivable that the "debate" between artificially opposed "national security" and "civil liberties" positions could denigrate to the level of competing political products.

102. Seth Stevenson, "In Cold Blood: A Nasty New Public Service Announcement from the American Red Cross," *Slate*, January 16, 2006. Available at http://www.slate.com/id/2134294/.

103. Tom Ridge, "Transcript of Secretary of Homeland Security Tom Ridge at the Launch of New Ready Campaign Public Service Advertisements," November 27, 2004, http://www.dhs.gov/dhspublic/display?content=4152 3891 (accessed October 15, 2006; site now discontinued).

104. Department of Homeland Security, http://www.dhs.gov/dhspublic/display?theme=11 &content=3891 (accessed October 15, 2006; site now discontinued).

105. "Risk Communication Defined," U.S. Department of Veterans' Affairs, http://www.va.gov/wriisc-dc/risk/definition.asp.

106. "HIV/AIDS Transmission," Visual Culture and Public Health Posters, National Library of Medicine online exhibit. Available at http://www.nlm.nih.gov/exhibition/visualculture/hivaidstransmission.html.

107. Peter Sandman, "Risk Communication and the War against Terrorism," November 2001. Available at http://www.psandman.com/col/9–11.htm.

108. Peter Sandman, "When People Are 'Over-reacting' to Risk" February 2004. Available at http://www.psandman.com/col/over-re.htm.

109. Aristotle, *On Rhetoric: A Theory of Civic Discourse*, trans. George A. Kennedy (New York: Oxford University Press USA, 2006), 130.

110. Edward R. Tufte, *Visual Explanations* (Cheshire, CT: Graphics Press, 1997), 27–53.

111. Edward R. Tufte, "PowerPoint Does Rocket Science—and Better Techniques for Technical Reports," online posting, September 6, 2005, *Ask E.T.* online forum, http://www.edwardtufte .com/bboard/q-and-a-fetch-msg?msg_id=0001yB&topic_id=1&topic=Ask+E%2eT%2e.

112. "How to Lead during Bioattacks with the Public's Trust and Help: A Manual for Mayors, Governors, and Top Health Officials," Center for Biosecurity, University of Pittsburgh Medical Center. Available at http://www.upmc-biosecurity.org/website/resources/leadership/index.html.

113. United States Federal Civil Defense Administration, *Duck and Cover* (filmstrip), Prod. Archer Productions, Inc., 1951. See also the films of the 1950s and 1960s in the 1982 documentary *Atomic Cafe*.

114. Brian Massumi, "Fear (The Spectrum Said)," *Multitudes Web*, January 4, 2006. Available at http://multitudes.samizdat.net/Fear-The-spectrum-said.html.

115. Spoof, *CODEPINK4Peace*, http://www.codepink4peace.org/downloads/codepinkpeaceSPOOF .pdf htm.

116. "Democracy Threat Alert System—Terror Alert Parody, *Political Humor About.com*, http:// politicalhumor.about.com/library/images/bldemocracythreat.htm.

117. "Terror Alert Level," *geek and proud*, http://www.geekandproud.net/terror/.

118. "Liberal Terror Alert System—Terror Alert Parody," *Political Humor About.com*, http:// politicalhumor.about.com/library/images/blpic-liberalterroralert.htm.

119. Steve Anderson, "Abuse of Power," 2006, http://ia301217.us.archive.org/1/items/ Abuseofpower/AbuseofPower.mov.

120. "New Al Qaeda Tape: Personal Injury Lawyer Zawihiri Vows to fight . . . FOR YOU," American Comedy Network, http://www.americancomedynetwork.com/.

121. Elizabeth Losh, "Boxing Day," online posting, December 30, 2005, *Virtualpolitik*, http:// virtualpolitik.blogspot.com/2005/12/boxing-day.html.

122. Julia Lupton, "Brand Aid," online posting, January 8, 2006, *Design Your Life*, http://www .design-your-life.org/blog.php?id=507.

123. "Public Diplomacy for Middle Eastern and MEPI Affairs," *USAID Public Diplomacy*. Available at http://www.usaid.gov/about_usaid/presidential_initiative/diplomacy/.

124. For more, see John Emerson, "An Introduction to Activism on the Internet," 2005. Available at http://backspace.com/action/.

125. The White House, "White House Interactive," http://www.whitehouse.gov/interactive/.

126. The White House, "White House Panoramic Tours," http://www.whitehouse.gov/history/whtour/360index.html.

127. See Elizabeth Losh, "The Horses of Elberfeld," online posting, July 7, 2006, *Virtualpolitik*, http://virtualpolitik.blogspot.com/2006/07/horses-of-elberfeld.html.

128. Ian Bogost, *Persuasive Games: The Expressive Power of Videogames* (Cambridge, MA: MIT Press, 2007), ix.

129. This point about how the ideological substrate of videogame play both encourages compliance and invites critical resistance was not developed by earlier rhetoricians. See Ken S. McAllister, *Game Work: Language, Power, and Computer Game Culture* (Tuscaloosa: The University of Alabama Press, 2004)

130. See Ian Bogost and Gonzalo Frasca's blog *Water Cooler Games* at http://www.watercoolergames .org/.

131. See Barbara Ehrenreich, *Bait and Switch: The (Futile) Pursuit of the American Dream* (New York: Metropolitan Books, 2006) for more on this topic.

132. Lee Rainie and Bente Kalsnes, "The Commons of the Tragedy: How the Internet was used by millions after the terror attacks to grieve, console, share news, and debate the country's response," *Pew Internet & American Life Project*, October 10, 2001. Available at http://www .pewinternet.org/PPF/r/46/report_display.asp, 8–9.

133. Note that I am looking at less publicized changes than in the agency's home page. I chose the Press Release section because the designer would anticipate a large audience, and yet its public profile is at least one layer down from the most public portal.

134. "Hijacking Letter Found at Three Locations," *The FBI*, September 28, 2001. Available at http://www.fbi.gov/pressrel/pressrel01/letter.htm.

135. The flag is less likely to be part of the web identity of federal websites associated with science, such as the National Institutes of Health, the Federal Drug Administration, the National Science Foundation, and the like.

136. The White House, "10 Improvements in the Lives of Iraqi Children," http://www .whitehouse.gov/infocus/iraq/part5.html.

137. The White House, "President Bush Discusses the Budget in Billings, Montana," March 26, 2001, http://www.whitehouse.gov/news/releases/2001/03/20010327.html.

138. The White House, "President Participates in Meeting on Comprehensive Immigration Reform," March 23, 2006, http://www.whitehouse.gov/news/releases/2006/03/20060323 .html.

139. The White House, "Interview of the President by Korean Broadcasting System," November 8, 2005, http://www.whitehouse.gov/news/releases/2005/11/20051108-4.html.

140. Lawrence Lessig, *Free Culture: The Nature and Future of Creativity* (New York: Penguin, 2004), 69.

141. Ibid., 117.

142. Ibid., 250.

143. Lisa Nakamura, *Cybertypes: Race, Ethnicity, and Identity on the Internet* (New York: Routledge, 2002), 107.

144. Ibid., 98.

145. Ibid., 133.

146. James D. Sewell, "Point of View: The Four Rs for Police Executives," July 1996. Available at http://www.fbi.gov/publications/leb/1996/july963.txt.

147. Kevin M. Gilmartin, "The Lethal Triad: Understanding the Nature of Isolated Extremist Groups," September 1996. Available at http://www.fbi.gov/publications/leb/1996/sept961.txt.

148. See the MLA Job Information List, http://www.mla.org/jil.

149. See "digital rhetoric" courses for WRA 415 at Michigan State University in fall 2006 at http://www.msu.edu/~devossda/415/index.html. There was also a fall 2005 course at Rennselaer Polytechnic Institute.

150. Richard Lanham, "Digital Rhetoric: Theory, Practice, and Property," in *Literacy Online: The Promise (and Peril) of Reading and Writing with Computers*, ed. Myron C. Tuman, Pittsburgh series in composition, literacy, and culture (Pittsburgh: University of Pittsburgh Press, 1992), 221–243; Richard Lanham, "Digital Rhetoric and the Digital Arts," in Richard A. Lanham, *The Electronic Word: Democracy, Technology, and the Arts* (University Of Chicago Press, 1995), 29–52.

151. Richard Lanham, interview with the author, Santa Monica, California, November 17, 2006.

152. Jeremy Campbell, *Grammatical Man: Information, Entropy, Language, and Life* (New York: Simon & Schuster, 1982).

153. Richard Lanham, "Digital Literacy," *Scientific American* 273, no. 3 (September 1995).

154. James J. O'Donnell, "Richard Lanham's *The Electronic Word*," *Bryn Mawr Medieval Review* (June 1994). Available at http://www.infomotions.com/serials/bmmr/bmmr-9406-o'donnell-electronic.txt.

155. George P. Landow, "The Electronic Word," *Computational Linguistics* 21, no. 1 (1995): 116–119.

156. "Rod Davis Interviewing Richard Lanham," http://130.238.79.99/ilmh/ren/lanham-interview.htm (accessed May 6, 2006; site now discontinued).

157. Richard Lanham, *The Electronic Word* (Chicago: Chicago University Press, 1993), 31.

158. Ibid.

159. Richard Lanham, "The Implications of Electronic Information for the Sociality of Knowledge," *Technology, Scholarship, and the Humanities: The Implications of Electronic Information*, Coalition for Networked Information. Available at http://www.cni.org/docs/tsh/Lanham.html.

160. Lanham, *Electronic Word*, 129–130.

161. See also Alan Liu on the need for scholars to be producers as well as critics, and Gregory Crane on the importance of scholarship as metadata authorship.

162. Lanham, *The Electronic Word*, 133.

163. George Landow, *Hypertext 3.0* (Baltimore: Johns Hopkins University Press, 2006), 14–15.

164. Lev Manovich, *The Language of New Media* (Cambridge, MA: MIT Press, 2001), 78.

165. Gregory Ulmer, *Teletheory: Grammatology in the Age of Video* (New York: Routledge, 1989), 9.

166. Ulmer, *Teletheory*, 5.

167. The digital rhetorician as indexer is an important role that includes other major figures in the study of digital culture in the United States, including Alan Liu at the University of California, Santa Barbara. See Landow's rings at http://www.victorianweb.org/cv/websites.html, in addition to his indexing work.

168. Lanham, *The Electronic Word*, 31.

169. Jay David Bolter, *Writing Space: The Computer, Hypertext, and the History of Writing* (Hillsdale, NJ: Lawrence Erlbaum Associates, 1991), 9.

170. Bolter, *Writing Space*, 19.

171. Jay David Bolter, personal webpage, http://www.lcc.gatech.edu/~bolter/mediatheory.htm.

172. Jay David Bolter and Richard Grusin, *Remediation: Understanding New Media* (Cambridge, MA: MIT Press, 1999), 19

173. Michael Joyce, *Of Two Minds: Hypertext Pedagogy and Poetics* (Ann Arbor: University of Michigan Press, 1995).

174. Michael Joyce, *Othermindedness: The Emergence of Network Culture* (Ann Arbor: University of Michigan Press, 2000), 3.

175. Joyce, *Othermindedness*, 2.

176. See Susan Jarratt, *Rereading the Sophists: Classical Rhetoric Refigured* (Carbondale: Southern Illinois University Press, 1991).

177. Kathleen Welch, *Electric Rhetoric: Classical Rhetoric, Oralism, and the New Literacy* (Cambridge, MA: MIT Press, 1999), 45.

178. Walter J. Ong, *Orality and Literacy*, 2nd ed. (Routledge, 2002).

179. See the work of Henry Jenkins, *Convergence Culture: When Old and New Media Collide* (New York: New York University Press, 2006) and *Fans, Bloggers, and Gamers: Exploring Participatory Culture* (New York: New York University Press, 2006).

180. In Lanham's later work on intellectual property, however, he points out how pop cultural icons, such as Barbie, have important implications about appropriation and reconfiguration that are also relevant to legal scholarship and disputes in religious studies over interpretive rights to the Dead Sea Scrolls. See Richard Lanham, "Barbie and the Teacher of Righteousness," in *The Economics of Attention* (Chicago: University of Chicago Press, 2006).

181. Ulises Ali Mejias, "Social Media and the Networked Public Sphere," *Ideant*, July 20, 2006. Available at http://ideant.typepad.com/ideant/2006/07/social_media_an.html.

182. Bruce A. Bimber and Richard Davis, *Campaigning Online: The Internet in U.S. Elections* (New York: Oxford University Press USA, 2003); Kirsten Foot and Steven M. Schneider, *Web Campaigning* (Cambridge, MA: MIT Press, 2006); Philip N. Howard, *New Media Campaigns and the Managed Citizen* (Cambridge: Cambridge University Press, 2005).

183. John Logie, *Peers, Pirates, & Persuasion: Rhetoric in the Peer-to-Peer Debates* (West Lafayette, IN: Parlor Press, 2006), available at http://www.parlorpress.com/pdf/PeersPiratesPersuasion-Logie .pdf; Laura J. Gurak, *Persuasion and Privacy in Cyberspace: The Online Protests Over Lotus MarketPlace and the Clipper Chip* (New Haven, CT: Yale University Press, 1999).

184. Barbara Warnick, *Rhetoric Online: Persuasion and Politics on the World Wide Web* (New York: Peter Lang Publishing, 2007).

185. Kenneth Burke, *A Rhetoric of Motives* (University of California Press, 1969), 26.

186. Laura J. Gurak, *Cyberliteracy: Navigating the Internet with Awareness* (New Haven, CT: Yale University Press, 2003), 5.

187. Ibid., 47–54 (on "techno-rage") and 81–109 (on hoaxes).

188. Of course, there are significant exceptions, particularly the work of N. Katherine Hayles and Mark Hansen.

189. Aristotle, *On Rhetoric: A Theory of Civic Discourse*, trans. George A. Kennedy (Oxford University Press, USA, 2006), 211.

190. Dilip Gaonkar, "Contingency and Probability," *Encyclopedia of Rhetoric* (Oxford: Oxford University Press, 2001).

191. C.P. Snow, *The Two Cultures and the Scientific Revolution* (New York: Cambridge University Press, 1959), 4.

192. Siva Vaidhyanathan, "Critical Information Studies: A Bibliographic Manifesto," *Cultural Studies* 20, no. 2–3 (Mar-May 2006): 292–315.

193. Definition from the *Oxford English Dictionary Online,* http://dictionary.oed.com/ via the California Digital Library. See also John Seely Brown and Paul Duguid, *The Social Life of Information* (Cambridge, MA: Harvard Business School Press, 2000), 120, in which knowledge is defined by its relationship to a knower, while information is treated as a self-contained substance.

194. Michael E. Hobart and Zachary Schiffman, *Information Ages: Literacy, Numeracy, and the Computer Revolution* (Baltimore: Johns Hopkins University Press, 1998), 3.

195. Claude Shannon, "A Mathematical Theory of Communication," *The Bell System Technical Journal* 27 (July and October 1948): 379–423 and 623–656.

196. Although if no terminal letter appears in the second case, the reader might assume that a linguistic shift has occurred and the word "chocolat" comes either from another language or a nonstandard or idiosyncratic English dialect.

197. Claude Shannon and Warren Weaver, *The Mathematical Theory of Communication* (Urbana: University of Illinois, 1949), 116.

198. Ibid., 22.

199. See, however, the research of Naomi Baron at American University, who argues that IM, or instant messaging, is surprisingly formal and unabbreviated. See Michael Schirber, "Study: Instant Messaging is Surprisingly Formal :-)," *Live Science*, March 1 2005. Available at http://www .livescience.com/technology/050301_internet_language.html.

200. E-mail from Janie Morris to the author, 2004.

201. The Cmabrigde e-mail, http://www.mrc-cbu.cam.ac.uk/~mattd/Cmabrigde/.

202. Claude Shannon and Warren Weaver, "Recent Contributions to the Mathematical Theory of Communication," *The Mathematical Theory of Communication* (Champaign, IL: University of Illinois Press, 1963), 24.

203. Lev Manovich, *The Language of New Media* (Cambridge, MA: MIT Press, 2001), 78.

204. Roman Jakobson, "Linguistics and Poetics," in *Style in Language*, ed. Thomas A. Sebeok (Cambridge, MA: The Technology Press of the Massachusetts Institute of Technology, 1960), 350–377.

205. Edward Tufte, "PowerPoint Does Rocket Science," *Ask E.T.*, http://www.edwardtufte.com/ bboard/q-and-a-fetch-msg?msg_id=0001yB&topic_id=1.

206. Albert-László Barabási, *Linked: How Everything Is Connected to Everything Else and What It Means for Business, Science, and Everyday Life* (New York: Plume, 2003), 4.

207. See http://www.u-r-connected.com.

208. James P. Zappen, "Digital Rhetoric: Toward an Integrated Theory," *Technical Communication Quarterly* 14 (2005): 323.

209. Andrew C. Revkin, "A Young Bush Appointee Resigns His Post at NASA," *New York Times*, February 8, 2006. Available at http://www.nytimes.com/2006/02/08/politics/08nasa.html.

3   The Desert of the Unreal: Democracy and Military-Funded Videogames and Simulations

1. Jerry Clark and John Vines, "Coding: What's All This Reality Sandwich Stuff, Anyhow?" *U.S. Army Research Laboratory Major Shared Resource Center*. Available at http://www.arl.hpc.mil/Publications/eLink_Spring03/flatworld.html.

2. The author's second visit to FlatWorld occurred October 3, 2006, and the first visit took place on June 5, 2006.

3. James Hebert, "Hollywood and the Military Join Forces, Using Virtual Reality to Train GI's and 'Help Keep People Alive,'" *San Diego Tribune* online edition, November 6, 2005. Available at http://www.signonsandiego.com/news/features/20051106–9999–lz1a06ictech.html.

4. Jarrell Pair and Diane Piepol, "FlatWorld: A Mixed Reality Environment for Education and Training," http://www.ict.usc.edu/publications/SCI-2002–Pair.pdf.

5. For more on "reality hacking" in *The Matrix*, see Stacy Gillis, ed., *The Matrix Trilogy: Cyberpunk Reloaded* (London: Wallflower Press, 2005).

6. This is a trope that also goes back to the allegory of the cave in Plato's *Republic*, from which the original virtual reality cave installations derived their name.

7. Slavoj Žižek, "Welcome to the Desert of the Real," *re:constructions*, September 15, 2001. Available at http://web.mit.edu/cms/reconstructions/interpretations/desertreal.html.

8. Ibid.

9. Ibid.

10. Bruno Latour, "From Realpolitik to Dingpolitik," in *Making Things Public: Atmospheres of Democracy*, ed. Bruno Latour and Peter Weibel (Cambridge, MA: MIT Press, 2005), 14.

11. Michael Schrage, *Serious Play: How the World's Best Companies Simulate to Innovate* (Boston: Harvard Business School Press, 2000).

12. Lev Manovich, *The Language of New Media* (Cambridge, MA: MIT Press, 2001), 143.

13. Karen Walker, "A Grown-Up Game: Scientists, Whiz-Kids Devise Lifesaving Trainer for Soldiers," *Training & Simulation Journal* (February 21, 2005). Available at http://www.tsjonline.com/story.php?F=567940.

14. Andrew Murr, "Arabic High-Tech Tutor," *Newsweek* (June 14, 2004). Available at http://www.newsweek.com/id/54008.

15. Alison McMahon, "Immersion, Engagement, and Presence: A Method for Analyzing 3–D Video Games," in *The Video Game Theory Reader*, ed. Mark J. P. Wolf and Bernard Perron (New York: Routledge, 2003), 75.

16. Michael Ostwald, "Identity Tourism, Virtuality and the Theme Park," in *Virtual Globalization: Virtual Spaces / Tourist Spaces*, ed. David Holmes (New York: Routledge, 2001), 194.

17. "Customs Check," *Foreign Policy* March/April 2005.

18. Christopher Miller, Marc Chapman, Peggy Wu, and Lewis Johnson, "The 'Etiquette Quotient': An Approach to Believable Social Interaction Behaviors," in *Proceedings of the 14th Conference on Behavior Representation in Modeling and Simulation (BRIMS)*. Conference held May 16–19, 2005, Universal City, CA. Available at http://www.sift.info/publications/PDF/MLCW-BRIMS05-v2.pdf.

19. Penelope Brown and Stephen C. Levinson, *Politeness: Some Universals in Language Usage* (Cambridge: Cambridge University Press, 1987), 86.

20. W. Lewis Johnson & Carole Beal, "Iterative Evaluation of a Large-Scale, Intelligent Game for Language Learning," in *Artificial Intelligence in Education*. Chee-kit Looi et al. (Amsterdam: IOS Press, 2005), 290–297.

21. For example, in evaluating foreign language multimedia software, Plass has argued that task-based, problem-solving, and role-playing activities that encourage critical thinking around decoding and selection are desirable. See Jan L. Plass, "Design and Evaluation of the User Interface of Foreign Language Multimedia Software: A Cognitive Approach," *Language Learning & Technology* 2, no. 1 (July 1998): 40–53.

Doughty and Long similarly make the case for task-based psycholinguistic environments in Catherine J. Doughty and Michael H. Long, "Optimal Psycholinguistic Environments for Distance Foreign Language Learning," *Language Learning & Technology* 7, no. 3 (Sept. 2003): 50–80.

22. Janet Murray, *Hamlet on the Holodeck: The Future of Narrative in Cyberspace* (Cambridge, MA: MIT Press, 1998).

23. Michael Heim, *Virtual Realism* (New York: Oxford University Press, 1998)

24. Albert Rizzo, Jarrell Pair, Ken Graap, Brian Manson, P.J. McNerney, Brenda K. Wiederhold, Mark Wiederhold, and James Spira, "A Virtual Reality Exposure Therapy Application for Iraq War Military Personnel with Post Traumatic Stress Disorder: From Training to Toy to Treatment," in *NATO Advanced Research Workshop on Novel Approaches to the Diagnosis and Treatment of Posttraumatic Stress Disorder* (Amsterdam: IOS Press, 2006), 235–250.

25. Jonathan Steuer, "Defining Virtual Reality: Dimensions Determining Telepresence," *Journal of Communication* 42, no. 4 (1992): 73–93.

26. Jarrell Pair, Brian Allen, Mathieu Dautricourt, Anton Treskunov, Matt Liewer, Ken Graap, Greg Reger, and Albert Rizzo, "A Virtual Reality Exposure Therapy Application for Iraq War Post Traumatic Stress Disorder," in *Proceedings of the IEEE VR2006 Conference*, (Washington D.C.: IEEE Computer Society, 2006), 62–72.

27. Ibid.

28. Cicero, *De Oratore* II.lxxxvii, *On Oratory and Orators*, trans. J. S. Watson (Carbondale: Southern Illinois University Press, 1986), 186–187.

29. See François G. Christen, *Updating Interactive Images: Proactive Effects in the Method of Loci* (Ph.D. dissertation, University of California, Los Angeles, 1980).

30. Frances Yates, *The Art of Memory* (Chicago: University of Chicago Press, 1966), xii.

31. Mary Carruthers and Jan M. Ziolkowski, *The Medieval Craft of Memory: An Anthology of Texts and Pictures* (Philadelphia: University of Pennsylvania Press, 2002), 3.

32. Janine Wong and Peter Storkerson, "Hypertext and the Art of Memory," *Visible Language* 31, no. 2 (1997). Available at http://www.id.iit.edu/visiblelanguage/Feature Articles/ArtofMemory/ArtofMemory.html.

33. Ian Bogost, *Unit Operations* (Cambridge, MA: MIT Press, 2006).

34. Nicholas Negroponte, *Being Digital* (New York: Vintage Books, 1995), 109.

35. Eric Fassbender, "The Virtual Memory Palace," 2005, http://www.ics.mq.edu.au/~eric/virschool/virschool.htm.

36. Albert Rizzo, J.Galen Buckwalter, and Cheryl van der Zaag, "Virtual Environment Applications for Neuropsychological Assessment and Rehabilitation," in *Handbook of Virtual Environments,* ed Kay Stanney (New York: Erlbaum, 2002), 1027–1064.

37. Cicero II.lxxv, *On Oratory and Orators*, trans. J. S. Watson (Carbondale: Southern Illinois University Press, 1986), 173.

38. "The Memory Stairs," handout to Los Angeles SIGGRAPH tour, October 4, 2006

39. Rebecca Tortell and Jacquelyn Ford Morie, "Videogame Play and the Effectiveness of Virtual Environments for Training," *Interservice/Industry Training, Simulation, and Education Conference (I/ITSEC) 2006*, Orlando, FL.

40. Max Boot, "Navigating the 'Human Terrain,'" *Los Angeles Times*, December 7, 2005. Available at http://www.cfr.org/publication/9377/navigating_the_human_terrain.html.

41. Michel de Certeau, *The Practice of Everyday Life*, trans. Steven Rendall (Berkeley: University of California Press, 1988), 98.

42. Patrick Crogan, "Gametime: History, Narrative, and Temporality in *Combat Flight Simulator 2*," in *The Video Game Theory Reader*, ed. Mark J. Wolf and Bernard Perron (New York: Routledge, 2003), 275–301. For a reading that develops the differences between the figure of the *flâneur* and the functionality of the flight simulator, see Todd Presner, "HyperCities, Google, and the Digital Dialectic" lecture presented at the University of California, Irvine, Irvine, CA, May 12, 2008.

43. Bob Rehak, "Playing at Being: Psychoanalysis and the Avatar," in *The Video GameTheory Reader*, ed. Mark J. Wolf and Bernard Perron (Routledge, New York, 2003), 103–128.

44. A. S. Canagarajah, *Critical Academic Writing and Multilingual Students* (Ann Arbor: University of Michigan Press, 2002).

45. Manuel Castells, *The Power of Identity* (Oxford: Blackwell, 1997), 22.

46. Ibid., 52.

47. Ibid.

48. Bruce Horner and John Trimbur, "English Only and U.S. College Composition," *College Composition and Communication* 53, no. 4 (June 2002): 594–630.

49. Georgi Lozanov, *Suggestology and Suggestopedia: Theory and Practice* (Paris: United Nations Educational, Scientific, and Cultural Organization, 1979).

50. James Paul Gee, *What Video Games Have to Teach Us about Learning and Literacy* (New York: Palgrave, 2003).

51. In 2006 versions of the game, the Skill Builder is populated by characters in the game world of the Mission Game. See Lewis Johnson, "Tactical Serious Games Development! The Creation and Usage of the TACTICAL IRAQI Language Trainer," lecture presented at the Serious Games Summit, Washington, D.C., October 30, 2006.

52. Alex Handy, "Video Game Trains Troops; Software Stresses Cultural Interaction, Not Fighting," *Atlanta Journal-Constitution*, February 22, 2005. Available at http://www.tacticallanguage.com/press-atlanta_constitution-2005–02–22.html.

53. Lewis Johnson, Stacy Marsella, and Hannes Vilhjálmsson, "Serious Games for Language Learning: How Much Game, How Much AI?" International Conference on Artificial Intelligence in Education (AIED), July 18–22, 2005, Amsterdam.

54. David Yau-Fai Ho, "On the Concept of Face," *American Journal of Sociology*, 81, no. 4 (1976): 867–884

55. Penelope Brown and Stephen C. Levinson, *Politeness: Some Universals in Language Usage* (Cambridge: Cambridge University Press, 1987).

56. Ibid., 74.

57. However, by the 1987 edition, they described the influence of speech act theory on their work as "dated" in Ibid., 10.

58. Ibid., 36.

59. Ibid., 1.

60. Ibid., 48.

61. Alex Handy, "Video Game Trains Troops; Software Stresses Cultural Interaction, Not Fighting," *Atlanta Journal-Constitution*, February 22, 2005. Available at http://www.tacticallanguage.com/press-atlanta_constitution-2005–02–22.html.

62. Tactical Iraqi website, "Tactical Iraqi: How It Works," 2005, http://www.tacticallanguage.com/tacticaliraqi/howitworks.htm (accessed October 1, 2006; site now discontinued).

63. See Paul Virilio, *The Information Bomb* (London: Verso, 2000) and Stuart Moulthrop, "From Work to Play: Molecular Culture in the Time of Deadly Games" and Simon Penny, "Representation, Enaction, and the Ethics of Simulation," in *FirstPerson: New Media as Story, Performance, and Game*, ed. Noah Wardrip-Fruin and Pat Harrigan (Cambridge, MA: MIT Press, 2004).

64. Jean Baudrillard, *Simulacra and Simulation*, trans. S. Glaser (Ann Arbor, MI: University of Michigan Press, 1994).

65. Tactical Iraqi website, "Tactical Iraqi: How It Works," 2005, http://www.tacticallanguage.com/tacticaliraqi/howitworks.htm (accessed October 1, 2006; site now discontinued).

66. James Paul Gee, *What Video Games Have to Teach Us about Learning and Literacy* (New York: Palgrave, 2003); Kurt Squire and Henry Jenkins, "Harnessing the Power of Games in Education," *Insight*, The Institute for the Advancement of Emerging Technology in Education, 2003. Available at http://website.education.wisc.edu/kdsquire/manuscripts/insight.pdf.

67. Steve Jones, "Let the Games Begin: Gaming Technology and Entertainment among College Students," *Pew Internet & American Life Project*, July 6, 2003. Available at http://www.pewinternet.org/report_display.asp?r=93.

68. Lewis Johnson, Stacy Marsella, and Hannes Vilhjálmsson, "The DARWARS Tactical Language Training System," Interservice/Industry Training, Simulation, and Education Conference (I/ITSEC) December 6–9, 2004, Orlando, FL. Available at http://ru.is/faculty/hannes/publications/IITSEC2004.pdf.

69. Ibid.

70. Lewis Johnson and Carole Beal, "Iterative Evaluation of a Large-Scale, Intelligent Game for Language Learning," International Conference on Artificial Intelligence in Education (AIED), July 18–22, 2005, Amsterdam.

71. Ibid.

72. Bernard Perron, "From Gamers to Players and Gameplayers," in *The Video GameTheory Reader*, ed. Mark J. Wolf and Bernard Perron (Routledge, New York, 2003), 237–258. See also Mia Consalvo, *Cheating: Gaining Advantage in Videogames* (Cambridge, MA: MIT Press, 2007).

73. Lewis Johnson and Carole Beal, "Iterative Evaluation of a Large-Scale, Intelligent Game for Language Learning," in *Artificial Intelligence in Education*. Chee-kit Looi et al. (Amsterdam: IOS Press, 2005), 290–297.

74. Andrew Murr, "Arabic High-Tech Tutor," *Newsweek*, June 14, 2004, http://www.newsweek.com/id/54008.

75. See Murthada Bakir, "Sex Differences in the Approximation to Standard Arabic: A Case Study," *Anthropological Linguistics* 28, no. 1 (1986): 3–9, and Hassan R.S. Abdel-Jawad, "Language and Women's Place with Special Reference to Arabic," *Language Sciences* 11, no. 3 (1989): 305–324.

76. Tactical Iraqi website, "Tactical Language—Iraqi Arabic Made Easy," 2005, http://www.tacticallanguage.com/tacticaliraqi/ (accessed October 1, 2006; site now discontinued).

77. James Paul Gee, *What Video Games Have to Teach Us about Learning and Literacy* (New York: Palgrave, 2003).

78. Ibid., 113–138.

79. Kurt Squire and Henry Jenkins, "Harnessing the Power of Games in Education," *Insight*, The Institute for the Advancement of Emerging Technology in Education, 2003. Available at http:// website.education.wisc.edu/kdsquire/manuscripts/insight.pdf.

80. Public Radio International, "Iraq Gestures Report," The World, February 20, 2006. Available at http://www.theworld.org/?q=node/982.

81. Tactical Iraqi website, "Tactical Iraqi in the Press," 2006, http://www.tacticallanguage.com/ tacticaliraqi/press.htm (accessed October 1, 2006; site now discontinued).

82. Albert Rizzo, "Recent Press on the ICT/USC Project," ftp://imsc.usc.edu/pub/uploads/ Skips%20Stuff/PTSD/ (accessed October 1, 2006; site now discontinued).

83. See Guy Debord, *The Society of the Spectacle* (New York: Zone Books, 1994).

84. Ian Bogost. *Persuasive Games: The Expressive Power of Videogames.* (Cambridge, MA: MIT Press, 2007).

85. "Learning Culture Through a Videogame," *ABC News*, April 12, 2006. http://abcnews.go .com/Video/playerIndex?id=183564/ (accessed October 1, 2006; site now discontinued).

86. This visit took place on June 5, 2006.

87. Ibid.

88. E. Ann Kaplan, *Trauma Culture: The Politics of Terror and Loss in Media and Literature* (New Brunswick, NJ: Rutgers University Press, 2005).

89. Bob Rehak, "Playing at Being: Psychoanalysis and the Avatar," in *The Video GameTheory Reader*, ed. Mark J. Wolf and Bernard Perron (Routledge, New York, 2003), 103–128.

90. Simon Penny, "Representation, Enaction, and the Ethics of Simulation," in *First Person: New Media as Story, Performance, and Game*, ed. Noah Wardrip-Fruin and Pat Harrigan (Cambridge, MA: MIT Press, 2004), 73–84; Timothy Lenoir, "All But War Is Simulation: The Military-Entertainment Complex, *Configurations*, 8, no. 3 (2000): 289–335.

91. Manuel Castells, *The Internet Galaxy* (Oxford: Oxford University Press, 2001).

92. Katrina vanden Heuvel, "Playstations for Peace," online posting, April 4, 2005, *The Nation Blog*, http://www.thenation.com/blogs/edcut?pid=2302.

93. It is worth noting, however, that there are exceptions. See Clive Thompson, "Saving the World One Video Game at a Time," *New York Times*, July 23, 2006. Available at http://www .nytimes.com/2006/07/23/arts/23thom.htm.

94. Stuart Moulthrop, "From Work to Play: Molecular Culture in a Time of Deadly Games," in *First Person: New Media as Story, Performance, and Game*, ed. Noah Wardrip-Fruin and Pat Harrigan (Cambridge, MA: MIT Press, 2004), 56–69.

95. Elizabeth Loftus and Gregory Loftus, *Mind at Play: The Psychology of Video Games* (New York: Basic Books, 1983).

96. Janet Murray, "The Last Word on Ludology v. Narratology in Game Studies," DIGRA 2005, June 17, 2005, Vancouver, Canada. Available at http://www.lcc.gatech.edu/~murray/digra05/lastword.pdf. This was not, however, the last word, as is shown by Ian Bogost's critical review of Henry Jenkins, *Convergence Culture: Where Old Media and New Media Collide* (New York, NY: New York University Press, 2006) at http://www.watercoolergames.org/archives/000590.shtml.

97. Nick Montfort, "Gestural Iraqi," online posting, February 19, 2006, *Grand Text Auto*, http://grandtextauto.gatech.edu/2006/02/19/gestural-iraqi/.

98. Gonzalo Frasca, "Shame on Tactical Iraqi," online posting, February 20, 2006, *Water Cooler Games*, http://www.watercoolergames.org/archives/000526.shtml.

99. Mark Marino, "Technological Tact in Tactical Iraqi," online posting, November 23, 2005, *WRT: Writer Response Theory*, http://writerresponsetheory.org/wordpress/2005/11/23/technological-tact-in-tactical-iraqi/.

100. Gonzalo Frasca, "Shame on Tactical Iraqi," online posting and following responses, February 20, 2006, *Water Cooler Games*, http://www.watercoolergames.org/archives/000526.shtml.

101. Ibid.

102. Ibid.

103. Ibid.

104. Ibid.

105. Ibid.

106. Ibid.

107. Alexander Galloway, "Social Realism in Gaming," *Game Studies* 4, no. 1 (November 2004). Available at http://www.gamestudies.org/0401/galloway/.

108. Bob Rehak, "Playing at Being: Psychoanalysis and the Avatar," in *The Video GameTheory Reader*, ed. Mark J. Wolf and Bernard Perron (Routledge, New York, 2003), 103–128.

109. Future versions of the game may include some instruction in written language, according to a presentation by the parent company Alelo to the Pasadena Angels venture capital group, Pasadena, CA,November 15, 2006.

110. Ludwig Wittgenstein, *Philosophical Investigations*, trans. G. E. M. Anscombe (New York: The Macmillan Company, 1965).

111. Jean-François Lyotard, *The Postmodern Condition: A Report on Knowledge*, trans. Geoff Bennington (Harmondsworth, Penguin, 1984).

112. Jacques Derrida, *The Monolingualism of the Other OR The Prosthesis of Origin*, trans. Patrick Mensah (Stanford, CA: Stanford University Press, Stanford, 1998), 7.

113. Kurt Squire, "Cultural Framing of Computer/Video Games," *Game Studies* 2, no. 1 (July 2002). Available at http://www.gamestudies.org/0102/squire/.

114. Elizabeth Losh, "In Country with *Tactical Iraqi*: Trust, Identity, and Language Learning in a Military Video Game," *Digital Experience: Design, Aesthetics, Practice* (Copenhagen, Denmark: IT University of Copenhagen, 2005): 69–78.

115. Bruno Latour, "From Realpolitik to Dingpolitik or How to Make Things Public," in *Making Things Public Atmospheres of Democracy*, ed. Bruno Latour and Peter Weibel (Cambridge, MA: MIT Press, 2006), 14–41.

116. Ibid., 31.

117. USC Institute for Creative Technologies, "ELECT," http://ict.usc.edu/projects/elect/.

118. Michel Foucault, *The Birth of the Clinic: An Archeology of Medical Perception*, trans. A. M. Sheridan Smith (New York: Vintage, 1963).

4 The War from the Web: An Atlas of Conflict, Government, and Citizenship

1. Jad Adbumrad, "Whitney's 'Listening Post' a Fly on Chat-Room Walls," *NPR Weekend Edition Saturday*, February 22, 2003.

2. Mark Hansen, "Time/Space, Gravity, and Light," artists' panel presented at the Skirball Cultural Center, Los Angeles, CA, December 2, 2004.

3. Lawrence K. Grossman, *The Electronic Republic: Reshaping Democracy in the Information Age* (New York: Viking, 1995).

4. Jeffrey B. Abramson, F. Christopher Arterton, and Gary R. Orren, *The Electronic Commonwealth: The Impact of New Media Technologies on Democratic Politics* (New York: Basic Books, 1998).

5. Bruce Bimber, *Information and American Democracy: Technology in the Evolution of Political Power* (Cambridge, UK: Cambridge University Press, 2003).

6. Siva Vaidhyanathan, *The Anarchist in the Library: How the Clash between Freedom and Control is Hacking the Real World and Crashing the System* (New York: Basic Books, 2004).

7. Richard Davis, *The Web of Politics: The Internet's Impact on the American Political System* (New York: Oxford University Press, 1999).

8. Anthony G. Wilhelm, *Democracy in the Digital Age: Challenges to Political Life in Cyberspace* (New York: Routledge, 2000).

9. Darin Barney, *Prometheus Wired: The Hope for Democracy in the Age of Network Technology* (Vancouver, BC: University of British Columbia Press, 2000), 264.

10. Similar arguments about the unjustified equation of "freedom" and "democracy" have been made by Geert Lovink and others.

11. Geert Lovink, *Zero Comments: Blogging and Critical Internet Culture* (New York: Routledge, 2008).

12. Henry Jenkins, *Convergence Culture: Where Old and New Media Collide* (New York: New York University Press, 2006).

13. Howard Rheingold, *Smart Mobs: The Next Social Revolution* (Cambridge, MA: Perseus Books, 2002), 205.

14. Jane Fountain, "Toward a Theory of Federal Bureaucracy for the Twenty-First Century," in *Governance.com: Democracy in the Information Age*, ed. Elaine Ciulla Kamarck and Joseph S. Nye, Jr. (Washington, D.C.: Brookings Institute Press, 2002).

15. Jane Fountain, *Building the Virtual State: Information Technology and Institutional Change* (Washington, D.C.: Brookings Institute Press, 2001), 18–19. See also the work of Jennifer Cool on Unix-based systems and the identity of the file as a unit in computing.

16. For more on this subject, see Anne Friedberg, *The Virtual Window: From Alberti to Microsoft* (The MIT Press, 2006).

17. Lev Manovich, *The Language of New Media* (Cambridge, MA: MIT Press, 2001), 94.

18. Ibid., 96.

19. Lee Rainie and Bente Kalsnes, "The Commons of the Tragedy: How the Internet was used by millions after the terror attacks to grieve, console, share news, and debate the country's response," *Pew Internet & American Life Project*, October 10, 2001, 8–9. Available at http://www .pewinternet.org/PPF/r/46/report_display.asp.

20. Overall, government URLs still rarely appear in the top 100 English-language websites by web traffic, according to http://www.alexa.com, even though government websites are also likely to be visited in connection with web traffic for genealogical research.

21. See the contrast between http://web.archive.org/web/20010815081729/http://www.whitehouse .gov/news/releases/ and http://web.archive.org/web/20011006060648/http://www.whitehouse.gov/ news/releases/ between August 15 and October 6 of 2001 that has been noted by Mark Marino.

22. Mark Boardman, *The Language of Websites* (New York: Routledge, 2005).

23. Elizabeth Losh, "Teaching, Terrorism, and Technology: Reading for Rhetoric in September 11 Documents on the Internet," *Kairos* 7, no. 1 (summer 2002). Available at http://english.ttu .edu/kairos/7.2/.

24. George W. Bush, "A Statement by the President in His Address to the Nation," September 11, 2001. Available at http://www.whitehouse.gov/news/releases/2001/09/20010911–16.html.

25. George W. Bush, "Address to a Joint Session of Congress and the American People," September 20, 2001. Available at http://www.whitehouse.gov/news/releases/2001/09/20010920–8.html.

26. George W. Bush completed a course in "American Rhetoric" as an undergraduate at Yale and frequently mentioned this experience in collaborating with speechwriters, according to D. T. Max, "The Making of the Speech," *New York Times*, October 7, 2001. Available at http://select .nytimes.com/search/restricted/article?res=F40714FF39590C748CDDA90994D9404482.

27. Karlyn Kohrs Campbell and Kathleen Hall Jamieson, *Deeds Done in Words* (Chicago: University of Chicago Press, 1990).

28. George W. Bush, "A Statement by the President in His Address to the Nation," September 11, 2001. Available at http://www.whitehouse.gov/news/releases/2001/09/20010911–16.html.

29. George W. Bush, "Address to a Joint Session of Congress and the American People," September 20, 2001. Available at http://www.whitehouse.gov/news/releases/2001/09/20010920–8.html.

30. See Roderick P. Hart, *Verbal Style and the Presidency: A Computer-Based Analysis* (Orlando, FL: Academic Press, 1984).

31. D. T. Max, "The Maxing of the Speech," *New York Times*, October 7, 2001. Available at http://select.nytimes.com/search/restricted/article?res=F40714FF39590C748CDDA90994D9404482.

32. George W. Bush, "Address to a Joint Session of Congress and the American People," September 20, 2001. Available at http://www.whitehouse.gov/news/releases/2001/09/20010920–8.html.

33. George W. Bush, "A Statement by the President in His Address to the Nation," September 11, 2001. Available at http://www.whitehouse.gov/news/releases/2001/09/20010911–16.html.

34. George W. Bush, "Remarks by the President Upon Arrival," September 16, 2001. Available at http://www.whitehouse.gov/news/releases/2001/09/20010916–2.html.

35. In contrast, missing persons signs for victims who were not first-responders that were posted after the World Trade Center disaster often gave as much information about the victim's class affiliation as about other distinguishing physical features.

36. See Mike McIntee, "White House Caught Doctoring 'Mission Accomplished' Video," 2006, http://www.youtube.com/watch?v=-u2ITs4yIAE and the response posted at http://www.youtube.com/watch?v=PkRHki5P6fc, which questions McIntee's conclusions.

37. "Translated Text: Hijackers' How-To, Terrorists' Papers Give Detailed Instructions for Their Missions," *CBS News* online edition, October 1, 2001, http://www.cbsnews.com/stories/2001/10/01/archive/main313163.shtml.

38. "Instructions for the Last Night," trans. *The New York Times, Frontline: Inside the Terror Network*, http://www.pbs.org/wgbh/pages/frontline/shows/network/personal/instructions.html.

39. See John Martin Collins, *Collatoral Language: A User's Guide to America's New War* (New York: New York University Press, 2002). See also President Bush on the "crusade against illiteracy."

40. See discussions of "educational reform" in Pakistan and other countries on whitehouse.gov. The U.N.'s "Arab Human Development Report," published in English and Arabic and downloaded off the Internet over a million times when it first appeared, presents these criticisms even more candidly in its 2003 report on the "knowledge deficit" in the Arab world, although publication of the current 2004 edition was delayed by the White House because of language critical of U.S. policy in the prologue. See Thomas L. Freidman, "Holding up Arab Reform," *New York Times*, December 16, 2004. Available at http://www.nytimes.com/2004/12/16/opinion/16friedman.html.

41. Plato famously disparaged this particular kind of text in the *Phaedrus*: "They will cease to exercise memory because they rely on what on that which is written, calling things to remembrance no longer from within themselves, but by means of external marks. What you have discovered is a recipe not for memory, but for reminder." Cited from *The Collected Dialogues of Plato* trans. R. Hackforth (Princeton: Princeton University Press, 1961), 320.

42. In contrast, see Jean Bethke Elshtain, *Just War against Terror: The Burden of American Power in a Violent World* (New York, Basic Books, 2003).

43. "Instructions for the Last Night," trans. The New York Times, *Frontline: Inside the Terror Network*, http://www.pbs.org/wgbh/pages/frontline/shows/network/personal/instructions.html.

44. Ibid.

45. Slavoj Žižek, "The Desert of the Real: Is This the End of Fantasy?" *In These Times*. October 29, 2001, http://www.inthesetimes.com/issue/25/24/zizek2524.html.

46. Salman Rushdie, "Fighting the Forces of Invisibility," *The Washington Post*, October 2, 2001. Available at http://www.washingtonpost.com/ac2/wp-dyn?pagename=article&node=&contentId=A55876-2001Oct1.

47. Stanley Fish, "Don't Blame Relativism," *The Responsive Community* (Summer 2002): 27–31. Available at http://www.gwu.edu/~ccps/rcq/Fish.pdf.

48. The text of the hijackers' letter as evidence is conspicuously lacking in the official September 11 Commision report.

49. "Transcript of Osama bin Laden videotape," *CNN* online edition, December 13, 2001, http://archives.cnn.com/2001/US/12/13/tape.transcript/.

50. Note the disclaimer below a catalog of print materials from the International Information Programs at http://usinfo.state.gov/products/pubs/.

51. See Lawrence Lessig, *Free Culture: How Big Media Uses Technology and the Law to Lock Down Culture and Control Creativity* (New York: Penguin Press, 2004) and Siva Vaidhyanathan, *Copyrights and Copywrongs: The Rise of Intellectual Property and How It Threatens Creativity* (New York: New York University Press, 2001).

52. *The New Public Diplomacy: Soft Power in International Relations*, ed. Jan Melissen (New York: Palgrave Macmillan, 2005).

53. Charlotte Beers, "Transcript: Charlotte Beers and Richard Boucher at the Foreign Press Center on November 9, 2001," U.S. Department of State: International Information Programs, November 14, 2001, http://208.243.114.93/usa/islam/t111401.htm (accessed June 15, 2002; site now discontinued).

54. See Peter Brooks, *The Melodramatic Imagination: Balzac, Henry James, Melodrama and the Mode of Excess* (New Haven: Yale University Press, 1976).

55. George W. Bush, "Address to a Joint Session of Congress and the American People," September 20, 2001. Available at http://www.whitehouse.gov/news/releases/2001/09/20010920–8.html.

56. Ibid.

57. Search on http://www.whitehouse.gov search engine on June 15, 2004.

58. George W. Bush, "President Urges Readiness and Patience," September 15, 2001. Available at http://www.whitehouse.gov/news/releases/2001/09/20010915-4.html.

59. George W. Bush, "Remarks by the President Upon Arrival," September 16, 2001. Available at http://www.whitehouse.gov/news/releases/2001/09/20010916-2.html.

60. Despite international outcry about use of the term "crusade," President Bush used the phrase as recently as June 15, 2004 in a press conference with Afghanistan president Hamid Kharzai at which he described a "crusade against illiteracy" in the region. See http://www.whitehouse.gov/news/releases/2004/06/20040615-4.html.

61. Osama bin Laden, *Messages to the World: The Statements of Osama Bin Laden*, ed. Bruce Lawrence and trans. James Howarth (London: Verso, 2005).

62. Edward W. Said, "The Clash of Ignorance," *The Nation* (October 22, 2001). Available at http://www.thenation.com/doc/20011022/said. Said and Žižek also both assert that much of this East/West rhetoric is repackaged from the Cold War.

63. Charlotte Beers, "Transcript: Charlotte Beers and Richard Boucher at the Foreign Press Center on November 9, 2001," U.S. Department of State: International Information Programs, November 14, 2001, http://208.243.114.93/usa/islam/t111401.htm (accessed June 15, 2002; site now discontinued).

64. Ibid.

65. Benjamin R. Barber, *Jihad vs. McWorld* (New York: Ballantine Books, 1996).

66. Charlotte Beers, "Transcript: Charlotte Beers and Richard Boucher at the Foreign Press Center on November 9, 2001," U.S. Department of State: International Information Programs, November 14, 2001, http://208.243.114.93/usa/islam/t111401.htm (accessed June 15, 2002; site now discontinued).

67. Stanley Fish, "Condemnation without Absolutes," *New York Times*, October 15, 2001. Available at http://select.nytimes.com/search/restricted/article?res=F50617FE385B0C768DDDA-90994D9404482.

68. For more on this campaign, see Patrick Lee Plaisance, "The Propaganda War on Terrorism: An Analysis of the United States' 'Shared Values' Public-Diplomacy Campaign After September 11, 2001," *Journal of Mass Media Ethics* 20, no. 4 (November 21, 2005): 250–268.

69. Charlotte Beers, "Transcript: Charlotte Beers and Richard Boucher at the Foreign Press Center on November 9, 2001," U.S. Department of State: International Information Programs, November 14, 2001, http://208.243.114.93/usa/islam/t111401.htm (accessed June 15, 2002; site now discontinued).

70. See news coverage on the use of triple-X websites by Al Qaeda operatives. Jack Kelley, "Terror groups hide behind web encryption," *USA Today*, February 5, 2001. Available at http://www

.usatoday.com/tech/news/2001-02-05-binladen.htm. Gina Kolata, "Veiled Messages of Terror May Lurk in Cyberspace," *New York Times*, October 30, 2001. Available at http://query.nytimes.com/gst/fullpage.html?res=9B01E3D91730F933A05753C1A9679C8B63.

71. At the same time in Internet reception history, anxiety about the amorphousness of our national identity produced visual gags about "If the Taliban Wins," widely distributed via e-mail, which humorously showed the manufactured presence of mosques in the landmarks and skylines of the United States. See http://www.coe.unco.edu/RosemaryHathaway/ENG238/Sept11archive/Icons/talibanwins2.html (accessed June 15, 2002; site now discontinued) for examples of this form of humor.

72. In contrast, the Department of Justice website "Rewards for Justice," which is intended to locate possible terrorist agents, employs considerably more languages in its hypertext wanted posters.

73. Donald Rumsfeld, "Secretary Rumsfeld Interview with Al Jezeera," *Defense LINK*, U.S. Department of Defense, June 15, 2001, http://www.defenselink.mil/news/Oct2001/t10172001_t1016sd.html (accessed October 16, 2001; site now discontinued).

74. Ibid.

75. Interviews with Joyce Rumsfeld appeared elsewhere on the Defenselink website.

76. Lee Rainie and Bente Kalsnes, "The Commons of the Tragedy: How the Internet was used by millions after the terror attacks to grieve, console, share news, and debate the country's response," *Pew Internet & American Life Project*, October 10, 2001, 8–9. Available at http://www.pewinternet.org/PPF/r/46/report_display.asp.

77. *Rewards for Justice*, United States Department of State, http://www.rewardsforjustice.net/ (accessed September 15, 2002; site now substantially changed).

78. See the debate between Pearl's father, computer scientist Judah Pearl, and free speech advocates about this webcast in the pages of the *Los Angeles Times*.

79. See Steven Livingston, *The Terrorism Spectacle* (Boulder: Westview Press, 1994).

5 Power Points: The Virtual State and Its Discontents

1. Michael Zyda, interview with the author, Venice, California, December 14, 2006.

2. andrewburton, "Giving a PowerPoint Presentation in Second Life," online posting, January 27, 2006, *Gaming Hacks*, http://www.oreilly.com/pub/h/5239/.

3. "YTMND—PowerPoint: Death Star Attack," http://lay-uh.ytmnd.com/.

4. Edward R, Tufte, *The Cognitive Style of PowerPoint* (Cheshire, CT: The Graphics Press, 2003).

5. Richard A. Lanham, *The Economics of Attention: Style and Substance in the Age of Information* (Chicago: University of Chicago Press, 2007).

6. Edward R. Tufte, "PowerPoint Does Rocket Science—and Better Techniques for Technical Reports," online posting, September 6, 2005, *Ask E.T.* online forum, http://www.edwardtufte .com/bboard/q-and-a-fetch-msg?msg_id=0001yB&topic_id=1&topic=Ask+E%2eT%2e.

7. Edward R. Tufte, "PowerPoint is Evil," *Wired* 11, no. 9, September 2003, http://www.wired .com/wired/archive/11.09/ppt2.html.

8. Edward R. Tufte, "Metaphors for Presentations: Conway's Law Meets PowerPoint," online posting, January 3, 2006, *Ask E.T.* online forum, http://www.edwardtufte.com/bboard/ q-and-a-fetch-msg?msg_id=00025o.

9. Barry Rubin, "British Government Plagiarizes MERIA Journal: Our Response," *MERIA: Middle East Review of International Affairs*, http://meria.idc.ac.il/british-govt-plagiarizes-meria.html.

10. Mark Bernstein, "Hypertext 2007 Conference Programme," http://www.sigweb.org/ht07/ programme/.

11. Thomas E. Ricks, *Fiasco: The American Military Adventure in Iraq* (New York: Penguin, 2007).

12. Paul Krugman, "Bullet Points Over Baghdad," *New York Times*, December 2, 2005. Available at http://select.nytimes.com/2005/12/02/opinion/02krugman.html.

13. The White House, *National Strategy for Victory in Iraq*, November 30, 2005. Available at http:// www.whitehouse.gov/infocus/iraq/iraq_national_strategy_20051130.pdf.

14. Scott Shane, "Bush's Speech on Iraq Echoes Analyst's Voice," *New York Times*, December 4, 2005. Available at http://www.nytimes.com/2005/12/04/politics/04strategy.html.

15. IMEF & MNC-I EFFECTS Exploitation Team, "Telling the Fallujah Story to the World (Third Cut)," PowerPoint presentation, Soldiers for the Truth Foundation, November 20, 2004. Available at http://www.sftt.org/.

16. "Fallujah Slideshow," online posting, November 30, 2004, *Little Green Footballs*, http:// littlegreenfootballs.com/weblog/?entry=13787.

17. Department of Defense Briefing, December 3, 2004, http://www.defenselink.mil/ transcripts/2004/tr20041203–1721.html.

18. Martha Raddatz, "Army Captain's Simple Demonstration: How to Win in Iraq," *ABC News*, December 15, 2006. Available at http://abcnews.go.com/International/story?id=2729584.

19. Martha Raddatz, "A Young Captain and Progress in Al Anbar," online posting, September 11, 2007, *ABC News* http://blogs.abcnews.com/theworldnewser/2007/09/progress-in-al-.html.

20. David Petraeus, "Slides from Petraeus' Testimony," U.S. Congress, September 11, 2007. Available at http://www.talkingpointsmemo.com/docs/petraeus-slides/.

21. Karen DeYoung, "Experts Doubt Drop In Violence in Iraq," *The Washington Post*, September 6, 2007. Available at http://www.washingtonpost.com/wp-dyn/content/article/2007/09/05/ AR2007090502466.html.

22. Seth Grimes, "Petraeus Does PowerPoint," online posting, October 15, 2007, *The Intelligent Enterprise Blog*, http://www.intelligententerprise.com/blog/archives/2007/10/petraeus_does_p .html.

23. The White House, FY07ITBudget, http://www.whitehouse.gov/omb/egov/documents/ FY07ITBudgetRollout_MarchUpdate.pdf.

24. Douglas L. Wilson, *Lincoln's Sword: The Presidency and the Power of Words* (New York: Knopf, 2006).

25. Peter Norvig, "PowerPoint: shot with its own bullets," online posting, August 2003, http:// norvig.com/lancet.htm.

26. Ian Parker, "Absolute Powerpoint," *New Yorker* 77, no. 13 (May 28, 2001): 76–87.

27. Peter Norvig, "The Making of the Gettysburg Powerpoint Presentation," 2007, http://norvig .com/Gettysburg/making.html.

28. John F. Raffensperger, "Gettysburg Address PPT, Raffensperger Version," March 21, 2005, http://www.mang.canterbury.ac.nz/people/jfraffen/Military/MakingGettysburg.htm.

29. To be fair to Norvig, many academic, government, and corporate events require the use of PowerPoint presentations to aid those providing technical support to organizational events and to provide more uniformity to a conference's visual identity.

30. David Byrne, *Envisioning Emotional Epistemological Information* (Göttingen, Germany: Steidel, 2003).

31. Ian Parker, "Absolute Powerpoint," *New Yorker* 77, no. 13, May 28, 2001, 76–87.

32. James Paul Gee, "Literacy, Discourse, and Linguistics: Introduction" *and* "What is Literacy?" in *Literacy: A Critical Sourcebook*, eds. Ellen Cushman, Eugene R. Kintgen, Barry Kroll, and Mike Rose (New York: Bedford/St. Martin's, 2001), 525–544.

33. Michael Heim, *Electric Language*, second edition (New Haven, CT: Yale University Press, 1987).

34. Astrid Klein and Mark Dytham, "Pecha Kucha / What," *Klein Dytham architecture*, http://www .klein-dytham.com/pechakucha/what.

35. The Yes Men, "Globalization of Textile Trade," Textiles of the Future, Tampere, Finland, August 16, 2001. Available at http://www.theyesmen.org/finland/ppt/index.html.

36. Edward R. Tufte, "Apple's Keynote Vs Microsoft's PowerPoint," online posting, November 10, 2006, *Ask E.T.*, http://www.edwardtufte.com/bboard/q-and-a-fetch-msg?msg_id=0000zF.

37. "History in a Nutshell PowerPoint," http://www.conceptwizard.com/conen/conflict_2 .html.

38. "Studio Homage Web site design," http://www.conceptwizard.com/.

39. "Nutshell Too," http://www.jewishvirtuallibrary.org/jsource/nutshell/nutshell3.html.

6 Whistle-Blowers: Traditional Epistolary Discourse and Electronic Communication

1. Massachusetts Historical Society, *Collections of the Massachusetts Historical Society* (Boston, MA: Massachusetts Historical Society, 1835), 61.

2. Essex Institute, *Essex Institute Historical Collections* (Salem, MA: Essex Institute Press, 1869), 87.

3. Janet P. Near and Marcia P. Miceli, "Whistle-Blowing: Myth and Reality," *Journal of Management* 2, no. 3 (June 1, 1996): 507–526.

4. Vitaly J. Dubrovsky, Sara Kiesler, and Beheruz N. Sethna, "The Equalization Phenomenon: Status Effects in Computer-Mediated and Face-to-Face Decision-Making Groups," *Human-Computer Interaction* 6 (1991). Available at http://www.leaonline.com/doi/abs/10.1207/s15327051hci0602_2.

5. Caroline Bland and Máire Cross, eds., *Gender and Politics in the Age of Letter-Writing, 1750–2000*, (Aldershot, Burlington, VT: Ashgate, 2004).

6. Sherron Watkins, "Twenty-First Century Corporate Governance: The Growing Pressure on the Board Toward a Corporate Solution," in *Leadership and Governance from the Inside Out*, ed. Robert P. Gandossy and Jeffrey A. Sonnenfeld (New York: John Wiley and Sons, 2004), 28–29.

7. Sherron Watkins, "Alleged Sherron Watkins August 2001 Letter to Enron C.E.O. Kenneth Lay." Available at http://news.findlaw.com/hdocs/docs/enron/empltr2lay82001.pdf.

8. Dan Ackman, "Sherron Watkins Had Whistle, But Blew It," *Forbes* (February 14, 2002). Available at http://www.forbes.com/2002/02/14/0214watkins.html.

9. Mimi Swartz and Sherron Watkins, *Power Failure: The Inside Story of the Collapse of Enron* (New York: Currency, 2004), 276.

10. Ibid.

11. Ibid.

12. Sherron Watkins, "Twenty-First Century Corporate Governance: The Growing Pressure on the Board Toward a Corporate Solution," in *Leadership and Governance from the Inside Out*, ed. Robert P. Gandossy and Jeffrey A. Sonnenfeld (New York: John Wiley and Sons, 2004), 30.

13. Coleen Rowley, "Coleen Rowley's Memo to FBI Director Robert Mueller," *TIME* (May 21, 2002). Available at http://www.time.com/time/nation/article/0,8599,249997,00.html.

14. Toby Ditz, "Formative Ventures: Mercantile Letters and the Articulation of Experience," in *Epistolary Selves*, ed. Rebecca Earle & Carolyn Steedman (London: Ashgate, 1999), 59–78.

15. John Poulakos, "Special Delivery: Rhetoric, Letter Writing, and the Question of Beauty," in *The Ethos of Rhetoric*, ed. Michael J. Hyde and Calvin O. Schrag (Univ of South CarolinaPress, 2004), 89–97.

16. Coleen Rowley, "Coleen Rowley's Memo to FBI Director Robert Mueller," *TIME* (May 21, 2002). Available at http://www.time.com/time/nation/article/0,8599,249997,00.html.

17. Janet Gurkin Altman, *Epistolarity: Approaches to a Form* (Columbus: Ohio State University Press, 1982), 117.

18. Ibid., 122.

19. Coleen Rowley, "Coleen Rowley's Memo to FBI Director Robert Mueller," *TIME* (May 21, 2002). Available at http://www.time.com/time/nation/article/0,8599,249997,00.html.

20. Gail Hawisher and Charles Moran, "Electronic Mail and the Writing Instructor," *College English* 55, no. 6 (October 1993): 632.

21. Lee Sproull and Sara Kiesler, *Connections: New Ways of Working in the Networked Organization* (Cambridge, MA: MIT Press, 1992), 42.

22. Coleen Rowley, "Coleen Rowley's Memo to FBI Director Robert Mueller," *TIME* (May 21, 2002). Available at http://www.time.com/time/nation/article/0,8599,249997,00.html.

23. Jonathan Steuer, "Defining Virtual Reality: Dimensions Determining Telepresence," *Journal of Communication* 42, no. 4 (1992): 73–93.

24. Rosalind W Picard, *Affective Computing* (Cambridge, MA: MIT Press, 1997), 87.

25. Ellen Strenski, "The Electronic Hybridity of E-Mail: Liminal Subject Formation Through Epistolary Gift Exchange," *RhetNet: The Rhetorical Dimensions of Cyberspace* (November 1996), http://wac.colostate.edu/rhetnet/rdc/strenski.html.

26. The Center for Public Integrity, "Profiting from Katrina," http://www.publicintegrity.org/katrina/report.aspx?aid=484.

27. Ibid.

28. David Shipley and Will Schwalbe, *Send: The Essential Guide to Email for Office and Home* (New York: Alfred A. Knopf, 2007), 3–4.

29. "Decision Making at NASA," *Columbia Accident Investigation Board Report*, August 2003. Available at http://caib.nasa.gov/news/report/default.html, 151.

30. Ibid., 157.

31. Ibid., 157.

32. Ibid., 164.

33. "FBI E-Mail Refers to Presidential Order Authorizing Inhumane Interrogation Techniques," online posting, December 20, 2004, *American Civil Liberties Union*, http://www.aclu.org/safefree/general/18769prs20041220.html.

34. Sibel Edmonds, "Sibel Edmonds—Official Web Site—www.JustaCitizen.org," http://www.justacitizen.com/.

35. Paul Elias, "Wikileaks Case Due Back in Court," *Associated Press*, February 27, 2008. Available at http://ap.google.com/article/ALeqM5iDWyWp3GfGD4juECC5_zs64xphOQD8V314PO0.

36. "Stifling Online Speech," *New York Times*, February 21, 2008. Available at http://www .nytimes.com/2008/02/21/opinion/21thu3.html.

37. "Wikileaks," http://wikileaks.org/wiki/Wikileaks.

38. "WikiLeak.org," http://wikileak.org/.

39. Sam Gregory, "DIY Video and Human Rights," online posting February 13, 2008, *The Hub: See It : Upload It : Share It : Take Action*, http://humanrightsvideo.wordpress.com/2008/02/13/ diy-video-and-human-rights/.

40. William Teesdale, "Guantanamo Unclassified," 2007, http://www.youtube.com/watch? v=D5E3w7ME6Fs.

41. Michael De Kort, "Original-See Other Copy If This Version Is Frozen," 2006, http://www .youtube.com/watch?v=qd3VV8Za04g.

42. Mark Klein, "AT&T Whistleblower Speaks Out Against Retroactive Immunity," 2007, http:// www.youtube.com/watch?v=b9aeKF-rOGA.

43. For more on the use of transnational networks by civil society organizations, see Jon Anderson, Jodi Dean, and Geert Lovink, eds. *Reformatting Politics: Information Technology and Global Civil Society* (New York: Routledge, 2006).

44. Sam Gregory, Gillian Caldwell, Ronit Avni, and Thomas Harding, eds., *Video for Change: A Guide for Advocacy and Activism* (London: Pluto Press, 2005).

45. The Humane Society of the United States, "Cheap Meat: Working in a Slaughterhouse," 2008, http://video.hsus.org/?fr_story=38247e8c8ea570aca40146c9477f280b28113254.

46. Ingrid Newkirk, "Re: Why Does PETA Use Such Graphic Imagery?," 2008, http://www .bigthink.com/media-the-press/7661.

47. Environmental Working Group, "Farm Subsidy Database," http://farm.ewg.org/sites/ farmbill2007/mappage.php.

48. "Campaign Donors: Fundrace 2008," *Huffington Post*, http://fundrace.huffingtonpost.com/.

49. Sunlight Foundation, "Earmark Map," http://www.sunlightlabs.com/earmarks/.

50. "Federal Funding Accountability and Transparency Act of 2006," http://thomas.loc.gov/ cgi-bin/bdquery/z?d109:S.2590:.

51. See Andrea Frisch, "*The Ethics of Testimony: A Genealogical Perspective Discourse* 25, no1&2 (Winter & Spring, 2003): 36–54 for how Jacques Derrida explored these subjects in his late work.

52. Maryland v. Craig, 497 U.S. 836 (1990).

7 Submit and Render: Digital Satires about Surveillance and Authentication

1. Christopher Soghoian, telephone interview with the author, November 8, 2007.

2. Christopher Soghoian, "Airport (in)security for the masses," online posting, October 25, 2006, *slight paranoia*, http://paranoia.dubfire.net/2006/10/airport-insecurity-for-masses.html.

3. Henry Jenkins, *Convergence Culture: Where Old and New Media Collide* (New York: New York University Press, 2006).

4. Jonathan Silverstein, "Web Site Lets Anyone Create Fake Boarding Passes," *ABC News*, October 27, 2006. Available at http://abcnews.go.com/Technology/story?id=2611432&page=1.

5. Congressman Edward Markey, "MARKEY: DON'T ARREST STUDENT, USE HIM TO FIX LOOP-HOLES," online posting, October 29, 2006, http://markey.house.gov/index.php?option=content &task=view&id=2336&Itemid=125.

6. Jonathan Silverstein, "Web Site Lets Anyone Create Fake Boarding Passes," *ABC News*, October 27, 2006. Available at http://abcnews.go.com/Technology/story?id=2611432&page=1.

7. Charles Schumer, "SCHUMER REVEALS NEW GAPING HOLE IN AIR SECURITY: IN SIMPLE STEPS TERRORISTS ON WATCH LIST COULD BOARD FLIGHTS NO QUESTIONS ASKED," online posting, February 13, 2005, http://www.senate.gov/~schumer/SchumerWebsite/pressroom/press _releases/2005/PR4123.aviationsecurity021305.html.

8. Andy Bowers, "A Dangerous Loophole in Airport Security," *Slate Magazine*, February 7, 2005. Available at http://www.slate.com/id/2113157/.

9. Christopher Soghoian, "Paging Osama, please meet your party at the Information Desk," online posting, October 18, 2006, *slight paranoia*, http://paranoia.dubfire.net/2006/10/paging-osama-please-meet-your-party-at.html.

10. Christopher Soghoian, "Airport (in)security for the masses," October 25, 2006, online posting, *slight paranoia*, http://paranoia.dubfire.net/2006/10/airport-insecurity-for-masses.html.

11. Ryland Sanders, The Church Sign Generator, 2003, http://www.churchsigngenerator.com/.

12. Adobe, "Adobe Photoshop: Photoshop and CDS," http://www.adobe.com/products/photoshop/cds.html.

13. Alan De Smet, "US Driver's License Numbers—Florida, Illinois, Wisconsin, perhaps others," *High Programmer*, http://www.highprogrammer.com/alan/numbers/dl_us_shared.html.

14. M. Borroff, "The Computer As Poet," *Yale Alumni Magazine* (1971).

15. Ellen Strenski and N. G. Esposito, "The Poet, the Computer, and the Classroom," *College English* 42, no. 2 (1978): 142–150.

16. Alan Turing, "Computing Machinery and Intelligence," *Mind* 236 (October 1950): 433–460.

17. Noah Wardrip-Fruin and Nick Montfort, *The New Media Reader* (Cambridge, MA: MIT Press, 2006).

18. Gary R. Hess, Dada Poetry Generator, http://www.poemofquotes.com/tools/dada.php.

19. Charles Fleming, "Spam, spam, spam, spam, and poetry," *The Los Angeles Times*, December 13, 2007. Available at http://www.latimes.com/news/printedition/asection/la-oe-fleming13dec13,1,3339208.story?ctrack=1&cset=true.

20. Mark Hansen, "Spam Poetry," Homepage for Mark Hansen, http://www.stat.ucla.edu/~cocteau/.

21. Douglas Giles, "Spam Poetry Institute," The Spam Poetry Institute, http://www.spampoetry.org/.

22. Charles Fleming, "Spam, spam, spam, spam, and poetry," *The Los Angeles Times*, December 13, 2007. Available at http://www.latimes.com/news/printedition/asection/la-oe-fleming13dec13,1,3339208.story?ctrack=1&cset=true.

23. Michael Smith, logopoeia ≫ emily dickinson random epigram machine, 2005, http://logopoeia.com/ed/.

24. Write an Instant William Carlos Williams Poem, http://ettcweb.lr.k12.nj.us/forms/williams.htm.

25. "Warholizer: Turn digital photos of you and your friends into pop art!," http://bighugelabs.com/flickr/warholizer.php.

26. Andrew C. Bulhak and Josh Larios, "Communications From Elsewhere," *Postmodern Essay Generator*, http://www.elsewhere.org/pomo/.

27. Andrew C. Bulhak, "On the Simulation of Postmodernism and Mental Debility using Recursive Transition Networks" 96/264, 1996, Dept. Computer Science Technical Reports, Monash University, Melbourne Australia. Available at http://www.csse.monash.edu.au/cgi-bin/pub_search?104+1996+bulhak+Postmodernism.

28. Ibid.

29. Ibid.

30. Andrew C. Bulhak, "Communications From Elsewhere," *Postmodern Essay Generator*, http://www.elsewhere.org/pomo/.

31. Alan Sokal, "Transgressing the Boundaries: Towards a Transformative Hermeneutics of Quantum Gravity," *Social Text* 46/47 (spring/summer 1996): 217–252.

32. Alan Sokal, "A Physicist Experiments With Cultural Studies," *Lingua Franca* (May/June 1996): 62–64.

33. Ibid.

34. C. P. Snow, *The Two Cultures* (Cambridge: Cambridge University Press, 1993).

35. Andrew C. Bulhak, "On the Simulation of Postmodernism and Mental Debility using Recursive Transition Networks" 96/264, 1996, Dept. Computer Science Technical Reports, Monash University, Melbourne Australia. Available at http://www.csse.monash.edu.au/cgi-bin/pub_search?104+1996+bulhak+Postmodernism.

36. Phillip Ball, "Computer Conference Welcomes Gobbledygook Paper," *Nature* 434 (April 8, 2005): 936. Available at http://www.nature.com/nature/journal/v434/n7036/full/nature03653.html.

37. Christopher Soghoian, telephone interview with the author, November 8, 2007.

38. Ryan Singel, "The Great No-ID Airport Challenge," *Wired*, June 9, 2006. Available at http://www.wired.com/science/discoveries/news/2006/06/71115.

39. Department of Homeland Security Data Privacy and Integrity Advisory Committee, "OFFICIAL MEETING MINUTES Wednesday, June 7, 2006." Available at http://www.dhs.gov/xlibrary/assets/privacy/privacy_advcom_06–2006_mtgminutes_PM.pdf.

40. Christopher Soghoian, telephone interview with the author on November 8, 2007. For more on the relationship between counterculture and corporate cyberculture at this annual event, see Fred Turner, "Burning Man at Google: How Art Worlds Help Sustain New Media Industries," presentation at the Society for Social Studies of Science (4S) conference, Montréal, Canada, October 13, 2007. Each year about 50,000 people attend what Burning Man organizers describe as "an annual experiment in temporary community dedicated to radical self-expression and radical self-reliance" held in the Black Rock Desert of Nevada. See http://www.burningman.com/.

41. Christopher Soghoian, telephone interview with the author, November 8, 2007.

42. Ian Bogost, "Persuasive Games—Airport Insecurity," http://persuasivegames.com/games/game.aspx?game=airportinsecurity.

43. Ibid.

44. Ibid.

45. Ibid.

46. http://nofly.s3.com/ (accessed April 1, 2007; site now discontinued).

47. Bruce Schneier, "Find Out if You're on the "No Fly List," online posting, March 14, 2007, *Schneier on Security*, http://www.schneier.com/blog/archives/2007/03/find_out_if_you.html.

48. Kathleen Schafer, "TSAin't—Keeping America Safe from Photographers: So what's your story?" http://tsaintgood.blogspot.com/2006/04/so-whats-your-story.html.

49. Transportation Security Administration, "TSA: Myth Busters Archive," http://www.tsa.gov/approach/mythbusters/index.shtm.

50. Christopher Soghoian, "Paging Osama, please meet your party at the Information Desk," online posting, October 18, 2006, *slight paranoia*, http://paranoia.dubfire.net/2006/10/paging-osama-please-meet-your-party-at.html.

51. Clive Thomson, "The Visible Man: An FBI Target Puts His Whole Life Online," *Wired*, March 22, 2007. Available at http://www.wired.com/techbiz/people/magazine/15–06/ps_transparency.

52. Hasan Ekahi, "trackingtransience.com," http://www.trackingtransience.com/.

53. Steve Mann, Jason Nolan, and Barry Wellman, "Sousveillance: Inventing and Using Wearable Computing Devices for Data Collection in Surveillance Environments," *Surveillance & Society* 1, no. 3 (2003): 333.

54. j0hn4d4m5, "Document Gennreator," http://j0hn4d4m5.bravehost.com/.

55. Ibid.

56. Mathew Waterman, http://www.dehp.net/fakewarrant/.

57. Ibid.

58. Gerard Vlemmings, *The Generator Blog*, http://generatorblog.blogspot.com/.

59. J. M. Balkin, *Cultural Software: A Theory of Ideology* (New Haven, CT: Yale University Press, 2003).

60. Corinne Kratz, "Genres of Power: A Comparative Analysis of Okiek Blessings, Curses and Oaths," *Man* 24, no. 4 (December 1989): 636–656.

61. Simon Jenkins, "Biblical Curse Generator," *Ship of Fools: the Magazine of Christian Unrest*, http://ship-of-fools.com/Features/Curses/.

62. Trevor Stone, "Elizabethan Curse Generator," http://trevorstone.org/curse.

63. Boingo Bill and Rhino, "Worldwide Blessing Generator," http://worldwideblessing.com/.

64. I.N.X.J.U./Banjo Ruthless Creations, "Surrealism Server: Surrealist Compliments For All," http://www.madsci.org/cgi-bin/cgiwrap/%7Elynn/jardin/SCG/.

65. Open Directory, "Recreation: Humor: Insults," http://www.dmoz.org/Recreation/Humor/Insults/.

66. InkStainedRetch, "Tell Zell: Go Down in Flames, Hack!*," http://www.tellzell.com/2008/06/go-down-in-flames-hack.html.

67. Autoreplace functions can have unintended consequences, of course. The Christian news service OneNewsNow.com automatically substituted the word "homosexual" for the word "gay" in its AP news feed in order to avoid a term that IT managers worried might be embued with overly positive connotations. In June of 2008 runner Tyson Gay was angered when he was repeatedly called "Tyson Homosexual" in the group's online coverage of his athletic achievements. See Mary Ann Akers, "Christian Site's Ban on 'G' Word Sends Homosexual to the Olympics," online posting, July 1, 2008, *The Sleuth*. Available at http://blog.washingtonpost.com/sleuth/2008/07/christian_sites_ban_on_g_word.html.

68. Bruce Schneier, "Random Identity Generator," online posting, June 22, 2006, *Schneier on Security*, http://www.schneier.com/blog/archives/2006/06/random_identity.html.

69. Jennifer Cool, "The Data Structures of Everyday Life (The Limits of Automagical Order)," *The Participant Observer*, online posting, January 9, 2007, http://cool.org/?p=20 (accessed January 15, 2007; site now discontinued).

70. Andrew Keen, *The Cult of the Amateur: How Today's Internet is Killing Our Culture* (New York: Currency, 2007).

71. Trebor Scholz and Geert Lovink, *The Art of Free Cooperation* (Amsterdam: Autonomedia/ Institute for Distributed Creativity, 2007).

72. Geert Lovink, *Zero Comments: Blogging and Critical Internet Culture* (New York: Routledge, 2007).

73. Siva Vaidhyanathan, "Me, 'Person of the Year'? No thanks," *MSNBC*, December 28, 2006. Available at http://www.msnbc.msn.com/id/16371425/.

74. Mia Consalvo, "Who Owns This FAQ?" paper presented at the Association of Internet Research Conference, Vancouver, Canada, October 19, 2007.

75. Lisa Nakamura, "Race 2.0: Identity, the Internet, and the Shift to New Media," keynote address, Association of Internet Research Conference, Vancouver, Canada, October 17, 2007.

76. Jaron Lanier, "Digital Maoism: The Hazards of the New Online Collectivism ," *Edge* no. 183 (May 30, 2006). Available at http://www.edge.org/3rd_culture/lanier06/lanier06_index.html.

77. Dan Lockton, "Architectures of Control," *Engineering Designer* (April 2006). Available at http://www.danlockton.co.uk/research/28–31–ED.pdf.

78. Paolo Ordoveza, "WWTQ | Buzz," http://what.was.the.question.whyblog.org/buzz/.

79. Mark Marino, "Generating Web 2.0 ," online posting, April 21, 2007, *WRT: Writer Response Theory*, http://writerresponsetheory.org/wordpress/2007/04/21/generating-web-20/.

80. Christopher Soghoian, telephone interview with the author, November 8, 2007.

81. Virgil Griffith, "My summer of dilettante data-mining," lecture, University of California, Irvine, November 16, 2007. Available at http://virgil.gr/1+Berkeley-WikiScanner_Presentation. ppt.

82. Ibid.

83. Ibid.

84. Ibid.

85. Ibid.

86. Ibid.

87. United States Holocaust Museum, "Crisis in Darfur," http://www.ushmm.org/googleearth/ projects/darfur/.

88. American Patrol, "American Patrol Report ©—Citizenship—Sovereignty—Law," http://www .americanpatrol.com/.

89. Tad Hirsch, "Dialup Radio," http://www.dialupradio.org/.

90. See Steven Levy, *Hackers: Heroes of the Computer Revolution* (Garden City, N.Y: Anchor Press/ Doubleday, 1984) and Pekka Himanen and Linus Torvalds, *The Hacker Ethic* (New York: Random House Trade Paperbacks, 2002).

91. Virgil Griffith and Markus Jakobsson, "Messin' with Texas Deriving Mother's Maiden Names Using Public Records." Available at http://www.informatics.indiana.edu/markus/papers/mmn .pdf.

92. Virgil Griffith and Markus Jakobsson, "Demo for Messin' with Texas: Deriving Mother's Maiden Names from Public Records," http://php.virgil.gr/mmn-demo/.

93. Ryan Singel, "Homeland Security Website Hacked by Phishers? 15 Signs Say Yes—UPDATED 3 Times," online posting, February 14, 2007, *Threat Level: Privacy, Security, Politics, and Crime Online*, http://blog.wired.com/27bstroke6/2007/02/homeland_securi.html.

94. Michel Foucault, "Governmentality," in *The Foucault Effect, Studies in Governmentality*, ed. Graham Burchell, Colin Gordon, and Peter Miller (Chicago: University of Chicago Press, 1991), 87–104.

95. Jane Fountain, *Building the Virtual State: Information Technology and Institutional Change* (Washington, DC: Brookings Institute Press, 2001).

96. Neil Zawacki, "DARKSITES.COM EVIL GUIDE PLAN," http://www.darksites.com/evilplan.php.

97. Lev Manovich, *The Language of New Media* (Cambridge, MA: MIT Press, 2002), 32.

98. Ibid., 121.

99. Michael Bérubé, "Instantaneous Citation Index," Meet the Bloggers: Blogging and the Future of Academia panel, Modern Language Association Annual Conference, Philadelphia, PA. December 30, 2006.

100. Geert Lovink, *Zero Comments: Blogging and Critical Internet Culture* (New York: Routledge, 2007), 9.

101. Jennifer Cool, *Cyborganic and the Birth of Social Media*, draft of unpublished dissertation, University of Southern California.

102. Ibid.

103. David Fleming, "Can Pictures Be Arguments?" *Argumentation and Advocacy* 33, no. 1 (1996): 11–22.

104. Corrie Pikul, "The Photoshopping of the president," *Salon*, July 1, 2004. Available at http:// dir.salon.com/story/ent/feature/2004/07/01/photoshop/index.html.

105. Bruno Latour and Peter Weibel, *Making Things Public: Atmospheres of Democracy* (Cambridge, MA: MIT Press, 2005).

106. David King, "The Commissar Vanishes," *Newseum*, http://www.newseum.org/berlinwall/ commissar_vanishes/.

107. Frank W. Baker, "Comparison of Alcatel," *Media Literacy Clearinghouse*, http://www.frankwbaker.com/comparison.htm (accessed February 28, 2006; site now partially discontinued).

108. "Ethics in Image Manipulation," panel at SIGGRAPH 2006, Boston, MA, August 1, 2006,. Available at http://www.siggraph.org/s2006/main.php?f=conference&p=panels&s=panel4.

109. L. M. Dario, Franca Agnoli Sacchi, and Elizabeth F.Loftus, "Changing History: Doctored Photographs Affect Memory for Past Public Events," *Applied Cognitive Psychology* 21, no. 8 (December 2007): 1005–1022.

110. Matt Mahurin, *Time* (June 27, 1994) cover.

111. David Hume Kennerly and Tim O'Brien, *Time* (March 26, 2007) cover.

112. Jane Hamsher, "About That Graphic . . .," online posting, August 2, 2006, *Firedoglake*, http://www.firedoglake.com/2006/08/02/about-that-graphic/.

113. Michelle Malkin, "Netroots vs. Rightroots; left-wingers love blackface," online posting, August 2, 2006, *Michelle Malkin*, http://michellemalkin.com/2006/08/02/netroots-vs-rightroots-left-wingers-love-blackface.

114. Steve Gilliard, "Simple Sambo wants to move to the big house," online posting, October 26, 2005, *THE NEWS BLOG*, http://stevegilliard.blogspot.com/2005/10/simple-sambo-wants-to-move-to-big.html.

115. Ann Althouse, "Bill Clinton, lunching with the bloggers," online posting, September 13, 2006, *Althouse*, http://althouse.blogspot.com/2006/09/bill-clinton-lunching-with-bloggers.html.

116. Ibid.

117. Ibid.

118. Ibid.

119. Ann Althouse, "Let's take a closer look at those breasts," online posting, September 15, 2006, *Althouse*, http://althouse.blogspot.com/2006/09/lets-take-closer-look-at-those-breasts.html.

120. Jessica Valenti, "The 'dirty pillow' line of attack," online posting, September 16, 2006, *Feministing*, http://www.feministing.com/archives/005716.html.

121. Ibid.

122. Amanda Marcotte, "Actually, the pubic hair lept off the soda can and told a joke, so really it was kinda funny," online posting, September 27, 2006, *Pandagon*, http://pandagon.blogsome.com/2006/09/27/actually-the-pubic-hair-lept-off-the-soda-can-and-told-a-joke-so-really-it-was-kinda-funny/.

123. Ibid.

124. Ibid.

125. Liza Sabater, "There are no black bloggers in Harlem or New York City," online posting, September 15, 2006, *The Daily Gotham*, http://dailygotham.com/blog/liza_sabater/there_are_no _black_bloggers_in_harlem_or_new_york_city.

126. Lindsay Beyerstein, "Burqas, Photoshop, and the feminist blogosphere," online posting, October 7, 2006, *Majikthise*, http://majikthise.typepad.com/majikthise_/2006/10/burqas_photosho.html.

127. Amanda Marcotte, "Actually, the pubic hair lept off the soda can and told a joke, so really it was kinda funny," online posting, September 27, 2006, *Pandagon*, http://pandagon.blogsome .com/2006/09/27/actually-the-pubic-hair-lept-off-the-soda-can-and-told-a-joke-so-really-it-was -kinda-funny/.

128. Elizabeth Losh, "Divide and Conquer," online posting, April 12, 2006, *Virtualpolitik*, http:// virtualpolitik.blogspot.com/2006/04/divide-and-conquer.html.

129. Siva Vaidhyanathan, "Uh. Maybe I am Gale Norton . . .," online posting, April 12, 2006, *SIVACRACY.NET,* http://www.sivacracy.net/2006/04/uh_maybe_i_am_gale_norton.html.

130. Forsman and Bodenfors, G*!rlpower Retouch* http://demo.fb.se/e/girlpower/retouch/.

131. Alan Becker, "Animator vs. Animation," *deviantART*, June 3, 2006, http://alanbecker .deviantart.com/art/Animator-vs-Animation-34244097.

132. Alan Becker, "Animator vs. Animation II," *deviantART*, March 14, 2007, http://alanbecker .deviantart.com/art/Animator-vs-Animation-II-50891749. For more on the window metaphor, see Anne Friedberg, *The Virtual Window: From Alberti to Microsoft* (Cambridge, MA: MIT Press, 2006).

133. Lev Manovich, *The Language of New Media* (Cambridge, MA: MIT Press, 2002), 175.

134. David G. Hale, "Analogy of the Body Politic," *Dictionary of the History of Ideas*, http://etext .virginia.edu/cgi-local/DHI/dhi.cgi?id=dv1-11.

135. ~shock-value, "Interactive Buddy v.1.02," *deviantART*, http://shock-value.deviantart.com/ art/Interactive-Buddy-v-1–02–11117398.

136. Wafaa Bilal, "Domestic Tension FAQ," http://www.crudeoils.us/wafaa/html/faq.html.

137. One of Bilal's later installations, which was held at the Rensselaer Polytechnic Institute, "The Night of Bush Capturing: Virtual Jihadi" was cancelled after a public outcry about its supposed incendiary content. Bilal had taken the crude anti-American *Night of Bush Capturing* videogame from the Global Islamic Media Front, which was a mod that had used the *Quest for Saddam* game engine to argue for its jihadist aggression. Bilal had inserted clips of himself and elements of his own autobiography into the digital work. See Bilal's explanation of events at "Wafaa Bilal Interviewed on the RPI Censorship," 2008, http://www.youtube.com/ watch?v=TGzb6lNLY98 and http://www.wafaabilal.com/media.html.

138. Gonzalo Frasca, "September 12th a toy world," *Newsgaming.com*, http://www.newsgaming .com/games/index12.htm.

139. Caroline Ewing, "Post-Domestic Tension," *FNewsmagazine.com: the Student Magazine of the School of the Art Institute of Chicago*, http://www.fnewsmagazine.com/summer/news/ bilal_postdomestic.php.

8   Reading Room: The Nation-State and Digital Library Initiatives

1. The Library of Congress, "U.S. Serial Set Home Page: U.S. Congressional Documents." Available at http://memory.loc.gov/ammem/amlaw/lwss.html.

2. Readex, *"U.S. Congressional Serial Set, 1817–1980* with American State Papers, 1789–1838: Bibliographic Records—Background Information," http://www.readex.com/readex/index.cfm ?content=208.

3. Anthony Grafton, "Future Reading," *New Yorker* (November 5, 2007). Available at http://www .newyorker.com/reporting/2007/11/05/071105fa_fact_grafton.

4. The National Archives, "About the National Archives and Records Administration," http:// www.archives.gov/about/.

5. John Y. Cole, "Jefferson's Legacy: A Brief History of the Library of Congress—THE LIBRARY OF CONGRESS, 1800–1992," http://www.loc.gov/loc/legacy/loc.html.

6. The Library of Congress, "About THOMAS (Library of Congress)," http://thomas.loc.gov/ home/abt_thom.html.

7. Thomas Jefferson, "Thomas Jefferson to Richard Price, January 8, 1789," January 8, 1789. Available at http://memory.loc.gov/cgi-bin/query/P?mtj:15:./temp/~ammem_x1dZ::.

8. Grace News Network, "Grace News Network," http://www.gracenewsnetwork.com/.

9. Shane Harris, "Government will launch news network to counter 'anti-American' image," June 2, 2003, *Government Executive*, http://www.govexec.com/dailyfed/0603/060203h1.htm.

10. Stephen Labaton, "ARCHIVES OF BUSINESS: A ROGUES GALLERY; Cortes Randell: Student Market Hoax," *New York Times*, December 7, 1985. Available at http://select.nytimes.com/search/ restricted/article?res=F50715FA345E0C748CDDAB0994DE484D81.

11. "WASHINGTON TALK: FEDERAL NEWS SERVICE; REPORTING EXACTLY WHAT IS SAID," *New York Times*, July 27, 1987. Available at http://query.nytimes.com/gst/fullpage .html?res=9B0DE6DE143EF934A15754C0A961948260.

12. Google Press Center, "Press Release: Google Checks Out Library Books," http://www.google .com/press/pressrel/print_library.html.

13. Keith Regan, "E-Commerce News: Internet: Publishers Raise Concerns About Google Print Project," *E-Commerce News*, June 22, 2005. Available at http://www.ecommercetimes.com/story/ HMu4OEh2cXVvuX/Publishers-Raise-Concerns-About-Google-Print-Project.xhtml.

14. Google Press Center, "Press Release: Google Checks Out Library Books," http://www.google .com/press/pressrel/print_library.html.

15. *Authors Guild v. Google*, Findlaw.com, http://fl1.findlaw.com/news.findlaw.com/hdocs/docs/google/aggoog92005cmp.pdf.

16. Eric Schmidt, "Books of Revelation," *The Wall Street Journal*, October 18, 2005. Available at http://online.wsj.com/article/SB112958982689471238.html.

17. *The McGraw-Hill Companies, Inc. et al v. Google Inc.*, Justia Docs, http://docs.justia.com/cases/federal/district-courts/new-york/nysdce/1:2005cv08881/275068/1/.

18. Google Book Search, "User Stories," http://books.google.com/googlebooks/testimonials.html.

19. Ibid.

20. Mia Consalvo, *Cheating: Gaining Advantage in Videogames* (Cambridge, MA: MIT Press, 2007).

21. Mary Sue Coleman, "Google, the Khmer Rouge and the Public Good—February 6, 2006," address given to the Professional/Scholarly Publishing Division of the Association of American Publishers, February 6, 2006. Available at http://www.umich.edu/pres/speeches/060206google.html.

22. Google Press Center, "Press Release: Google Checks Out Library Books," http://www.google.com/press/pressrel/print_library.html.

23. Mary Sue Coleman, "Google, the Khmer Rouge and the Public Good—February 6, 2006," address given to the Professional/Scholarly Publishing Division of the Association of American Publishers, February 6, 2006. Available at http://www.umich.edu/pres/speeches/060206google.html.

24. Ibid.

25. Ibid.

26. Ibid.

27. The Library of Congress, "Jefferson's Library," *Thomas Jefferson (Library of Congress Exhibition)*, http://www.loc.gov/exhibits/jefferson/jefflib.html.

28. James Conaway, *America's Library: The Story of the Library of Congress*, 1800–2000 (New Haven, CT: Yale University Press, 2000), 30.

29. Hillel Schwartz, *The Culture of the Copy: Striking Likenesses, Unreasonable Facsimiles* (New York: Zone Books, 1998).

30. Laura Graham, interview with the author, Washington, D. C., 2002.

31. Mary Sue Coleman, "Google, the Khmer Rouge and the Public Good—February 6, 2006," address given to the Professional/Scholarly Publishing Division of the Association of American Publishers, February 6, 2006. Available at http://www.umich.edu/pres/speeches/060206google.html.

32. Siva Vaidhyanathan, "A Risky Gamble with Google," *The Chronicle of Higher Education*, December 2, 2005. Available at http://chronicle.com/weekly/v52/i15/15b00701.htm.

33. Diane Harley, Jonathan Henke, and Shannon Lawrence, *Use and Users of Digital Resources: A Focus on Undergraduate Education in the Humanities and Social Sciences* (Berkeley, CA: University of California, Berkeley, 2006). Available at http://cshe.berkeley.edu/research/digitalresourcestudy/report/.

34. Siva Vaidhyanathan, "A Risky Gamble with Google," *The Chronicle of Higher Education*, December 2, 2005. Available at http://chronicle.com/subscribe/login?url=http%3A%2F%2Fchronicle.com%2Fweekly%2Fv52%2Fi15%2F15b00701.htm.

35. Ibid.

36. Jim Zwick, e-mail message to the author, November 9, 2007.

37. See Albert-László Barabási, *Linked: How Everything Is Connected to Everything Else and What It Means* (New York: Plume, 2003) for more on large hubs.

38. Claus Schmidt, "Page Hijack Exploit: 302, redirects and Google," online posting, March 14, 2005, *clsc.net*, http://clsc.net/research/google-302–page-hijack.htm.

39. Henry Jenkins, *Textual Poachers: Television Fans & Participatory Culture* (New York: Routledge, 1992).

40. John Seely Brown and Paul Duguid, *The Social Life of Information* (Cambridge, MA: Harvard Business School Press, 2002), 44.

41. Jim Zwick, e-mail message to the author, November 18, 2007.

42. Ibid.

43. Jim Zwick, e-mail message to the author, November 9, 2007.

44. Steve Lohr, "This Boring Headline Is Written for Google," *New York Times*, April 9, 2006. Available at http://www.nytimes.com/2006/04/09/weekinreview/09lohr.html.

45. Kevin J. Delaney, "You're a Nobody Unless Your Name Googles Well," *The Wall Street Journal*, May 8, 2007. Available at http://online.wsj.com/article/SB117856222924394753.html.

46. Siva Vaidhyanathan, "Critical Information Studies: A Bibliographic Manifesto," *Cultural Studies* 20, no. 2 & 3 (March 2006). Available at http://www.sivacracy.net/archives/CriticalInformationStudies.pdf.

47. Tom Zeller, "House Member Criticizes Internet Companies for Practices in China," *New York Times*, February 15, 2005. Available at http://www.nytimes.com/2006/02/15/technology/15cnd-internet.html.

48. Siva Vaidhyanathan, "Has the Library of Congress Surrendered Its Role in Standardizing How We Catalog Knowledge?" online posting, January 29, 2008, *Sivacracy.net*, http://www.sivacracy.net/2008/01/has_the_library_of_congress_su.html.

49. The Library of Congress, *Report of The Library of Congress Working Group on the Future of Bibliographic Control* (Washington, D.C.: The Library of Congress, January 9, 2008). Available at http://www.loc.gov/bibliographic-future/news/lcwg-ontherecord-jan08–final.pdf.

50. "FutureOfBibliographicControl—Open Knowledge Foundation Wiki," http://www.okfn .org/wiki/FutureOfBibliographicControl.

51. Library Juice, "Thomas Mann's New One," online posting, June 16, 2007, http:// libraryjuicepress.com/blog/?p=272.

52. Douglas K. Smith and Robert C. Alexander, *Fumbling the Future: How Xerox Invented, Then Ignored, the First Personal Computer* (New York: Morrow, 1988).

53. American Library Association, Chicago, Press Release dated March 16, 1938, TS, Box 8, "Microphotography" folder, Albert Boni Collection of Material about Photography (Collection 1046). Department of Special Collections, Charles E. Young Research Library, University of California, Los Angeles.

54. August Imholtz, "Albet Boni: A Sketch of Life in Micro-Opaque," *The Proceedings of the American Antiquarian Society* (Worcester) 115 (2006): 253–277.

55. Ibid.

56. Paul Avrich, "Albert Boni," in *Anarchist Voices: An Oral History of Anarchism in America* (Princeton: Princeton University Press, 1995), 65–66.

57. August Imholtz, "Albet Boni: A Sketch of Life in Micro-Opaque," *The Proceedings of the American Antiquarian Society* (Worcester) 115 (2006): 253–277.

58. Marvin Lowenthal, "Too Small to See But Not to Read," *Saturday Review of Literature*, November 16, 1944.

59. August Imholtz, "Albet Boni: A Sketch of Life in Micro-Opaque," *The Proceedings of the American Antiquarian Society* (Worcester) 115 (2006): 253–277.

60. Edgar L. Erickson, "Microprint: A Revolution in Printing," *Journal of Documentation* 7, no. 4 (September, 1951): 184–187.

61. "Condensed Library," *Business Week* (December 9, 1939): 48.

62. August Imholtz, "Albet Boni: A Sketch of Life in Micro-Opaque," *The Proceedings of the American Antiquarian Society* (Worcester) 115 (2006): 253–277.

63. Marvin Lowenthal, "Too Small to See But Not to Read," *Saturday Review of Literature*, November 16, 1944.

64. American Library Association, Chicago, Press Release dated March 16, 1938, TS, Box 8, "Microphotography," Albert Boni Collection of Material about Photography (Collection 1046). Department of Special Collections, Charles E. Young Research Library, University of California, Los Angeles.

65. Marvin Lowenthal, "Too Small to See But Not to Read," *Saturday Review of Literature*, November 16, 1944.

66. Ibid.

67. Albert Boni, Untitled Typescript, Albert Boni Collection of Material about Photography (Collection 1046). Department of Special Collections, Charles E. Young Research Library, University of California, Los Angeles.

68. *The Scientists Speak*, ed. Warren Weaver (New York: Boni and Gaer, 1947).

69. John Tennant, "Miniprint: Is It a Practical Way to Cut Publishing Costs? or If You Read This You Can Read Miniprint," *Essays of an Information Scientist* 3, no. 2 (January 9, 1978).

70. Pierre Metz to Albert Boni, 11 September 1963, Box 3, Folder 8, Albert Boni Collection of Material about Photography (Collection 1046). Department of Special Collections, Charles E. Young Research Library, University of California, Los Angeles.

71. J.R. Madden to Dorothy S. Gelatt, Morgan & Morgan reader survey for *Photographic Literature*, Box 3, Folder 8, Albert Boni Collection of Material about Photography (Collection 1046). Department of Special Collections, Charles E. Young Research Library, University of California, Los Angeles.

72. For more on the connection between Bush's ideas and the microphotography movement, see Lawrence A. Harper, "Microphotography and History," *Pacific Historical Review* 15, no. 4 (1946): 427–434.

73. John Tennant, "Microprint and Readex," 11 December 1939, TS, Box 8, "Microphotography" folder, Albert Boni Collection of Material about Photography (Collection 1046). Department of Special Collections, Charles E. Young Research Library, University of California, Los Angeles.

74. Marvin Lowenthal, "Too Small to See But Not to Read," *Saturday Review of Literature*, November 16, 1944.

75. Kevin Kelly, "Scan This Book!," *New York Times*, May 14, 2006. Available at http://www .nytimes.com/2006/05/14/magazine/14publishing.html.

76. Siva Vaidhyanathan, *The Anarchist in the Library* (New York: Basic Books, 2004), 170.

77. Roland Barthes, *Mythologies*, trans. Annette Lavers (New York: Hill and Wang, 1972).

78. Jacques-Alain Miller, "Google," *Le Nouvel Observateur*, March 15, 2007, http://hebdo .nouvelobs.com/hebdo/parution/p2210/articles/a335903.html.

79. Siva Vaidhyanathan, "The Googlization of Everything," http://www.googlizationofeverything .com/.

80. Jacques-Alain Miller, "Google," *Le Nouvel Observateur*, March 15, 2007. Available at http:// hebdo.nouvelobs.com/hebdo/parution/p2210/articles/a335903.html.

81. Jean-Noël Jeanneney, *Google and the Myth of Universal Knowledge: A View from Europe*, trans. Teresa Lavender Fagen (Chicago: University Of Chicago Press, 2007), 85.

82. Ibid., 71.

83. Jean-Noël Jeanneney, e-mail message to the author, March 4, 2008.

84. He has certainly been willing to acknowledge these shortcomings in other venues, however, and explain his efforts at remediation. Jean-Noël Jeanneney, e-mail message to the author, March 4, 2008.

85. Jean-Noël Jeanneney, interview with the author, Paris, France, September 17, 2007.

86. Michael Lorenzen, "Deconstructing the Philanthropic Library: The Sociological Reasons Behind Andrew Carnegie's Millions to Libraries," http://www.michaellorenzen.com/carnegie .html.

87. Jean-Noël Jeanneney, interview with the author, Paris, France, September 17, 2007.

88. Ibid.

89. John Battelle, *The Search: How Google and Its Rivals Rewrote the Rules of Business and Transformed Our Culture* (New York: Portfolio Trade, 2006).

90. Jean-Noël Jeanneney, "La culture gratuite? Illusions et hypocrisies," *Le Débat* 146 (September–October 2007): 158.

91. Pierre Lévy, *Collective Intelligence*, 1st ed. (New York: Basic Books, 1997).

92. Jean-Noël Jeanneney, "Wikipédia, une encyclopédie pas si Net," *Le Point*, June 21, 2007. Available at http://www.lepoint.fr/actualites-societe/wikipedia-une-encyclopedie-pas-si-net/920/ 0/189153.

93. Erkki Huhtamo, "Tracing the Topoi-On media Archeology," lecture, University of California, Irvine, Irvine, CA, January 25, 2006. See also Eric Kluitenberg, "Archaeology: Discourse Analysis, Media Archaeology, the Megamachine, Libidinal Mechanics," in *Delusive Spaces: Essays on Culture, Media, and Technology* (Amsterdam: NAi Publishers Institute of Network Cultures, 2008), 38–73.

94. Richard Stallman, "The Right to Read," *Communications of the ACM* 40, no. 2 (February 1997). Available at http://www.gnu.org/philosophy/right-to-read.html.

95. Jessica Litmann, "Exclusive Right to Read," http://www-personal.umich.edu/~jdlitman/ papers/read.htm.

96. Robert Darnton, *The Forbidden Best-Sellers of Pre-Revolutionary France* (New York: Harper Collins Publishers, 1997).

97. William J. Mitchell, *City of Bits: Space, Place, and the Infobahn* (Cambridge, MA: MIT Press, 1996) and *E-Topia* (Cambridge, MA: MIT Press, 2000).

98. Adam Gopnik, *Paris to the Moon* (New York: Random House Trade Paperbacks, 2001).

99. Colin St John Wilson, *Design and Construction of the British Library* (London: British Library, 1998).

100. Stanley Chodorow, "The Medieval Future of Intellectual Culture: Scholars and Librarians in the Age of the Electron," *ARL: A Bimonthly Newsletter of Research Library Issues and Action* 189 (December 1996): 1–3. Available at http://www.arl.org/bm~doc/medieval.pdf. Although Chodorow

is probably best known as the former Provost of the University of Pennsylvania, he also later served as Vice President of the online paid content service Questia.

101. Neil Smith, interview with the author, London, England, 2002.

102. This experience is also reflected in my own research on first-year freshmen at the University of California, where students were encouraged to use the California Digital Library to complete writing assignments. Although this digital library project was initiated to reduce demand on the physical collections by students in large enrollment courses, comparable numbers of students said that electronic resources increased their use of the library to those who said they decreased their use of the library. A recent study on "Generation Y" students, who are assumed to be frequent cut-and-paste consumers of online digital texts, confirms that they are in fact more likely to use the physical spaces of traditional libraries than their older counterparts.

103. Walter Benjamin, "The Work of Art in the Age of Mechanical Reproduction," *Illuminations: Essays and Reflections*, ed. Hannah Arendt, trans. Harry Zohn (New York: Schocken, 1969), 217–252.

104. Aly Conteth, interview with the author, London, England, September 14, 2007.

105. Neil Fitzgerald and Aly Conteth, interview with the author, London, England, September 14, 2007.

106. Michael Alexander and Alexander Prescott, "The Initiatives for Access Programme: an overview," in *Towards the Digital Library: The Initiatives for Access Programme,* ed. Leona Carpenter, Simon Shaw, and Andrew Prescott (London: The British Library, 1998), 15.

107. "Turning the Pages™, the British Library," http://www.bl.uk/onlinegallery/ttp/ttpbooks .html (accessed January 21, 2008; site now discontinued).

108. Elizabeth Losh, "Reading Room(s): Building a National Archive with Digital Spaces and Physical Places," *Literary and Linguistic Computing* 19, no. 3 (September 2004): 373–384.

109. Aly Conteth, interview with the author, London, England, September 14, 2007.

110. Nicholson Baker, *Double Fold: Libraries and the Assault on Paper* (New York: Vintage, 2002).

111. Michael Alexander and Alexander Prescott, "The Initiatives for Access Programme: an overview," in *Towards the Digital Library: The Initiatives for Access Programme,* ed. Leona Carpenter, Simon Shaw, and Andrew Prescott (London: The British Library, 1998), 28.

112. Laura Campbell, "The Library of Congress's National Digital Library: reaching out to schools and libraries through the Internet," in *Development of Digital Libraries: An American Perspective*, ed. Deanna B. Marcum and Kakugyo S. Chiku, (Westport, CN: Greenwood Press, 2001), 213.

113. Lester Haines, "Google Book Search Reveals Scanner's Sleight of Hand," *The Register*, December 5, 2007. Available at http://www.theregister.co.uk/2007/12/05/google_books/.

114. Asher Moses, "Book Scans Reveal Google's Handiwork," *The Age*, December 6, 2007. Available at http://www.theage.com.au/news/web/book-scans-reveal-googles-handiwork/2007/12/06/ 1196812901631.html.

115. LibraryThing, "Catalog Your Books Online," http://www.librarything.com/about.

116. "Member: Thomasjefferson | LibraryThing," http://www.librarything.com/profile/thomasjefferson.

117. "Michael's Library," http://books.google.com/books?uid=12844878399470761018.

118. Laura Graham, "Tales from the Vault: A Journey Over the Mountains," *Common-place* (January 2003). Available at http://www.historycooperative.org/journals/cp/vol-03/no-02/tales/.

119. H.A. Olson, *The Power to Name: Locating the Limits of Subject Representation in Libraries* (Berlin: Springer, 2002).

120. Laura Graham, "Tales from the Vault: A Journey Over the Mountains," *Common-place* (January 2003). Available at http://www.historycooperative.org/journals/cp/vol-03/no-02/tales/.

121. Flickr, "Photos from The Library of Congress," http://www.flickr.com/photos/library_of_congress/.

122. Henry Jenkins, *Convergence Culture: Where Old and New Media Collide* (New York City: NYU Press, 2006).

123. Christophe Dessaux and Sonia Zillhardt, interview with the author, Paris, France, September 18, 2007.

124. William Y. Arms, *Digital Libraries* (Cambridge, MA: MIT Press, 2001).

125. Alexander Hars, *From Publishing to Knowledge Networks: Reinventing Online Knowledge Infrastructures* (Berlin: Springer, 2003), 102.

126. Ibid., 90–95.

127. Aly Conteth, interview with the author, London, England, September 14, 2007.

128. Christine L. Borgman, *From Gutenberg to the Global Information Infrastructure: Access to Information in the Networked World* (Cambridge, MA: MIT Press, 2003).

129. Laura Graham, interview with the author, Washington, D. C., 2002.

130. James Billington, "The Library of Congress and the Information Age," in *Books, Bricks, and Bytes: Libraries in the Twenty-First Century*, ed. Stephen Graubard and Paul LeClerc (New Brunswick, NY: Transaction Publishers, 1997).

9   Waiting Room: Serious Games about National Security and Public Health

1. John Mintz, "Homeland Security Employs Imagination," *The Washington Post*, June 18, 2004. Available at http://www.washingtonpost.com/wp-dyn/articles/A50534-2004Jun17.html.

2. Michel Foucault, *The Birth of the Clinic: An Archaeology of Medical Perception*, trans. A. M. Sheridan Smith (New York: Vintage, 1994), ix.

3. Ibid., 1.

4. Federation of American Scientists, "Immune Attack," http://www.fas.org/immuneattack/.

5. Donna Haraway, "The Promises of Monsters: A Regenerative Politics for Inappropriate/d Others," in *Cultural Studies*, ed. Lawrence Grossberg, Cary Nelson, and Paula Treichler (New York: Routledge, 1991), 295–337.

6. HopeLab, "Re-Mission: a game & community for young people with cancer," http://www.re-mission.net/.

7. Ian Bogost. *Persuasive Games: The Expressive Power of Videogames*. (Cambridge, MA: MIT Press, 2007).

8. Anna Munster, *Materializing New Media: Embodiment in Information Aesthetics* (Dartmouth, NH: Dartmouth College Press, 2006).

9. Merrilea Mayo, "Games for Science and Engineering Education," *Communications of the ACM* 50, no. 7 (July 2007).

10. As Peter Rauch has pointed out, some games of crisis have an extremely simple game logic that rewards torture with information, much as the television show *24* frequently shows questioning procedures that violate human rights protocols as time-efficient ways to solve mysteries and thus defuse the crisis. See Peter Rauch, "Severe Pain or Suffering: Videogames, Morality and Torture," paper presented at Philosophy of Computer Games Conference, Reggio Emilia, Italy, January 27, 2007. Available at http://game.unimore.it/Papers/Rauch_Paper.pdf.

11. E. Lofgren and N.H. Fefferman, "The Untapped Potential of Virtual Game Worlds to Shed Light on Real World Epidemics," *The Lancet Infectious Diseases* 7 (2007): 625–629.

12. John Markoff, "Something Is Killing Off the Sims, and It's Not by Accident," *New York Times*, April 27, 2000. Available at http://partners.nytimes.com/library/tech/00/04/circuits/articles/27sims.html.

13. J.M. Bower, "Constructivism on the World Wide Web: Whyville.net" presentation at the Serious Games Summit 2006, Washington, D.C., October 30–31.

14. Ian Bogost. *Persuasive Games: The Expressive Power of Videogames*. (Cambridge, MA: MIT Press, 2007).

15. Carnegie Mellon's Entertainment Technology Center, "About Hazmat: Hotzone," http://www.etc.cmu.edu/projects/hazmat_2005/about.php.

16. Frank Boosman, "SGS 2006: "Serious Games Case Study Blasts," online positng, March 21, 2006, *pseudorandom*, http://www.boosman.com/blog/2006/03/sgs_2006_serious_games_case_st.html.

17. Richard Winton, "LAPD defends Muslim mapping effort," *The Los Angeles Times*, November 10, 2007. Available at http://www.latimes.com/news/local/la-me-lapd10nov10,0,3960843.story?coll=la-home-center.

18. USC Gamepipe Labs Projects, "Firescope," http://gamepipe.usc.edu/Projects/Firescope.

19. "Lockdown," http://gamepipe.usc.edu/USC_GamePipe_Laboratory/R%26D/Entries/2008/5/13_Lockdown.html.

20. "Incident Commander: A Crisis Training Simulation," http://www.incidentcommander.net/index.shtml.

21. Ogilvy Public Relations, "Topoff Case Study," http://www.ogilvypr.com/case-studies/topoff.cfm.

22. Ibid.

23. Johan Huizinga, *Homo Ludens*, 1st ed. (Boston: Beacon Press, 1971).

24. Mia Consalvo, *Cheating: Gaining Advantage in Videogames* (Cambridge, MA: MIT Press, 2007).

25. Alexander R Galloway, *Gaming: Essays On Algorithmic Culture* (Minneapolis: University of Minnesota Press, 2006).

26. Max Boisot, *Information Space: A Framework for Learning in Organizations, Institutions, and Culture* (New York: Routledge, 1995).

27. Joseph Henderson, "Comprehensive Technology-Based Clinical Education: The 'Virtual Practicum'," *International Journal of Psychiatry in Medicine* 28, no. 1 (1998): 51.

28. Interactive Media Laboratory, "HIV Prevention Counseling: A Client-Centered Approach," http://iml.dartmouth.edu/education/cme/HIV_Prevention/index.html.

29. Lynn Miller, "Using Games to Deliver Key Health Messaging," panel presentation, Games Health Day, Los Angeles, CA, May 9, 2007.

30. "Mysexycity.com," http://www.mysexycity.com/.

31. inSPOT LA, "[HIV/STD] Internet Notification Service for Partners, Los Angeles," http://www.inspotla.org/.

32. Kaiser Family Foundation, "mtvU and Kaiser Family Foundation Launch Search for Best Video Game Concept to Reduce Spread of HIV/AIDS," http://www.kff.org/hivaids/phip012507nr.cfm.

33. "In the Moment," 2008, http://inthemoment.ning.com/.

34. Justin Peters, "World of Borecraft," *Slate*, June 27, 2007. Available at http://www.slate.com/id/2169019/.

35. Joseph Henderson, interview with the author, Hanover, New Hampshire, July 31, 2006.

36. Noah Falstein, comment in question-and-answer session, Creating Games & Simulations for Learning, Long Beach, CA, January 23, 2006.

37. Joseph Henderson, interview with the author, Hanover, New Hampshire, July 31, 2006.

38. Ian Bogost, *Persuasive Games: The Expressive Power of Videogames* (Cambridge, MA: MIT Press, 2007).

39. James Paul Gee, *What Video Games Have to Teach Us About Learning and Literacy* (New York: Palgrave Macmillan, 2004).

40. Joseph Henderson, interview with the author, Hanover, New Hampshire, July 31, 2006.

41. Peter Sandman, "Risk Communication and the War against Terrorism," Novermber 10, 2001, http://www.psandman.com/col/9-11.htm.

42. Global Security, "Flu Pandemic Mitigation—Social Distancing," http://www.globalsecurity.org/security/ops/hsc-scen-3_flu-pandemic-distancing.htm.

43. The Yes Men official website, http://www.theyesmen.com.

44. Department of Homeland Security, "Ready.gov: Stay or Go — Shelter in Place," http://www.ready.gov/america/makeaplan/shelter_in_place.html.

45. Federation of American Scientists, "Analysis of Ready.gov," updated July 31, 2007, http://www.fas.org/reallyready/analysis.html.

46. Ad Council, http://www.adcouncil.org/campaigns/homeland_security/ (accessed November 1, 2005; website now discontinued).

47. Federal Bureau of Investigation, "Federal Bureau of Investigation – Kids' Page," http://www.fbi.gov/fbikids.htm.

48. Bill Viola and Tracy Fullerton, "The Night Journey," http://www.thenightjourney.com/.

49. Jane McGonigal, "World Without Oil," http://worldwithoutoil.org/.

50. Michel de Certeau, *The Practice of Everyday Life*, trans. Steven Rendall (Berkeley: University of California Press, 2002).

51. "World Without Oil—UCI—Episode Five," 2007, http://www.youtube.com/watch?v=6oz_2OWHHC0.

10   The Past as Prologue: Cultural Politics and the Founding Narratives of Information Science

1. John Markoff, "MCI and a Software Partner Set to Offer Video Network," *New York Times*, August 5, 1997. Available at http://query.nytimes.com/gst/fullpage.html?res=9400E4D9113DF936A3575BC0A961958260.

2. John Noble Wilford, "A Month on Mars and the Pathfinder Is Declared a Total Success," *New York Times*, August 9, 1997. Available at http://query.nytimes.com/gst/fullpage.html?res=9C01E5D9123CF93AA3575BC0A961958260&scp=2&sq=mars+pathfinder&st=nyt.

3. Mars Missions, "Welcome to the Mars Missions, Year 2000 and Beyond!" http://web.archive.org/web/19971211025839/http://mpfwww.jpl.nasa.gov/.

4. John Markoff, "MCI and a Software Partner Set to Offer Video Network," *New York Times*, August 5, 1997. Available at http://query.nytimes.com/gst/fullpage.html?res =9400E4D9113DF936A3575BC0A961958260.

5. Edward R. Tufte, *The Cognitive Style of PowerPoint: Pitching Out Corrupts Within*, Second Edition (Cheshire, CT: Graphics Press, 2006).

6. Columbia Accident Investigation Board, *The Colombia Accident Investiation Board Report*, August 2003. Available at http://caib.nasa.gov/news/report/default.html.

7. Karen Kaplan, "THE CUTTING EDGE; NASA Is Reaching for the Moon—Via E-Mail; Innovation: Engineers Are Developing a Computer Network for the Era of Interplanetary Travel," *The Los Angeles Times*, July 27, 1998.

8. For other such areas of "regional advantage" in the United States, see AnnaLee Saxenian, *Regional Advantage: Culture and Competition in Silicon Valley and Route 128* (Cambridge, MA: Harvard University Press, 1994).

9. Sigmund Freud, *New Introductory Lectures on Psychoanalysis* (London: Hogarth Press, 1933).

10. John Von Neumann, *Theory of Self-Reproducing Automata* (Urbana: University of Illinois Press, 1966), 43.

11. Thomas S. Kuhn, *The Structure of Scientific Revolutions* (Chicago: University of Chicago Press, 1962).

12. Vannevar Bush, "As We May Think," *The Atlantic Monthly*, July 1945. Available at http://www .theatlantic.com/doc/194507/bush.

13. Ibid.

14. Vannevar Bush, "The Art of Management," in *Science Is Not Enough* (New York: William Morrow & Company, Inc., 1967), 50–74.

15. Wendy Hui Kyong Chun, "The Enduring Ephemeral, or the Future is a Memory, lecture, University of California, Irvine, Irvine, CA, February 22, 2008.

16. G. Pascal Zachary, *Endless Frontier: Vannevar Bush, Engineer of the American Century* (Cambridge, MA: MIT Press, 1999).

17. Paul N. Edwards, *The Closed World: Computers and the Politics of Discourse in Cold War America* (Cambridge, MA: MIT Press, 1997).

18. Bush also discusses diverting institutional computing for recreational purposes when a Harvard physicist decides to study trajectories in the game of baseball. See "When Bat Meets Ball," in *Science Is Not Enough* (New York: William Morrow & Company, Inc., 1967), 102–122. For more about the rhetoric of institutional computing, see Brian Rajski, *Mainframes: Computers, Corporations, and Mid-Century American Fiction*, unpublished dissertation, University of California, Irvine.

19. Vannevar Bush, "As We May Think," *The Atlantic Monthly* (July 1945). Available at http:// www.theatlantic.com/doc/194507/bush.

20. W. Russell Neuman, *The Future of the Mass Audience* (Cambridge: Cambridge University Press, 1991).

21. Vannevar Bush, "As We May Think," *Life* (September 1945).

22. Vannevar Bush, "As We May Think," *The Atlantic Monthly* (July 1945). Available at http://www.theatlantic.com/doc/194507/bush.

23. Ibid.

24. Ibid.

25. For more about the ways that Bush did not adequately account for intellectual property regimes in his 1945 report "Science: The Endless Frontier," in *Science for the Twenty-First Century: The Bush Report Revisited* (Washington, D.C: AEI Press, 1997), 19–23.

26. Vannevar Bush, "As We May Think," *The Atlantic Monthly* (July 1945). Available at http://www.theatlantic.com/doc/194507/bush.

27. Evelyn Fox Keller, *Reflections on Gender and Science* (New Haven: Yale University Press, 1985).

28. IEEE Virtual Museum, "Nurturing the Network: Women and the Communications Industry," http://www.ieee-virtual-museum.org/exhibit/exhibit.php?id=159251&lid=1.

29. J. C. R. Licklider, "Man-Computer Symbiosis," *IRE Transactions on Human Factors in Electronics*, HFE-1, nos. 4–11 (March 1960). Reprinted in *Digital SRC Research Report* 61 (August 7, 1990). Available at http://gatekeeper.dec.com/pub/DEC/SRC/research-reports/abstracts/src-rr-061.html.

30. See also Alice Gambrell, "Stolen Time" *Vectors* 1 (winter 2005). Available at http://vectors.iml.annenberg.edu/index.php?page=7&projectCurrent=Stolen%20Time%20Archive.

31. For more on the role of printed tables in book culture see the research of Adrian Johns in *The Nature of the Book: Print and Knowledge in the Making* (Chicago: Chicago University Press, 1998) and other works.

32. David Alan Grier, *When Computers Were Human* (Princeton: Princeton University Press, 2007).

33. Anne Balsamo, *Technologies of the Gendered Body: Reading Cyborg Women* (Durham: Duke University Press, 1995), 158.

34. Erik Conway, "NASA—Women Made Early Inroads at JPL," http://www.nasa.gov/centers/jpl/news/historyf-20070327.html.

35. Ibid.

36. Jet Propulsion Laboratory, "JPL Computers," http://www.jpl.nasa.gov/explorer/captions/computers.php.

37. See Bush's reminder that "we must not forget the women, whose ambition nearly always was just to marry the right man, and then to mold his ambitions, sometimes by boosting him up, and sometimes by just driving him ragged" in "Poverty and Opportunity," in *Science Is Not*

Enough (New York: William Morrow & Company, Inc., 1967), 136. See also the numerous mentions of "boys" in the office and the role of paternal authority in "The Art of Management," so that the employees of an effective manager fear him in the "same way that a boy should be afraid of his father."

38. Vannevar Bush, "As We May Think," *The Atlantic Monthly* (July 1945) Available at http://www.theatlantic.com/doc/194507/bush.

39. It is interesting to note that when Bush revisited this essay two decades later, he relabeled the "girl" as a "stenographer" and removed the gendered references, although he keeps references to the operator who "strokes its keys languidly" and discomforts the speaker with a "disquieting gaze." See Vannevar Bush, "Memex Revisited," in *Science Is Not Enough* (New York: William Morrow & Company, Inc., 1967), 93.

40. Claude E. Shannon and Warren Weaver, *The Mathematical Theory of Communication* (Champaign, IL: University of Illinois Press, 1949), 27.

41. Jacques Derrida, *Spurs: Nietzsche's Styles; Esperons: Les Styles De Nietzsche* (University of Chicago Press, 1979).

42. Claude E. Shannon and Warren Weaver, *The Mathematical Theory of Communication* (Champaign, IL: University of Illinois Press, 1949), 8.

43. Warren Weaver, *Lady Luck; the Theory of Probability* (Garden City, NY: Anchor Books, 1963), 45.

44. Claude E. Shannon and Warren Weaver, *The Mathematical Theory of Communication* (Champaign, IL: University of Illinois Press, 1949), 31.

45. Ibid., 27.

46. Ibid., 28.

47. Paul Dourish, "Rethinking Information and Space in Ubiquitous Computing," EXP Lecture Series, University of California, Los Angeles, January 30, 2007.

48. Jane Jacobs, *The Death and Life of Great American Cities* (New York: Vintage, 1989). For more on the connection between information science and urban development, see Jennifer S. Light, *From Warfare to Welfare: Defense Intellectuals and Urban Problems in Cold* (Baltimore: JHU Press, 2003).

49. Warren Weaver, ed., *The Scientists Speak* (New York: Boni & Gaer, 1947).

50. Claude E. Shannon and Warren Weaver, *The Mathematical Theory of Communication* (Champaign, IL: University of Illinois Press, 1949), 5.

51. Ibid., 4–5.

52. Ibid., 5.

53. Ray Hyman, "How People are Fooled by Ideomotor Action," 1999, *Quackwatch*, http://www.quackwatch.org/01QuackeryRelatedTopics/ideomotor.html.

54. "Subservient Chicken," http://www.subservientchicken.com/.

55. Zachary Rodgers, "Questions for Jeff Benjamin, CP+B's Interactive Head," January 3, 2005, *ClickZ*, http://www.clickz.com/showPage.html?page=3453941.

56. "Subservient Programmer," http://www.subservientprogrammer.com/main.aspx.

57. "Subservient Blair," http://www.subservientblair.com/.

58. "Subservient President," http://www.subservientpresident.net/.

59. Harry Miles Johnson, "The Talking Dog," *Science*, New Series, 35, no. 906. (May 10, 1912): 749–751. The talking dog trope continues to be popular on YouTube, where one popular talking dog video has received over eight million views. See "Talking Dogs," 2006, http://www.youtube.com/watch?v=ZCYaw5tGYAs.

60. Karl Lashley, "Persistent Problems in the Evolution of Mind," *The Quarterly Review of Biology* 24, no. 1 (March 1949): 28.

61. Norbert Wiener, *Cybernetics, Second Edition: Or the Control and Communication in the Animal and the Machine* (Cambridge, MA: MIT Press, 1965), 157.

62. Gregory Bateson, *Steps to an Ecology of Mind: Collected Essays in Anthropology, Psychiatry, Evolution, and Epistemology* (Chicago: University of Chicago Press, 2000).

63. Richard Grusin, "The Affective Life of Media," talk presented at the University of California, Irvine, February 21, 2008.

64. Flo Conway and Jim Siegelman, *Dark Hero of the Information Age: In Search of Norbert Wiener The Father of Cybernetics* (New York: Basic Books, 2006).

65. Norbert Wiener, *Cybernetics, Second Edition: Or the Control and Communication in the Animal and the Machine* (Cambridge, MA: MIT Press, 1965), 157.

66. Ibid., 50.

67. Gregory Bateson, "Form, Substance, and Difference," in *Steps to an Ecology of Mind: Collected Essays in Anthropology, Psychiatry, Evolution, and Epistemology* (Chicago: University of Chicago Press, 2000), 465.

68. N. Katherine Hayles, "Liberal Subjectivity Imperiled: Norbert Wiener and Cybernetic Anxiety," *How We Became Posthuman: Virtual Bodies in Cybernetics, Literature, and Informatics* (Chicago: University of Chicago Press, 1999), 87.

69. See Wiener's repeated critiques of Von Neumann in *Cybernetics, Second Edition: Or the Control and Communication in the Animal and the Machine* (Cambridge, MA: MIT Press, 1965).

70. Ibid., 160.

71. His criticism of specific laboratories, however, is very muted. There are four mentions of Bell Laboratories in *Cybernetics*. Two are references to Shannon, and two are references to the Vocoder admired by Bush.

72. Siva Vaidhyanathan, "Critical Information Studies: A Bibliographic Manifesto," *Cultural Studies* 20, no. 2 & 3 (March 2006). Available at http://www.sivacracy.net/archives/002930.html.

73. Norbert Wiener, *Cybernetics, Second Edition: Or the Control and Communication in the Animal and the Machine* (Cambridge, MA: MIT Press, 1965), 160.

74. John R. Pierce, *An Introduction to Information Theory* (New York: Dover Publications, 1980).

75. Norbert Wiener, *I Am a Mathematician* (Cambridge, MA: MIT Press, 1964).

76. Norbert Wiener, *Ex-Prodigy: My Childhood and Youth* (Cambridge, MA: MIT Press, 1964).

77. Norbert Wiener, *Cybernetics, Second Edition: Or the Control and Communication in the Animal and the Machine* (Cambridge, MA: MIT Press, 1965), 158.

78. Ibid., 5.

79. To see how some of these phallic rites were eventually taken to excess, see John Carter, *Sex and Rockets: The Occult World of Jack Parsons* (Los Angeles: Feral House, 1999).

80. See the National Association of Rocketry at http://www.nar.org/ for more.

81. Steve Hargadon, "John Seely Brown on Web 2.0 and the Culture of Learning (School 2.0, Part 6)," online posting, January 20, 2007, *Steve Hargadon*, http://www.stevehargadon .com/2007/01/john-seely-brown-on-web-20–and-culture.html.

82. John Seely Brown, "New Learning Environments for the 21st Century," http://www .johnseelybrown.com/newlearning.pdf.

83. Although the data visualization is obviously much less dramatic than Hollywood blockbuster films such as *Armageddon* and *Deep Impact*, the availability of this telnet data also shows that information about possible future cataclysmic planetary impacts would hardly be secret knowledge.

84. For more on the use of data visualization at JPL in the context of scientific deliberation among project team members, see Janet Vertesi, "'It's Too Red': The Construction of Visual Knowledge on the Mars Exploration Rover Mission," paper presented at the Society for the Social Studies of Science Annual Meeting, Montréal, Canada, October 9, 2007. Vertesi has examined the scientific practices of deliberation associated with the rover mission that now depend on the relationship of drawing to photography in the digital interface. With attention to the rhetoric of science of the project team, she explains how those who must decide where the rover goes next are presented with data in which green represents drivable regions and red represents the unnavigable territory. As they negotiate the visual field of the "lilypad," each must register approval for the consensus that emerges from their discussions of their collective markup of the planet's surface. Acts of naming also have important rhetorical functions in their discourse, because a geological structure resembling "home plate" in baseball has inspired them to name landmarks after those in the All-American Women's Baseball Team and—during Black History Month—the Negro Players League.

85. See the work of Chris Kelty on electronic voting and the failure of election officials to consider novel procedures for deliberation as one example.

Index